Massive Resistance and Southern Womanhood

POLITICS AND CULTURE IN THE TWENTIETH-CENTURY SOUTH

Massive Resistance and Southern Womanhood

WHITE WOMEN, CLASS, AND SEGREGATION

Rebecca Brückmann

The University of Georgia Press
ATHENS

Athens, Georgia 30602
www.ugapress.org

Set in 10/13 Minion Pro Regular
by Kaelin Chappell Broaddus

Most University of Georgia Press titles are
available from popular e-book vendors.

Printed digitally

Library of Congress Cataloging-in-Publication Data

Names: Brückmann, Rebecca, 1983– author.
Title: Massive resistance and southern womanhood : white women, class, and segregation / Rebecca Brückmann.
Other titles: Politics and culture in the twentieth-century South.
Description: Athens : The University of Georgia Press, [2021] | Series: Politics and culture in the twentieth-century South | Includes bibliographical references and index.
Identifiers: LCCN 2020025508 | ISBN 9780820358352 (hardback) | ISBN 9780820358628 (paperback) | ISBN 9780820358345 (ebook)
Subjects: LCSH: White supremacy movements—Southern States—History—20th century. | Women, White—Political activity—Southern States—History—20th century. | Women, White—Southern States—Attitudes—History—20th century. | Women, White—Southern States—Social life and customs—History—20th century. | Segregation—Southern States—History—20th century. | Race discrimination—Southern States—History—20th century. | Racism—Southern States—History—20th century. | Southern States—Race relations—History—20th century.
Classification: LCC F220.A1 B78 2021 | DDC 305.800975—dc23
LC record available at https://lccn.loc.gov/2020025508

CONTENTS

ACKNOWLEDGMENTS

Writing this book has taken a decade. During this time and beyond, I was, and I am, fortunate enough to rely on the practical and moral support and valuable advice of many people.

I am very grateful for the generous financial support of the Graduate School of North American Studies of the John F. Kennedy Institute for North American Studies at Freie Universität Berlin, which has made this research possible, and I am equally thankful for the vibrant intellectual exchange with and, at times, tough questions from many colleagues. I would like to especially thank my dissertation advisers, M. Michaela Hampf and George Lewis, for their support, insight, and humor throughout this journey. Many thanks to the other members of my dissertation committee, Jessica Gienow-Hecht and Ulrike Schaper, and to David Bosold, Gabriele Bodmeier, and Andreas Etges. The archivists and librarians at various institutions in Arkansas, Louisiana, South Carolina, and Washington, D.C. have been extraordinarily generous to me with their time and their expertise—thank you. I am also thankful for the time and the astute research advice of scholars who happily conversed with an obscure early career researcher from Germany: Valinda Littlefield, Daniel C. Littlefield, and Connie Schulz, who graciously opened their homes to me, John Kirk, John White, Jacquelyn Dowd-Hall, Phoebe Godfrey, Karen Anderson, and Bryant Simon. I am grateful for the University of Georgia Press's team, particularly James Patrick Allen, Nathaniel Holly, and Walter Biggins who have been kind and patient in their support for this publication, and to MJ Devaney for her incisive editing. I have discussed this project and many more of life's conundrums at workshops, on coffee breaks, at kitchen tables, on subway cars, in emails, and on walks by the Paul-Lincke-Ufer in Berlin with colleagues and friends who have lent an open ear and gave empathetic guidance. I appreciate you, Ahu Tanrisever, Stefanie Rauch, Natalia Klimina-Schultz, Sonja Longolius, Dorothee Booth, Peter Hartig, Eva Bischoff, Barbara Lüthi, Tiffany Florvil, David Prior, Marieke Schippert,

Anita Röder, Heidi Renée Lewis, Kimberly Singletary, Anke Ortlepp, Norbert Finzsch, Claire Litchfield, Rebecca Williams, Teresa Kerntopf, Tabea Koch, Katrin Gorogranz, Florian Gröhl, Ruth Steinhof, Florian Plum, Silke Hackenesch, Kristoff Kerl, Katharina Kloock, and the M team. Finally, my biggest thanks of all is to my family: Gudrun Schwarz-Brückmann, Wilfried Schwarz, Barbara Brückmann, and Bernhard Brückmann.

Massive Resistance and Southern Womanhood

INTRODUCTION

White Supremacy, White Women, and Desegregation

Two people died and hundreds were injured when the Air Force veteran and native Mississippian James Meredith desegregated the University of Mississippi in 1962. Local resident Ray Gunter and journalist Paul Guihard suffered fatal gunshot wounds in the battle that erupted on campus more than eight years after the U.S. Supreme Court declared racial segregation in public schools unconstitutional in *Brown v. Board of Education of Topeka, Kansas* (1954). Federal agents, highway patrolmen, and the university's police chief escorted Meredith to his dormitory on September 30, 1962. By nightfall, a mob had assembled; an estimated three thousand people gathered and yelled segregationist slogans, attacked federal agents, and threw bottles and bricks. The federal government answered Mississippi's massive resistance with an armed intervention. Federal guardsmen arrived on campus, followed by army troops during the night. By the early morning hours, the riot had been quelled. James Meredith's enrollment stood firm, and he successfully graduated the following year.[1]

Thirty days after the segregationist riot at the University of Mississippi, Cornelia Dabney Ramseur Tucker, an eighty-one-year-old South Carolinian, wrote a letter to U.S. attorney general Robert Kennedy to protest the federal government's actions at Oxford. For decades, Tucker had been a conservative grassroots campaigner, and she addressed Kennedy in a matriarchal manner. Opening her letter with "My dear Attorney General," Tucker boasted that from her "accumulated wisdom of more than eighty years of sympathetic study of human nature I presume to write you this letter as one from mother to son."[2] Tucker explained that while she was "assuming—as a mother would of her son—that your purpose in this Mississippi military action is to improve race relations, it is now definitely proven that such action has served only to inflame the passions of both races."[3] Tucker sought to put the attorney general in his place by insinuating that though he might have had good intentions, his inexperienced handling of the situation proved that he was in need of motherly advice.

Tucker's advice for Kennedy was that of a white supremacist. Figuratively taking him by the hand—"Let us reason together—you and I"—she lectured Kennedy on human nature, arguing that allowing Meredith to attend Ole Miss was tantamount to "mental cruelty" to the veteran, perhaps even leading to his "mental derangement." Tucker claimed that violent segregationists and the prevalence of white supremacy were not the problem; rather it was the very presence of Meredith, who was "a constant incentive to rebellion by other students." Closing with a patronizingly racist statement about black people's "loveable qualities," Tucker urged Kennedy to "entertain some confidence" in states' rights and to trust officials, "who know that their own states are not yet prepared for this innovation."[4]

Tucker's letter derived its legitimacy from her status and authority as a mother and as an elderly southern lady. Her self-presentation as a benign advisor, however, clashed with her political actions. Tucker interwove motherly advice with racism, white supremacy, and an emphasis on states' rights.

Tucker was an advocate of massive resistance. Beginning in the 1950s, southern segregationist politicians as well as grassroots activists organized against *Brown* specifically and the civil rights movement more generally, building on decades of segregationist ideology, laws, policies, and customs.[5] Proponents of massive resistance attacked the ruling from a variety of hostile positions. They invoked states' rights, attempted to find biblical justifications for the continuance of racial segregation, and denounced civil rights activists as communist agents. Southern white women played pivotal roles in the defense of white supremacy. They were vocal segregationists who actively campaigned for the racial hierarchization of society. White women policed the boundaries of white supremacy and ensured its stability in their communities, using a variety of tools.[6]

Historian Stephanie Jones-Rogers has shown that not only did white mistresses of enslaved people profit economically from their ties to slavery before abolition, but after the Civil War, such white women became "co-conspirators" in the construction of the South's racial caste system designed to sustain white privilege.[7] Women benefited from the white supremacist culture in which they lived, and so they supported it. The everyday culture of white supremacy made white privilege and the sense of race-based entitlements seem normal, and that sense of normalcy permeated the everyday lives of housewives, working women, mothers, and longtime grassroots agitators like Cornelia Tucker who connected white supremacy to her prior, broader conservative activism in support of anticommunism and traditionalist values.

Tucker's emphasis on maternal authority, moreover, can be ranked with traditional framings of women's activism in the realm of politics. Early on in U.S. history, the idea of Republican motherhood tasked women with the political duty to both raise patriotic male citizens and maintain public virtues through their domestic influence. Women's abolitionist activism, the temperance movement, and the suffrage movement, too, created "rhetorical links between political ideas and maternal practices," which served both as a justification for white, upper- and middle-class women's activism and as the foundation for it.[8] Motherhood gave women a social status in a patriarchal society, and it served as a tool for creating spaces for women in the public sphere.

Race and class differences among women delimited their maternalist activism and dictated how it was perceived and received. Particularly pronounced differences in the framing of black and white mothers emerged during the period that saw the ascendance of the civil rights movement and the countercampaign launched by the massive resistance movement. The "discourse on motherhood was not incidental" to either movement, historian Ruth Feldstein argues.[9] The actions taken by black and white women in the name of motherhood render portrayals of mothers as apolitical in the 1950s as inadequate.[10]

Certainly, Tucker capitalized on her motherhood to justify her intervention. Similarly, many segregationist women used their role as mothers to legitimize their challenges to court-mandated desegregation. Sociologist Beth Roy concludes that school desegregation in particular "was a struggle that especially evoked women's activism; who else could better claim the moral authority to speak up when the site of contestation was the domain of children?"[11] While segregationist women's support for massive resistance was a matter of white supremacist principle and so not limited to the issue of school desegregation, school desegregation crises offered them the opportunity to publicly intervene by making tactical use of the idea of maternalism. Of course, the desegregation of schools was linked to every other segregationist fight against integration and to the defense of a white supremacist social system more generally. But school desegregation battles were prime sites of female massive resistance, spaces where the actions of segregationist women, in particular working-class women, became most prominent and most effective. The publicity generated through media reports was critically important in sustaining these groups' actions.

Maternalism proved to be one of the linchpins of segregationist women's activism in the 1950s and 1960s, but many of these women continually expanded their strategies for battling desegregation and adapted their arguments against it in the South and across the nation to fit different audiences and political purposes. By creating performative spaces in interaction with the media, white supremacist women expanded the traditional frames of mothers' and women's roles and activism in the public sphere. They showed that their maternalism was invested in white supremacy and often a means to this end.

A masculinist rhetoric, the concomitant idea of white southern womanhood, and the belligerence and chauvinist undertones of the showdowns between segregationists and the federal government can create the impression that women were relegated to the sidelines or merely used as pawns in massive resistance. *Massive Resistance and Southern Womanhood*, however, shows that white women were self-conscious agents in the segregationist countermovement. This book offers a gender, cultural, and social history of segregationist women's activism in massive resistance. Historian Elizabeth McRae suggests that women in massive resistance assumed the role of "segregation's constant gardeners."[12] *Massive Resistance and Southern Womanhood* examines how these activities were entwined with factors of social differentiation, particularly class, social status, and space, and how white supremacist women steadily expanded the frames of their public activism.

The book presents three case studies: the Mothers' League of Central High School during the school desegregation crisis in Little Rock, Arkansas, between 1957 and 1960; the so-called cheerleaders who were active in the school desegregation crisis in New Orleans, Louisiana, in 1960 and 1961; and the female citizens' council and fellow white supremacist grassroots agitators in South Carolina's Lowcountry, particularly in Charleston, between 1954 and 1963. This comparative study explores the scale, scope, and characteristics of women's support of and role in massive resistance and the defense of white supremacy in these different southern metropolitan areas, showing the strategies women employed to bridge the discursive and practice gaps between urban and rural spaces and between domestic and public spaces.

The women who are the protagonists in this book all believed in white supremacy, and their support for continued segregation and opposition to legal and social equality became one expression of their discriminatory views. While they—along with all massive resistance proponents in this multifaceted and changeable movement—might hold different views on broader political topics, including political party affiliations, they shared a belief in the superiority of whites that underwrote how they lived their everyday lives.

The book asks how these segregationist women created public spaces for their activism in the 1950s and 1960s, how ideas about gender, race, and class informed their strategies and actions, how their activism related specifically to these different spatial and social settings, and how they expanded the roles they developed for themselves beyond their local contexts. In view of women's exclusion from formal power structures in the 1950s and early 1960s, *Massive Resistance and Southern Womanhood* reevaluates the role of grassroots activists and their relationship with political and economic elites in massive resistance, thereby adding to our understanding of segregationist grassroots activism and political action in the 1950s and 1960s.[13]

Until recently, few studies focused on women in massive resistance.[14] This historiographical neglect is striking, given the central role gender discourses play in segregationist ideology. Since Reconstruction, the ideological construct of (white) southern womanhood has been a battleground for proponents and opponents of desegregation and social equality for African Americans. Historian John Ruoff argues that southern womanhood became a collective symbol for the "southern way of life" itself. According to segregationists, the social equality of white and black Americans posed a critical threat to southern womanhood, the "integrity of the races," and, thereby, to the South.[15] White women, however, were not merely mute icons of white supremacy but vocal segregationists themselves. They took part in the defense of segregation and they injected their idea of the "integrity of the races" into massive resistance's masculinist discourse. This raises the question how interactions between class and status concerns, race, space, and gender shaped these women's views and actions.

Given the separate spheres paradigm in the era of domestic containment and thus the limited opportunities for women to participate in public activities, this study stresses what women chose to protest and the methods they used to mount their objections effectively within massive resistance and the broader political discourse of the era. Women's groups in massive resistance transcended a thematically narrow focus on children and family surrounding an immediate school desegregation. Well versed in the rhetoric of massive resistance writ large these women created performative spaces through which they defied the behavioral expectations attached to their race, class, and gender, which enabled them to play key roles in segregationist political action. The women expanded the social and spatial scripts that limited the actions of white working-class women.[16]

Segregationist women at the forefront of protests walked a thin line between motherly respectability and impropriety, according to conventions of the time. Their activism was acceptable to male segregationists when women emphasized their maternal capabilities and when they relied on their supposedly special ability to enter disputes surrounding schoolchildren. Male segregationists also supported female groups when they used their alleged delicate constitutions to their advantage in publicity and political lobbying campaigns and when women portrayed their activism as the work of just another parent association. In her study of housewives from the opposite end of the political spectrum in 1940s and 1950s Canada, Julie Guard shows that housewives employed their identities to "claim political space" and to justify actions that would otherwise have been deemed unpalatable. Like these Canadian housewives, segregationist women frequently "used maternalism strategically to overcome the limitations imposed on them because of their gender."[17]

Gender essentialist maternalism, then, served as a "cover" for women's political participation and public protest and gave them "license to deploy the kinds of strategies of resistance available to those with little power."[18] Female massive resisters across socioeconomic backgrounds used this strategy to justify their presence and their actions in the public political discourse and on the streets.

Through this maternalist framing of their actions, segregationist women extended their household duties to caring for and policing the community, and conflicts surrounding schools and schoolchildren were easily portrayed as essentially domestic issues. Segregationist women did not confine their activism to maternalist politics in the service of white supremacy, however. All continuously adapted and expanded the frames of their political activism. Maternalism served as a cover, but the women eventually and consciously blew that cover and publicly presented themselves as political agents of white supremacy.

Historian Michelle Nickerson's work on 1950s, conservative California housewives also lends itself to the study of women in the massive resistance. Nickerson describes housewives' engagement as a "housewife populism" that spanned "the political spectrum" and used maternalism as a means of forming networks with "centers of power."[19] Nickerson argues that conservative women represented themselves as the selfless advocates of children, families, and households and as defenders of local communities. Harking back to discourses that styled communities as the bulwark against overbearing state interventions and communism in the 1930s, conservative women in the 1950s made anti-elitist and antistatist arguments the cornerstones of their campaigns.[20] The housewife populism of middle- and upper-class California, conservative housewives, who also opposed racial desegregation and organized against social movements, exemplifies the long history of women as community activists and the long, national history of white supremacy. But there were also many differences among conservative women activists. The social status of the Charleston supporters of massive resistance was similar to that of the California women, and the Charleston women had also been active in their neighborhoods and community for decades and shared many of Californian conservative housewives' political outlooks, but while the women most prominent in Charleston's and South Carolina's Lowcountry massive resistance were antistatist and anticommunist they most certainly were not anti-elitist, neither in their self-conception nor in their rhetoric. Agitators like Cornelia Tucker saw themselves as part of a racialized caste system and class-based society, and they expressed contempt for people they deemed poor and uneducated.

The working-class and middle-class women in Little Rock and New Orleans, in turn, had networks in their own neighborhoods, but they did not have a social standing in their larger communities. In fact, locals described them as "unknowns," or as white trash, a social group without social capital. These women frequently attacked political and social elites and expressed disdain for what they saw as the hypocritical establishment, but despite their continuous efforts, their public activism was not sustainable because of their lack of economic, cultural, and social capital. They had a public presence during crises and when there was a power vacuum to fill, but then they disappeared from sight.

The fact that the prominent female segregationists in Arkansas and Louisiana were working women, moreover, could also be used to advantage. These women were not "just" housewives; they shared the traditional responsibility of breadwinning with their husbands out of economic necessity. Female segregationist agitators in Little Rock, New Orleans, and Charleston transgressed their roles as maternal massive resisters frequently and forcefully.

Working-class women's modus operandi differed significantly from those of middle- and upper-class fellow female segregationists. Members of the Mothers' League of Central High School entered local and regional electoral politics on right-wing platforms in pursuit of upward mobility, whereas the cheerleaders in New Orleans became notorious for their foul-mouthed tirades and physical violence. The women's socioeconomic backgrounds informed their actions. Both groups exhibited a clear class consciousness, and the women frequently criticized and mocked affluent whites who advocated moderation while living in firmly segregated spaces, the "silk-stocking" districts of the respective cities. The upper- and middle-class women active in Charleston's and South Carolina's Lowcountry massive resistance similarly transgressed seemingly harmless maternalism by deploying the organizational and mobilizational experience they had amassed in prior club activism for the benefit of organized white supremacist resistance.

A wave of scholarship in the past decade has explored racialization and its intersection with class and region, particularly the history of poor whites. Historians Keri Leigh Merritt and Nancy Isenberg have shown that evolving definitions of whiteness, class, and social status in the South and in the nation further complicate the history of white supremacy. Merritt argues that poor whites in the nineteenth century "possessed class consciousness" and chronicles the tense relationship between poor whites and emancipated blacks particularly after Reconstruction.[21] The working-class women of Little Rock and New Orleans were both heirs to and producers of class-based resentment against a white elite as well as a white supremacist hostility toward black people. African Americans' acquisition of economic and cultural capital through desegregation threatened what segregationists viewed as a socially mandated racial hierarchy and the idea of "whiteness as treasured property," which afforded everyday privileges even to white working-class people.[22]

In its basic definition, class denotes the "economic stratification" created by access to the means of production, material assets, and, as historian Barbara Fields notes, the "ideological mediations" of these markers of "inequality of human beings from the standpoint of social power."[23] Class, therefore, is also gendered, racialized, spatialized. In order to trace the multifaceted aspects of the working-class street politics in defense of white community assets of segregationist women in Little Rock and in New Orleans and the white supremacist agitation and network building with right-wing and conservative players of middle- and upper-class segregationist women in Charleston, my analysis employs the sociologist Pierre Bourdieu's conceptualization of social classes and different forms of capital. To Bourdieu, class is at once an economic circumstance, derived from "material differences," and a sociocultural circumstance, "expressed in lifestyles," habitus, and representations.[24] In this view, the social world is a "multi-dimensional space that can be constructed by discovering the main factors of differentiation." This social differentiation results from the unequal distribution of the immanent power of different forms of capital.[25]

Whereas capital is, at its core, an economic condition, it can, Bourdieu argues "present itself in three fundamental guises": as economic capital, as cultural capital (broadly translatable as culture, representation, and knowledge), and as social capital (comprised of social connections and networks that promise to be mutually beneficial to its members and to offer resources).[26] Bourdieu's notion of cultural capital directly relates to the school desegregation struggles in Little Rock and New Orleans. In its institutionalized state, Bourdieu argues, cultural capital encompasses education, including schools and universities. The prior cultural capital of one's family plays a role in the level of education one achieves, and the educational system can make it possible for one to acquire knowledge and, therefore, cultural capital, which in turn can be converted into economic capital—the path to upward social mobility.[27]

The Mothers' League of Central High School and the cheerleaders of New Orleans protested the desegregation of formerly white public schools in their respective working-class districts. Bourdieu states that people who occupy "neighboring positions" in social space "are placed in similar conditions and are therefore subject to similar conditioning factors." Through this economic, social, and cultural proximity of individuals of a similar social class, mutual dispositions and views arise. These dispositions and views create a "sense of one's place" in society, which produces a desire to define and police boundaries between social groups.[28]

Physical space, too, expresses this relational, changeable social matrix. In *Postmodern Geographies*, Edward Soja shows that while primordially given, the organization and the meaning of geographical space are socially constructed, translated, and transformed. Space is not a structure separate from a society's framework but is imbricated in modes of production and sociocultural hierarchies.[29] The social structure shaped the space in which white supremacy asserted itself through the legal segregation of public facilities, federal and local housing policies that fostered residential segregation, suburbanization and white flight, zoning laws and ghettoization, busing and property value controversies, and expressed fears that the close proximity of black and white students in desegregated schools would encourage miscegenation. The actions of segregationist women across the socioeconomic spectrum were spatialized, too: they defended their turf—geographically and socially.

Simultaneously, the social backgrounds and the public behaviors of the working-class and lower middle-class women in Little Rock and New Orleans located them at the margins of this white supremacist space. In contrast to their fellow segregationist agitators in Charleston, South Carolina, and to their moderate white counterparts, the women of the mothers' league and the cheerleaders had little economic, cultural, and least of all social capital in their communities. In fact, upper and middle-class whites referred to these women as "white trash." Adolphine Terry, the patron of the moderate Women's Emergency Committee to Open Our Schools in Little Rock, a group of elite white women who campaigned to reopen Little Rock's high schools after their closure in the 1958–59 school year, called the women of the Mothers' League of Central High "a group of poor whites and a portion of the lunatic fringe that every town possesses." The league embarrassed the "better class" of Little Rock's whites.[30] Similarly, opponents of the cheerleaders of New Orleans dismissed them as "white trash." The cheerleaders, in turn, reclaimed the term and used the same insult to describe every white person who was not, in their view, sufficiently white supremacist.[31] The segregationist women active in Little Rock's mothers' league oscillated between being seen as respectable, although marginal, working-class whites who aimed to defend their social position within the community and being labeled white trash as a result of the transgressive actions they took to ensure their social position. The cheerleaders, in contrast, were not concerned with their reputation, and the majority of the group embraced and co-opted their media portrayal as vulgar and improper.

The term "white trash" is historically and culturally loaded.[32] It emerged in the mid-nineteenth century, bound to a long national history in which class and race were entangled, and was used to express disdain for the supposed idleness and destitution of lower classes and their supposedly genetic inferiority. By 1850, northern commentators as well as southern elites were derisively portraying a distinct caste of "southern white trash," a permanent social class of poor white laborers and landless farmers. The concept of southern white trash encompassed class and race as well as gender and space: elite whites viewed "white trash" women as "a wretched specimen of maternity" who did not "care properly for their offspring," Nancy Isenberg argues. Variations of these themes reemerge in critics' descriptions of working-class women who were massive resistance proponents in Arkansas and Louisiana. During Reconstruction, Isenberg shows, "Republicans designated white trash as a 'dangerous class' that was producing a flood of bastards, prostitutes, vagrants, and criminals," violating sexual and social norms. In social and in spatial terms, commentators perceived the individuals whom they deemed southern white trash as a "stagnant" people who exhibited geographical, cultural, social inertia. The category white trash, Annalee Newitz and Matt Wray argue, is a "naming practice" that has helped define "stereotypes of what is and is not acceptable or normal" behavior for white people in the United States.[33] The cases of the mothers' league and the cheerleaders reveal how such designations were deployed within communities in a supposedly solid white South.

For an understanding of the political escalations in Little Rock and New Orleans, it is vital to recognize the entanglement of class and race. This entanglement figured in white supremacist grassroots activism, including the women's groups, but it equally permeated the actions of state politicians in dispute with the federal government. National media portrayed Arkansas governor Orval Faubus as an Ozark hillbilly, and Faubus, in turn, embraced this idea of himself to ramp up support from grassroots segregationists in his home state, who had theretofore chided Faubus for his inadequate backing of white supremacy.[34] In Louisiana, Governor Jimmy Davis represented himself as the voice of rural, poor people in his campaigns. The singer, actor, and son of sharecroppers presented himself as "a hillbilly with a touch of style," as Isenberg aptly summarizes. Both Faubus and Davis were aware of their white trash reputation in Washington, D.C., and in the national media, and both defiantly toyed with it.[35]

Many historians have addressed the complex relationships between the white and the black working classes, instances of interracial cooperation, white working-class racism, and the "psychological wage of whiteness" that set white workers apart from black workers.[36] The mostly working- and lower middle-class female segregationists in Little Rock and in New Orleans had an acute sense of their place and the place in society they designated to others. The women regarded Central High School, Frantz, and McDonogh 19 elementary schools, and public space as rightfully theirs. The middle and upper-class female massive resistance supporters in Charleston and South Carolina's Lowcountry, too, were acutely aware and supportive of their region's racialized caste system, and they defended what they saw as the naturally owned spaces and privileges of white people. A "legitimizing theatricalization" of everyday practices goes hand in hand with the exercise of power, according to Bourdieu's conceptualization of social classes and space. These theatrical practices are designed to justify domination.[37] *Massive Resistance and Southern Womanhood* applies Bourdieu's theory of power and performance to the activism of female segregationist who, through theatricalization and medialization, created performative spaces by which they could justify their actions and have an impact.

Space is a dynamic, practiced place, shaped by different actors.[38] Women in massive resistance were actors in this process, and they constructed different, performative spaces for themselves in the public sphere based on their socioeconomic and sociocultural backgrounds. Historians and political scientists have theorized the public sphere as spaces that are essentially democratic due to their open access, use of common resources, and employment for the performance of public roles.[39] However, public spaces also reflect and reconstruct social hierarchies, which means that they are gendered and racially compartmentalized, and those hierarchies are reflected in the fact of segregated facilities and separate spheres.[40] The ideology of separate spheres and domestic containment in the 1950s and early 1960s complicated the access to public roles that segregationist women had owing to white privilege.

What constitutes a performative space? Erving Goffman's seminal study, *The Presentation of Self in Everyday Life*, defines a performance as "all the activity of an individual which occurs during a period marked by his continuous presence before a particular set of observers and which has some influence on the observers."[41] Performance is not only an individual activity; people can also form "teams" that cooperate to maintain "a given projected definition" of a situation. Segregationist agitators in all three locales formed such teams, and they sought to define desegregation as a state of emergency to their observers to legitimize their actions and elicit support.[42]

Performances, whether on a theater stage or in the streets, are "a microcosm of social structure."[43] According to Judith Butler, gender and sex, for example, are codetermined and constituted by performative, corporeal acts.[44] Female massive resistance proponents were self-conscious agents in their gendered self-portrayals. The women of Little Rock's mothers' league publicly presented themselves as white damsels in distress and Charleston's Cornelia Tucker dressed herself in delicate chiffon robes at dinner parties she used for political networking, while the New Orleans cheerleaders consciously transgressed gender lines with their violent behavior and were subsequently labeled unfeminine.[45]

In his work on the public performances of street theater by civil rights activists and activists of the New Left in the 1960s, Martin Bradford points out that public performances contributed to the permeation of life by everyday politics and broadened the definition of politics and political engagement.[46] Segregationist women, too, broadened the political arena with their public performances on the street, through their lobbying campaigns, and with publicity stunts. Through the media-conscious theatricalization of their protests, segregationist women not only sought to justify white domination but to push against public scripts, that is, explicit and implicit social rules and customs of legitimate behavior, and social frames that defined women's social roles and political positions.[47]

All segregationist women sought to justify their public activism through performative acts, but the performances of working-class women in Little Rock and New Orleans were very different from those of middle- and upper-class women in Charleston and South Carolina's Lowcountry owing to economic, social, and cultural capital or a lack thereof. The predominantly working-class and lower middle-class women in Little Rock and New Orleans were unable to rely on the resources of social elite networks in their communities, and their lack of financial resources further complicated their protest. These women were not considered power players in the grand scheme of things, and their social positioning as working- and lower middle-class housewives or working mothers meant they did not have an influential public voice. Drastic measures seemed to be in order to rationalize their public actions and generate influence, which resulted in the construction of performative spaces that deviated from the norm. Both in Little Rock and in New Orleans, observers commented on the apparent "carnival-like" atmosphere that surrounded the protests, at least until their violent escalations, an atmosphere in which certain "social constraints" were "suspended."[48] In his study on behavioral scripts and power relations, historian James Scott argues that carnival allows "certain things to be said, certain forms of social power to be exercised that are muted or suspended outside this ritual sphere."[49]

Women's activism in Little Rock and in New Orleans emerged out of an impending desegregation crisis, one they helped create. This perceived emergency served as an opportunity structure that made the public sphere more accessible to women's activism. A variety of factors, including shifting political circumstances and social relations and the actions taken by participants in crisis situations can create opportunity structures, that is, enhanced possibilities for grassroots mobilization and impact on "mainstream institutional politics and policy."[50]

The state of emergency that the working-class and lower middle-class women in Little Rock and New Orleans contributed to and capitalized on never occurred in Charleston because, in part, segregationist women in Charleston and the Lowcountry did not have to escalate that far in order to be effective on behalf of white supremacy. To be sure, these segregationist agitators also employed theatrical and media-conscious strategies, but Cornelia Tucker and other grassroots white supremacist women mostly had the social networks, organizational experience, and resources to influence local and regional politics. Middle- and upper-class women used maternalist discourses and hardline white supremacist rhetoric, their participation in lobbying and grassroots mobilization campaigns, and their successful establishment of links to broader conservative networks in the region and the nation to create performative spaces that justified their public interventions and deviation from the Old South southern belle ideal. In Charleston, moreover, segregationist politicians and grassroots officials were reassured by the higher age and social rank of the women who were prominently active in segregationist campaigning. Women's actions on behalf of massive resistance were presented and perceived as a natural extension of their Daughters of the American Revolution or United Daughters of the Confederacy memberships.

Although strategies, methods, and some ultimate goals varied, the common denominator for the proponents of massive resistance was the defense of white supremacy and the continuation of segregation. Women deliberately created group- and region-specific popular images for their organizations and for themselves as individuals. They were aware of journalists' role as actors in the desegregation crises rather than mere observers. Women consciously enlisted the help of the press in order to gain attention and to widen their spaces of influence. The public image of the women's groups varied and was related to class, but there was a sexist undertone in the coverage of all of them. Media either concentrated on women's appearances or described their behavior in a stereotypically gendered way, including labeling some of the women as hysterical.

White supremacist women's activism was entwined with external influences, such as their geographical region or the progress made by the civil rights movement at the time. In a classic definition formulated by social scientists Friedhelm Neidhardt and Dieter Rucht, social movements are "organized and sustained" of a "collectivity of inter-related individuals, groups and organizations to promote or to resist social change with the use of public protest activities."[51] In this sense, massive resistance was a social movement that sought to counter civil rights progress, starting different campaigns, employing different strategies, and serving as an overall identificatory tool for diverse, elite and grassroots white supremacist agitators from the 1950s onward. Segregationist women's actions were at times responsive to perceived civil rights "threats," at times proactive, and always adaptive.

Massive resistance was a countermovement to increasing political and judicial pressure that threatened the legal codification of segregation and to the civil rights movement that captured the national stage from the 1950s to the 1970s. While massive resistance was part of a long history of white supremacy and the oppression of African Americans that transcended a southern sectional struggle, it was also a distinct phase in a regional response to the post–World War II phase of the black freedom struggle, which challenged discriminatory laws and practices in the South as well as the systematic, institutionalized discrimination against African Americans across the nation.[52] White supremacists perceived the *Brown* ruling in particular as a fundamental attack on segregation and its legal and habitual underpinnings. Massive resistance was a diverse, dynamic, and concerted effort by a conglomerate of white supremacist actors who sought to expand their opposition to legal and social equality beyond their own region. In the late 1960s and in the 1970s, massive resistance branched out, inserting itself into desegregation clashes in Chicago, Detroit, and Boston, where segregationists mimicked the tactics they had seen unfold in southern communities a decade earlier.

Massive resistance's trajectory was longer than the federal legislation that supposedly ended segregation with the Civil Rights Act in 1964, the Voting

Rights Act in 1965, and the Fair Housing Act in 1968, and it is this sustained mobilization and agitation of elite and grassroots white supremacists that distinguishes massive resistance from earlier white supremacist protest. Segregationist politicians and grassroots activists in the South began to mount a determined campaign in the late 1940s against the civil rights platform of the national Democratic party, desegregation verdicts by federal courts, and the federal government's changing attitudes toward the long-standing demands of black civil rights activists. Segregationist agitators began to launch concerted actions against this fundamental challenge to segregation and white supremacy between the establishment of the States' Rights Party, known as the Dixiecrats, in 1948 and the first *Brown* verdict in 1954. With the *Brown* decision, massive resistance came into full force.[53]

Massive resistance was characterized by its aggressive defense against the perceived assault on legally codified and customary everyday white privileges by the actions of civil rights activists, federal court decisions, and federal legislation.[54] The rallying point of working-class and lower middle-class women in massive resistance was the imminent desegregation orders in their communities, although they all had long espoused a belief in white supremacy. They decisively acted on these convictions only after *Brown* and were able to cultivate support from white elites, and thus the period of their public segregationist protest agitation was more truncated than in the case of the predominantly middle- and upper-class women supporters of massive resistance whose ideologies and actions Elizabeth McRae rightly traced back to the 1920s.[55]

Working-class and lower middle-class women, exemplified by the mothers' league and the cheerleaders, were unable to sustain their political influence after the imminent desegregation crises had faded. With few exceptions, these women did not have the social capital and, therefore, neither the social networks nor the resources to establish a more permanent presence in public conservative activism. Although a number of massive resistance supporters, most notably members of Little Rock's mothers' league attempted to transcend their previous actions and translate them into a career in right-wing politics, they had no stable connections to their community's civic and political elite and could not amass continued support. In addition, the stain of the "white trash" label white elites had given these women, immortalized in newspaper and television pictures that showed them screaming in front of the schools, was difficult to wash off.

Nevertheless, some middle-class and upper-class women segregationist actors were able to incorporate broader political tropes into their campaigns, which had the effect of aligning these campaigns with regional and national conservative organizations.[56] Intellectuals and grassroots activists formed an organized, conservative social and political movement after the Second World War.[57] The tenets and ideological roots of modern conservatism are diverse, but the conservative political spectrum houses social and moral traditionalism, fervent anticommunism, political opposition to racial equality and other social equality movements, laissez-faire capitalism, opposition to federal interventions on the state level and antistatism, and libertarian views on individualism and freedom of choice. The formation of the *National Review* in 1955 by William F. Buckley Jr. functioned as a consolidating space for different currents of conservatism and for the movement's self-identification. After the Second World War, these ideologies were embraced by both white upper- and middle-class communities in suburbia and by urban and rural working-class communities in the Old and the modernizing Sunbelt South.[58] If we understand the modern conservative movement as "a collective identity" that developed and evolved "in the course of struggles and collaborations over meaning," we can see how a number of segregationist female activists might have seen their quest for continued white supremacy as compatible with conservative ideologies. A shared belief in everyday white supremacy, which afforded white people across the socioeconomic spectrum race-based privileges, included preferential treatment, the belief in white people's essential superiority, and spatialized power, resting on the assumption that all spaces, public and private, physical and social, belonged to white people, and nonwhite people were intruders, could serve as the tool for fusing and consolidating diverse views.[59]

Proponents of massive resistance advocated a reactionary worldview rooted in white supremacy. The relationship between the segregationist structure of the state and segregationist grassroots campaigns was both symbiotic and mutually reinforcing. Massive resistance was not solely a top-down phenomenon—at times, segregationists' resistance was driven by the activism of grassroots groups.[60] The relationship between massive resistance's grassroots groups' male-dominated leadership and women's activities within the movement was likewise symbiotic. Although massive resistance was undeniably male-led, the movement's women's groups and individual activists were not necessarily subordinate to men. Women's activism at times complemented, at times dominated, and at times prompted men's activism.

Tucker taunted Kennedy in her letter by infantilizing him, thus implicitly questioning his masculinity. This was a tried and true tactic that the Mothers' League of Central High School also consciously employed to stir men into action. It is within this network of interdependent conversations about white supremacy, race, gender, class, region, and space, in which segregationist women in Arkansas, Louisiana, and South Carolina initiated and executed their activism in massive resistance. *Massive Resistance and Southern Womanhood* uncovers their paths.

Chapter 1 analyzes and compares Arkansas's, Louisiana's, and South Carolina's respective massive resistance campaigns, in particular the civil rights activism and segregationist backlash leading up to the desegregation crises in Little Rock from 1957 to 1959, in New Orleans from 1960 to 1962, and the extended defiance in South Carolina that centered around Charleston and its metropolitan area from 1954 to 1963. This chapter highlights central argumentative lines in massive resistance in these states and locales, emphasizing the positions adopted at the regional grassroots level and the concomitant gender aspects of segregationist resistance.

Chapter 2 presents the first case study: the formation, strategies, and activities of the Mothers' League of Central High School between 1957 and 1960. The league's segregationist activism was both dynamic and adaptable. It widened its activism from participation in a local desegregation crisis to working for regional elections and ultimately to an attempt to form a national organization. It created performative spaces through both stereotypically gendered displays of hyperbolic emotion and through aggressive actions. The women thus carved out a space for a white working-class, female politics in Arkansas. Ultimately, however, the group's lack of economic and social capital and its branding as the city's "white trash" thwarted it, and it dissolved in 1960.

Chapter 3 analyzes the emergence and actions of the so-called cheerleaders during the desegregation crisis surrounding two elementary schools in New Orleans, William Frantz and McDonough 19, tracing the name of the group and presenting a social history of these predominantly working-class women. The chapter also examines the women's verbal and physical violence and their social status, focusing in particular on their creation of performative spaces, the conscious corporeality of their actions, and the relationship between them and the media. The core group of cheerleaders was more diverse in terms of their social background and education level than previously assumed, thus complicating the "white trash" label often associated with their image.

Chapter 4 examines segregationist women's groups and individual female activists in Charleston and South Carolina's surrounding Lowcountry between 1954 and 1963. South Carolina's campaign of massive resistance avoided a localized, highly publicized school desegregation crisis, and the state defied *Brown* until 1963. The state had several enclaves of white supremacist activism, however, and one of the most active was in Charleston and its metropolitan area. Here, the most prominent women who engaged in massive resistance were middle to upper class; this chapter thus provides an excursus into a different social space. Female segregationists in South Carolina had previously been politically active in patriotic societies and civic clubs, and they were able to align their segregationist activism with broader conservative values. Female activists in Charleston's massive resistance grassroots movement could, therefore, muster more economic and social capital, and their history provides a contrast filter to the working-class segregationist women in Arkansas and Louisiana. South Carolina segregationists were the most successful in framing what appeared to be a sectional struggle as a question of national and even international importance.

The conclusion points to the central similarities and differences of the women's groups and individuals analyzed in the case studies and assesses their significance for the study of women in massive resistance, linking these women's activism to right-wing and new conservative politics from the 1950s onward. White women employed varied tactics in their activism in defense of white supremacy. Creating performative spaces through their actions, which generated publicity value, allowed them to extend the frames that limited their public roles. "Ordinary" white women as well as women who were previously politically active were motivated by a culture of everyday racism that inscribed racialized expectations and privileges. Segregationist women helped to create crises in order to avoid desegregation and to police the boundaries of white privilege. They were as versed in the ideology and just as committed to the defense of white supremacy as their fellow male activists.

CHAPTER 1

Massive Resistance in Arkansas, Louisiana, and South Carolina

The United States Supreme Court decision *Brown v. Board of Education*, rendered on May 17, 1954, served as a rallying point for massive resistance. The court declared that racial segregation was unconstitutional in public schools but refrained from giving instructions as to how this ruling should be implemented, instead inviting the defendants and every southern state that practiced segregation to hand in their opinion on the topic.[1] Nonetheless, civil rights activists were enthused by the ruling. In her memoir, Daisy Bates, president of Arkansas's NAACP state conference, writes that to "the nation's Negroes the Supreme Court decision meant that the time for delay, evasion, or procrastination was past."[2]

On May 31, 1955, the Supreme Court followed up with its implementation decision, commonly known as *Brown II*. Putting the responsibility for public school desegregation on local school boards and district courts, the court requested a "prompt and reasonable start toward full compliance." The fact that the Supreme Court refused to give a firm deadline but prompted the defendants to proceed "with all deliberate speed" was criticized by civil rights activists and historians alike.[3]

The *Brown* verdicts represented a fundamental challenge to legal segregation in public education and, therefore, one of the bases of white supremacist rule and the discriminatory retention of cultural and economic capital. Even before *Brown II*, organized resistance to the desegregation ruling was already under way. Two days after the first *Brown* decision, Democratic U.S. representative John Bell Williams of Mississippi coined a segregationist term by naming the day of the verdict "Black Monday." Mississippi and Georgia politicians vowed to abolish the public school system rather than to desegregate, while Louisiana simply proclaimed that *Brown* did not apply to the Pelican state.[4] After *Brown*, the South readied itself to defend Jim Crow.[5] But contrary to the picture that segregationist politicians were trying to paint, southern states were not homogenous in their resistance against the desegregation ruling. Democratic populist governor Francis Cherry of Arkansas announced that Arkansas would "obey the law" because "it always has," when he was questioned about *Brown* in 1954, and upper southern states initiated desegregation processes for the 1954–55 school year.[6]

In an attempt to unify the South, the southern delegation in Congress drafted the Declaration of Constitutional Principles, known as the Southern Manifesto. Authored by Democratic U.S. senators Richard B. Russell of Georgia, Sam Ervin of North Carolina, John Stennis of Mississippi, and Strom Thurmond of South Carolina, the manifesto bore the signature of almost every southern congressman.[7] The declaration earned the support of "both intransigents and moderates within the Southern Congressional Delegation," historian John Kyle Day shows, and was introduced in Congress on March 12, 1956. The manifesto condemned what it saw as the "unwarranted exercise of power by the Court, contrary to the Constitution," and proclaimed that the South would resist *Brown* by "all lawful means." The congressmen announced the common goal of eventually overturning the verdict.[8] The expression "massive resistance" itself was coined by Harry Byrd in February 1956. Although reporters were unsure whether the senator had called for "passive" or "massive" resistance at his press conference, the *New York Times* quoted Byrd as saying the latter, and with that, the segregationist movement had found a name.[9]

Weeks after *Brown*, segregationist activists formed the first citizens' council in Indianola, Mississippi, a movement of various segregationist organizations soon to appear in all southern states. These white supremacist grassroots groups proclaimed that they were fighting desegregation in a respectable manner and distanced themselves from the KKK. The councils did not shy away from issuing physical threats or implementing economic and social reprisals for refusal to toe the line, however. The councils recruited many members from the white working class and also received the support of middle-class whites, business owners, and politicians.[10]

Gender was a mobilization tool of massive resistance that was equally accessible to white supremacist elites and grassroots organizations, and the idea that segregationists would be saving white women from a racialized threat by preventing desegregation was a useful instrument for them. Gender was not only used by politicians as a way to invoke the collective symbolism of racial purity embodied by white southern women but also served as a recruitment device at the grass roots. An anti-integration flyer that circulated in Arkansas in 1958 illustrates the strategy.[11] With a frightened, alarmed face, "Southern Womanhood," embodied by a white southern belle with long hair, heavy makeup, and a flowing dress, flees before a demon-like creature that is chasing after her. The picture is entitled "Conquer and Breed," and that, coupled with the rip in "Southern Womanhood's" dress, which bares her leg, insinuates a sexualized

Anti-integration propaganda flyer, circa 1958 (Arkansas State Archives)

context. The ape-like demon in pursuit is named "Integration," and he casts a long shadow. He is tall, dark-skinned, has a naked and unshapely upper body, and his pants are already untied. His hair is curly, the nose is broad, and he has full lips, all of which are physical traits stereotypically attributed to black people. With a seemingly lusty gaze and open arms ready to snatch, he pursues white "Southern Womanhood." The integration demon is reminiscent of racist "black beast" depictions of black men at the turn of the century, which sought to justify racial segregation through tales of black degeneracy and monstrous sexuality.[12]

This handbill, disseminated by an unknown segregationist grassroots group, exemplifies the perception of miscegenation as an existential danger for the South. The flyer is also an example of segregationist grassroots activism and its defense of white supremacy. At the intersection of race and gender, the fight for an everyday culture of white privilege not only resonated with a large portion of the white southern population but was proactively propagated by many. The grassroots nature of this flyer is indicated by the writing on the arms of the integration demon, which reads "Demo. Party" and "Repub. Party." The author of this flyer regarded both the Republican and the Democratic Parties not only as inefficient institutions in the fight against desegregation but also literally as the political arms of integration, as part of the demon that had to be fought by the southern people.

The next part of the flyer exposes the alleged hidden agenda behind demands for school desegregation. It quotes several members of the NAACP, including former executive secretary Walter White, who it alleges stated that "the association of the Races in public schools leads to friendship, love and marriage". The integration demon's goal, then, becomes fully clear: to conquer white women and, through miscegenation, conquer the white race. The means by which black people would conquer white women is through children's association in desegregated public schools, which would result in "interracial" marriages. The peaceful, friendly, and fabricated Walter White quote is contradicted by the violence of the flyer's imagery and wording. It suggests that a relationship between white women and black men can only ever be the result of force.

Finally, the flyer calls for resistance against this supposed grim scenario: "The South Must Fight or Perish!" The long shadow cast by the demon integration, then, not only threatened white women but southern womanhood, the white race, white supremacy, and the entire "Southern Way of Life."[13] Although this depiction of white southern womanhood strips white women of any agency, historian Nell Painter notes that white women of all classes discovered that "they could raise themselves to the status of ladies in their own and in white men's eyes by joining the outcry against black men."[14] Gendered, racist propaganda sought to evoke a strong emotional reaction from whites and thereby rally support for white supremacy. It also served as a means of white upward social mobility. White women of lower social strata used their skin color as a tool to gain respect and influence in a white supremacist, patriarchal society. White women accessed white privilege to employ agency.

Traditional sexual norms were part of massive resistance's ideology, propagating not only the ideal of white southern womanhood but also its binary counterpart of hegemonic masculinity.[15] Segregationists' rhetoric expressed fear that white masculinity would be threatened by "forced" integration and that integration would lead to a loss of gendered and racialized privileges. Segregationists presented federal interventions as assaults not only on states' rights but on white men's virility. Defiance, in contrast, was associated with manhood, serving as an indicator of one's hegemonic masculinity. The allegedly insufficiently segregationist stance of the student newspaper at the University of Georgia, for example, led former Democratic state senator Roy Harris to declare that "those little sissy boys" should be "made to play football."[16] A segregationist comic entitled "White Man of Today" that was circulated throughout several southern states, moreover, depicted a white man beneath a tree, telling a bird to "go ahead" with its droppings: "I've let everyone else."[17] The native Louisianan judge James Skelly Wright, who issued several desegregation orders for News Orleans's public schools, received scornful letters from Louisiana segregationists who questioned not only his patriotism and his whiteness but also his manhood. Wright should leave the bench if he was "not man enough to protect the rights" of his own people, an anonymous letter from "A Southern Gentleman" charged. Another self-named "New Orleans segregationist" condemned Wright for his stance and asked whether Skelly wanted any of his female relatives to be raped by black men. The anonymous letter writer went on to praise the lynching of Emmett Till and the men of Mississippi for having "plenty of guts what the [Louisiana] men lack." Finally, an anonymous letter from "an old Grandma" asked Wright to read her protest "and think what am I a man or a half man."[18] Gender served as an emotional, agitating rhetorical device at the grassroots and for white elites.

Segregationist women's activism relied on tried and tested gendered and racialized scripts for their public activism, but they also created performative spaces that extended these traditional frames. Segregationist women took advantage of perceived power vacuums created by the entanglements between federal, regional, and local authorities and the inertia of civil elites, which left room for nontraditional actors to intervene publicly. They co-created and exacerbated crises in order to maintain and expand their influence.[19]

Massive resistance was never uniform across the South. Historian George Lewis has identified it as a "conglomeration of concomitant conversations of resistance," which housed "a multitude of groups and individuals . . . under the banner of southern resistance."[20] Segregationist politicians and grassroots activists joined together to defend white supremacy. Within this network of interdependent conversations about white supremacy, race, gender, class, and region, segregationist women's groups in Arkansas, Louisiana, and South Carolina undertook their activism. Each group confronted a different stage of the civil rights movement and massive resistance's countercampaign.

The desegregation crisis surrounding Little Rock, Arkansas, was one of the hardest tests. "In 1958, Little Rock was a different city," concluded superintendent of schools Virgil T. Blossom two years after the peak of the school desegregation crisis. Despite its prior reputation as a progressive southern city, Little Rock had been the stage for racist violence in the past, and it ended up being the center of white resistance to desegregation.[21] The city had served as headquarters for the Women of the Ku Klux Klan since 1923, and Little Rock's assistant superintendent of schools at the time, Annie Griffey, was a member of the organization, foreshadowing the ties between children's education, white women, and white supremacy.[22]

After the Second World War, Little Rock became Arkansas's most important economic center. Little Rock's increasing urbanity contrasted with the rural character of the state's Ozark Mountains in the northwest and the delta in the southeast. Arkansas's geographic diversity was mirrored in differing social compositions and political mentalities. Whereas almost 25 percent of the 107,000 people of Little Rock in the 1950s were African American, only 4 percent of Arkansas's rural and financially strapped northwestern region's inhabitants were black. Fifteen of the state's seventy-five counties had no African American pupils at all, whereas in other counties up to 60 percent of the student population was African American.[23] In 1952, Arkansas's expenditures per pupil amounted to $102.05 for whites compared to $67.75 for African Americans. Little Rock had already desegregated parts of its public facilities in the late 1940s and early 1950s, but its city planning, slum clearance and block-busting techniques became effective tools, which were implemented starting as early as the 1930s and used into the 1970s, for maintaining de facto segregation.[24]

While the state's northwest was less prone to the politics of white supremacy and had traditionally supported politicians with populist platforms, including Sid McMath and Orval Faubus, in Arkansas's southeastern region, where up until the early 1950s, plantations were an economic staple and the percentage of African Americans averaged 50 percent, the ideology and politics of white supremacy flourished, personified by influential members in the state legislature.[25] Delta politicians initiated the state's protest against *Brown* and took the first legal steps to preserve Arkansas's public school segregation. In March 1955, two months before *Brown II*, Democratic state senator Fletcher Long of Forrest City introduced a bill designed to circumvent school desegregation. The bill ordered every school district to nominate an official who would have to place students individually according to a variety of factors, excluding race, thus allowing for a justification of continued segregation by obscuring racial discrimination.[26]

Democratic state senator Max Howell of Little Rock, the bill's only outspoken opponent, succeeded in using an array of tactical maneuvers, resulting in the tabling of the bill, although Little Rock and other locales were able in the end to use the strategy to maintain segregation.[27] Distinguishing Arkansas from neighboring states and their white supremacist tactics, Howell warned his fellow senators that "just because some other dyed-in-the-wool southern state jumped in haste to preserve [segregation] doesn't mean that Arkansas should."[28] Evidently, the political climate in Little Rock regarding race relations was moderate enough to allow Howell the opportunity to speak up against more extreme measures of defiance to *Brown*. This more moderate climate owed in part to the initiative of several black activists, such as attorneys Scipio Jones and Harold Flowers, voter registration campaigns, and the 1941 founding of the *Arkansas State Press* by L. C. Bates and his wife, Daisy Bates, which helped the black community establish its political presence in Little Rock. In the 1940s, the NAACP began to challenge racial discrimination in court.[29]

Shortly after the *Brown* decision, Arkansas seemed on the path of relative compliance. Within days, the Little Rock School Board advised Blossom to work out a plan to desegregate the city's public schools.[30] The state's newly elected Democratic governor, Orval Faubus, made no mention of desegregation in his inaugural address, while three school districts in northwest Arkansas had immediately drawn up plans to desegregate without encountering resistance. Daisy Bates, who had been elected president of the NAACP's Arkansas State Conference of Branches in 1952, stated that the NAACP had no immediate plans for action but was waiting for the Arkansas legislature to announce their position on the subject.[31]

In September 1954, Blossom presented the original "Blossom Plan" to the executive board of Little Rock's NAACP. Desegregation would begin in September 1956 at the high schools, where enrollment would be determined by racially unspecified city school zones. A year later junior high schools would follow and, finally, the elementary schools.[32] After *Brown II*, however, politicians and Little Rock school officials adopted a policy of minimum compliance, using the Supreme Court's implementation order as a justification for tokenism and delay.[33] In August 1955, Bates issued a request to the Little Rock Board of Education calling for the immediate integration of Little Rock's public schools, which the board rejected. The Little Rock NAACP branch subsequently filed suit in federal district court.[34] Federal district court judge John Miller endorsed the Blossom Plan and attested that the Little Rock Board of Education practiced "the utmost good faith."[35] Little Rock's first phase of public school desegregation was officially set for September 1957 with the token integration of Little Rock Central High and Hall High. Segregationist resistance in the city spiked. After both of its candidates lost to moderate opponents who vowed to uphold the Blossom Plan in the school board elections of March 1957, Little Rock's white supremacist Capital Citizens' Council opted for an extrainstitutional approach to circumvent desegregation.[36]

Echoing the strategy of fellow activists across the South, the council's campaign against public school integration focused on a racialized framing of gender and class issues in an attempt to unite and solidify white resistance in the city.[37] Segregationists who had employed the same tactics and rhetoric during the school desegregation crisis at Hoxie, Arkansas, in the summer and fall of 1955 came to the fore, most notably L. D. Poynter and his group White America, Inc., which included former Democratic state senator Jim Johnson of Crossett and the council's attorney, Amis Guthridge. They executed a vigorous publicity campaign that relied on and generated white people's opposition to "miscegenation" in order to stir fears of whites' losing privileges and that attacked Faubus, Blossom, and the Little Rock School Board for their perceived prointegration stances.[38]

Given that the previous redistricting of Little Rock's Hall High School's attendance area had left the school with only six potential African American students, none of whom sought enrollment, Central High became the first and only school in Little Rock to be scheduled for desegregation in 1957.[39] Segregationist activists used the already present anxiety related to social mobility to their advantage while exacerbating the existing resistance of parents and students who lived in Central High's attendance area. In contrast to Hall High School, which had been built in 1956 for students living in Pulaski Heights, otherwise known as the prosperous "silk-stocking district," Central High School was located in a neighborhood that was predominantly lower middle and working class.[40] Central High had traditionally served white children of these families, giving them a chance for upward social mobility.[41]

Blossom and the school board members had virtually ignored the residents of the Central High School district, and Blossom also failed to call on the aid of the city's white moderate business and social elite.[42] The Capital Citizens' Council began a sustained campaign to prevent desegregation. The group would show over the summer of 1957 how much segregationist grassroots activism could alter official local and state policy. The council asked Arkansas's governor to exercise his executive power to prevent school integration. The group continued the stream of segregationist organizations' attacks on Faubus for his perceived gradualist and noncommittal attitude toward segregation.[43] To pressure Faubus, the council published newspaper advertisements that instructed white readers to "write, wire or phone the Governor" to prevent "Race-Mixing."[44]

The council was adept at stirring up underlying currents of a culture of white supremacy. Through the constant reiteration and bold printing of words like "race mixing," the council insinuated that the desegregation matter was not merely one of school integration but of looming miscegenation. The group created a state of crisis, which it proclaimed could only be solved by a white leader rising up to his duties.[45]

In their antidesegregation campaign, council officials Amis Guthridge and James Wesley Pruden Sr. repeatedly alluded to potential "interracial" dating and "miscegenation."[46] Ultimately, this segregationist offensive put enough pressure on Blossom to cause him to once again alter his plan. Having insisted on individual screening processes by the principals of Horace Mann und Dunbar for each student who was contemplating a transfer to Central, Blossom personally interviewed the thirty-two remaining candidates who were suggested by the black high schools' principals. Blossom used this opportunity to discourage or dismiss over 70 percent of the preselected students from enrolling at Central High School, leaving only nine black pupils who were allowed to register at Central High School for the 1957–58 school year.[47]

Still, it was hard to imagine that "Remember Little Rock" would soon become the battle cry of segregationists across the South. Three years after Central High School's desegregation, however, Arkansas's Deep South neighbor Louisiana evoked the slogan in order to rally against school desegregation in New Orleans. Compared to other southern states, Louisiana was much more culturally diverse, boasting French and Spanish colonial heritages as well as Cajun and Creole traditions.[48] In 1960, New Orleans had a population of over 600,000 people, 233,000 of whom were black. New Orleans housed a quarter of Louisiana's total population as the fifteenth biggest city in the United States and the second biggest port in the South.[49] Black and white New Orleanians traditionally lived in mixed neighborhoods, although residential subdivisions built after the Second World War were more strictly segregated. And after years of unsuccessful petitioning, New Orleans's prominent NAACP activist and Seventh Ward resident Alexander Pierre (A. P.) Tureaud had reached an out-of-court settlement with the Orleans Parish School Board that ensured the equalization of salaries for black and white teachers in *McKelpin v. Orleans Parish School Board* in 1942.[50] New Orleans was known as a cultural and ethnic mosaic, and its "lazy, hedonistic culture seemed to discourage extreme racism," historian Adam Fairclough asserts.[51]

The contrast to Little Rock was substantial. But despite this distinct cultural history and southern Louisiana's predominant Catholicism, the state was entrenched in an everyday culture of white supremacy. Many Catholic churches were segregated, and the Archdiocese of New Orleans did not employ black priests until the 1950s.[52] The Catholic Church played an ambivalent role in the New Orleans schools desegregation crisis of 1960. The church opposed segregation on moral grounds but failed to establish a precedent with its own parochial schools. As the existence of deeply religious Catholic cheerleaders shows, individuals' belief in Catholicism and white supremacy were not mutually exclusive either but could serve to support segregationist activism. The color line was part of New Orleanians' daily lives from street cars to schools.[53]

Although when deLesseps Morrison became mayor in 1946, an office he would hold for four consecutive terms until 1961, a progressive spirit seemed on New Orleanians' side, as Morrison was not only affiliated with the moderate white city elite but also swiftly established ties to the black community. He never questioned the underlying system of racial segregation however. Aspiring to the governor's office, he made little effort to distance himself from race-baiting campaign tactics and stayed silent on the desegregation of New Orleans's public schools until the desegregation of William Frantz and McDonogh 19 elementary schools became imminent in 1960.[54] Segregationists, nonetheless, accused him of fraternizing with the black community.[55]

During the 1940s and 1950s, black activists intensified their fight for equal access to educational opportunities.[56] Black children constituted between 50 and 57 percent of the city's pupils over the years, but New Orleans's black public schools were overcrowded and understaffed. Due to the lack of educational facilities and teachers, over ten thousand black pupils in New Orleans were forced into the platoon system, that is, a system of rotating school hours whereby half of the pupils attended school in the morning and the other half in the afternoon. Whereas the Orleans Parish School Board operated eighty-seven schools for white children, there were only thirty-four schools for black pupils. Even after *Brown*, Orleans Parish School Board president Clarence Scheps admitted that "very definitely an unequal situation" existed between black and white students.[57]

In November 1951, after years of unsuccessfully petitioning the school board, black parents and the NAACP abandoned their accommodationist stance. Tureaud presented the school board with a petition asking for the immediate integration of New Orleans's public schools. The Orleans Parish School Board denied the request.[58] Already working on his legal strategy with the support of the NAACP's Legal Defense and Educational Fund, Tureaud proceeded to file suit on September 5, 1952. *Bush v. Orleans Parish School Board* asked for the desegregation of the city's public schools.[59] For the next eight years, the school board engaged the NAACP in court battles to circumvent desegregation. The school board believed, Scheps declared, that "New Orleans schools were never going to be integrated." Meanwhile, Tureaud agreed to suspend the *Bush* case while awaiting the Supreme Court's decision on *Brown*.[60]

Education and state officials' initial reactions to *Brown* in May 1954 were calm. Governor Robert Kennon assumed a "wait-and-see position," Louisiana's State superintendent of education Shelby M. Jackson declined to comment, and both New Orleans's superintendent of schools James Redmond and Orleans Parish School Board president Scheps said they needed more time to study the verdict.[61] Louisiana's black activists celebrated. Tureaud said it was "a momentous decision which has very serious implications that seem to outlaw segregation," optimistically speculating that "the court decision may make unnecessary filing suits in the various parishes for Negro applicants to Louisiana schools." The state's black newspaper, the *Louisiana Weekly*, commented that the "stamp of approval is no longer on second class citizenship" but urged its readers to go vote in the upcoming years "to make the decision stick."[62]

Louisiana's legislature was one of the few in session when news of the ruling broke. Unlike educational officials, the state legislature was outright defiant and passed several bills in order to obstruct the ruling. One legislative resolution adopted the rhetoric of massive resistance, calling *Brown* "a usurpation of power" and dismissing integration as "intolerable, impractical, and in the ultimate sense unenforceable."[63]

During June 1954, three additional bills were passed and signed into law. They prohibited the state board of education from allotting financial support to desegregated public education institutions and provided local superintendents with the power to implement pupil placement plans. Only the lobbying work of the Catholic Church prevented these provisions from also applying to parochial and other private schools, attended by almost half of New Orleans's schoolchildren. Francis Rummel, archbishop of the Archdiocese of New Orleans, had "at one time announced that he was considering a plan for the integration of Catholic schools" before the *Brown* verdict, the *Southern School News* reminded its readers, but had then given in to the overwhelmingly negative public reaction. Eventually, he declared that "the Catholic Church will make no move toward integration in advance of similar steps in the public schools."[64] The Louisiana state legislature's initial reaction to *Brown* was indicative of its attitude toward desegregation over the course of the next decade. The legislators passed more than 131 segregationist measures by 1964. Up until late 1960 the Orleans Parish School Board supported these actions.[65]

Little more than a month after the Supreme Court issued *Brown II*, the school board received a letter from Tureaud. Tureaud included the signatures of parents who petitioned to enroll their children in officially white schools. In its response, the board merely stated that state laws did not allow integration. Tureaud then filed an amended *Bush* suit with the federal district court on August 20, 1955.[66] On Ash Wednesday in February 1956, federal district court judge James Skelly Wright issued the first ruling in the *Bush* case. He ordered the school board to "make arrangements" for public school desegregation with all deliberate speed. In its response to the verdict, the school board reiterated its belief that "there will be no desegregation." It challenged Wright's rulings for the next four years, filing seven appeals through the board's attorneys.[67] Whereas Little Rock's Superintendent Blossom and the Little Rock School Board officials opted for a strategy of minimum compliance, the Orleans Parish School Board chose wholesale rebellion.

Archbishop Rummel welcomed Wright's ruling. In a letter to the clergy and laity of the Archdiocese of New Orleans, Rummel declared that racial segregation was "morally wrong and sinful because it is a denial of the unity and solidarity of the human race as conceived by God" and because it violated "the dictates of justice and the mandate of love."[68] Both Catholic priests and lay people strongly objected to Rummel's stance. Catholic New Orleanians, who made up approximately two-thirds of the city's population, ran a successful grassroots campaign to circumvent the desegregation of the Crescent City's parochial schools in 1957. New Orleans's clergy leadership then stayed silent on the topic until Wright's second *Bush* ruling in 1959, when Wright ordered the Orleans Parish School Board to finally take action and present a desegregation plan to the court by March 1, 1960.[69] Massive resistance in Louisiana, however, was not ready to concede.

The Pelican State's first citizens' council had been founded in April 1955. The chapter was established in Homer, the seat of Claiborne Parish. Homer was predominantly rural and economically dependent on cotton production. Fifty-two percent of its residents were nonwhite. The area's best known politician, Democratic state senator William Rainach, became the first president of the Association of Citizens' Councils of Louisiana in January 1956. When the Citizens'

Council of America, a national network organization for the council movement, was formed in April 1956, Rainach again presided.[70]

By the first anniversary of Louisiana's council movement, twenty-eight of Louisiana's sixty-four parishes had chapters, claiming seventy-five to one hundred thousand members in total.[71] One of the most influential councils in the state was the Citizens' Council of Greater New Orleans, whose strength historian Neil McMillen attributes to the "high quality of its leadership," including that of Plaquemines Parish's leader Leander Perez and Dr. Emmett Lee Irwin, the former chief of surgery at Louisiana State University's Medical School and president of the council from 1956 until his death in 1965.[72] Several local councils joined together to form the Citizens' Council of Greater New Orleans. In the mid-1950s, thousands of people attended the group's rallies, and it claimed a membership of up to fifty thousand.[73] In 1958, Jackson Ricau, Joseph Viguerie, and others withdrew from the group over internal rifts and political disputes and formed the South Louisiana Citizens' Council, which became the second most active group in southern Louisiana.[74] It attempted to steer clear of the Citizens' Council of Greater New Orleans's increasing anti-Semitism and presented itself as "the more 'respectable' wing" of the local council movement, counting about two thousand members in 1960.[75]

About 10 percent of the Association of Citizens' Councils of Louisiana's membership was female by late 1958, and women also took leading positions within the council hierarchy.[76] Mrs. Sam K. Baldwin was the treasurer of the council in Ruston, Louisiana. Helen Price and Grace Jones were both directors of the Red River Parish council. Mrs. J. D. Eunice was listed as a Citizens' Council of Greater New Orleans officer alongside her husband. Clarisse Thaxton and Mrs. George Lindsey Jr. were directors of Union Parish's Bernice council. Mrs. A. J. Thompson was the secretary-treasurer and Mrs. L. T. Brown the director of Doyline council in Webster Parish.[77] In New Orleans's adjacent St. Bernard Parish, Leander Perez assisted the formation of the St. Bernard Citizens' Council in November 1955. Of the 513 members at the time, 216 were women, constituting 42 percent of the council. Mrs. Leslie Fagout of Meraux was the council's first incorporator alongside four men. As the extant membership list shows, often whole families joined the council in St. Bernard, and several small communities in the New Orleans metropolitan area, including Chalmette, were represented. Located only a ten-minute drive from William Frantz Elementary School and within walking distance of McDonogh, Chalmette's female council members could quickly join segregationist protests in front of the schools, and their fellow segregationists in southeastern Meraux or Yscloskey were not far, either.[78]

Although most women could only hold such positions of power in the smaller councils in rural communities, the fact that Mrs. J. D. Eunice rose to the rank as one of the officers of the Citizens' Council of Greater New Orleans and that Leslie Fagout was one of the first incorporators of the St. Bernard council shows the extent of the political conviction and organizational dedication women could bring to the council movement.[79]

In 1960, tensions escalated between the Orleans Parish School Board, Judge Wright, and black parents. By March 1960, Wright's deadline for a desegregation plan had come and gone. Having successfully secured additional time from the judge to formulate a plan, the board used it to send out a postcard questionnaire to all seventy thousand parents of New Orleans schoolchildren. The school board inquired whether parents preferred to keep the schools open despite a "small amount of integration" or to shut them down rather than accept token integration. The majority of replies indicated that parents preferred to keep schools open, primarily due to black parents' overwhelming vote for option one. Eighty-two percent of white parents, however, made it known that they would rather see the schools close than desegregate. The new president of the Orleans Parish School Board, Lloyd Rittiner, announced that the board would only take white parents' votes into account and would "abide" by their wishes, as they were "the people who support the school system."[80] Of further help to the segregationist cause was Emile Wagner, who had been a member of the board since 1952. Wagner was an attorney, a member of the Citizens' Council of Greater New Orleans, and president of the Association of Catholic Laymen, an organization that had been established to oppose Archbishop Rummel's bid for desegregation.[81]

When Orleans Parish School Board's final deadline for a desegregation plan passed on May 16, 1960, Judge Wright devised his own. Declaring the start of the new school year, September 1, 1960, as the date for desegregation in New Orleans, Wright ordered the desegregation of all first grades of the city's public elementary schools. Every subsequent year, the first grade would be desegregated until all classes were integrated. The school board vowed to continue fighting the order. Not until August 14, 1960, when Redmond delivered a report on potential economic loss of up $8.7 million if the city's schools closed did the school board begin to back down, except for the ardently segregationist Emile Wagner.[82]

A day after Wright's ruling, grassroots segregationists held a rally at the New Orleans Municipal Auditorium.[83] The South Louisiana Citizens' Council called the style of Wright's order "significantly reminiscent of the evil Reconstruction period" and painted a horrid picture of desegregated schools in Washington, D.C. The group now placed its hopes in Democratic governor Jimmy "Sunshine" Davis, whose pledge to go to jail rather than to allow integration distinguished him, in its estimation, from unsuccessful massive resistance actors, such as Democratic governor Lindsay Almond of Virginia, who had "lost ground on the school mixing issue because he simply did not have the intestinal fortitude to stick to his guns." Segregationists saw massive resistance as a matter of political principle and a test of individuals' masculine perseverance in a showdown with the federal government.[84]

New Orleans's white business and social elite remained mostly mute, but a few civil organizations formed in New Orleans to preserve public education.[85] Save Our Schools, a group of white elites with close ties to Tulane University staff, had already organized in 1959. It now began a public campaign against school closures. Carefully avoiding a stand on integration itself, its publications focused on the harm caused by the abolition of public education. Its pamphlet "Our Stake in New Orleans Schools" cited Little Rock, Arkansas, as the prime example of the economic and educational damage that could result from eliminating public schools.[86] Save Our Schools had spoken out in favor of racial integration before and was modeled after groups like Help Our Public Education in Atlanta and the Women's Emergency Committee to Open Our Schools in Little Rock. Segregationists thus decried Save Our Schools as an " integration front" and referred to it as "Sabotage Our Schools."[87]

In the summer of 1960, Louisiana's segregationist politicians did not rest either. Davis defeated Morrison and took the governor's office for the second time in May 1960. He pledged to "maintain our way of life without compromise."[88] Louisiana's grassroots segregationists persisted in urging the Crescent City's white population to resist integration. They organized several public rallies, where members of both the Citizens' Council of Greater New Orleans and the South Louisiana Citizens' Council came together and insisted that New Orleans's situation was "not at all comparable" to that of Norfolk, Virginia, or Little Rock, Arkansas, where massive resistance had ultimately failed to prevent desegregation. Louisiana, they claimed, had "the advantage of their experiences," and the state's segregationists sought to optimize their strategies accordingly.[89]

Louisiana's legislature proceeded to pass several more segregation laws during the first month of Davis's term, including one authorizing the governor to close public schools and one creating a thirteen-member state sovereignty commission, modeled after Mississippi's. After the Orleans Parish School Board petitioned Davis to use interposition and order the continued segregation of public schools in June 1960, the governor seized control of the city's public schools. He planned to turn over the administration to a committee of the Louisiana legislature and issued an order for schools to reopen on a segregated basis on September 8, 1960.[90] After a federal district court struck down the legislature's Act 496, which had allowed Davis to seize control from school boards and close individual schools, and the United States Supreme Court confirmed the ruling on September 1, 1960, Orleans Parish School Board president Rittiner conceded that "it doesn't seem that any of us can defy the ruling of the Supreme Court."[91] Wright granted the school board an extension until November 14 to work out a desegregation plan for the first grades. Begrudgingly, the board began to prepare for token desegregation. Emile Wagner boycotted the board's meetings because he believed it had been voided of its authority by the Louisiana legislature.[92]

By the summer of 1960, the national black civil rights movement had intensified its strategy of direct action. New Orleans activists gained momentum not only with the immediate prospect of elementary school integration but also with the city's first wave of downtown sit-ins.[93] With this momentum against them, the school board adopted an intricate pupil placement procedure in order to have as little integration as possible.[94] The school board submitted the 135 black applicants to a battery of application requirements and short deadlines and eventually approved only five requests by black first graders to attend a formerly white school, constituting a success rate of 3.7 percent. One of the children later withdrew her request, hence, four first-grade girls would be the first children to desegregate public schools in New Orleans. Ruby Bridges was assigned to William Frantz, while Gail Etienne, Tessie Prevost, and Leona Tate were assigned to McDonogh 19. Both schools were located in New Orleans's Ninth Ward.[95]

The board only admitted black pupils whose test scores were "equal [to] or above the median" of schools to which they applied. This approach necessitated finding schools whose "grade median was low enough" to match those of black children who had been discriminated against in educational opportunities.[96] The board could have adopted a different approach, identifying schools where white parents would have accepted black students more readily and then finding black pupils "who could fit in." In fact, the parent-teacher associations of both Wilson and Luther elementary schools and Save Our Schools stronghold neighborhoods near Tulane University had explicitly petitioned the board to consider their schools for desegregation. Their requests were denied.

The fact that both chosen schools were located in the same neighborhood facilitated segregationists' resistance campaign. The Ninth Ward, like Little Rock Central High School's neighborhood, was a working- class and poor area. Speculation arose as to whether the schools had been chosen because the families lacked economic and social capital, and resistance would, therefore, be weak. Alternatively, historian Morton Inger suggests, perhaps the thinking was that if the start of desegregation in one of the areas "where the tension was greatest" failed, desegregation might be defeated altogether "by showing it just can't work."[97] The cheerleaders' loud, vulgar, and violent protests in front of the elementary schools in 1960 and 1961 put this theory to the test.

The state legislature and the superintendent of education made last-ditch efforts to circumvent the elementary schools' token desegregation. A three-judge federal court that included Wright knocked down the new statutes. The court instructed 775 state, parochial, and local officials not to interfere with desegregation. In 1960, "Desegregation-Day" had finally come to New Orleans, three years after Little Rock and six years after *Brown*. This is when the segregationist women nicknamed the cheerleaders gathered in front of Frantz and McDonogh 19 elementary schools.[98]

For segregationists, Louisiana was another Deep South state that had fallen with the token desegregation of two New Orleans schools. South Carolina, however, would defy the court's ruling even longer and became the last state to integrate a public educational facility in 1963. Although among "the original hard core of resistance to school desegregation," South Carolina was a quiet bastion of white supremacy that avoided the outbursts of violence that shook Little Rock, New Orleans, Oxford, Mississippi, and other locales.[99] When Harvey Gantt desegregated Clemson University in January 1963, he became the first African American to enter a formerly white public educational facility in South Carolina since Reconstruction. This peaceful desegregation event earned the Palmetto State the reputation of having accomplished "integration with dignity."[100]

Twenty years after *Brown*, Strom Thurmond, South Carolina's former governor and long-time U.S. senator, 1948 Dixiecrat presidential candidate, coauthor of the Southern Manifesto, and record holder for a twenty-four-hour-long filibuster against the 1957 Civil Rights Bill, claimed that in his advocacy for segregation there "was no idea in view that any race is inferior, it's just so that the schools are desegregated." As governor, it was his duty "to uphold" segregation until "it was changed or stricken down. . . . I never advocated defying the law."[101] In fact, South Carolina's politicians had embarked on a strategy of "preparedness" before the Supreme Court delivered its first *Brown* verdict. Preparedness, or at least swift reactions, to stifle any threats to the continuation of segregation was a central theme in the Palmetto State's racial policies throughout the 1940s, 1950s, and 1960s. When the Supreme Court invalidated the all-white Democratic primary in *Smith v. Allwright* in 1944, South Carolina's Democratic Party continued to bar all black South Carolinians from joining by presenting it as a private club. This development catalyzed the founding of the Progressive Democratic Party, led by John McCray and James M. Hinton.[102] When civil rights activists protested the continued segregation of recreational facilities in South Carolina, including the fact that seventeen of the twenty-two state parks were reserved for white people, the state legislature closed Edisto State Park rather than lose its case in federal court in 1956.[103] When South Carolina faced the *Brown* ruling, white politicians initiated a hasty program to bring black schools' funding and facilities up to the levels of white schools.

One of the key concerns of South Carolina's black communities was education. The state of public education in South Carolina's Clarendon County, on the edge of the state's Lowcountry, became the focus, a place that was hard to surpass in terms of its poverty and brutal oppressiveness for black people.[104] By 1947, Clarendon County's black activists had begun to search for a case that could be brought to court in an attempt to challenge the racial inequalities in public education. Forty black parents, including Harry Briggs, who agreed to be the official plaintiff, prepared a legal suit with the support of the NAACP.[105] After decades of unsuccessful reform appeals and petitions, South Carolina NAACP attorneys Harold Boulware and Thurgood Marshall filed suit with *Briggs v. Elliott* in May 1950, in a quest not for integration but for school equality.[106] The segregationist backlash was instantaneous. Black teachers who had signed the petition lost their contracts, sharecroppers lost credit, and local KKK chapters threatened activists, including the Briggs family, who relocated to New York City in 1961.[107]

At the suit's first pretrial hearing in November 1950, Charleston native and civil rights ally Judge Waties Waring asked Marshall to take on *Plessy v. Ferguson* and challenge the principle of racial segregation directly. When *Briggs v. Elliott* was refiled a month later, the suit asked that public school segregation itself be declared unconstitutional under the Fourteenth Amendment. Marshall made *Briggs* a test case and laid out the psychological and sociological studies that would also underpin his case in *Brown*. One of the two defense lawyers for Clarendon County, S. Emory Rogers of Summerton, would become a leading figure in the state's citizens' council movement.[108] The county's lawyers readily admitted that the school facilities of white and black pupils were unequal. They asked for more time to remedy the situation. Although the three-judge court ordered Clarendon County to equalize their school facilities, it ruled two-to-one against *Briggs*, upholding the view that segregation as such was not unconstitutional. Judge Waring filed a scathing dissent. Marshall appealed the verdict in the U.S. Supreme Court, and *Briggs* became one of the cases consolidated under *Brown*.[109]

As soon as Democratic governor James F. Byrnes took office in 1951, he embarked on an ambitious political program to circumvent public school desegregation in South Carolina and to counter the state's notoriety for racial inequalities. Byrnes, who had had a forty-year career as a member of Congress and U.S. secretary of state, had comfortably won the governorship of his home state. Although Byrnes had not associated himself with the Dixiecrat campaign in 1948, he had broken with the national Democratic Party when supporting the election of Dwight D. Eisenhower in 1952.[110]

Byrnes's opposition to federal intervention was linked to the question of black civil rights and not solely to a principle of abstract states' rights. This became clear in his gubernatorial inaugural address in January 1951. Byrnes stated that school equality was not only the "right" thing to do, but also "wise." Byrnes sought to fix the problem of the state's unequal educational facilities for black and white students in order to circumvent an unfavorable court decision. A new school equalization program went into effect in 1951, and $75 million and the revenue of a 3 percent sales tax were invested in school construction.[111] In

1951, South Carolina's general assembly created the South Carolina School Committee, also referred to as the Segregation Study Committee. The segregationist task force was proposed and headed by Calhoun County senator L. Marion Gressette. Known as the Gressette Committee, the group organized the Palmetto state's "defense of segregated schools" and "secured the passage" of state segregation laws.[112]

The preparedness measures made South Carolina one of the first states to institutionalize massive resistance prior to and in anticipation of *Brown*. Alongside Virginia, South Carolina led the way for other southern states' top-down resistance.[113] When the Supreme Court decided *Brown*, Byrnes announced that he was "shocked," nonetheless.[114] Democratic lieutenant governor George Bell Timmerman Jr., who after having served in this post for eight years would be elected governor later that year and take office in 1955, asked for "calm courage, determination and fairness to the end that we can find means of preserving separate schools in accordance with the wishes of the vast majority of the parents of this state." In his gubernatorial inaugural address, however, he chose more belligerent words, declaring that even token desegregation was "cowardly because it seeks to minimize opposition by careful selection of a few victims from time to time." When Timmerman was interviewed on *NBC*'s "Meet the Press" in July 1956, he stated that "not in a thousand years" would South Carolina abolish school segregation.[115]

South Carolina NAACP state conference president James M. Hinton was careful in his reaction to the *Brown* ruling. He commented that the state's black South Carolinians, "though happy, are most mindful of the seriousness of the decision and will welcome the appointment of a committee composed of leaders of both races to sit down and work out plans for the best interest of all citizens."[116] South Carolina's white officials tried to prepare the state for the ruling, but they were not ready to accept it yet. In its 1955 and 1956 sessions, the state legislature enacted several segregation measures. The general assembly repealed compulsory attendance laws, eliminated tenure for teachers, and extended local school officials' pupil assignment powers. They also passed a resolution asking Congress "to enact legislation limiting the appellate jurisdiction" of the Supreme Court and "the jurisdiction of the Federal Courts." The lawmakers petitioned the U.S. Supreme Court to not implement *Brown* on the grounds that it would cause "hatred, strife, chaos and confusion" in the Palmetto state.[117] In July 1955, the U.S. district court in Columbia decided in *Briggs v. Elliott* that, given the Supreme Court's recent *Brown* decisions, South Carolina's school segregation laws were "null and void." The presiding Judge John J. Parker, however, stressed that the U.S. Supreme Court's *Brown* decisions did not necessitate racial integration. In the court's view, the U.S. Constitution does "not forbid such segregation as occurs as the result of voluntary action. It merely forbids the use of governmental power to enforce segregation."[118] Known as the Briggs dictum, the ruling set no deadline to the end of governmentally enforced segregation, and it enabled segregationist politicians and school officials to implement supposedly colorblind measures, including pupil placement laws, to maintain the status quo. In Charleston, school superintendent Robert Gaines denied J. Arthur Brown's and other African American parents' petition for school desegregation on the grounds of their pupil placement practice. In 1968, the Supreme Court rejected the interpretation of the Briggs dictum in *Green v. County School Board of New Kent County*.[119]

In the fall of 1955, South Carolina businessmen and civil leaders, some with close ties to the emerging citizens' council movement, established the Committee of Fifty-Two. The committee published a resolution condemning *Brown* and started a publicity campaign to counter the verdict and attack the NAACP. The resolution amassed seven thousand additional signatures within a week.[120] The group exemplified the blurred lines between the segregationist resistance of a political, business, and civil establishment and the grassroots activism of the state's citizens' council movement.

South Carolina also pursued massive resistance from the bottom up. Grassroots activists tirelessly agitated against desegregation. The councils in South Carolina, however, never reached the membership numbers or direct influence of the movement's strongholds in Mississippi and Alabama. In 1958, the *Charleston News and Courier* lamented the lack of vigor in the Palmetto State's council movement, urging "men of substance in their community" to play "an active role in council affairs."[121] But although the council movement in South Carolina never drew more than forty thousand members, there were enclaves where citizens' council activism flourished and exercised considerable influence. The councils' numbers and impact were strongest in Charleston County and in Orangeburg County.[122]

As the Association of Citizens' Councils of South Carolina reported, the first state council was organized in Elloree, Orangeburg County, in August 1955 and was rapidly followed by the formation of councils throughout the Lowcountry.[123] By the end of the summer in 1955, council meetings were drawing as many as three thousand white participants.[124] Despite their small number, grassroots segregationists in the state were not only able to exert pressure on black South Carolinians but were also assured of receiving protection and sympathy from the state's elite citizens. Segregationist women joined citizens' councils all over the state, but Charleston became a hub for their activism.

In the first half of the twentieth century, Charleston, South Carolina's oldest and largest city, appeared to outside observers to be frozen in time, to be a space apart from the modernizing New South, owing to its preoccupation with caste, class, and family pedigree and to the traditional siestas businessmen took before returning to work later in the afternoon.[125] "No town better represented the Old South," historian Robert Korstad notes, in a state that was "tethered to the myths of the past."[126] Antebellum mansions, Fort Sumter, and Confederate monuments in the Battery and White Point Gardens' promenade alongside the harbor gave spatial expression to Charleston's enduring Old South culture and self-understanding. The city stressed its old world charm in marketing itself as a tourist destination. From its inception, Charleston was bound to Atlantic slavery and trade, giving rise to a "wealthy planter-merchant elite" in the Lowcountry.[127] The emerging class structure rested on genealogy, wealth, and conduct. Expectations pertaining to conduct called forth a paternalistic sense of Christian duty on the part of slave owners toward the enslaved, behavior designed to uphold racialized, gendered, and class hierarchies. By the 1950s, historian Scott Baker argues, Charleston's "close-knit and self-consciously aristocratic white leadership" had adapted this veneer of white paternalism to mask "a savage system of white supremacy," while upper and middle-class white Charlestonians publicly and privately lauded their supposedly amicable relationship with the city's always sizeable black population.[128] Segregation was nonnegotiable in this worldview. Charleston was both traditionalist and eccentric.

Despite these attitudes and the impression of stasis, Charleston underwent profound modernization in the 1940s and 1950s. Federal defense programs invested millions into the military shipbuilding industry in the port city and thus revived its economy. Charleston's population grew with its job market, and suburbs sprang up in the city's metropolitan area. Charleston's black population had risen to 44 percent in 1950 and continued to increase. Charleston's society, however, remained a segregated, racial hierarchy with stringent social codes.[129] Charleston's local politics was a Democratic one-party system, and, as historian Steve Estes has shown, "Old Charleston families" wielded disproportionate influence over elections and social politics.[130]

When civil rights activists began to systematically attack this order in the 1940s and 1950s, the white establishment met them with forceful resistance. Again, educational facilities proved to be a battleground. By 1960, due to white flight to suburbs and private schools, 75 percent of the city's school children were black. But whereas white students in Charleston had access to several, increasingly empty high schools and colleges, black elementary school children, similar to those in New Orleans, were forced to learn in a platoon system due to underfunding and overcrowding.[131] Black students were excluded from higher education in Charleston and only had one public high school. Burke High School served every black high school student in South Carolina's school district 20, which included the city of Charleston. A Burke High School graduate, Harvey Gantt, later desegregated Clemson University in 1963, and he, alongside fellow Burke students, staged the first sit-ins at S. H. Kress & Co. five-and-dime store in downtown Charleston in the spring of 1960.[132] Charleston's civil rights movement gained momentum in 1960. PTA groups and the American Teachers' Association, a professional association of black teachers in the South, organized a school boycott in the fall of 1960 to bring attention to the black schools' desolate financial state. J. Arthur Brown organized a "selective buying-campaign" to protest the refusal of white store owners to hire African American Charlestonians for white-collar jobs. On October 15, 1960, fifteen black students "applied for admission to white schools" and fought for their admission for nearly three years. When South Carolina again started into a completely segregated school year in 1962, South Carolina's NAACP president and Charlestonian J. Arthur Brown announced that the state NAACP would soon be "flooding the state with additional lawsuits."[133]

The year 1963 marked a watershed moment for the civil rights movement in Charleston. In the autumn of 1963, Millicent Brown, one of the two daughters of J. Arthur Brown, became the first black pupil to enter a formerly white public school in South Carolina, Rivers High School in Charleston. Her lawsuit, *Millicent Brown et al. v. Charleston County School District Number 20*, was decided by federal judge J. Robert Martin on August 23, 1963: all black student plaintiffs, including Millicent, were to be admitted to previously all-white schools. The following school year, Charleston's entire public school system had to desegregate.[134] Following the verdict, a network of Charleston's citizens' councils created the Foundation for Independent Schools and set a goal to open new private schools by February 1964. The College of Charleston held a meeting to explore the options of creating a private prep school. Between the first legal challenge to legal segregation and substantial school desegregation in 1964, South Carolina's political establishment and grassroots white supremacists tried everything in their power to circumvent it.[135]

Harvey Gantt later mused that in the fall of 1963, one year after the deadly escalation at Ole Miss, South Carolina's politicians had to realize that the only way to prevent violence and a federal intervention was to begrudgingly tolerate the start of desegregation. Indeed, Governor Ernest Fritz Hollings told the press that South Carolina would not have "a Little Rock or an Oxford if integration comes to our state."[136] *The State*, Columbia's biggest newspaper, editorialized that the Palmetto State should "go the last mile in legal resistance," but that "beyond that, as has been clearly demonstrated in state after state, there would appear to be no 'last mile' to truly law-abiding, non-violent people.'" In 1963, the combination of civil rights activism and looming federal intervention stifled the state's open resistance, notwithstanding Thurmond's and Gressette's continued calls for defiance. But before South Carolina had to accept desegregation, the state intensified its private schools tuition grants provisions, which served as tools for white supremacist Carolinians to elude school desegregation for their children while espousing a colorblind language.[137]

Across the region, segregationist politicians and grassroots activists coalesced to defend white supremacy. Arkansas's massive resistance escalated in Little Rock. The state, however, continued to pursue a policy of minimum compliance, only allowed token desegregation, and sought ways to bypass integration without referring to race. Louisiana, conscious of the crisis in Little Rock three years earlier, opted for a strategy of outright defiance. Aided and abetted by the executive branch of the state government, grassroots segregationists stirred communities into a frenzy. South Carolina, in contrast, was successful in keeping a low profile while simultaneously taking on preparedness measures that sought to sidestep desegregation in the Palmetto State by preemptive strikes of various magnitudes.

Arkansas's, Louisiana's, and South Carolina's segregationists understood their massive resistance campaigns as a fight against a shared threat, desegregation and social equality. In the course of massive resistance, each state looked to the other, as the gains of the civil rights movement gained steam, and feared a domino effect. Segregationists in New Orleans evoked Little Rock as a cautionary tale, and Charleston's segregationists warned that Chucktown could become another New Orleans.

Each of these segregationist campaigns was steeped in gendered rhetoric. Massive resistance was a test of virility and stamina and a quest to preserve (imagined) racial purity embodied in white southern womanhood. All three states, however, also proved fertile ground for the emergence of white supremacist women's groups; in their activism, these groups not only mirrored their state's massive resistance strategies but extended them by linking their defense of white supremacy to broader political themes and by co-creating states of emergency that legitimized their public activism.

CHAPTER 2

The Mothers' League of Central High School

"Two, four, six, eight—we don't want to integrate!" Hundreds of segregationists marched toward Little Rock Central High School shortly before noon on August 12, 1959. They hoped to prevent the school's second desegregation. However, they were received differently from the protesters who had assembled in front of Central High two years earlier chanting the same slogan. The protesters displayed United States and Confederate battle flags and blared a customized version of Dixie from loudspeakers: "In Arkansas in the state of cotton, federal courts are good and rotten. Look away, look away, look away, Dixieland." The demonstration soon found their route blocked by police. The crowd came to a halt one block from Central High. "Your behavior is a disgraceful matter," declared Little Rock police chief Eugene Smith via megaphone. "Clear the street. Go home."[1]

When the demonstrators refused to follow Smith's order, police officers with billy clubs moved in and made twenty-one arrests. The fire department used hoses to disperse the crowd.[2] An hour later, Elizabeth Eckford and Jefferson Thomas, two of the Little Rock Nine who had already desegregated Central High School two years earlier, quietly walked into their school and accomplished token desegregation for the second time.[3] The day signaled the end of offensive massive resistance against the desegregation of Little Rock's high schools, as public mobilization efforts and direct, obstructive action by Little Rock's segregationists started to become ineffective.[4] A two-year conflict had preceded this breakdown, leading to a year-long closure of all of Little Rock's high schools.[5]

Owing to the events surrounding Central High School in the fall of 1957, Little Rock has come to be known as "the epitome" of massive resistance.[6] Arkansas's Democratic governor Orval Eugene Faubus and segregationist mobs defied the federal court order to desegregate Central High School for nearly three weeks. President Dwight D. Eisenhower's move to federalize Arkansas's National

Guard and deploy the U.S. Army's 101st Airborne Division to Little Rock became a rallying point for massive resistance supporters across the South. "Remember Little Rock" was their battle cry and a tool of collective symbolism.[7]

The Women's Emergency Committee to Open Our Schools and white civil and business leaders were committed to reopening Little Rock's high schools in August 1959. Segregationists were determined to interfere with the desegregation again. City and police officials as well as Little Rock School Board members had issued a warning against interference with the integration of Central High School and Hall High School that fall term.[8] But Capital Citizens' Council attorney Amis Guthridge released a statement that condemned the "cowardly yellow quitters," and he proclaimed that segregationists' "answer to the leaders of this diabolical race-mixing plot is NEVER."[9]

Less belligerent but just as unwavering was the Mothers' League of Central High School, which had been continuously active in mobilizing resistance to public school integration in the two years since the crisis's peak in September 1957. The league's president, Margaret Jackson, invited "every patriotic citizen to meet us on the state capitol grounds" on the day of public school desegregation. The rally was "to pay tribute to our great governor and tell him that we need and want his continued leadership in our fight against federal dictatorship."[10] Following the league's invitation, several hundred segregationists, made up of adults and children alike, assembled on the morning of August 12. Carrying signs that read "Race Mixing Is Communism" and "Governor Faubus Save Our Christian America," the protesters listened to a speech by Faubus. The governor condemned school desegregation but asked his audience to resist peacefully and battle it out at the ballot box. Faubus said that "nothing was to be gained by being 'beaten over the head,'" alluding to rumors that "simulated, wide-spread violence" was going to be "staged" to artificially create an escalating situation at Central. Segregationist organizations denied this charge, and Jackson called it "real fancy."[11]

The story of the Little Rock crisis has been told many times.[12] At the grassroots level, several women played major roles in Little Rock's desegregation struggle. Daisy Bates, head of the Arkansas State Conference of Branches of the NAACP, was on the front line of the legal disputes in the NAACP's Little Rock school desegregation case *Cooper v. Aaron*. Bates stood firm against the increasing legal and political harassment of the NAACP by segregationist organizations and Arkansas's attorney general Bruce Bennett, refusing to divulge the organization's membership list.[13] Central High School's principal for girls, Elizabeth Huckaby, became segregationists' target for supposedly favoring the African American students. And hundreds of middle and upper-class white women in the Women's Emergency Committee to Open Our Schools lobbied for more than a year for Little Rock's public high schools to be reopened in 1959.[14]

School desegregation battles enabled women to publicly speak out as moral authorities on children's welfare. The Mothers' League of Central High School relied on this perception. Although the league faced belittlement from both its opponents and fellow male segregationists, who portrayed the women either as white trash bullies or the pawns of male-led segregationist organizations, by consciously modifying its segregationist rhetoric and activist strategies and pursuing working-class, maternalist, white supremacist identity politics, it was able to play a vital role in circumventing and sabotaging desegregation. Its tactics were dynamic and versatile. The league was able to intervene in Little Rock's public discourse, establish political influence, and adapt and diversify its responses to changing circumstances, and at times, these changing circumstances were the result of its own interventions. It relied on grass roots organizing, public rallies, racialized and gendered fear mongering, political lobbying, and judicial action. When it failed to circumvent Little Rock Central High's desegregation in the courts, it resorted to direct action in front of the school, including taking part in the mob violence, and it supported a campaign of sabotage and segregationist agitation inside Central High School.

The group expanded its prosegregationist approach by shifting its rhetoric from one that focused on the maternalistic impulses that justified its intervention in the first place to one that allowed it to support broader political issues. The league attempted to form a national organization whose platform was to focus on freedom of choice, anticommunism, and states' rights. League officers Margaret Jackson and Mary Thomason ran for seats on the Little Rock City Citizens' Council in 1957. They campaigned for a segregationist amendment to the state constitution and later for the closing of Little Rock's high schools. Thomason ran in the Democratic primary for the United States House of Representatives in 1958.

The league was well aware of the spatialization of power in Little Rock. Early on, the group took issue with the decision to integrate Central High School but no other ones. The women linked this decision to the fact that the school was located in a predominantly lower middle-class and working-class neighborhood that had much less influence than the civil and political elite living in Pulaski Heights. They attempted, therefore, to mark and occupy Central High School as a white space, and they realized that in order to access Little Rock's power network despite their lack of social capital, they would need to enter the public space with their protest and take up room in physical and media spaces.[15] However, the city's white elites ultimately defeated the league. The league could not muster enough economic, social, and cultural capital to sustain its activism, and in 1960, it dissolved, leaving the public realm of segregationist activism to right-wing fringe groups, including the female-headed Little Rock chapter of the National Association for the Advancement of White People.

The league faced several other hurdles in its activism. Traditional gender roles in the era of domestic containment and its lack of formal (access to) power through social capital were obstacles that this working-class group of women overcame by creating performative spaces that enabled it to extend the social and political frames that had previously limited its influence. Members of the league created and affirmed their members' white southern womanhood through a "stylized repetition of acts," such as by consciously displaying emotionality and calling on white men to help save them from desegregation.[16] The league also used these gendered and racialized performances to rewrite the scripts to which their activism had to adhere in public and to develop a dynamic, counterrevolutionary agenda.

Capital Citizens' Council official Amis Guthridge, whose wife, Ellen, was league member, credited his fellow officer and later president Merrill B. Taylor with the women's group's formation. He claimed that the council "worked hand in glove" with the league.[17] In 1957, however, the mothers' league constituted almost a fifth of the council's female supporters, historian Graeme Cope asserts.[18] Among the twenty-one people on the council's board of directors, four were women: Mrs. H. O. Anderson, Mrs. Fred Atkinson, and the league members Mrs. Bob Cook and Mrs. Theo A. Dillaha.[19] If the council indeed invented the league, it was not just men who were responsible for its creation. Despite their denials, male council members did provide organizational and financial assistance to the league, however, particularly during the group's early phase.[20] But female segregationists in Little Rock were as committed to massive resistance as their male counterparts and as well versed in the strategies and rhetoric of the movement as the men, and from 1957 to 1959, the league was a primary actor in the school desegregation crisis in Little Rock.

Little Rock's segregationist organizations had a significantly lower membership than those in other southern states. This resulted in a tightly woven segregationist network and overlap of segregationist activists in the city. Organized grassroots agitation for white supremacy and segregation was not unlike a cartel structure, in which several smaller groups formed a bigger collective and tried to imitate the city elite's social networks that they were lacking.

Little Rock grassroots segregationists labored to fill a power and publicity vacuum created by the silence of Little Rock's social elite, and their propaganda reached a bigger audience than the group's small membership numbers suggest.[21] It was within this tense climate that the Mothers' League of Central High School took to the stage for the first time at a fundraising dinner for the Capital Citizens' Council on August 22, 1957. That same evening, Daisy Bates had just sat down in her living room when a large object crashed through the window. Bates, who had thrown herself to the floor, was covered in shattered glass. The uninjured Bates and her husband, L. C., who had rushed into the room, picked up the rock that had been hurled through their window. "Stone this time. Dynamite next," said a scribbled note that was tied to the rock. "A message from the Arkansas patriots," Bates told L. C. sarcastically. Bates had listened to a radio broadcast that reported on a Capital Citizens' Council rally with Democratic governor Marvin Griffin of Georgia and former Georgia state senator Roy V. Harris, who also served as the executive director of Georgia's segregationist States Rights' Council. Griffin and Harris addressed their audience as "patriots."[22] Superintendent Blossom later described the Capital Citizens' Council's fundraising dinner as "the biggest and most effective blow" against token desegregation.[23]

At the ten-dollar-a-plate affair, which 350 segregationists attended, Griffin announced that Georgia had "stemmed the tide" of desegregation through decisive actions by the Peach State's legislature and administration.[24] To enthusiastic applause, rebel yells, and a few amens, Griffin urged the entire South to resist desegregation "by every legal means."[25] Delivering a roundup of massive resistance's rhetoric, Roy Harris proceeded to denounce *Brown* as the product of the court's reliance on "fuzzy-minded theorists," and he warned against communist subversion.[26]

The evening was the first time the newly formed Mothers' League of Central High School presented itself to the public. Master of ceremonies and Capital Citizens' Council member Rev. Lawton D. Foreman of the Antioch Missionary Baptist Church introduced Nadine O. Aaron. Foreman's wife Mary, both a council and league member and mother of four daughters, also spoke for the group.[27]

Aaron, a Sheridan, Arkansas, native pictured in the *Arkansas Gazette* with dressed hair and wearing a smart dress, took to the podium.[28] Aaron was a machine operator at Hankins Container Corporation and had previously been a secretary at the University of Arkansas Medical School. Her husband, Russell, was a manager at the Mathison Chemical Company's Acid Plant.[29] Aaron stated that the mothers' league had been formed in order to find "ways and means to prevent integration of the races at Central High School and to provide a rallying-point for all parents who are like-minded" and announced that "about 100 mothers of Central High students" were calling for a public rally the next day at Little Rock's Hotel Lafayette to discuss the issue.[30] In a prepared statement to the press, she claimed that the women's group was formed on Tuesday, August 20, 1957, just two weeks before Central High was due to open on a desegregated basis, "by about 30 mothers" and that "this is a matter for the mothers to settle, and it is time for the mothers to take over."[31]

Aaron's statement emphasizes the supposed special expertise of white mothers and implies that they were going to infuse Little Rock's resistance movement with a particular effectiveness that it had been lacking so far. Her reference to their determination and ability "to settle this matter" stresses women's responsibility for social and educational matters and creating a public space for their actions through the legitimizing force of maternalism. The *Arkansas Democrat* described the league as putting up "new resistance to integration."[32]

Outside the Silk-Stocking District: Motivations and Mobilization

The following evening at the league's first public meeting, Capital Citizens' Council attorney Amis Guthridge was the main speaker to an audience of a hundred people equally divided by gender. Even though Aaron claimed that the league "was not affiliated with any pro-segregation group," the council had arranged the venue and later paid the bill.[33] Furthermore, not only were there several council members present but council officer and former school teacher Arthur Bickle and league's vice president Margaret Jackson both worked at the W. H. Goodman Fireworks Company, which guaranteed tight networking and shared mobilization.[34]

Guthridge was chosen as the main speaker because he had been asked by another league member, Eva Wilbern, to file a mandamus suit in Pulaski Chancery Court for her fourteen-year-old daughter, Kay, who attended Central High School, and for "all others similarly situated." In later interviews, league members would thus present the group's first rally as a private meeting. Willie Webb, the league's only official male member and a Southern Paper Box employee and freelance photographer, reported that at this meeting the group discussed the possibilities of keeping Little Rock's schools segregated "through peaceful means." His wife, Lucille, also attended the meeting. Even though the Webbs did not have children, they both became league members. Lucille Webb said that the segregationist speakers stressed school choice as their right and had stated that "the white children should have the privilege of going to an all-white school, as well as the Negroes have the privilege of going to all Negro schools."[35]

Wilbern's suit stated that she had asked the Little Rock School Board to transfer her daughter out of Central High School in June. Since the board had "arbitrarily and discriminatorily" denied her request, she now asked that it be ordered "to furnish educational facilities substantially equal" to Central High School for white students who wished to be transferred.[36] Chancellor Guy E. Williams refused to hold a hearing on Wilbern's mandamus action on August 29, 1957, and the courts ultimately dismissed her case.[37] Wilbern's effort to halt integration at Central High shows how future league members first attempted to take individual action to preserve their children's white privileges. Segregationist women had already initiated the attack on Central High School's integration and were testing the waters in terms of resistance strategies.[38]

Throughout the summer of 1957, the Capital Citizens' Council had bombarded

Arkansas's newspapers with segregationist propaganda. Amis Guthridge and Wesley Pruden, minister of Little Rock's Broadmoor Baptist Church, often attended Little Rock School Board meetings.[39] At a school board meeting in July 1957, several organized segregationists were present among the partially recorded names of forty-two external attendees. At least two of the six women listed, Eva Mitchell and Evelyn Bennett, were future members of the league. Indeed, Superintendent Blossom later noted that "the Mothers League officers and members attended various meetings of the school board, seeking delay or changes in our plan."[40] Weeks before the organization of the league was announced, then, future members of it were already trying to directly intervene in the course of integration in Little Rock, and it was their failure on this front that inspired the formation of the group. Choosing the name "mothers' league" was strategic; it not only ensured the respectability and activist legitimacy awarded to white mothers who supposedly had children's welfare in mind but also obfuscated the fact that the mothers' league was a white supremacist interest group, not an alternative Parent-Teacher Association (PTA). The league embraced the strategy of some massive resistance groups of dropping racialized terms from their official names so as to appear more respectable and accessible and also to present their cause as more than just a southern sectional struggle and so rally broader support from other parts of the country.[41]

On August 20, 1957, Grace Fitzhugh received a telephone call from an unidentified person who invited her to attend a meeting that same evening. The meeting would take place at the home of Mary Thomason, the mother of two teenaged daughters and an inspector at the Westinghouse Lamp Plant. When the anonymous caller asked Fitzhugh how she felt about her "daughter going to school with colored persons," the forty-two-year-old replied that she "did not like it." The caller informed her that the meeting was being held to discuss this issue.[42] Only a few blocks away, Neva Harden received a personal visit from Mary Thomason who invited her to a meeting at Thomason's residence that day. Thomason, too, promised Harden that they would discuss means of avoiding Central High's desegregation and the peril of violent disorder should the school be desegregated.[43] Fitzhugh and Harden accepted the invitation and were present at the Mother League of Central High School's inaugural meeting. Both became group members.

Between thirty and forty people assembled that evening, including about ten men.[44] Thomason described herself as "a working mother" and stated that she "was definitely against her daughter going to an integrated school" due to "her background and the way she had been reared." Thomason, whose husband, Clyde, was a salesman for the Muswick Beverage Company, had heard rumors that one of the children of Margaret Stephens, the president of Central High's PTA, was attending Hall High School after their mother had successfully intervened with Blossom.[45]

Thomason told the group that she had telephoned Superintendent Blossom to ask that her daughter Louise be transferred from Central High School to Hall High School and that he had turned her down.[46] Thomason felt that she "was being forced" to send Louise to Central High School. She repeatedly called Blossom to ask him "what he was going to do about it." She tried to arrange a meeting with him, claiming that she was "speaking for about a hundred people who had the same problem." Thomason contended that the superintendent never returned her phone calls, although he supposedly met "at least twice a week" with black civil rights groups.[47] Used to preferential treatment through everyday white privilege, Thomason expected more, and she resented Blossom's actions. Illustrating the racially coded expectations that white men would protect white women against integration and the assumed danger of miscegenation, Thomason appealed to an implicit meme of white solidarity and white male chivalry when she asked Blossom what he was "going to do about it." Thomason considered herself betrayed by his perceived lack of racial solidarity and his refusal to grant white parents special privileges.[48]

Thomason was angry that a working mother neither had the social status nor the formal power or influence of upper middle-class parents whom Blossom had advised to move to Pulaski Heights or of a PTA president. Huckaby described the women of "the lily-white Central High School Mothers' Club" and their children as "unknowns" in "school life" and "in the community." Organizing a segregationist pressure group was Thomason's most promising option to compensate for the working-class mother's lack of social capital and thus access to power and recognition in Little Rock's community. What Thomason and fellow lower middle class and working-class mothers needed was a space where their voices would be heard.[49]

Blossom acknowledged that there had been "requests from Central High School to Hall High School which we were unable to grant." He tried to minimize the problem, however, by stating that although the parents were "disgruntled," "that is as far as it went."[50] This was a mistake because it gave the parents an opening to lament the lack of freedom of association pertaining to school choice, which proved to be a useful rhetorical tool for segregationists, allowing them to entwine broader political themes with massive resistance without explicitly resorting to open racism.[51]

In her interview report with the FBI describing this first meeting of the league, Margaret Jackson, a thirty-four-year-old divorcée and native of the small town of Houston in Arkansas's Perry County, whose two daughters, Charlene and Sandra, attended Central High, said that the women had "suddenly realized" they had "fallen asleep at the switch" and so they decided to "form an organization for the purpose of doing whatever they could to prevent integration at Central High School, by legal means only."[52] Jackson was elected vice president of the league, while Aaron became president and Thomason the recording secretary.[53]

As she herself admitted, Jackson had been brought up in a town that did not have a single black resident, which led one Mrs. Robert Wilson of North Little Rock to question how prepared she could be for the role she had assumed. Writing to the *Arkansas Gazette*, she stated that "Mrs. Margaret Jackson, coming from the metropolis of Houston, Arkansas, . . . probably knows all about how to run city and government affairs."[54] In a similar vein, she observed that Faubus "appears to be incredibly stupid," and with her tongue in her cheek, she blamed former governor Sidney McMath for paving "that road to Huntsville and let[ting] Orval out." To Wilson, the protagonists of Little Rock's desegregation crisis were unsophisticated hillbillies who were neither educated nor worldly enough to run the state's politics, a class and region-related theme that would reemerge, particularly in the context of the league's opposition to the Women's Emergency Committee to Open Our Schools. Adolphine Terry, a patron of the Women's Emergency Committee, referred to the league and other Little Rock segregationists as "a group of poor whites and a portion of the lunatic fringe that every town possesses." In Terry's view, they had "disgraced" the city and embarrassed its "better class."[55] To the city's elite, the league was white trash.

Three main factors led to the establishment of the league, then, all of them related to the women's social status and their belief in white supremacy. The most pressing reason was several future members' failure to secure individual remedies for their children in response to Central High's impending desegregation. The disappointment of being unable to avoid public school desegregation individually was related to the second reason, namely, Blossom's refusal to grant them exceptions from the rule as white parents. In addition, he refused to discuss his plan with residents in the working- and lower middle-class neighborhood in which the school was located, even though he did speak with traditionally influential community members. League members thus felt they had been let down by the city's white establishment, which, in their view, should have shown solidarity with white fellow citizens. Organizing a league promised more social capital and lobbying power, which could be put to use not merely in seeking personal solutions for a number of white children but in attacking the desegregation of Little Rock's public schools altogether. Finally, the first two factors were entwined with the members' underlying white supremacist convictions and their expectation of preferential treatment. The formation of a segregationist organization that worked closely with other white supremacist groups would provide a means through which to act on these convictions.[56]

The league's official purpose was defined in a statement the group had to file alongside its financial status and membership list to the city clerk in October 1957. The statement declared that the group existed to "find legal ways and means to prevent integration of the races at Central High School and to rally all parents of this school area to our supports [*sic*]."[57] The group's existence was thus built on the premise that race mixing at the school must be stopped. That fear of miscegenation was a driving force behind the league's activism is reflected in a publicity campaign it ran in early September. Answering the public call by an interfaith coalition that had invited the public to a "prayer meeting" to restore peace to Little Rock, the league published an open letter in the *Democrat* on September 7, 1957, which was paid for by Jackson and appeared next to a Capital Citizens' Council advertisement that asked why "the 'moderates' [were] advocating Race-Mixing," addressed to "the Clergymen, Catholic, Jewish, and Protestant" who were promoting the interfaith meeting.[58] Stating that "many people are having some difficulty in understanding some things about this Prayer Meeting," the letter suggested that the preachers who called for the meeting were renowned for their "activities toward race-mixing." The league accused the clergymen of having "agitated [for] the integration of our schools" for years by using "the 'Law of the Land' argument," and the group urged them to finally admit they were pursuing integration and to "fight the matter out on its own merits."[59]

More blatantly, the letter stated that "the South has lived under the Plan of Segregation of the races. It has been our code of life" and asked "How can you advocate race-mixing and pray to escape the fruits of race mixing?" The league thus not only publicly addressed its opposition to "race mixing" as one of its prime reasons for resisting the desegregation of Central High but explicitly thematized miscegenation. By asking how "the fruits of race mixing" could be escaped, the league brought up the subject of miscegenation, using religious nomenclature to refer to the offspring that could result from interracial relationships.

In a *New York Times* interview with Mrs. Walter Jones on October 5, 1957, the league and Capital Citizens' Council member spoke openly about believing in white supremacy and opposing racial equality, referring to black people as "niggers" in her interview with the national newspaper. She stated that every black person was "an inferior being who should remain in his place."[60] Jones based her opposition to desegregation on an alleged biblical foundation for segregation. She contended that God did not intend for races to mix, and she feared that desegregation would ultimately lead to miscegenation. "You can't bring them . . . into the schools and then tell your children that it's wrong to intermarry," Jones stated. "Intermarriage? I just know it's wrong. The cat and the dog don't mate."[61] Jones, a Central High School graduate whose daughter was supposed to attend the school, too, gave a glimpse into her time-consuming league and council activism. It included circulating petitions, attending meetings, and participating in telephone campaigns. According to the article, Jones's husband wished his wife "were at home more" but encouraged her actions, nonetheless. The housewife proudly stressed her strong commitment to the white supremacist cause. She found an outlet in her segregationist activism, and she was not subject to the directions of her husband. She joined the Capital Citizens' Council at the height of the group's very active phase in the summer of 1957, and she enthusiastically participated in the mothers' league's campaigns on her own time. Segregationist activism could also serve as a space for the self-realization of white supremacist working-class and lower middle-class women outside of their households and marriages. Mrs. Walter Jones felt alive.

Aaron claimed that "the effects of integration were discussed" at the group's first meetings, including "inter-racial marriages and resulting diseases which might arise."[62] The league thus recycled the miscegenation-related rhetorical strategies that the Capital Citizens' Council had previously employed when attacking the Little Rock School Board. Alluding to miscegenation, interracial dating and sex, and the supposed dangers desegregation posed particularly for white girls in an integrated Central High School proved to be a successful, gender- and class-conscious strategy that the league employed for recruiting new members and gaining publicity. Ideologically, the Mothers' League of Central High School and the Capital Citizens' Council were alike.

Mapping Strategies

In late August, the league intensified and diversified its approach, undertaking several measures to strengthen collective action. It held rallies, took further judicial action, and petitioned Faubus. The league invented itself as the voice of nonviolence at its public rally on August 27, 1957, but as reports of the league's rally show, speakers made inciting comments to stir the crowd, even as the league simultaneously distanced itself from violence and assumed the position of a "Christian" and "nonviolent" organization.

Guthridge and Pruden again played prominent roles at the league's second segregation rally on Tuesday, August 27, 1957.[63] Two hundred and fifty men, women, and children packed the room.[64] Guthridge, representing the Capital Citizens' Council, claimed that the council would "go all the way legally, morally and honorably" to retain segregation in all public schools, not only in Little Rock but also in the Ozarks in the northwest and Hoxie in northeastern Arkansas.[65] Pruden gave a speech on the importance of fighting integration "in a Christian way," and the meeting was opened and closed with a prayer.[66] By a standing vote, the segregationist rally adopted a petition. Citing the interposition measures approved by Arkansans in the last general election and several segregationist acts passed in 1957 by the Arkansas General Assembly, the petition asked Faubus to intervene to prevent desegregation.[67]

League president Aaron selected a committee to hand deliver the petition to Faubus. Five women, including Margaret Jackson, went to the state capitol.[68] Committee member Mrs. A. T. Forbess recalled that "the Governor appeared to be sympathetic" but "made no promises and no commitments of any kind and made no mention that he would stop integration," although Forbes added that Faubus had "said that he would do what he could."[69]

None of the league members made public what they had discussed with the governor. The relationship established between the group and Faubus was a friendly one. Faubus agreed to appear as a key witness to Mary Thomason's antidesegregation suit before Pulaski's Chancery Court only a day later. In view of this association and continual support, Women's Emergency Committee to Open Our Schools member Sara A. Murphy wondered whether the league's goal was in fact "to help launch a third term as governor for Faubus."[70] In contrast to the Capital Citizens' Council, which had run an accusatory campaign against Faubus earlier that year, the league sought a political alignment with him. They courted him as their most influential ally over the course of the following two years.

At the league's public rally on August 27, its officials Thomason, Jackson, and Aaron were also on the speakers' platform, from where they introduced the thirty members of the Mothers League of North Little Rock, which was said to have been formed a day earlier.[71] The North Little Rock league was an exact replica of the Mothers' League of Central High School. Mrs. Vernon Davis was the group's president, Mrs. Robert Fithen was the vice president, and Shirley Roberts was the recording secretary. Fithen announced to the press that the group had been organized "with 75 mothers at the home of one of the members" the night before. According to Fithen, the North Little Rock league's purpose was "to find ways and means . . . to prevent integration of the city's schools," copying the Mothers' League of Central High School's first public statement almost verbatim.[72]

Token desegregation of North Little Rock High School was set to take place on September 9, 1957, starting at the twelfth-grade level.[73] The Mothers' League of North Little Rock never developed as pronounced a public voice as its counterpart at Central High School. Media reports of the desegregation crisis at North Little Rock High School made no explicit mention of the women's group. The northern branch disappeared after the North Little Rock School Board decided to postpone integration indefinitely when the six African American pupils slated to begin at the school were refused entry in September by a segregationist mob of students and adults. The *Gazette* reported that members of the North Little Rock group, however, provided vocal support to the Central High league's protest in front of Central High School in September. The league expanded its segregationist network early on.[74]

The league used its ties to the Capital Citizens' Council to secure W. R.

Hughes, a Texas attorney and spokesman of the Association of Citizens' Councils of Texas, as their main speaker for the August 27, 1957, rally. This choice of speaker and the audience's reaction to his remarks demonstrate the league's reliance on both independent grassroots activism and direct council associations, as well as the ongoing paradox between the league members' desired respectability as Christian mothers and their penchant for blatant race baiting.

Hughes's tirades against the NAACP, the *Brown* decision, and communism were met with enthusiastic applause by the rally's attendees. His rhetoric stood in sharp contrast to the league's claims that its members sought to resist integration "as mothers" and to find strictly "legal ways and means" to do so. In his thirty-minute diatribe, Hughes claimed that communism was "behind every effort of the NAACP to desegregate," and that "a nigger in your school is a potential Communist in your school." Hughes advised his listeners to "stand up and fight for your children, schools, way of life and right to manage our affairs."[75]

As the rally drew to a close, an unidentified young man who stood at the rear asked "how many persons would be at Central when classes begin" to "push back" any African American pupils, adding that he "imagine[d] there a few shotguns in Little Rock too." The evening's only direct mention of violent resistance did not receive a friendly welcome. According to newspaper accounts, the man's remarks were met with "cold silence" and "a few moans."[76] Aaron took the microphone and declared that her group was "trying to keep down violence." Guthridge echoed her stance and claimed that the Capital Citizens' Council fought "only with the court of public opinion."[77]

Thomason reaffirmed the group's commitment to nonviolence when talking to the press the next day. Claiming that neither she nor any of the people whom she had talked to at the rally knew who the unidentified man was, Thomason stated that league was "working as a group of Christian mothers in a Christian-like way."[78] The league made good use of this incident as a performative opportunity. It absolved itself of responsibility for violence, and it portrayed itself as the agent of peace.[79]

Yet a contradiction lingered between the group's official claims and the women's actual behavior. Despite members' insistence that they were a group of Christian mothers who were independent of the Capital Citizens' Council, the league's political mobilization through rallies, the endorsement of W. R. Hughes and his incendiary rhetoric, and its framing of desegregation as a state of emergency showed that league was not solely an independent association of disgruntled or frightened mothers. It was a racist grassroots organization that helped organize massive resistance; its members were enraged by the attack on everyday white privileges, and so it was not just performing as southern mothers but as white southern mothers concerned for white children's welfare only. The league was a white supremacist interest group.

While the league denounced violence and declared itself the voice of reason, several prominent group members constantly stirred fears of an impending escalation. They exaggerated rumors, used loaded rhetoric, and ultimately displayed aggressive behavior themselves or demanded that male segregationists violently interfere with desegregation on their behalf. The league's initial performance as concerned Christian mothers enabled the group to progressively expand its activism and behavioral scripts and thus create a performative space for its public actions.

Hours before the league held its August 27 rally, Thomason had filed suit in Pulaski Chancery Court. Thomason asked for an injunction against the Little Rock School Board and Superintendent Blossom. She also demanded that "neither her child nor any other white child be required to attend Central High if Negroes attended."[80] Thomason's suit was argumentatively far reaching and named a number of high-profile witnesses, including Faubus, Blossom, and Little Rock police chief Marvin Potts.[81] She claimed that the prospect of admitting black pupils "had created a genuine danger of violence and civil commotion."[82] Other witnesses were not afraid to talk about the man at the rally who had intimated to the audience that segregationists might show up at the school with shotguns. They quoted him as an example for potential outbreak of violence due to integration.[83] Members of the league showed no sense of responsibility for this incident.[84]

As the first witness, Thomason appropriated the language of civil rights activism for her cause of maintaining white privilege. She stated that Central, among all other high schools in Little Rock, had been "singled out" and that the school was thus "being discriminated against."[85] To Thomason, the loss of white privilege for working- and lower middle-class whites was a form of bigotry against white people of lower social strata. In her view, white people were being equated with black people, which she took to be an insult to people at the intersection of stable white working class and lower middle class.

She testified that "violence was brewing" and that the league had been told that two armed gangs were forming, black boys against white boys. Thomason refused to name her sources, but she alleged that "one store sold all of its knives" to supposed gang members.[86] She said that she and other women had canvassed the city and that she personally had talked to people at her place of employment, the Westinghouse Lamp Plant. According to her survey, all the interviewed parents opposed desegregation. When questioned by the FBI in September, Thomason gave a more detailed account and claimed that she had received multiple anonymous phone calls "telling her to cease interfering with integration."[87] Another league member, forty-year-old Hilda Thevenet whose children were soon to attend Central High School, told the FBI that she had also heard there were pupils who had armed themselves with knives.[88]

Thomason concluded that "the mothers were 'terrified' at the situation and were afraid to send their children to school."[89] She emphasized an apolitical, maternalist role, claiming self-awarded authority as a representative for the imagined entity of Central High pupils' white mothers. She conveniently exaggerated the number of league members, estimating it at three hundred.[90]

It might have been this strategy of inflating the league's membership numbers that freed Thomason from having to give Judge Reed more detailed information about her supposed informants. After having called Thomason to his chamber to question her on her sources, he decided that he would "not require her to name any informants" until she had had "a chance later to obtain their permission." Thomason's report on rumors of alleged imminent violence was sufficient evidence for a real threat, despite the school board's attorney, A. F. House, opening his statement by saying that "an allegation that bloodshed will occur doesn't make it so" and despite the concurrence with that statement of Little Rock's police chief Marvin Potts, Little Rock's School Board director William Cooper, and Superintendent Blossom.[91]

Faubus was the last person to testify. As he made his way through the crowded court room to the witness stand, "a pretty unidentified mother rushed up to him with her hands clasped," according to the *Gazette*, and said, "Please governor, just see to it that there is no violence. We don't want our children mixed up in any violence." Faubus played to the theatrical quality of this incident, literally taking a bow to the enthusiastically applauding court room audience after he gave his testimony.[92]

While it is unclear why the *Gazette* concluded that a "pretty, unidentified" woman could automatically be described as a "mother," the woman's behavior and rhetoric were indicative of the mothers' league's strategy. Unlike the Capital Citizens' Council, the Mothers' League of Central High School was not in the business of alienating Governor Faubus. Instead, the league saved its contempt for the Little Rock School Board in general and Superintendent Blossom in particular, aiming to unify moderately to rigidly segregationist protagonists.

The young woman's action and plea in the court room illustrate a political and tactical ambivalence on the league's part; on the one hand, it performed a need for a chivalrous savior for white women and children, but on the other, it took decisive action on its own. This ambivalence is mirrored by the woman's plea: her action was quite possibly an expression of genuine moral panic about desegregation, and yet it could also be read as a tactical means of attracting the attention of the court and the media and thereby furthering the cause of Thomason's suit and her credibility. Other women engaged in similar displays over the following weeks, contributing to the escalation of the Central High School crisis.

Faubus told the court that "the present time" was "one of the worst possible times to integrate" because "revolvers" had been confiscated from both white and African American students recently—a claim he refused to substantiate and Police Chief Marvin Potts denied.[93] Faubus's statement had the desired impact, nonetheless: Reed granted the temporary injunction.[94] On the day of the verdict, the *Democrat* published a photograph of a cheerful Thomason, surrounded by several white middle-aged women and teenaged girls, including her daughter Louise. Mrs. Willie Chastain, "who described herself as 'just a housewife,'" is pictured congratulating Thomason.[95] The ruling was the public coup of unknown women who described themselves as just housewives and mothers and who were bolstered by Faubus's political authority. Through a mixture of hyperbolically performed maternal anxiety and the political hard line of invoking state segregation laws to prevent integration, Thomason and the league had earned a preliminary victory for their segregationist cause.

Although the league's actions have been deemed "peripheral" to the political processes of desegregation and a mere "thorn in the side" of the true protagonists of the Central High crisis by some contemporary witnesses and historians alike, the league turned the political periphery of publicly unknown housewives and working-class mothers into a space of nonconforming activism.[96] It seems unlikely that Thomason or the league initiated or even planned this suit by themselves. The group would indeed have been handy as pawns for Faubus's tactics. This alignment, however, proved mutually beneficial for the women's group and established political forces. The governor's actions legitimized the league's official stand against violence and earned it publicity, and the governor's actions were in turn legitimized by the women's group's public display of white female emotionality.[97]

The Thomason suit and its verdict established a segregationist framing of the Central High School crisis. Segregationists used a fear of violence as a strategy for creating performative spaces for their actions. Fear mongering served as justification for delaying desegregation.[98] While a fear of a violence surrounding Central High's desegregation was not wholly irrational in view of the school desegregation struggles in nearby communities such as Clinton, Tennessee, there was no evidence that a forcible conflict was inevitable in Little Rock. Segregationists, however, were able to circumvent desegregation without resorting to overt racism or belligerently challenging the federal courts by relying on the idea that violence would break out.[99]

Members of the league who asserted that their prime concern was working to prevent violence offered little more than vague rumors and circular reasoning—if everyone was talking about the danger of violence, then the danger of violence had to be real.[100] Segregationist politicians and grassroots activists supported each other's narratives of merely resisting impending violence, and they successfully deflected their own responsibility. Approaching the fight against desegregation by invoking parents' fear for their children and politicians' responsibility for preserving public order proved to be a solid political strategy for both the league and Faubus.

Bates gave an account as to how segregationists celebrated the ruling that night. Driving by her and L. C.'s house, they blew their car horns and yelled, 'Daisy! Daisy! Did you hear the news? The coons won't be going to Central!"[101] Segregationists' victory was short lived, however. On the same day that the Pulaski's Chancery Court granted Thomason the injunction, the Little Rock School Board asked the U.S. district court in Little Rock, temporarily presided over by Ronald N. Davies from North Dakota, for an injunction against interference with the board's desegregation plans. A day later, Davies nullified the chancery court's verdict and enjoined Thomason and all others from hindering the school board's desegregation plans.[102]

Thomason, who was present at the hearing, told the *Democrat* that she was "heart broken over the judge's ruling." She claimed that Davies "just did not understand the problem," implying that he neither had the knowledge nor capacity to decide on desegregation in the South.[103] Although the league's judicial action against the desegregation of Central High School thus came to a halt only four days before the new school term was supposed to start, its resistance to Central High's desegregation was far from over. The group shifted its focus to political action by lobbying Faubus. It also put a new emphasis on direct action by bringing its protest to Central High School's grounds.

"Where's your manhood?" The League's Role in the September Crisis

The three weeks of strife that followed are often depicted as the zenith of massive resistance. Central High was set to desegregate on September 3, 1957. The night before Central's desegregation was to begin, Faubus appeared on local television and radio channels and proclaimed that he had prayerfully reached the decision to dispatch Arkansas's National Guard to Little Rock. Its official mission was to keep "peace and order" and stifle violence should it occur. Yet instead the guardsmen acted as gatekeepers of segregation and refused to let any of the black students enter the school building for the next three weeks.[104]

Local segregationists were encouraged by this move. Although the day before the Little Rock Nine were to enter Central High School, Thomason, the league's recording secretary, had stated that she had "no plans whatsoever" to further interfere with the school's desegregation, noting that she was "not a lawbreaker," and as the federal court had handed down its ruling, that was that, the league sprang back into action.[105] Reviving its method of mobilization through a telephone chain, members of the league started to call mothers of Central High School students on September 2, 1957. The women invited fellow segregationist parents to attend a rally at 6:00 a.m. the following morning at Central High. The callers stated that their peaceful protest might circumvent integration after all and that they were scheduling their gathering at 6:00 a.m. so that working mothers would have a chance to attend as well.[106] Mrs. Hodge Alves reported that league member Minnice "Minnie" Sandusky called her and asked her to attend a prayer meeting that morning in front of the school. Sandusky told Alves that photographers would be on the scene and that it had been the governor himself who thought that their proposed action would be "a peaceful way of protesting integration."[107] Sandusky thus presented the rally as an officially sanctioned intervention.

While most league members emphatically denied any organized telephone campaign, Anita Sedberry admitted to the FBI that she had "done everything in her power to preserve segregation," including making "approximately 200 calls to other mothers along this line, . . . calling day and night." Sedberry, whose son attended Central High School, worked at the division of the Arkansas's welfare department for disabled children. The FBI agents described her as "very emotionally upset" during the interview. Sedberry asked the agents how they felt about desegregation; they declined to answer.[108] Aaron, who did not attend the morning gathering because she had "small children whom she had to get ready for school that morning," disclosed to the FBI that she had been given "a list of members" by Thomason two days before the school was scheduled to open and that she was instructed to contact members by telephone and invite them to "a sunrise service" at the school.[109]

Despite many league members' denials, at least parts of the group were invested in agitating other members and segregationist sympathizers and encouraging them to attend their protests. Female callers directly mentioned or alluded to Faubus having allegedly given his blessing to them to hold protests, seeking to portray their event as an official, political citizens' action that was legally sanctioned.[110] The callers were not merely concerned parents, however, but parents with a segregationist agenda. The telephone chain was a means by which league members tried to locate segregationist actors and protesters, not moderate bystanders. The women were not solely protesting desegregation but seeking to prevent it. During her phone call with Alves, who was the mother of a daughter at Central, Sandusky more than tripled the number of black students who were slated to attend Central High School. She warned Alves that there would be "30 Negroes eligible" to attend and insinuated that Alves's daughter would be in danger. Lying about the number of black pupils that would be entering the school was a tactic designed to heighten the fear of a black takeover of Central. By connecting a white mother's daughter to this threat, moreover, Sandusky used the coded rhetoric of branding black boys and men as sexual predators and white girls as their potential prey.[111] The majority of league members' children were indeed female. Alluding to white supremacist fears of miscegenation and the perceived threat to allegedly defenseless white southern womanhood posed by desegregation was a powerful mobilization tool.[112]

This rhetoric, however, was not mirrored in the segregationist women's actions. Although the callers presented themselves and their daughters as helpless victims of black and federal aggression, they were the ones who were taking steps to defend themselves. The women created a performative space for themselves that enabled white men to assume protective roles while they continued their own political activism, a space that they expanded through their publicly questioning the hegemonic masculinity of fellow male segregationists by criticizing their allegedly lackluster response.[113] The league legitimized its aggressive actions at the school by portraying them as filling a void and fulfilling the white community's duty.

Several hundred people showed up in the early morning hours at Central High School on September 3, despite the fact that Faubus had deployed the National Guard.[114] The mood in front of the school was one of elation in the wake of Governor Faubus's having called in the National Guard to stop desegregation. Small groups gathered to talk to each other or simply observe the scene in what historian Elizabeth Jacoway describes as a "carnival atmosphere . . . outside the school."[115] They watched as 1,878 white students walked past the guardsmen and entered the school. The earliest protesters had arrived at 5:30 o'clock that morning. Thomason followed shortly thereafter. The *Democrat* identified Thomason as the secretary of the league. She was again wearing the dress and hat that she had worn to her court hearing in August, suggesting that this was the outfit she used when she wanted to "dress up" and that as a working-class mother, she did not have a variety of choices. Thomason claimed that she was just accompanying her daughter to school, even though she had claimed after the court had handed down its ruling that she had withdrawn Louise from the school. By 6:00 a.m., it became clear that there "would be no mothers' march as had been reportedly scheduled," the *Gazette* wrote. The newspaper made no mention of the peaceful vigil that was advertised to white Central High School mothers the day before, and Thomason refused to say why the march had been canceled, thus confirming that there had indeed been a plan for the women to carry out a segregationist protest march instead of just passively standing by until the governor's preemptive strike forced them to call it off.[116]

Even though most protesters were men, according to the *Gazette*, Thomason's behavior was so noticeable that it warranted a newspaper mention.[117] At 7:00 a.m., two teenagers "unfurled a Confederate flag in the middle of the street and held it up while cameramen took pictures." Thomason and four other unidentified women started to sing Dixie, upon which the teenagers, encouraged by the singing and the applause of the adult crowd, paraded the flag up and down the street. When the boys were ordered by the guardsmen to put the flag away, Thomason picked it up. The segregationists' performance created the media interest that their grassroots activism needed, and the league's white supremacist, maternalist politics benefited from the public inclusion of children and teenagers in the protests.[118]

Jackson joined her fellow league members that morning, too. She stated that she had come to the school grounds with her two daughters merely "out of curiosity." But then Jackson proceeded to distribute petitions that called for the removal of Superintendent Blossom, disproving that claim.[119] Central High PTA president Stephens reported that Jackson had personally called her on September 2, 1957, asking Stephens to attend "a meeting" at the school the following morning. Jackson had stated that she and others "had been told to gather at the school," but when Stephens asked who had given them these orders, Jackson refused to answer her question. Jackson claimed that the organizers "had the approval of Gov. Faubus for the meeting," and that the police would be there. When Stephens remarked that the police would be on the scene to protect the Little Rock Nine, Jackson contradicted her: "She said no it was the other way around, that the police would be there to protect them, meaning the Mother's [*sic*] League and the other parents." Stephens then warned that "some unscrupulous person might take over the mob" and violence could result, to which Jackson replied that "that was a risk they would have to take."[120] In her view, the mere presence of black pupils posed a threat to white women and their children and increased the probability of violence. In reality, the league and other segregationists were the ones who posed the threat to the black children and integration sympathizers.

It is not coincidental that Stephens received a call from the league's vice president, whereas other mothers were invited by anonymous callers or less high-profile members of the women's group, given that Stephens had repeatedly asked all parents to accept Central High's desegregation. It was also not the first phone call she had received from concerned mothers who would ultimately become league officers: in August 1957, Thomason had called her to invite her to the league's inaugural meeting, an invitation that she declined.[121] The league officers sought to establish ties to the formal power structures of parental influence at Central High School, not only to empower their activism but to legitimize their cause. However, they did not have the social capital to bring this off.

When Stephens made a telephone call to Thomason on September 4 to inquire what the league's "next move was," Thomason told her untruthfully that the league "had no connection with the White Citizens Council" and that its first meeting "had been private." Thomason reiterated her claim that there was a danger of violence due to desegregation at Central High School. She told Stephens that "she had names of people, sealed in an envelope that could testify to the facts that negroes [*sic*] had been buying knives and acid but that she wouldn't open this envelope unless she needed to," changing the story she and other league mothers had previously told about how both white and black gangs alike were arming themselves.[122] The recording secretary shifted the blame and created another justification for white parents' protests. Withholding evidence for her claims, Thomason made her warnings unassailable.

When the black pupils did not appear on September 3, 1957, the crowd eventually dispersed. The following morning, however, the first black pupil who tried to enter Central High School, fifteen-year-old Elizabeth Eckford, became the target of the segregationists' wrath.[123] By eight o'clock, hundreds of segregationists had gathered in front of the school. The photograph of Elizabeth Eckford making her way through a crowd of irate segregationists in front of Central High while fifteen-year-old Hazel Bryan (walking next to her friend, fellow Central High School student and daughter of a league member, Sammie Dean Parker) followed behind her yelling, became the iconographic symbol of this crisis.[124]

As Eckford sought an entry point into the school, a segregationist mob of approximately two hundred jeering and taunting people closed in on her. She was subjected to verbal abuse, as segregationists spat on her, made threats that included "Lynch her!," and told her, "Nigger, go on to your own school, you have better schools than we do!"[125] The insults were not only racist; they also gave voice to a class-related hostility toward African American pupils breaking down the racial and spatial barriers of a formerly white school, one of the few local assets promising cultural capital to the white working-class residents' children.[126]

Despite the league's claims of passivity, the *Gazette* observed that "pleasant looking mothers, some members of the Mothers' League of Central High and some from its North Little Rock sister group, exploded into bitter vocal tirades" when black pupils showed up that day. Moreover, mothers' league members "seemed to form the hard core of the crowd and were seen each day of the last week."[127] The newspaper's description of the women's behavior captures the contrast between the group's self-description and its actions. Officially on a nonviolent observation mission, league members were part of the mob and harassed the black students. Officially in pursuit of middle-class respectability and southern mothers' gentility, the pleasant-looking mothers burst out racist insults and lost their composure. Their performance of white southern bellehood had given way to the aggressive defense of white supremacy. The group's political convictions made a colorblind, concerned mother performance difficult to sustain, and the women broke this behavioral frame while protesting outside of Central High.

Throughout the days of early September, Capital Citizens' Council and league members were among the segregationist crowds. Guthridge, Pruden, Foreman (whose oldest of four daughters attended Central High School), Bickle, and

Thomason were at the scene.[128] While it remains unclear whether league members were among the women and men who harassed Elizabeth Eckford, at least one member made her position clear. Sedberry told the FBI that she had not been on the scene on September 4, 1957, but, alluding to a stereotypically feminine type of physical fight, she disclosed that if the National Guard had not protected Eckford that morning and she had been there, she "would have snatched her hair out."[129] Even though Sedberry was employed in the handicapped children's division of the state's welfare department, black children apparently were not deserving of welfare in her view, and she was not above attacking them. The league's idea of motherhood clearly extended only to the protection of white children.

The level of organization, determination, and concerted action belies the statements of league members, who told FBI agents that the league was a spontaneous parents' gathering and not an organized group. Most league affiliates lied about their connection to the group in their FBI interviews, except for the group's officers who had previous media exposure in their official capacities. Whereas Aaron, Jackson, Thomason, and Mrs. A. T. Forbess admitted that they belonged to the mothers' league, Sedberry as well Thevenet and Flora Shatzer obfuscated their affiliation. The women divulged that they had been in contact with the group yet added that the league was not a formal organization but an informal gathering of mothers or parents.[130]

Thevenet's impression that the league was more of an informal group than an organization during the first week of September, however, might not have been a conscious deception, as by that time the league had been in existence for three weeks, members had neither received membership cards nor were they expected to pay dues, and the membership could have still have been fluctuating. Nevertheless, the group had three elected officers, had circulated several petitions, had supported a lawsuit, had organized two telephone campaigns, and then congregated with its North Little Rock counterparts in front of Central High School. The group could not be described as entirely informal either. Earl K. Lightcap outright lied in his FBI interview about his wife's membership, as did Sandusky, Lorraine Elrod, Lucille Webb, and Mary Opal Foreman, wife to Capital Citizens' Council member Lawton D. Foreman.[131] At least some members had legal counsel and had perhaps been advised to not reveal too much to the FBI, and entered the interviews cautiously. Foreman, for example, declined to sign her statement and referred the agents to her attorney, Guthridge. Thomason, too, eventually asked the two special agents interviewing her whether she could speak to her attorney, Arthur Frankel, and subsequently broke off the interview after their conversation.[132]

League members were ambivalent FBI witnesses. Eager to prove that Central High's desegregation would lead to violence, which they thought would increase their chances of circumventing its implementation, the league's officers provided vague information to the agents. Hesitant interviewees like Thevenet and outright hostile interviewees like Foreman objected to what they perceived as outside interference by the federal government. They were thus uncooperative on principle. The repeated downplaying of the league's organizational structure as well as of its activities was an attempt to protect the group's structure, affiliates, and members from potential prosecution.

During the first week of September, the federal Justice Department petitioned the federal district court for an injunction against Faubus and the National Guard commanders. Judge Davies ordered a federal investigation into the rumors of impending violence, which resulted in a four-hundred-page-long FBI report that rejected such claims. On September 20, Judge Davies ruled that Faubus's deployment of National Guard had "thwarted" the court-approved plan of integration and that desegregation would proceed.[133] Up until this ruling, black students had continued to be barred from entering Central High School. Although the "cool-off period" until the trial proceeded did ease tensions after the first week of strife and the crowds shrunk, segregationists still assembled in front of the school.[134] The scene drew truants from other white schools in the city, and citizen councils in Arkansas urged fellow council members to come to Little Rock to join the protests. Little Rock's segregationists did not relent in their campaigning.[135] Guthridge spoke to a citizens' council rally of 750 people in Greenville, Alabama, on September 16, 1957. He asserted that Arkansas had been "selected as the target state for integration" because it was considered "the weakest link in the Southern chain." Uplifted by the strengthened segregationist resistance in his state, he exclaimed that "we're going to dis-integrate every place that is integrated in Arkansas."[136]

The exacerbation of the Little Rock crisis was based on the mutual influence, if not symbiotic relationship, of the state's executive and grassroots activists.[137] On September 17, league member Katherine Dame telephoned the governor's mansion and left a message: "Tell the Gov. I am one of the Mothers at Central and we are still behind him 100%." If the governor had to "withdraw the guard," she stated, he should let the mothers know and they would "take the guns and guard the school themselves."[138] Having warned that they were prepared to "dis-integrate" every desegregated place in Arkansas, segregationists were now threatening to dismantle the rule of law and to incite violence in public spaces.

However, officially, league and Capital Citizens' Council officers had called for nonviolence after Davies's ruling. Thevenet, now identified by the *Gazette* as "a founder of the League," declared, "I just hope there won't be any violence and I'm praying today that there won't be any."[139] Thomason told the *Democrat* that the league was "praying the leaders" would "see the will of [the] people and not try to force on us something we cannot and will not accept." Thomason elaborated on this point by referencing massive resistance's insistence on states' rights: "If this injustice of the states losing their rights continues, we will be losing everything that has made America a great and Christian nation." She warned that "dictatorship" would "set in" if the people's will was ignored. "The mothers in the League," she concluded, would not "ever accept integration in our heart and it has never been the American way of life to . . . have something forced on us that we cannot accept."[140] Thomason thus framed the activism of the league in broader political, patriotic terms. By omitting mention of the fact that racism was at the heart of the league's resistance to desegregation, Thomason sought to elevate her cause and secure respectability for it. She presented the league as a fighter for freedom, states' rights, and American values. Although Thomason made no mention of communism, she alluded to the centralization of power in communist countries as being anathema to the subsidiary model of politics in the United States and thereby transformed the issue of desegregation from a southern sectional crisis into a question of American principles.

Thus the league once more publicly performed nonviolence while laying the groundwork for an escalation. No longer content with its prior plan to stand prayerfully by, it announced a demonstration against the desegregation of Central High. Faubus had removed the National Guard from Central High after Davies handed down his ruling and had then left the state for the Southern Governors' Conference in Sea Island, Georgia. Little Rock's police was left on its own to enforce desegregation starting on September 23, 1957, which proved to be an impossible task.[141] At seven o'clock in the morning, seventy-five people assembled in front of Central High School. Before noon, the mob had grown to over one thousand people, and approximately every eighth member of the mob was female.[142] Mothers' league members were among this mob and incited segregationist men from the Capital Citizens' Council to exercise violence. Although Jackson's presence was not mentioned in any newspaper report, the *Gazette*'s reporter Jerry Dhonau told the FBI that he had observed the league's vice president "pushing, yelling, shouting, and trying to break through the police line," when the news broke that the Little Rock Nine had made it inside the school. An FBI report stated that Jackson was "a leader of the trouble makers at the high school" that morning.[143]

Thevenet, whose children had not yet reached high school age, was described by three witnesses "as a mob leader," too. She was "yelling loud insults at Negroes and others she suspected of being in favor of integration" and kept haranguing the crowd. According to reports made to the FBI, Thevenet "made a constant effort to influence the crowd and cause general unrest around the high school," thus contradicting her previous FBI statement that the league attempted to circumvent Central High's desegregation "in a peaceable way within the law."[144] *As-*

sociated Press reporter Sy Ramsey disclosed to the FBI that he had also noticed Thevenet in front of the school on September 23 and that "she seemed to be enjoying all of the activity in that she was doing a lot of talking to newsmen and posing for cameramen." He concluded that Thevenet was not an agitator but an "exhibitionist."[145] Thevenet was in fact both. Her performance served to agitate the crowd, and the crowd's and her own agitation, in turn, fed her performance. Thevenet created a performative space and played to an audience.

Thomason, who, along with Thevenet, was among the crowd from the start, also tried to break through police lines.[146] She exhibited the most aggressive behavior of all the members of the league that day. According to five reporters and a Little Rock policeman, she "was verbally agitating the crowd" in front of the school throughout the morning.[147] Thomason's public voice in the desegregation crisis and her presence at Central High School earned her the title "segregationist leader," as the *Gazette* captioned her picture. The photograph showed her dropping money into a hat that was passed around the crowd to collect money for Tommy Dunaway, a patrolman who had quit his job on the scene and had joined the segregationist protests.[148] Thomason grew more belligerent. Stifled in her own attempt to break through police lines when she realized that the black students had arrived, she shouted at men in the crowd, "Where's your manhood, why don't you do something to get these people?," before she started crying, saying "My daughter's in there with those niggers. Oh, my god! Oh, God!"[149]

Thomason's emotional response was not at odds with her displays of aggression, and as sociologist Phoebe Godfrey argues, Thomason's "emotional responses to integration" were "vehemently instrumental in leading the mob" at Central. Indeed, several newspaper reports of the scene at Central High School on September 23 depicted segregationist girls and women in a stereotypically gendered way by emphasizing the "wails of hysterical women," "hysteria [that] swept from the shrieking girls to members of the crowd," and "women crying hysterically, tears running down their faces."[150] While a group of white girls left the school and chanted "2-4-6-8, we ain't gonna integrate" and "Are we going to school with niggers? Hell, no," other girls exited Central in tears, which reporters interpreted as a state of shock. The *Democrat* published a picture of two crying girls who were led away from the school by two women who had each placed an arm around the shaken teenagers.[151]

The media depiction of the mood of girls and women at Central High School that morning was one of anger, panic, and fear. Whether this display of emotions was a genuine reaction caused by prejudicial fear rooted in their racism, group dynamics of anger and frustration, or a conscious performance intended to escalate the situation by dramatization, the seemingly terrified white women and girls legitimized the mob's cause. They were highly visible in the crowd, so visible, in fact, that FBI director J. Edgar Hoover advised President Eisenhower not to send federal troops to Little Rock, as the perceived "presence of so many women and church ministers in the midst of those crowds suggested . . . that they could not be seen as legitimate targets."[152]

Members of the crowd initially mistook three black newspaper reporters and a black freelance photographer for a delegation of the Little Rock Nine and set upon them shortly before nine o'clock.[153] Although the protestors had tried to cover every entrance of the Central High building to prevent black students from entering the school, as parts of the crowd attacked the newspapermen and photographer, the Little Rock Nine slipped into Central High's south entrance.[154] Finally realizing that the black students had entered the school, members of the crowd began to yell "They're in!," and the situation descended into chaos, which the meager police presence of seventy officers and fifty state troopers assigned to the school could (or would) not control. A woman shouted, "I want my child out of there," to which a man responded, "Let's go in there and get those niggers." Inciting the crowd to follow him with shouts of "Come on, let's go. Let's go get 'em," he and approximately thirty other white men unsuccessfully tried to break through the police lines, while another woman screamed, "I hope they drag eight dead niggers from that school." A steady stream of white parents, including many mothers, entered the school to withdraw their children from classes, and a number of white students took part in a walkout to the cheers of the crowd.[155]

The crowd, the sound of which one of the Little Rock Nine, Melba Pattillo, described "as having an 'animal quality,'" surrounded the school building, In view of the escalating violence in front of the school and the failure of Little Rock's police to disperse the crowd, the Little Rock Nine were removed from the building at 11:00 a.m. After the Little Rock Nine were escorted from the school premises, a police officer announced their departure to the crowd. The segregationist mob did not believe him. The demonstrators were invited to choose a member of the crowd to verify the policeman's statement. After initial "We want Faubus" shouts, Thevenet was chosen alongside the city attorney O. D. Longstreth Jr., and the two entered the school building. When Thevenet returned, she declared that she had visited "several rooms and that the students remaining in the School were under the impression the Negroes had left." Thevenet carried enough segregationist credibility for the mob to disperse after her announcement.[156] The segregationists dispersed gradually, moving on to break car windows and storefronts in downtown Little Rock and even attacking black passersby. By the evening of September 23, Little Rock's police department had made forty-two arrests, and the homes of the Little Rock Nine and Daisy Bates had been put under police protection.[157]

Daisy Bates, afraid for the black children's lives, did not return with the group on September 24. Still, a crowd of several hundred people formed in front of the school again. Little Rock mayor Woodrow Mann asked President Eisenhower to intervene.[158] Eisenhower federalized Arkansas's National Guard, and on the evening of September 24, units of the 101st Airborne Division arrived. That same evening, seven hundred people crowded a ballroom at Little Rock's Hotel Lafayette. Little Rock's segregationist network invited everyone who was "against race-mixing in our schools." They proclaimed the launch of "a crusade against public enemy no. 1," which was desegregation.[159] Little mention was made at this rally of the troops. Speakers called for the dismissal of Woodrow Mann, the mayor, Marvin Potts, the police chief, and Gene Smith, the assistant police chief. The segregationists demanded a special session of the state legislature to abolish public schools altogether and to set up segregated private schools. Capital Citizens' Council president Robert Ewing Brown urged nonviolent resistance and added that "we feel the minorities as well as the majorities have rights." Brown echoed the position Thomason had taken in her testimony during her August suit, appropriating civil rights language and applying it to the perceived violation of white supremacists' freedom of choice and freedom of association.[160]

Shifting Gears

Little Rock's segregationist countercampaign did not end here. The league broadened its campaign and remained a voice in Little Rock's public discourse about Central High's desegregation throughout the school year. The interplay between a silent majority and the league's persistent agitation (and that of other segregationist groups) afforded it a disproportionate amount of influence, particularly considering the group's size, its lack of established social networks within Little Rock's civil society, and its limited financial means.[161] The league diversified its strategy, abandoning its protests in front of the school and resuming its political lobbying, judicial action, and publicity campaigns. The league also started to intervene with school life at Central High, attempting to thwart desegregation by harassing black pupils and sabotaging the daily routine, and sought to directly influence local and national policies by running for office. The group claimed Central High School as white people's exclusive space, bemoaning its occupation by not only federal troops but also black pupils, whom they deemed intruders. They wanted to reclaim Central High. By entwining the desegregation struggle with broader questions of states' rights and the preservation of individual (white) rights, the league aimed to give its struggle national appeal—a quest that was frequently sabotaged by its overt racism.

Faubus, despite his prior reluctance, was now firmly on their side. Addressing the United States over a nationally broadcast speech on the ABC network on September 26, 1957, he held up a photograph of two white girls who were seemingly being forced forward by soldiers pointing bayonets at their backs.[162] "We are now an occupied territory. Evidence of the naked force of the federal government is here apparent in these unsheathed bayonets in the backs of school girls," he added.[163] Upon closer inspection, the audience would have noticed that the girls were laughing and that none of the bayonets were touching their backs, a fact obscured by the photograph's angle. The photograph made the front covers of Little Rock's newspapers, and segregationists all over the South subsequently used it in their "Remember Little Rock" propaganda.[164] Faubus accused the FBI of haven "taken" teenaged girls who were then "held incommunicado for hours of questioning while their frantic parents knew nothing of their whereabouts" and accused the federal government of employing "police state" methods.[165]

The teenaged girls were fourteen- and fifteen-year-old Central High students Beverly Burks and Annette Harper. They had indeed been questioned by the FBI on September 7, 1957. The FBI issued a statement that they had interviewed the girls for an hour and that their mothers had known where they were. According to this statement, one of Faubus's lawyers had supplied the FBI with a list of students who could provide information pertaining to its investigation of potential violence at Central High. Beverly and Annette were among those listed.[166] The girls' mothers, Maxine Burks and Mrs. Kenneth Harper, were members of the mothers' league. They refused to elaborate on the incident when talking to the *Gazette* but made clear their sentiments toward the FBI. Harper stated that "she was angry because she had told her daughter not to accompany the agents to the FBI office," while Burks said that "she didn't want to discuss the interview or the statement," adding that she "wasn't very pleased about it. I'm sick and tired of this whole thing."[167]

That Faubus propagated the story of the supposed detainment of the league members' daughters suggests that the women's group continued to be in contact with him, feeding him information. League members followed their by-now established pattern of reiterating their dislike of the FBI's intervention while simultaneously wanting to give information on impending violence. Disseminating the false information that the girls had been held for hours was a conscious act aimed at discrediting the FBI. Annette Harper would be suspended for her segregationist activism at Central High School in October 1957.[168] The league's collusion with Faubus continued. On the morning of September 28, 1957, more than 130 league members and six white children assembled at the governor's mansion.[169] During their visit, Thomason boasted to the press that the league probably had thousands of members. The league again sought to present itself as the only legitimate parental agent in the desegregation crisis and presumed a silent majority behind their actions.[170] This tactic did not go unnoticed. Elsie D. Jones, in a letter to the *Gazette*, wrote that she was "one of the 1,865 mothers of Central High School students who were not at the Governor's Mansion Saturday." Jones sought to clarify that the league was not representing all mothers,

Orval Faubus with members of the mothers' league, 1957 (Bettman, Getty Images)

not even a majority. She did not believe that a school closing was necessary, and she wanted her son in school. Jones added that she was "not in favor of integration" and was not "criticizing these mothers for expressing their views, but they are only 135. Do they speak for all parents of high school children?"[171]

The league was neither elected nor otherwise authorized to speak for all white mothers of Central High. Not even all of the 137 mothers present at the governor's mansion were members of the league. The petition that the league presented to Faubus stated that the women were from Little Rock, North Little Rock, and other parts of Arkansas.[172] The league called on its North Little Rock sister group and other segregationist women to boost its numbers and create the perception that they had a broad support base. That most white parents of Central High students stayed mute and failed to establish a coherent counterpublic served as an opportunity structure for the league. It had carved out a space between established but complacent or competing powers in the city and the state, which allowed it to step into the spotlight and claim public space.

The women waited at the front gate until Faubus was ready to receive them. Jackson, representing the league in lieu of the group's president Aaron who Jackson said was ill that day, spoke to numerous journalists in the meantime.[173]

Jackson, whom one journalist described as "a slim, alert looking brunette with a mercurial temperament which she tries very hard to keep under control," reiterated the league's claim that Central High was on the brink of a violent altercation. She proclaimed that violence would erupt at the school as soon as the federalized troops were removed. When prompted for evidence, however, Jackson responded that this was "just the way the children talk."[174] The league had not abandoned its fear mongering and continued to ignore demands for substantiation of these claims.

Jackson remarked that her two daughters, Sandra and Charlene, had not attended Central High since September 20, 1957, and that they would not go back until Central was resegregated. When prompted about her daughters' educational prospects if the school remained desegregated, Jackson replied, "There are still schools in Georgia, Mississippi and Alabama where there are no Negroes."[175] Invoking a supposed biblical foundation for segregation, Jackson claimed that the league "held no personal animosity" toward African Americans but that "God himself set us apart by boundaries and language," without further explaining this statement. She stressed that she was in favor of the 1896 separate-but-equal doctrine, set out by the U.S. Supreme Court's *Plessy v. Ferguson* ruling. She advocated for black people having "exactly the same facilities that we have—but keep them separate." Finally, Jackson alluded to broader ideological principles about white people's freedom of association and states' rights. When a news reporter inquired whether the league would ask the governor to remove his son from the desegregated Arkansas Tech College, Jackson stated that the league was "not trying to tell others what to do. That's what we dislike—people trying to tell us what to do about our own schools."[176] Jackson was well versed in segregationist rhetoric, and she presented several arguments for the group's opposition to Central High's desegregation. Stressing individual choice and states' rights, Jackson expanded the women's group's public frame beyond maternalism, and she elevated her group's politics above the immediate opposition to Central High desegregation by embracing supposedly colorblind, more abstract political principles.

Leaving the news reporters outside, the league met with Faubus for thirty minutes. The group presented Faubus with a petition that asked him to "call into Special session the Arkansas State legislature and close Central Hight [*sic*] School and open it again on some basis that would remove it completely from Federal Jurisdication [*sic*]." The league made no suggestion as to how the legislature was to achieve this aim, and Faubus remained noncommittal. The spelling and grammatical mistakes in the league's petition only contributed to the perception that the women were uneducated white trash.[177]

The governor personified the white male champion for the league, and the women made a show of it as they left the mansion and posed for photographs with him. Emphasizing the group's name and supposed purpose, the petition stressed that the league's approaching Faubus in this way was not only "in the interest of Good Government" and "good Human Relations" but, "most of all," in "the interest of their children." Never reluctant to dramatize the perceived evils of integration for white children and society as a whole, the league again resorted to a public performance of concerned maternalism and claimed that the desegregation of Central High School had left its children "emotional[ly] sick," had prevented the children from studying, and had led to "unspeakable" conditions at the school. The group begged Faubus "to lift from the parents, and the children of Little Rock this humiliation, this unspeakable reproach, this atrocity that has been visited upon us, our children and the name of our state."[178]

The apocalyptic vision laid out in the league's petition was echoed in a letter by "A Mother" to the *Democrat* on September 30, 1957. The letter writer stated that in her view, Central High's state was "repugnant to the people of Arkansas, as well as to entire South." She added that she was outraged by a federal government "that would force to make a whole section of the country accept something that is so alien and repugnant to our accepted ideas and customs. Why doesn't President Eisenhower have his own grandchildren attend a school with Negroes?"[179] Whether the petition expressed genuine terror in the face of desegregation, rooted in racist perceptions of black people and the assumption of white supremacy, or the League's words were strategic and indicative of the rhetoric accessible to segregationist women in the public eye at the time, the league styled itself and white children once more as the victims of a plague visited upon their city.

By performatively appealing to white men to take the lead, the league was able to legitimize its actions in public space. Sammie Dean Parker, an eleventh-grade Central High student, became an icon of this southern damsel-in-distress tactic when, after the league had left the mansion to meet the waiting reporters, she rushed forward to hug Faubus. She began to sob in his arms in front of the press cameras, as the women benignly smiled and the white children surrounding them, all dressed up for the occasion, curiously looked on. This symbolic expression of feminine fragility and powerlessness, however, clashed with segregationist white women's actions in Little Rock.[180] Parker became one of the white students who continuously harassed the black pupils and distributed segregationist literature at the school, and she was eventually expelled from Central High School in 1958. She served as the Capital Citizens' Council's poster girl for alleged injustices against white students. Her expulsion was widely publicized by segregationists, including her mother, a league member, and Guthridge, who was the family's attorney.[181] She and other white women's performances of helpless white womanhood, then, were the means by which they sought to avoid accountability for their transgressive actions. Parker's behavior also show that white students, too, were conscious agents in their actions.

The league's visit to the governor's mansion is a nutshell example of its activist tactic of creating a performative space for maternalist, white supremacist politics. The performance of mothers concerned about the "unspeakable" conditions at Central High School evoked the traditional scripts of female activism on behalf of children's welfare and white women's reliance on white men's chivalry. This performance allowed members of the league to find the spaces between these traditional frames to expand the scripts of their everyday practices and enactments as white southern women.[182]

Simultaneously, the league and its sympathizers accused white moderate and prointegration citizens of putting on a performance. The league, the Capital Citizens' Council, and the letter writer who identified only as "Mother," questioned the sincerity of white moderates' support for desegregation. "Mother" asked why President Eisenhower's grandchildren attended racially segregated private schools, and Little Rock's segregationists doubted white upper-class Pulaski Height residents' commitment to desegregation in their predominantly white neighborhood. This class-based reproach of white moderates enabled segregationists to reframe their resistance as a fight against a hypocritical establishment. The mothers' league and other segregationists stressed the spatial separation of upper-class whites from Central High neighborhood's lived spaces and daily struggles. Space, both physical and social, was an expression of power, which was not easily accessible to the working-class and lower middle-class members of the league.[183] The treatment that the league received at the governor's mansion further revealed this lack of formal power and social capital, although the league and the governor mutually benefited from their alliance. Not only was the group made to wait outside, but later on, Governor Faubus quipped that he did not want to share his press conference with the women and had asked them to step aside.[184] Despite the league's representation as a group of white damsels in distress, it did not stand idly by as Faubus refused to call a special session of the legislature. Demonstrating once again its fluid trial-and-error approach in pursuit of Central High's eventual resegregation, the league resumed the judicial path of attack. Five days after the league's visit to the governor's mansion, Jackson filed suit in federal district court seeking the removal of the federal troops from Central High's premises. Jackson filed the suit on behalf of her daughters, Sandra and Charlene.[185] Judge Davies dismissed Jackson's suit on October 17, 1957, after which Jackson challenged his verdict in the Eighth Circuit Court of Appeals. On April 28, 1958, the court unanimously dismissed her case.[186] By late November, however, the 101st Airborne had withdrawn from Central High School, leaving only the federalized National Guard to keep watch.

The league persevered. Misleading the public by stating that the league had grown to a size of four to five hundred members, Jackson claimed that despite her recent loss in court, the group's determination was "firmer than ever," adding that "there is a great deal of resentment against the Negroes inside the school. The white children are determined to get them out of there."[187] In fact, the group had 163 official members in October 1957. Two of these, Mary Foreman and Ethel Childers, were also official citizens' council members before joining the league.[188] Jackson became the league's president on October 24 after Aaron moved to Beaumont, Texas. The league elected Jewell Payne as vice president and Thevenet, Sedberry, Marjorie Maters, and Margaret Douglass to the group's board.[189]

Occupying the Territory

Jackson was correct that there was a campaign under way at Central High School to force the Little Rock Nine out but failed to mention the league's pivotal role in it.[190] Unlike those protesting desegregation at William Frantz and McDonogh 19 elementary schools in New Orleans, the mothers' league and the Capital Citizens' Council never directly called for a comprehensive boycott of Central High School nor directly sanctioned white parents who continued to send their children to the school. They wanted to defend what they saw as their space, not abandon it, and the women enlisted the help of white Central High students to do so. Children of league officers had not attended school since the Little Rock Nine were escorted back into the school on September 25, 1957, after having stayed home on September 24. Both Jackson and Thomason stated that their children would not go to Central High as long as the school was desegregated. Jackson's statement regarding her daughters' absence was carefully phrased. She said that she was only speaking for herself and did not imply that her position was either the official policy of the league or that of any other white mother of a Central High School child.[191] At the same time, Jackson sought to present her cause as one of constitutional principles when she told the *Gazette* that "people all over the United States are going to know that this is not just a fight of segregation or integration but a fight for states [*sic*] rights and the right to govern ourselves. We believe in freedom of choice, that the government is actually by the consent of the governed with majority rule."[192]

Jackson's daughter Sandra, a junior, started to reattend school again in early October, according to Huckaby, but Charlene, the elder daughter, was absent for the rest of the year.[193] The *Gazette* reported that members of the league "sent their children back to School" as soon as October 1, 1957. The group's stance on the matter was far from uniform or consistent.[194] Perhaps Jackson's younger daughter had asserted a desire to return to school or perhaps even to Jackson, her daughters' education ultimately trumped her dislike of desegregation. Jackson could also have decided that returning at least one daughter to school would give her better access to daily proceedings and events that, in turn, fueled the league's activism.

Central High's attendance rates had been steadily increasing since the federal troops' intervention. While the absentee rate was 43 percent on September 25, 1957, it sunk to 30 percent only two days later. An anonymous letter to the *Gazette* clarified more moderate Central High School parents' attitude toward the league's boycott. A "Reader" from Little Rock ironically asked the newspaper not to "put anything in your paper that would discourage the Mother's [*sic*] League at Central High. My daughter assures me it has never been so good since the brats of such harpies are absent. It is a pleasure to think of this spawn draped around the living rooms of these biddies during school hours. In time, a well deserved mutual disgust should develop so please let them stew in their own juice."[195] The league's reputation (as well as that of their children) was that they were a group of misbehaved, vicious, and ignorant women whose antics had disturbed the other children's and parents' school routine. By implying that the mothers, and by proxy their children, were unpleasant people whose character and behavior would eventually lead to strain even among each other, "Reader" joined the chorus of middle- and upper-class Little Rockians who depicted league families as misbehaved white trash.

The terms "harpies" and "biddies," moreover, amounted to classist and sexist devaluations and referred not just to the fact that the women were from working- and lower middle-class backgrounds but also to their chosen field of activism, seemingly occupied with brooding over and indoctrinating teenagers. Critics ridiculed and belittled the women's segregationist activism by depicting them as badly mannered mothers, hovering over equally rude children.[196]

A letter from "White Native" from Little Rock sarcastically stated that everyone should vote for Jackson for governor. "Wise up, Mrs. Jackson, your agitation is one of the causes of this damn mess." The letter writer asked Jackson to send her daughters to private school if she did not like the situation at Central High and to "please let us have peace." "White Native" suggested that Jackson was primarily a seeker of attention: "You got your name in the papers, so now pipe down."[197]

The letter writers made a point about the league members' repeated attempts to disrupt the day-to-day proceedings of Central High School. Its interferences with Central's school life provide insight into the various strategies that the mothers' league employed. Part of the reasoning behind the mothers' league's interventions at Central during the 1957–58 school year echoed the group's previous line of argument. To them, Central High belonged to the white community, and black pupils violated their everyday white rights. The league stressed white children's supposed entitlement to preferential treatment by the school officials, particularly in the face of desegregation.[198]

In two letters sent to Central High's principal Jess Matthews in December 1957, Jackson expressed her group's dismay at Matthews's perceived lack of white supremacist, racial solidarity and concomitant lack of masculinity. Copies of Jackson's open letter also reached Blossom, the *Arkansas Gazette*, and the *Arkansas Democrat*—the league was staging a publicity campaign to reclaim space and regain the spotlight. Jackson charged that Central High School's morale was at "a disgraceful low" and that the league was protesting "with every impulse and energy of our soul" the school administration's alleged discriminatory behavior against white students. Jackson wrote that the "common decencies of one white person to another are being outraged—to say nothing of the respect a white child has a right to expect of a white school official."[199]

Lamenting the loss of white privilege, Jackson claimed that white pupils were disciplined more severely than black pupils. Matthews and other school officials had put "an iron clad censorship" on this alleged maltreatment of white children. To the members of the league, the normal social order had been reversed inside of Central High School: the black teenagers, perceived as intruders and outsiders, were displacing the school's rightful owners. Even worse, in segregationists' view, black pupils received the preferential treatment that should have been allotted to white children.

Jackson charged that the school administration was "negro dominated" and that Bates was secretly manipulating everyday proceedings. This led to a "fear campaign" against white children and a "prison-like . . . mental paralysis," as children had "been told that anytime a child crossed one of Bates' children" the child would have "to give an account to Daisy Bates personally." The league and the Capital Citizens' Council also circulated a pamphlet that stated that Bates was allowed to cross-examine white students at Central High School. This was a "fabricated" account, Blossom later stated, which derived from a visit of the NAACP's state president to the principal's office during which she had discussed an incident at the school with Matthews.[200]

The members of the league viewed Matthews's perceived lack of white solidarity with their children as being secretly steered by Bates. The group depicted Bates as the guardian of the nameless and faceless deindividualized group of black students she controlled alongside the white school officials. In the league's view, white school officials bowed to Bates's wishes and thus betrayed their own people. A segregationist card passed around Central High School read: "That White Trash Matthews Named Jess, Sure Got Central High in a Mess, The Kids—If They're White, He Deprives of their Rights, He's a Kansas Nigger-Lover, I guess."[201] Segregationists, including the mothers' league, charged that white people who did not actively support them were race traitors.

Matthew's supposed acquiescence to black people's demands was reiterated in the league's second letter. The group charged that one of the "continuing outrages" to which white children were "being forced to submit" was the supposed ban on students singing "the beautiful and time honored Christmas song, 'White Christmas.'" Jackson, who believed that a complaint from one of the Little Rock Nine had led to the song's ban, lamented that "nineteen hundred white children must give in to the silly ridiculous whinings [*sic*] of one negro girl," while the "feelings of white children" seemed irrelevant to Matthews. "If a negro complains that the 'White' section of our American flag offends their sensitive soul," Jackson continued, "shall we haul down the flag? How far shall the white people be expected to go in appeasing the whims of the African race?" If Matthew had "enough manhood," he would give an explanation.[202]

Jackson's letter was simultaneously published in the *Democrat*, where it was entitled "Goodbye 'White Christmas' at Central High School" and attributed to the segregationist Freedom Fund for Little Rock. The "White Christmas" campaign was a concerted effort by segregationist grassroots activists in Little Rock to stir controversy.[203] "White Christmas" and its reference to snow had not been banned at Central High School. According to Huckaby, some teachers objected to a parody sung by a number of segregationist students during gym class: "I'm Dreaming of a White Central."[204] A group of girls performed the parody at a league meeting in December.[205]

Exemplifying the cognitive dissonance inherent in white supremacy and the mental gymnastics required to support it, Jackson dismissed and ridiculed the feelings of black students while emphasizing the importance of those of white pupils. Both letters stressed the alleged deteriorating psychological state of white Central High pupils due to a loss of white privilege while mocking black students' demeanor as unreasonably frail and implicitly uppity. The league's white supremacist reasoning allowed it to conclude that white students were the victims despite the disparity in power relations between black and white pupils and officials. The group did not shy away from explicit racism in its protests, referring to black people as "the African race," implying that they were not only outsiders at Central High but also in the country. To these segregationist women, Central High and the United States was a space that belonged to whites. The league again linked white masculinity to segregationist resistance. Adhering to court orders and not treating white pupils preferentially was proof of one's effeminacy, which in turn resulted in a lack of protection for white children and women. The league was determined to claim and defend Central High School as its territory, and its members continually took steps to remind school officials and the public of their claim.

One of the most well-known controversies created in an attempt to keep the crisis alive at Central High School was the so-called changing room incident in October 1957, which can be traced back to the women's group.[206] Just as he had sought to capitalize on rumors that two daughters of league members had been held incommunicado by the FBI, Faubus made use of rumors disseminated by members of the league to attack the federal troops stationed at the school. According to Huckaby, Carlotta Walls had been escorted by a guardsman to her gym class. He accompanied her to the landing that led to the girls' dressing rooms and left, after which a white girl, later identified by the press as the fifteen-year-old Kathleen Craighead, alleged that the guard might have been able to peek inside the girls' dressing room. Jackson's daughter Sandra overheard this remark and passed it on.[207]

Illustrating the league's influence with the governor, Faubus sent a letter to the Edwin Walker, commander of the federal troops, in which he stated that he had "received a number of complaints from parents, mostly mothers, about your troop's accompanying the girl students to their dressing rooms" and asked whether the Women's Army Corps could be deployed to take over if Walker considered "the invasion of the privacy of the girls' dressing rooms . . . necessary in order to protect fully the negro students."[208] Simultaneously, Faubus released this information to the press, putting the league at the forefront of the publicity campaign once again. Jackson stated that Sandra had not seen soldiers inside the girls' dressing rooms but that she had complained that the soldiers "might as well be because they stand outside and see right in through a glass door," a charge that other Central High students denied. Jackson made no mention of the fact that it was her daughter who had circulated the rumors. Instead, she remarked that she had received several telephone calls from parents who decried this and other alleged incidents.[209]

Huckaby described the charges as having "undertones of sex" and concluded that Faubus and the league leveled them "to titillate the prurient," and not only Walker but also Central High School officials, Blossom and his assistant Fred Graham, FBI director Hoover, the army secretary Wilber M. Brucker, and the White House denied them, the latter calling them "vulgar and untrue."[210] The incident, nonetheless, showed once more that members and proxies of the league were capable of interfering with school life, had the ear of the governor, and were not opposed to using sexualized images to incite the fears of white parents. Previously, the league had stirred those fears by referring to miscegenation. Now, it added "outsiders" and an intruding federal government to the threats to white girls' purity.[211] The league sought to create moral outrage in order to put its white supremacist agenda back on the offense. The group created a performative space not only for the white mothers but also their children at Central High, enabling both the women and the female students to entangle a need for attention with a political mandate to fight desegregation.

This was not the only time that children of league members spread rumors or instigated segregationist agitation at the school. The Little Rock Nine were especially subjected to a bullying and harassment campaign by segregationist students after the federal troops departed and only the National Guard remained.[212] As the group was unsuccessful in preventing Central High's desegregation by judicial, political, or direct action, its new tactic was to instead end the school's integration through inside agitation and acts of sabotage. Sandra Jackson began to distribute segregationist literature at school in late October. One of these was a sign that read "Refugee from Occupied Arkansas," which a student paraded down Central High's hall. When asked where he had gotten the sign, he gave Sandra away. After Huckaby advised Sandra Jackson to stop distributing the literature and to take the signs home, Margaret Jackson withdrew her daughter from Central High.[213]

Other daughters of league members also bullied the Little Rock Nine while simultaneously claiming to be victims. Darlene Holloway, the daughter of league member Mrs. Fred Gist, got into an altercation with Elizabeth Eckford. Holloway was shoved into Eckford and Eckford grabbed her arm to keep from falling, resulting in a "light pink color line" on Holloway's arm, according to Huckaby. Holloway's mother told newspapers that Darlene had been so badly "scratched and clawed" by Eckford that she felt it necessary to take her to the hospital to get a tetanus shot.[214] Huckaby noted that Holloway's name, like Parker's, had become familiar to her in regard to segregationist agitation inside Central High. Both Holloway and Parker were suspended several times.[215] Huckaby remarked that the parents who contacted her to complain about the alleged mistreatment of white students at Central "were easily identifiable as Mothers' League members or their sympathizers."[216] The league and some of their daughters put on hyperbolic performances of white female victimhood to legitimize their actions at Central.

Miscegenation informed segregationist resistance in Little Rock at every turn. A segregationist flyer in card format that was passed around Central High School rhymed "Little Nigger at Central High, Has Got Mighty Free with His Eye, Winks at White Girls, Grabs Their Blond Curls; Little Nigger Sure Is Anxious to Die."[217] According to Huckaby, the card referred to Sammie Dean Parker, who had accused Ernest Green of trying to flirt with her. Sammie Dean's father, J. D. Parker, called the principal to complain. Huckaby stressed that "it was hard to believe that Ernest was showing any familiarity with Sammie Dean since this was the first complaint we had had of this nature." Green said that he had only encountered Parker in the school cafeteria and that he had never spoken with or looked at her. Nonetheless, Matthews advised him "to continue avoid looking in Sammie Dean's direction." Parker's performance of a white girl threatened by the sexuality of a black boy took some effort. According to the cafeteria supervisor Mrs. Means, Parker repeatedly attempted to gain Green's attention.[218]

In March 1958, after several suspensions for distributing segregationist material and harassing the Little Rock Nine, Sammie Dean was expelled when she and her mother physically attacked Huckaby.[219]

The league continued to instigate shows of defiance at Central High. On October 3, 1957, it organized a student walkout in protest of the school's desegregation. A disappointing number of about fifty white students participated and joined league picketers in front of the school. Some of them hung a black effigy from a tree and set it on fire. Two daughters of league members, Darlene Holloway and Annette Harper, participated in the protest and were subsequently suspended from school along with the other walkouts.[220] Although the league failed to achieve its goal of inciting 200 to 250 students to walk out, it was successful once again in interfering with Central High's school life.[221]

Another tactic was devised at a February 1958 Capital Citizens' Council meeting, where league and council member Mrs. Bob O. Cook advised students to buy spoons and instructed them, according to the FBI, "to bend the handles and burn and black the spoons and place them in spots around and inside the school. She said this would drive Virgil Blossom . . . crazy because the burned spoons would make it appear that narcotics were being used by the students." League members sought to sabotage school life by fabricating a crisis that could not only have ruined Central High's reputation but could have led to school officials and the city's superintendent losing their jobs.[222]

Jackson repeatedly called for both Blossom's and Matthews's resignations. She accused them of having endangered students by not evacuating the school building, despite repeated (but ultimately false) bomb scares. Jackson charged that school officials were concerned with "making it appear that integration is proceeding gloriously" and so would not admit "the ugly facts of failure."[223] The league also circulated letters among white Central High School's students' parents to encourage the white community to take action and to recruit white parents. One of the letters that came to Huckaby's attention illustrates the league's attempts to frame its fight for desegregation as activism for freedom and states' rights and to infuse it with religious zeal. The November 29, 1957, letter was an invitation to a league meeting on December 2 that was to deal with the question what white parents could do about Central High School's situation.[224]

Stating that people "must awaken, arouse, and alert those who do not as yet understand the wickedness" of the supposedly extraordinary "conspiracy of evil forces confronting men," the league claimed in this letter that "the control of our schools, the education of our children, the sanctity and dignity of human freedom—in fact every thing that free men hold dear is in the process of being gradually taken away from us." "A divine providence, it seems," the league continued, had "decreed that a most critical phase of this conflict is to be fought in Little Rock, Arkansas. We are now in that conflict." The meeting, the letter concluded, was "open to everyone who believes in States rights, racial integrity and that our public schools should be kept segregated."[225]

The league's propaganda transcended the desegregation fight surrounding Central High and employed conservative rhetorical tropes. Aiming at a wider audience, including moderates who might have disapproved of the league's and the Capital Citizens' Council's methods but not white supremacy itself, the league avoided direct mention of racial arguments in its letter. It focused on states' rights and the defense of freedom against an alleged vast conspiracy, thereby entering the territory of rhetorical and ideological paranoia.[226] The league insinuated that, in fact, states were in a fight against the overpowering forces of the federal government and the federal judiciary. The league also alluded to miscegenation in its invitation. The group declared that everyone who favored "the integrity of the races" was invited to attend this meeting—a code for the group's opposition to "race mixing" and an expression used in white citizens councils' and other segregationist group's pamphlets across the South. The league's invitation promulgated a paranoid fatalism infused with anticommunist and Christian fundamentalist propaganda.[227]

Little Rock's segregationists followed the rhetorical lead of other massive resistance proponents who denounced integrationists as communist agents. The group attempted to stir controversy and exaggerated or invented student claims of maltreatment to instigate negative media coverage. They supplied and supported segregationist students in their distribution of segregationist literature and tried to rally other white parents by putting an emphasis on states' rights and the group's fight against an allegedly vast conspiracy. The league's political tactics and rhetorical strategies were dynamic, versatile, and adaptable to different audiences.

White Maternalist Working-Class Politics

The league sought to broaden its appeal further, aiming not only to establish a regional but national networks, and attempted to strengthen its influence on local and even national politics by encouraging its members to run for office. The league had come to the conclusion that direct, legal, and lobbying action were insufficient to achieve its goal of Central High's resegregation, and so its two most prominent officers, Jackson and Thomason, filed last-minute candidacies to Little Rock's board of directors in late September 1957, hoping to fill two seats in the November 1957 elections. Jackson and Thomason sought to redirect the city's policy.[228]

Thomason, running for position 3 on the board, opposed the housewife Mrs. Edgar F. Dixon who was an incumbent and was backed by the informal Good Government Committee, comprised of the capital's moderate political and economic white elite. Jackson, meanwhile, opposed two other well-established figures on Little Rock's political scene for position 1, the Good Government candidate and real estate broker Warren Baldwin and the public relations consultant William Hadley.[229] The *Gazette* remarked that with the candidacies of Jackson and Thomason, the "fuss over integration" had reached the election. Indeed, Jackson stated that desegregation was "a major issue in the city manager board race." Little Rock's segregationist grassroots movement initiated a vigorous campaign to support segregationist candidates running for the city board, including funding public Capital Citizens' Council rallies and running newspaper advertisements.[230] Hilda Thevenet placed an advertisement in the *Democrat* under the name "Parents Committee," insinuating Central High's parents were a uniform front opposing desegregation. The ad urged people "to vote for Jackson, Heer, Thomason, Lauderdale and Langford as city board directors because they are against RACE MIXING."[231] On the day of the election, the Gazette published a letter to the editor by an anonymous reader named "Neighbor" from Conway, Arkansas, that highlighted the league's and particularly Thomason's role in local segregationist politics. The author titled the league officers Aaron, Jackson, and Thomason "the Big Three" and noted that while Aaron had moved to Texas, even though the state had "enough trouble of their own," and while the *Gazette* had leveled criticism at Jackson, "Mrs. Clyde Thompson's [*sic*] name hasn't appeared in your column yet." The author wrote that Thomason would "be remembered as the distinguished trouble-maker whose picture appeared in the Gazette as a leader of the September 23 mob." The letter writer asked readers to not "blame it all on Mrs. Jackson," and that voters should "beware" both Jackson and Thomason, who had "been mentioned as being in the running for a position on the city manager board of Little Rock." Voters should "vote right" to keep their "fair city clean," the author urged.[232]

The league members lost their races on November 5, 1957. Given that Thomason and Jackson were relatively unknown in Little Rock's public life before the desegregation crisis broke, that they did not have the backing of the broad political and civil coalition of the city represented in the Good Government Committee, and that they had been branded as segregationist radicals by the press, their defeat was narrow. Although the Good Government Committee won six of seven races for the city board (for which the coalition had been campaigning for over a year), the segregationist candidates, including Jackson and Thomason, amassed thousands of votes. Awaiting the final tally, league members and their supporters assembled at the real estate office of Mrs. F. E. Bates, premises that also served as the Capital Citizens' Council's headquarters. When it became clear that their candidates had been defeated, a female supporter declared: "You can say us provincials went down fighting!"[233] Indeed, the segregationist candidates had made an unanticipated "strong showing" and received "healthy vote totals," the *Gazette* admitted.[234]

League members felt that they "had given the 'integrationists' a run for their money." And Jackson hoped segregationists would "do as well with a third party as we've done with this," indicating that she and others contemplated an independent party run in the state's elections.[235] After a recount, Thomason was defeated by only 479 votes, and both Jackson and Thomason received more than 10,000 votes. The league might have been an often belittled spearhead of female segregationist activism in Little Rock, but the group's aims were compatible with the views of a significant segment of the city's population, and its perceived antiestablishment fight resonated with thousands of people.[236] Thomason, moreover, was elected as one of eight new members to the board of the Capital Citizens' Council in December 1957, alongside the wife of former council president Robert Ewing Brown.[237]

Thomason's narrow loss in the city board elections gave her a taste for electoral campaigns. The league's recording secretary ran for office again in 1958, this time in the Democratic primaries for the U.S. House of Representatives in Pulaski County. The *Democrat* pointed out that never before had the House seats in the county been contended for by so many women, as four of the eight seats were being sought by women.[238] Thomason stated that she was running because she wanted to broaden her agenda. She proclaimed that she was "interested in any problems that arise, not only the racial issues," when the newspaper reminded its readers that Thomason had first become "prominent" during the desegregation crisis at Central High.[239] Little Rock's state of crisis and the prominent role women had assumed during it had expanded white women's access to institutional politics.

This time, however, Thomason suffered a clear defeat. While she received 10,712 votes, her opponent and incumbent Joel Y. Ledbetter accumulated over 16,000.[240] However, Thomason's election campaign shows how the league developed rhetorically and the connections between massive resistance and emerging trends in national politics. Thomason ran on an explicitly segregationist platform, stating that she opposed "any and all efforts to FORCE THE MIXING OF THE RACES." She declared that she supported legislation that would keep schools under local control and by opposing federal intervention in what she perceived as state affairs. Thomason's pledges not only reiterated her commitment to segregationism but illustrated the compatibilities between massive resistance and broader politics. Thomason also stated that she opposed "any tax increase" and supported "legislation to increase economy and efficiency in our State Government."[241]

Thomason interweaved several strands of conservative politics, including traditionalism and advocacy for small government and low taxation, with her prosegregation stance. By opposing what she perceived as unlawful federal intervention in local issues and becoming a public advocate of a small, economically run government, she tried to appeal to a broader base of conservatives. She framed her politics as being that of limited government and free market conservatism by linking it to her opposition to federal intervention in Little Rock, vastly extending the league's original maternalist platform.[242]

Thomason did not belong to the political establishment. Her status as a working-class mother worked in her favor, as she opposed governmental intervention not only in the educational sector but also in the economic realm of the small people. Thomason promised to "represent ALL of the people of Pulaski County, fairly and without special favor" granted to the county's elites.[243] Her relative fringe status, however, meant she could not accumulate enough social capital to win the race.

In October 1957, while Central High School was still occupied by troops, the league announced its plans to extend "into other cities and states and hopes to establish a Mothers' League of America to oppose school integration." According to Jackson, a league chapter had just been organized in Pine Bluff, and she had received requests to assist in the formation of further chapters in other Arkansas communities. Jackson declared that the league was "going to organize all over Arkansas" and then tackle Louisiana. The group stated that it had also received invitations to form chapters from across the nation, including in Washington, D.C.[244]

By March 1958, the group was officially meeting once a month.[245] It proceeded with its plan of forming a national organization. Shortly after newspapers announced its initiative to found a national group named "Strike Back—the Mothers' Leagues of America," Margaret Jackson placed an advertisement for this national group in the *Democrat*. The short announcement read "STRIKE BACK" and asked readers to donate $1 to "strike back" against the NAACP's "dangerous power" in regional and national politics. "The battleline is drawn," the advertisement stated. "Arkansas and the South can win or lose at the 'Battle of Little Rock.'" Now was the time for the entire south to rally around Arkansas and to come to Little Rock's aid.[246]

Despite the emphasis on the South in the advertisement, Thomason claimed that the national organization would focus its efforts "on forming segregationist blocks in the north and west, since the South already has many strong organizations."[247] In late October, Jackson stated that the national league would be headed by her group and that Strike Back was in the process of drafting bylaws and a charter.[248] On November 7, 1957, the league met again and appointed committees to draw up the national organization's bylaws and constitution. At that point, members of the Mothers' League of Central High School and their sister groups in North Little Rock and Pine Bluff made up Strike Back's board of directors.[249]

Thomason proclaimed that Strike Back would target "the unlawful use of federal troops, the Supreme Court decisions based on political and sociological reasons, unlawful loading of the court with politicians instead of experienced judges, undue political power wielded by the NAACP and forced integration" on a national level. She thus not only addressed segregationists' demands but again adapted her language to befit changing audiences and a shifting agenda.[250]

Strike Back never made it past the initial stages, however, and quickly vanished from the public eye. Strike Back was more of a grand posture than a reality. The women of the Mothers' League of Central High School did not have enough economic and social capital to move beyond established institutions and groups within Little Rock's and Arkansas's social networks. The women's social background prevented them from easily associating with established, more prestigious middle- and upper-class women's groups, and the league remained separated from conservative women's clubs.

Despite the league's mainstreamed rhetoric, its association with the screaming mobs in front of Central High School extinguished the potential for more "respectable," politically established support by a national audience. The transparency of its racism also made their supposedly colorblind arguments less palatable. Strike Back's failure signaled the slow but steady demise of the group as a distinct women's group active at the forefront of Little Rock's grassroots segregationist movement. When the political, civil, and business establishment reasserted its power and advocated for moderation in Little Rock, the league struggled to keep its grip on the space it had created for itself.

The Little Rock School Board made a show of minimum compliance as an obstructionist tactic in February 1958 and asked the federal district court for a delay in desegregation, bemoaning "extraordinary opposition of the state" of Arkansas.[251] The board's wish came true when Judge Lemley granted a stay to the city to effect desegregation plan until 1961. Blossom publicly declared his relief, and Jackson stated that she was "grateful and glad for the two and a half years delay. I hope the U.S. Supreme Court may reverse its decision in that period."[252] The league was still optimistic that massive resistance would succeed in the end.

Lemley's decision was swiftly overruled by the federal appeals court. On September 12, 1958, the U.S. Supreme Court rendered its verdict in *Cooper v. Aaron*. The court declared that political, even violent opposition to desegregation was not a legitimate reason for the delay of integration, and it ordered the Blossom Plan to proceed. In response, Faubus closed all four of Little Rock's high schools the day after the ruling, a move that the league supported. The group had been lobbying for the passage of school closing legislation throughout the summer.[253]

League members Ellen Fifthen, Rena Coffman, and Anita Sedberry approach a voter near the polls on September 27, 1958, with a petition to recall the Little Rock School Board (Alliance/Associated Press)

In the subsequent state election, the referendum on Faubus's high school closures passed overwhelmingly. Faubus was reelected governor, which Jackson touted as "the second mandate from the people within two or three months" against desegregation. "The people of Little Rock have said again they do not want integration in their schools. We feel that the Supreme Court should listen to the voice of the people of Little Rock."[254] The league's president was routinely quoted alongside other segregationists and school officials in the media. The league was still perceived as a primary grassroots actor in the desegregation crisis.

Segregationists in other southern states supported the group's actions. In a full-page advertisement, Louisiana segregationists, including Democratic state senator William Rainach and state representative John Garrett, saluted "the brave people of Little Rock" for their defiance. They declared that Louisiana was "proud to stand by your side."[255] Sensing a chance for another resegregation bid, the league began to circulate a petition to recall the Little Rock School Board's four moderate members.[256]

Jackson, moreover, was not the only league member publicly speaking out for segregation. Fellow member Pauline McLendon urged voters to cast their ballots in favor of the school closing in an advertisement published in her name in the *Democrat* on September 24, 1958. McLendon warned that even token desegregation would inevitably lead to complete integration. Asking whether people were prepared to see their children "dating any or all their classmates" when integration was allowed to proceed, the former teacher stated that she, too, felt "compelled to make a 'stand' for the proper education of our children." According to McLendon, she had worked too many years in Little Rock's public schools to see them "ruthlessly destroyed" by desegregation. To her, the "real vote" in the state election was "not, repeat not, 'for or against public schools,'" but "for integration in the schools and in your homes and in your churches."[257] Members of the league, then, publicly urged Little Rock's voters to support the closing of public schools by stirring white supremacists' fears of "complete" integration that was likely to follow public school desegregation.

Little Rock's public high schools stayed closed throughout the 1958–59 school year. Several initiatives were undertaken to continue public education; a TV schooling program was piloted and a private segregated school was established by the newly formed Little Rock Private School Corporation. The incorporators included Capital Citizens' Council president Malcolm Taylor and Mrs. Gordon P. Oates, who had run alongside Thomason in the 1958 Democratic primaries for the U.S. House of Representatives and was now a nominee.[258] The newly formed, segregated high school was named after Thomas Jefferson Raney, president of the cooperation and Faubus's physician. The school was financed by donations from throughout the South. League children who had attended Central High School, including Sammie Dean Parker, transferred to this school. White student protests erupted when T. J. Raney closed only a year later due to a lack of funding.[259]

Despite segregationists' public display of strength and the support of the Little Rock community for segregation, evidenced in the election of three segregationists to the school board in November 1958, the mounting economic and educational repercussions of segregation for the city began to expose cracks in the community. When school board members purged teachers whom they considered "integrationists" from Little Rock's public schools in May 1959, Little Rock's civil community finally reacted. Little Rock journalists and businessmen organized the group Stop This Outrageous Purge (STOP), which asked for a recall of the segregationist school board members and joined the Women's Emergency Committee to Open Our Schools' already months-long campaign for the reopening of the city's high schools. The upper-class women of the organization relied on their social capital, amassed as wives of influential businessmen in Little Rock's community, which helped them change public perceptions of token integration.[260] The Women's Emergency Committee to Open Our Schools also profited from decades of middle- and upper-class club activism, their reputable community status, and their ability to lobby more effectively than the league had ever done.[261]

Women's Emergency Committee to Open Our Schools member Sara Murphy concludes that the women of the league were women "who could not afford to flee west" like the affluent families of Pulaski Heights. Just as league members "felt superior to blacks," so committee members "were into feeling a liberal superiority" to league members. Murphy thus reflects on the middle and upper classes' own performance: the demand for moderation and acceptance of integration, which they could easily practice because they lived in separate, segregated, affluent spaces. Indeed, the social status-based habitus of the women could not have been more different. As Murphy notes, when lobbying the state legislature, for example, committee members "could easily pick out who was on which side. Our women were bareheaded and casually dressed while the mothers' league women were usually overdressed and wore fussy little hats."[262] League members' dressing up when they lobbied was a strategy they used to bypass their working-class status and achieve middle-class respectability. It was part of their performance.

Defeat and Decline

Despite setbacks, the Capital Citizens' Council and the league did not give in to the formal power of the city elite. In May 1959, Jackson and Thomason purchased a half-page advertisement for the league in the *Democrat*. "They Said . . . 'It Can't Happen Here,'" the advertisement stated, quoting Sinclair Lewis's book title. Once again, the league took on the role of grassroots organizer, activating and policing the white community in an attempt to establish a united white supremacist front. The women again appropriated antifascist and antiracist rhetoric for segregationist purposes, comparing desegregation and federal interventions to the rise of Nazism and creating a performance of righteous resistance. "It Happened Here," the advertisement continued, repeating the phrase several times, the theme illustrated each time with a different newspaper clipping. The clippings showed, for instance, an African American woman receiving a crown from a white woman for the title of Miss Sacramento 1959, a newspaper headline that said "3 Children and White Wife Gone, Negro Post Reward," and a clipping of Bates as a distinguished guest. "And It Will Happen Here," the ad stated, "Unless Tucker, Lamb, and Matson," the three moderate school board members, were recalled.[263] For the members of the league, the school board election, then, was a battle for the preservation of white supremacy and everyday white privileges. The group dramatized this battle by staging it as a question of freedom or dictatorship. "If the integrationists win this school board fight, the schools will be integrated this fall. There will be absolutely nothing you or we can do to stop it," the league warned.[264]

The league's prediction proved to be accurate. In the end, its activism was no match to that of the city's social, political, and economic elite. By a small margin effected by the city's black population and upper-class whites, the segregationist school board members were recalled in the May 1959 election. The newly elected moderate school board immediately announced the reopening of Little Rock's high schools for the same year.[265] Led by the mothers' league, segregationists had failed in their quest to preserve segregation, and the group and its protagonists vanished from the public eye by 1960. Their performative, public space collapsed with the crisis.

The local National Association for the Advancement of White People chapter, which by 1958 had three members and was headed up by Margaret Morrison, a local housewife, did provide one outlet for organized segregationist female activism (apart from the Capital Citizens' Council).[266] When the league members, including Jackson and Sedberry, filed signatures with the city clerk in support of Little Rock School Board's segregationist members in May 1959, Morrison accompanied them. At the time, Jackson stated that Morrison was not affiliated with the league. According to Murphy, "Morrison liked Jackson, whom she called 'a very nice person . . . level headed and well organized,'" but the National Association for the Advancement of White People member never joined the league. Instead, the members of the association "preferred their own guerilla warfare."[267]

Morrison ran for a school board seat in December 1959. In the Little Rock School Board winter election, Morrison and Mrs. H. H. Ray, whose husband was a railroad brakeman, opposed the moderate school board members Everett Tucker and Frank Mackey. The women claimed that they were "more segregationist" than the current school board members. The women proclaimed that female board members would have "more time to devote to school problems and activities," that the board needed "a woman's touch," and that they were "more interested in the WELFARE of the children" than in "BIG BUSINESS."[268] Morrison and Ray were soundly defeated by their opponents. They responded by threatening to contest the election and stated that they would seek the replacement of officials they deemed to be "connected with" the Women's Emergency Committee to Open Our Schools.[269] Although the women never did complain to the election commission, they delivered a letter to U.S. attorney Osro Cobb demanding "the grand jury and the federal Civil Rights Commission to investigate," a request that was swiftly denied.[270]

In June 1960, Margaret Morrison was among three other women who officially incorporated the National Association for the Advancement of White People's Little Rock chapter with the help of Louisiana barber and association official Carl Olson. The group opposed "further centralization of federal power" and the NAACP. It campaigned "for the preservation of states' rights," the repeal of the federal income tax, and for "any and all things necessary to further the Caucasian people" in the United States.[271] Topically, the National Association for the Advancement of White People was closely aligned with the league, and members of each group were not only acquainted with one another but provided assistance to members in the other group in their quest for the repeal of moderate school board members. The league was also rubbing shoulders with the most extreme white supremacist strands in Little Rock—a league member's husband, Alton Clarence Hightower, filed the papers for the establishment of a Klan chapter in Arkansas and became its grand dragon.[272]

Despite the league's last show of defiance in August 1959, in the 1959–60 school year, at least fourteen league members reenrolled their children at Central High School, including Jackson. They had few other choices. T. J. Raney School had been closed, and Jackson, a single mother of two, was not affluent enough to move her family at her leisure, even if, as she had announced, there must be parts of the South that would not be integrated. The fact that Jackson became prominent due to her role in the desegregation dispute is remarkable. Newspapers rarely mentioned Jackson's status as a divorcée. Jackson was referred to as a mother or as the league's president. Her status as a single mother did not deter her from public activism and did not evoke negative reactions. Perhaps Jackson was even freer as a single woman to intervene on what she perceived as the defense of her children because she was the head of her household.

Jackson's status as a single mother, however, was unusual for the league. Nearly every other member of the league is listed either under their husbands' first name or is otherwise identified as married. The majority of the league's members, moreover, were not self-identified "working mothers." Still, being a (house)wife clearly did not limit the women's activism to the home, and they repeatedly justified their activism on the grounds that it was an extension of motherhood. As working-class white women, the league sought to defend the one privilege afforded to them: whiteness. By stressing their motherhood, league members attempted to further their respectability and give their actions legitimacy, even though not all members of the league had children at Central High School. That the media made frequent reference to the members of the group as "mothers" proves their success in this regard. The group used stylized, repetitive acts when performing white southern womanhood, including strong emotionality, thereby creating a performative space for its activism, which it expanded beyond traditional frames, including that of maternalism.

The league functioned as a political outlet for working-class women who were not "fit" for traditional organizations and contributed to Little Rock's massive resistance by lending credibility to the cause, linking segregationism to broader conservative ideas in their rhetoric, and continuously keeping the crisis alive through media-conscious, performative actions. However, the women's social backgrounds and their inexperience in organizing and lack of social networks were detrimental to their aspirations, and their performative space disappeared with the end of the immediate crisis.

CHAPTER 3

The Cheerleaders of New Orleans

John Steinbeck's description of the New Orleans school desegregation crisis in 1960 in his *Travels with Charley* includes what has become an infamous characterization of a segregationist women's group called the cheerleaders. Steinbeck admitted that what lured him to go see the cheerleaders in action were reports about "stout middle-aged women" who "gathered every day to scream invectives at children." Throughout his narrative, Steinbeck emphasizes the theatrical quality and appeal of the cheerleaders' activism, noting that "a crowd gathered every day to enjoy and applaud their performance." The cheerleaders were an attraction for locals and tourists alike. When Steinbeck arrived at William Frantz Elementary School, his expectation of a show was fulfilled. "Suddenly I was pushed violently and a cry went up: 'Here she comes. Let her through. . . . Come on, move back. Let her through. Where you been? You're late for school. Where you been, Nellie?' The name was not Nellie, I forget what it was. But she shoved through the dense crowd quite near enough to me so that I could see her coat of imitation fleece and her gold earrings. She was not tall, but her body was ample and full-busted. I judge she was about fifty. She was heavily powdered, which made the line of her double chin look very dark."[1]

Steinbeck notes that the cheerleaders reviewed their newspaper coverage with "little squeals of delight." He nods to the show elements of their activism when he stresses that at "three minutes to nine," men "all around looked at their watches" and the "crowd grew restless, as an audience does when the clock goes past curtain time." The tension finally erupted in an outbreak of jeers when police motorcycles and two cars with federal marshals arrived on the scene. The marshals escorted the only black pupil of William Frantz, six-year-old Ruby Bridges, inside the school. When the show started, writes Steinbeck, "a jangle of jeering shrieks went up from behind the barricades," frightening little Ruby.

The cheerleaders' vilest treatment was reserved for the Reverend Lloyd Andrew Foreman, a Methodist minister. His appearance was the occasion of the "big show," according to Steinbeck: "A shrill, grating voice rang out. The yelling was not in chorus. Each took a turn and at the end of each the crowd broke into howls and roars and whistles of applause."[2]

Steinbeck notes that newspapers reported the obscene phrases the cheerleaders used and that television reports had resorted to blurring out their language. But hearing their actual words, "bestial and filthy and degenerate," left him shocked. It was not just that their words were "dirty" and "carefully and selectedly filthy." He was witnessing "something far worse . . . than dirt, a kind of frightening witches' Sabbath." Steinbeck thus elevates the cheerleaders' behavior to a new level of immorality, a unique expression of anger and hate. The women's group lacked manners and class and also is awarded the historical, gendered badge of a supernatural, incomprehensible, and unpredictable female threat. Steinbeck implies that he witnessed a ritual and not just a coincidental gathering and states that he did not see a "spontaneous cry of anger, of insane rage," but rather "theater," as the women's shouts were, he claims, "tried and memorized and carefully rehearsed. . . . I watched the intent faces of the listening crowd and they were the faces of an audience. When there was applause, it was for a performer." The cheerleaders were not only performing for the local and national press but also for their onlookers, seeking applause and recognition. Steinbeck contends that the "blowzy women with their little hats and their clippings hungered for attention. . . . They simpered in happy, almost innocent triumph when they were applauded. Theirs was the demented cruelty of egocentric children, and somehow this made their insensate beastliness much more heart-breaking."[3]

Steinbeck also described the cheerleaders' unattractive physical and sartorial appearance and deemed their behavior to be that of "egocentric children," stating that the cheerleaders were "not mothers, not even women." From Steinbeck's perspective, the behavior and physical appearance of the cheerleaders served to negate their roles as mothers; they were outside of accepted norms of maternalism, womanhood, and behavior defined as feminine and either monstrous in their roles as "witches" or "demented" in their egocentric childishness. Steinbeck goes further by masculinizing, even dehumanizing, his objects of study when he describes the voice of one of the cheerleaders as " the bellow of a bull, a deep and powerful shout with flat edges like a circus barker's voice." Steinbeck accentuates the lack of femininity and class in both the cheerleaders' physical traits and conduct.[4]

Vulgarly racist, physically aggressive female segregationists in public was not a common sight. The public and the media reacted with curiosity and shock to the women's demeanor. The cheerleaders defied written and unwritten rules about how white women were expected to behave. Steinbeck's description conveys the sense of scandal that surrounded the cheerleaders in 1960 and 1961.[5] This chapter analyzes the women's group and traces its emergence, as well as the social and political backgrounds, actions, rhetoric, and media and self-representations of its members. Cheerleaders were identifiable both by their distinct performance and as a core group of female segregationist protesters. Both their working-class backgrounds, actual and perceived, and the performative nature of their protest are vital to understanding them. Their exhibition of vulgarity and an imminent corporeality resulted in class- and gender-related somatophobic responses to their actions and self-representations. The media coconstituted this phenomenon by serving as an audience to the cheerleaders, who reveled in the attention. Most Cheerleaders were indeed working-class women, but not all fit the description media observers ascribed them. Being associated with the cheerleaders spatially and behaviorally, however, was enough for critical observers and reporters alike to assign the women a collective low social status, to assume that they had little education—in a word, to paint them as akin to white trash.

The Cheerleaders' Emergence

The cheerleaders seemed to emerge out of nowhere in November 1960. The Orleans Parish School Board did not release the names of the schools that were to desegregate until Monday, November 14, 1960.[6] New Orleans' superintendent of police, Joseph I. Giarrusso, stationed local police around every elementary school in the city. The federal marshals who escorted the black children to school had been instructed by Judge James Skelly Wright and handed a copy of the desegregation decree, to be shown to any officials if they encountered trouble. The marshals drove the children and some of their parents to the schools in unmarked cars and accompanied them inside. White "onlookers jeered and booed," whereas black bystanders "applauded and cheered," newspapers reported, which shows that a number of black New Orleanians felt safe enough to occupy the same vicinity as segregationist protesters and cheer for the African American elementary school children that day. That would no longer be the case in the coming few weeks. In contrast to Little Rock, there was no physical violence initially. Louisiana state troopers did not attempt to hinder Ruby Bridges and her four accompanying federal marshals from entering William Frantz, or Gail Etienne, Tessie Prevost, and Leona Tate and their six accompanying marshals from entering McDonogh 19.[7]

The absence of physical violence on November 14 read as an early victory to many state officials. Orleans Parish School Board president Lloyd Rittiner declared that "the worst is over. The lack of any appreciable amount of demonstration indicates the people of New Orleans are going to accept the inevitable." Mayor deLesseps Morrison said that the "crowds at the two schools" had "behaved quite well and attempted no violence. The booing and jeering and the applauding is all part of the American way of life." He praised New Orleans's citizens for their restraint and the city police for their "effective planning," asking New Orleans to refrain from "the trouble that have befallen many of our sister Southern cities."[8] But whereas the former battleground of Little Rock quietly admitted eleven black students to Central and Hall high schools and one six-year-old black girl started to attend the formerly lily-white Dollarway Elementary School near Pine Bluff, the scene at New Orleans's desegregated schools could hardly be described as quiet or peaceful. Having lost the battle in his own state, moreover, Arkansas Governor Orval Faubus repeated his mantra that desegregation was "a complete thwarting of the people's will." He claimed that the "New Orleans judicial action" to desegregate William Frantz and McDonogh 19 was similar to the kinds of things Hitler did in Nazi Germany and would "lead to crushing people completely."[9] Echoing Faubus's argumentative line, the South Louisiana Citizens' Council issued a statement denouncing the Orleans Parish School Board, except for the segregationist member Emile Wagner, as "dedicated integrationists." The council asserted that black schoolchildren in New Orleans were being "used as pawns" to promote the federal government's "annihilation" of states' rights and freedom. Segregationists encouraged resistance and attempted to elevate New Orleans's elementary school desegregation to the level of a national political crisis.[10]

As word spread in the neighborhoods of Frantz and McDonogh, the crowds in front of the two schools grew to up to a thousand people who jeered and booed. The mob remained outside until the African American children left the schools in the afternoon. Women who became part of the cheerleaders were among the crowd of the five to six hundred hecklers that had gathered in front of William Frantz. When Bridges entered, a woman yelled that "the niggers are going to take over . . . , they're going to run us all out there."[11] Another white woman shouted that "they ought to take Judge Wright out and hang him by his toes." Within fifteen minutes after Bridges had entered the school, several mothers and fathers went inside Frantz to take their children out of it, and as they left, they were applauded and cheered by the crowd. As one white mother left the building with her daughter, a white man shouted that she was "a real white woman," the *Shreveport Journal* observed. Another mother of a white first grader stated that she would take her "boy back to school when they . . . go back to their school." The *Baton Rouge States-Item* estimated that between fifty and seventy-five students were taken out of school throughout the morning. Only 105 of the school's 575 pupils had attended that day in the first place. The *Times Picayune* reported that "mothers clad in slacks and pedal pushers arrived to take their children home."[12]

At 10:00 a.m., a group of two hundred male students from close-by Francis T. Nicholls Senior High School arrived at Frantz. Police hindered them from entering. The group chanted the Little Rock slogan—"Two, four, six, eight, we don't want to integrate"—and sang "glory, glory segregation, the South will rise again" to the melody of "Onward Christian Soldiers." Many people in the crowd joined in with the teenagers, waving small Confederate flags.[13] Just as the newspapers highlighted the protesting mothers' lower-class status by referencing the "slacks" they were wearing, they also noted that several of the signs the teenagers carried were "crudely printed" and some misspelled. One sign said, "We Don't Want Intagration," an error the black-owned newspaper *Pittsburgh Courier* sarcastically attributed to "the basic intelligence of mob leaders."[14]

The protesting crowds at McDonogh 19 were even more formidable. Angry adults as well as children ranging from preschoolers to teenagers hurled insults at the few white mothers who did not take their children out of school. Their protests were "electrifying the scene," the *Times Picayune* reported. Following the lead of the white parents of Frantz School children, white parents entered McDonogh and removed their children from school. In the process, one white mother yelled: "Those black . . . ," the expletive being left implicit. "I'm going in there and get my children out. I'm no nigger lover."[15] As at Frantz, a group of Nicholls students arrived at McDonogh. The teenagers carried segregationist signs, rebel flags, and a piece of cloth with the letters KKK written on it. They began chanting white supremacist slogans, inciting "others to greater heights of emotion," according to one newspaper reporter. In fact, one mother "hastily printed some placards and handed them to children to display."[16] On the first day of desegregation protests, the *Alexandria Daily Town Talk* commented that "almost Mardi Gras spirits prevailed" at the schools, as protesters paraded the streets, "playing kids danced up and down," and "neighborhood bars and soda fountains did brisk business."[17]

The absence of physical violence did not indicate an absence of determination on the part of segregationists. Even after the parents had withdrawn their children from school, loudly protesting the black girls' admission, and made threats against black people and white nonsegregationists, the crowds still did not disperse. In a letter to the *Shreveport Journal* in support of the legislature's interposition legislation, former state representative and Citizens' Council of Greater New Orleans member Harry P. Gamble Sr., contended that the situation was one of "sink or swim; win or lose." Gamble predicted that "confusion, disturbance, and per-chance, another Little Rock here, will shock indifference in all the other States into greater vigilance."[18]

Operation Out

New Orleans did not devolve into another Little Rock. Both the city's and the region's segregationists saw this desegregation struggle, nonetheless, as crucial to the fate of white resistance. The cheerleaders were at the forefront of the segregationist resistance at the two schools, starting their campaign on the following day. With about ten thousand of the thirty-eight thousand white public school children in New Orleans already not attending school, segregationists began a boycott called "Operation Out" on November 15, 1960.

Not all white parents who withdrew their children from school did so for ideological reasons. Margie Arbon, a white mother, was chiefly concerned with her son's safety. In an interview with the *Alexandria Daily Town Talk*, Arbon stated that she was only temporarily taking her son out of school until "all this has quieted down." She added that although she did not "hold with Negroes going to school with him," her son's education was more important.[19] According to James F. Redmond, New Orleans superintendent of schools, 65 out of 517 pupils had remained at Frantz, and 20 pupils had attended McDonogh 19 on Tuesday, November, 15, 1960, out of the school's total enrollment of 467 pupils. Redmond called these numbers "magnificent" and encouraging. In order to assuage segregationists' fears that the interaction between young black and white children would eventually lead to miscegenation, he announced that William Frantz would separate its pupils by gender. Redmond also answered reproaches that desegregation had been confined to a lower-class, politically powerless section of the city. He asserted that the schools' locality was coincidental and that the black children had been chosen by the automated pupil placement procedure. Redmond thus also insinuated that the school board did not consider concerns pertaining to the working-class district in which the schools where located and that it had not entertained the offer of the uptown PTA to be the first to open their affluent district's schools for desegregation.[20]

"Operation Out" urged white parents to keep their children out of schools as long as they were desegregated. Like the women of the mothers' league, then, the New Orleans segregationists thought the elementary schools were rightfully theirs, that they were white spaces, although they chose a different tactic with their boycott. "This school has been here 30 years and they haven't had any niggers in it and we don't want them now," declared a white woman in front of McDonogh 19. Segregationists waved U.S. flags, and some women carried small children on their arms at the protests. "We ought to go in there and beat the hell out of them," one of the women shouted, and another replied, "Yeah, they can't put us all in jail." Newspaper reports started to specify that the black children were booed with particularly "lusty hoots by angry mothers," who were "aided and abetted by children ranging from preschool age to truant students." New Orleans police moved the crowds behind barriers on the sidewalk across from McDonogh. The *New York Times* published a picture of yelling and sign-waving young to middle-aged women, observing that armed and mounted police units had to hold back the demonstrators.[21]

Throughout the second day of desegregation, white mothers broke through the police lines so they could go in and remove their children from the schools. One of the women, named Alita Drews, whose daughter attended fifth grade at William Frantz, "vehemently echoed by scores of others," proclaimed to reporters that she "would leave the state if her children could not attend segregated schools." Drews became involved with the cheerleaders shortly thereafter.[22] The newsreel service *Telenews* showed some of the female protesters in front of William Frantz School on this second day of desegregation. When Bridges arrived in the car with federal marshals, the crowd in front of the school broke into the "2, 4, 6, 8—we don't wanna integrate" chorus. Several women among the throng of people shouted along enthusiastically. A middle-aged, dark-haired white woman amid the crowd told the reporter, with a smile on her face, "Well, I have three daughters in school and I mean, I wouldn't want them to be in contact with. . . . You know, if they start, uh, integrating with the high schools, and . . . after a point . . . a mixture like that. So, I mean, as far as I'm concerned, I'd rather keep my children out. Till they get this thing settled."[23] A younger blonde white woman next to her chimed in: "What if innocent children get hurt," to which the interviewee responded, "That's right!" Another protesting woman, standing next to the two and holding a cigarette in her hand, proclaimed: "I'll keep mine home, until it's decided one way or another. But as long as all this emotion is going on, I prefer to have mine at home with me." She smiled benignly and continued: "Then, in the event they do integrate, I'll just keep them home." Finally, another middle-aged, dark-haired white woman reported that she kept her two children, attending Frantz's first and sixth grades, out of school that morning because she "didn't want them to go to school with the niggers."[24] Despite the women's composed demeanor in front of the press cameras and their timid smiles during their interviews, footage from just minutes earlier shows that all of the interviewees had been viciously screaming at Bridges in the federal marshals' car. Acting coyly in front of the camera would not be a long-term strategy for the cheerleaders. They soon discovered that aggressive performances, employing violent imagery, and physically attacking supposed integrationists resulted in bigger headlines and more public space for their actions.

November 15, 1960, also marked the day of the first police arrests of several protesters outside of McDonogh and Frantz.[25] The noisy crowds did not disperse despite police orders, and eventually, the police made twelve arrests. Among them were the neighboring St. Bernard Parish's sheriff and two women, one of them thirty-two-year-old neighborhood resident and mother Ethel Arieux. Arieux, too, was a cheerleader. Police arrested her for "interfering with police, being loud and boisterous and simple escape." Another arrested white woman and a fellow cheerleader was Julie Otto, apprehended for being "loud and boisterous." Otto, mentioned in the *Baton Rouge States-Item* merely as a "blond girl," was hauled into a police car after she physically resisted being taken into custody. Otto had been carrying a sign that said "Police go home. Your kids may sit with niggers." Some cheerleaders, then, were already protesting so vehemently that they grabbed the attention of the media and the police and were being arrested for their aggressive behavior.[26]

That same evening, New Orleans segregationist grassroots activists were joined by the state's segregationist elite. The Citizens' Council of Greater New Orleans held a rally at the New Orleans Municipal Auditorium that lasted over three hours and that between five and six thousand people attended. Children, waving Confederate flags, darted between the seat rows. The *Times Picayune* noted the "large numbers" of "young people," many of whom "appeared to be leading the singing and chanting." The defense of white supremacy was a multigenerational affair.[27] The speakers included Democratic state senator Willie Rainach of Claiborne Parish, segregationist Orleans Parish School Board member Emile Wagner, and the Jackson, Mississippi, citizens' council president John Wright. Segregationists circulated a petition to the U.S. House of Representatives, which asked for the impeachment of Judge Wright. Claiming Wright had shown "malfeasance and gross misconduct in office," the petition charged that Wright had "in effect" attempted the "dissolution of the State Legislature," and his actions thus "constituted a gross and tyrannical usurpation of ungranted power."[28] The *Pittsburgh Courier* called the meeting a fanning of "the flames of race hate, defiance, insurrection and open rebellion."[29]

Signifying the ties between the council movement and protesting mothers in front of William Frantz and McDonogh 19, at the beginning of the rally it was announced that a march would be held the next day, starting at 10:00 a.m. downtown at Canal Street and Elk Place and proceeding to the school board premises on Carondelet Street. Speakers emphasized that this march would be "sponsored" by the "ladies of Frantz School." White women, among them later cheerleaders, not only sympathized with the council movement's ideology and policies but actively contributed to the council's agenda, announcing their own protest event. Like the mothers' league, the cheerleaders sought to use established segregationist organizations' networks and infrastructure for mobilization and publicity purposes. And like mothers' leagues members, the cheerleaders also shared the council's ideology, and indeed, some cheerleaders were already citizens' council members.[30]

Drews, the cheerleader who had proclaimed to reporters that she would leave the state if her daughter could not continue to attend segregated schools, also announced to the media that there had been a plan for a mothers' march. There had been "an attempt" on Monday night, November 14, she stated, "to organize a march of 500 mothers on the school" for Tuesday, November 15, but the "the plan fell through."[31] Using the Citizens' Council of Greater New Orleans's platform promised more success. It is not clear whether the cheerleaders at this stage were in fact a group that had been established quickly during the first day of desegregation or whether it had in fact been established prior. On the one hand, the latter hypothesis finds support in the fact that the group was able to immediately act and had already been networking with the council; the swiftness of the cheerleaders' concerted action raises doubts regarding the spontaneity of their formation, and at least some of the group's members were previously active for segregationist causes. On the other hand, that the march fell through shows a lack of organizational or institutionalized power within the desegregated schools' neighborhoods.

Closing the Citizens' Council of Greater New Orleans's evening event was Leander Perez, who gave a rabidly racist and anti-Semitic speech. Fourteen alleged victims of police brutality were introduced on stage, and Perez accused the New Orleans Police Department "of getting rough and brutalizing segregationist demonstrators." He added that the officers were "merely acting on the orders of the real culprit, malefactor and double-crosser, the weasel, snakehead mayor of yours." Perez concluded his speech by relentlessly attacking the NAACP and "Zionist Jews" and urged his audience to not "wait for your daughter to be raped by these Congolese. Don't wait until the burr-heads are forced into your schools. Do something about it now."[32] Perez not only evoked racist and gendered fears of miscegenation and the white supremacist ideological figure of the "black beast" rapist that threatened white southern womanhood but consciously used the 1960 Congo crisis, newspaper reports about which had detailed alleged acts of cannibalism by Congolese troops against white soldiers in the newly independent Central African state.[33] These reports illustrated, in Perez's view, the primitive character and habits of black people.[34] Perez's remarks, linking black U.S. citizens to central Africa, also spoke to racist notions of dark magic and alluded to South Louisiana voodoo narratives. Such ideas had not only once fostered fears of slave rebellions and black insurrection in antebellum Louisiana and during the Reconstruction period but "helped cultivate the ground" for "black 'beast rapist'" propaganda, according to historian Michelle Gordon.[35] The fear mongering accomplished its goal: by morning, the march the "ladies of Frantz School" had intended to hold would turn into one of New Orleans's biggest downtown riots.

With only Frantz and McDonogh 19 marginally desegregated by the four black first graders, Louisiana's public schools had an integration rate of 0.001 percent, compared to 84.1 percent in Washington, D.C., at the time. Only Alabama (after Autherine Lucy's expulsion from the University of Alabama in 1956), Georgia, Mississippi, and South Carolina had managed to completely circumvent desegregation.[36] Nonetheless, another Deep South state had a chink in its armor, and segregationist politicians were determined to force New Orleans to become a successful Little Rock. The desire to make this strategy work encouraged grassroots segregationists to intensify their protests.

On November 16, the morning after the Citizens' Council of Greater New Orleans rally, "mothers of Frantz school pupils" assembled downtown to start their announced march on the Orleans Parish School Board's offices. The *Times Picayune* minimized the women's agency by stating that they "were told" to gather. Only a day earlier, the same newspaper had reported that the "ladies of Frantz School" were the ones sponsoring the demonstration and who had called on those who were at the Citizens' Council of Greater New Orleans's meeting to participate in it. Indeed, the reason the segregationist crowd at McDonogh 19 and William Frantz was "much smaller and quieter than on the two previous days," as the *Times Picayune* reported, was because the cheerleaders and others mothers were participating in the downtown protest, which shows that the women played an active role in planning and executing the segregationist protest march.[37]

Police attempted to quell the demonstration before it began, because the women did not have a parade permit. The group, however, said it was "going to parade anyway" and started its march. The women carried signs such as "Down with Redmond," "God Demands Segregation," and "Keep Our Race White." At city hall, a group of teenagers joined the mothers' march. When asked which schools the teenagers were from, some of them responded, "We're from all the schools."[38] The *Times Picayune* underestimated the crowds' numbers by counting them "in the hundreds" and only acknowledged the presence of "tumultuous teenagers," but national media like the *New York Times* estimated the demonstrators' numbers "upward from 2,000." The black-owned *Louisiana Weekly* stated that "thousands of white teenagers and adults paralyzed the business district early Wednesday," and the local *Bogalusa Daily News* wrote that "more than 5,000 mothers and teenagers, urged to 'civil disobedience' by segregation leaders, ran screaming through the streets of New Orleans." The ensuing segregationist riot encompassed the New Orleans business district and the French Quarter, and during the riot, the crowd burned a cross on St. Charles Avenue. Again chanting "2-4-6-8, we don't [want] to integrate; 8-4-6-2, we don't want a jig-a-boo," the mob swept through Louisiana's supreme court building and the city library. Five hundred members of the crowd then stormed city hall and demanded to see Mayor Morrison, who refused. Finally, the demonstration converged on the school board offices on downtown Carondelet Street. Groups of teenagers and adults, among them participants from the mothers' march, attacked several black citizens, shop fronts, and cars. Demonstrators attempted to shake a black paint worker off a building's scaffolding and hurled rocks and large pieces of ice at city buses and cars with black occupants. White demonstrators also attacked nineteen-year-old black porter Donald Campbell who was returning to his job from lunch and beat several other African Americans in the vicinity. When a segregationist female protester attempted to grab a police officer's nightstick, he placed her under arrest. Giarrusso could not "remember anything like this in New Orleans before." He added that "the people who instigated this"—in his view, the speakers of the Citizens' Council of Greater New Orleans's rally the previous night—were "conspicuous with their absence at the scene today." Indeed, none of the most vocal segregationist leaders participated in the demonstration, although Rainach had visited McDonogh 19 that morning, telling reporters he had come "to observe."[39]

When the mob tried to enter the school board offices, New Orleans police called on the city's firemen, who tried to disperse the crowd by using fire hoses set on low pressure because they did not wish to injure anyone. The police's manner of dealing with the mob and the use of low-pressure hoses to disperse the crowd directly contrasted with the law enforcement's martial reaction to black civil rights demonstrations. As a photo of the scene published in the *Times Picayune* and the *Baton Rouge States-Item* shows, the police lines and the use of fire hoses prevented the mob from entering the board's offices but had little effect on its dispersal. An unabashed crowd of young to middle-aged women in summer dresses continued to assemble, one of them smiling at the officers in front of them. Teenaged boys posed arm in arm for the photographers, and a few cheerful men stood in the background. As the police moved into the demonstrators, Muriel Schneider, a mother of two children, "grabbed" Giarrusso and "tearfully" begged him to "help us, not the United States government." The police superintendent replied that the police would if the protesters did "it in an orderly manner," but that the police would not let them "take over the city." Anita Mendoza, Gloria Dibos, and Genevieve Long, all described as mothers of public school children, were among other female protesters who were more defiant in the face of police intervention; one of them jokingly remarked that she was "sorry that I didn't bring my shampoo," while another quipped that she was "going to send Morrison a note thanking him for the free bath." Mendoza was a cheerleader. She proceeded to hand out "soggy slips of paper asking the parents of McDonogh No. 19 to attend a meeting of the Frantz Co-operative Club." The club was a segregationist organization presided over by plumber Armand Duvio, and it aimed to establish a private, white school. Mendoza stated that the desegregation of New Orleans schools was "not Americanism" but "just what the Communists want." She had five children and was determined that they would not be "going to school with Negroes," a sentiment that was echoed by the women next to her.[40]

Telenews TV material also confirms the participation of not only teenagers but many men and women in the downtown riot. The television report shows a group of young to middle-aged women walking and talking as some of them wield placards, while other young women in the crowd are laughing and jeering, some of their voices distinctly discernable in the crowd. They seem to be enjoying being doused by the low-pressure water hoses the fire department deployed. The atmosphere is reminiscent of New Orleans's Mardi Gras season.[41] Although Mendoza was not identified in the subsequent *Telenews* interview and newspapers made no mention of an arrest, the young, dark-haired woman is shown in the news segment, being led to the sidewalk by a police officer. Handing out wet slips of paper to the crowd, she states that she has five children who were "not going to school with no niggers," adding, "I say for the mothers to keep their kids out of school, all together. . . . We are white people, we don't want them to go to school with niggers." As she continues to hand out flyers, she proclaims in an agitated voice, "I'm willing to go to jail every day. I will not have my daughter go to school with a nigger." When the women who surround the interviewee ask why she has been arrested, she repeats that she is willing to go to jail every day but says she does not know why she was arrested. A policeman, with a friendly smile on his face, carefully asks, "You don't know why you're arrested? What did you throw?" "A tomato!" she answers emphatically, at which the two police officers next to her nod and smile.[42]

Although the regional media outlets as well as the police downplayed the activism of women during this first demonstration and riot, they soon acknowledged the force that they represented. The women were among the initial crowds that gathered outside the schools, but it was not until they began incessantly verbally abusing and physically attacking white parents who disregarded the segregationists' school boycott that the group's contours became more evident. They also became more visible because their behavior toward white parents evoked a stronger media reaction from (white-owned) newspapers than "regular" expressions of racism against black pupils and civil rights activists did.

Shock Value

"Cheerleaders" was not a self-chosen description by the segregationist women gathering at the schools, although they did not publicly object to it. The description emerged in the media two weeks after their initial protests. The *Bogalusa Daily News* was the first to refer to the reappearing female protesters by this name, a day after it had first reported on physical violence toward a white parent by female segregationist protesters in front of Frantz. This newspaper explained that the women's group had been thusly named by the police.[43]

A day later, the *Shreveport Journal* followed suit when describing the attack on civil rights ally Sydney Goldfinch by "fanatical women." That same day, the *Alexandria Daily Town Talk* likewise identified "some 40 women" as the "cheerleaders," explaining that this was what the police called them. By the time John Steinbeck visited New Orleans in the winter of 1960–61, the cheerleaders were a household name. None of the black-oriented newspapers covering the story, however, referred to the women's group by the name "cheerleaders." The *Louisiana Weekly* repeatedly portrayed the group as a crowd of "yelling, cursing and jeering white women," while the *Pittsburgh Courier* and *Chicago Defender* made a small but significant change in the group's commonly used name by dubbing them the "jeer-leading group" and "jeerleaders" respectively. *Time Magazine* picked up the name "cheerleaders" in December 1960, but neither the *New York Times* nor *Southern School News* nor Louisiana's bigger regional papers, that is, the *Times Picayune* or the *Baton Rouge States-Item*, identified the women as cheerleaders when reporting on segregationist women's activism surrounding the two New Orleans schools.[44] Regional and national media never honored the group by bestowing it with a distinct name.

The cheerleaders' title, then, originated with New Orleans police officers at the scene and was popularized by local newspapers and word of mouth. The name was also apt in a somatic sense. The women worked, commanded attention, and boosted their cause by publicly staging their bodies to evoke a reaction. The emphasis on the immediate somatic quality of the cheerleaders' protest was related to perceptions of the women's group as working class. The cheerleaders did manual labor, working (that is, protesting) with their bodies rather than with their minds. Their actions thus invited dismissals of white supremacy as an expression of a lack of education. Although some cheerleaders derived their legitimacy from their identity as mothers, just as some of the members of the Mothers' League of Central High did, the cheerleaders did not adhere to the premise of ladylike protest that featured in the mothers' league rhetorical emphasis on Christian motherhood and nonviolence, which relied on white male chivalry. Instead—defying their name—the cheerleaders both created and entered the battlegrounds themselves.

The fact that police christened female segregationists with this name speaks to the gendered and conflicting reactions that the group evoked. Not only is the word "cheerleaders" one that designates a primarily female group, but it is also a condescending marker that reduced their protest to an entertaining performance. Calling the women "cheerleaders" erased their clearly demonstrated potential for violence and their personal convictions. It also negated their political impact. The police indicated by their name for the women that they believed the women posed no threat to the black children or to integration advocates, despite their actions. The nickname delegated the group to a mere supportive role on the figurative sidelines of the desegregation crisis "game."

Massive resistance's proponents were used by now to the use of sports metaphors and sports-related names to describe them. Massive resistance's masculinist rhetoric emphasized that resistance against desegregation and federal interventions was also a test of political and personal virility. Similarly, football, stereotypically defined as a men's sport, is a test of the right mix of tactics and physical force. It seems appropriate, then, that the New Orleans Police Department assigned white segregationist women the role of vocal supporters and encouragers to those they believed to be the actual agents: segregationist men.

Paradoxically, the group earned its name at exactly the same time newspapers reported on the first physical attacks by segregationist women on white parents who ignored the call for a boycott at Frantz. The cheerleaders were not standing on the sidelines. They were the players on the field. To make light of them was thus to deny them political agency, and it indicated the sexist prism through which the New Orleans Police Department and concurring local newspapers viewed these women. The choice of words also served to mask the fact that they were neither an ordinary group of segregationist protesters nor a stereotypically ladylike behaved gathering of white southern belles, obscuring the vulgarity and violent nature of white supremacy's spearhead at the scene. The cheerleaders were a throng of vulgar racists the New Orleans Police Department should have been responsible for keeping under control.

"Cheerleader" also designates a position in a hierarchical support system. There are leaders among supporters who command cheers of encouragement, and they occupy a middle ground between audience and players, or the general population and (male) politicians. In this sense, the New Orleans cheerleaders were designated white supremacist bridge leaders. Still, this description is inadequate because these women consciously incited a perpetual state of emergency that sought to highlight resistance against desegregation. The cheerleaders did not rely on chivalrous white men—the strong football players—to defend white supremacy but put themselves on the frontline. The women repeatedly alerted the public to segregationist opposition, taking on the seemingly impossible task of establishing a united segregationist front. Like the mothers' league, the cheerleaders created performative spaces for their group in public, albeit choosing different and more radical expressions and measures.

That whites called them "cheerleaders," while blacks called them "jeerleaders," moreover, illustrates the difference in perception and classification of the group's activism. White police officers (and the newspapers that took up this term) rhetorically dismissed the women's group as noisy but harmless. The *Courier*'s and *Defender*'s choice to describe the women's behavior as "jeerleading," in contrast, emphasized the negativity and segregationist fervor present in the group's activism. They also emphasized the unusual sight of women leading a group of segregationist protesters at the scene. In addition, the term "jeerleaders" put the women's actions into context for black people and acknowledged their proclivity toward violence.

In a letter to the *Times Picayune*, former New Orleans resident James F. Moldenhauer commented on the seemingly curious choice of name for the protesters. Stating that he had "for some two years in the recent past" lived in New Orleans and had always known that desegregation would be a serious problem, he explained that he "really didn't expect a mob of woman [*sic*], whom your police have nicknamed the 'cheerleaders,' to be the loudest voice in New Orleans. I am wondering if 'cheerleader' isn't a rather elevated title for these women. After all, a cheerleader does try to lead, through her cheers, the home team on to victory, but she doesn't resort to spitting on the opposing team, nor does she give a Bronx cheer, nor does she use the tactics of a street fighter in doing so. When her team has been defeated, she accepts this defeat gracefully."[45] Here, the cheerleaders are viewed as not graceful, dignified, and ladylike enough to merit the name.

Finally, the fact that the female segregationists at the schools were dubbed "cheerleaders" is a testament not only to their volume but to the performative, theatrical quality of their activism that overshadowed that of other protesters. Steinbeck asserts that the cheerleaders' behavior was that of a rehearsed show, a spectacle with an audience, which might explain why the group did not acquire its name until two weeks after it had begun protesting. Theater studies scholar Benjamin Wihstutz writes that a performance takes place "when a space is divided, when a stage is created" and a marker has designated "the separation between the theatrical sphere and the everyday social sphere," thus enabling "the theatrical space to become apparent."[46] The cheerleaders only acquired the moniker after they had created this performative space through their activism. Be it through their tenacity, their volume, or their actions, they distinguished themselves from the crowd. There were "ordinary" protestors and onlookers, and then there was the cheerleaders' particular quality of protest that drew bystanders, even visitors like Steinbeck, to watch their performance. The cheerleaders literally made a name for themselves through their performances, which earned them notoriety, and they built a public space for their actions.

The police and the press were not only observers but active players in the group's establishment. By uncritically adopting the police's name for the group and by providing a public stage and a wide audience for their actions, the press allowed the cheerleaders to create performative routines. The cheerleaders' performances were tried and tested to have maximum impact, ensuring their continued visibility and the perpetuation of the crisis, which in turn led to constant media attention that molded the public's perception of the schools as sites of mayhem. The cheerleaders were critically dependent on this publicity. Their existence required an audience. The relationship between the press and the cheerleaders was pivotal and reciprocal.

The lack of formal membership and the fluidity between protesting segregationist women at the schools and the emerging core group of the cheerleaders makes it difficult to estimate how many women made up the group. Being a cheerleader was a behavioral marker, not a personalized identifier at this stage. A core group would emerge, but "cheerleaders" was used as an umbrella term for women who exhibited the loud and rowdy demeanor of the female segregationists described in newspaper reports and eyewitness accounts. Reporters employed the term "cheerleading" both as a description of a belligerent female presence at the scene as well as an indication of an emerging core group.

When describing the protests, newspaper reports fluctuated in their estimation of the number of women who formed the cheerleaders. By the end of November 1960, their estimations were ranging between twenty-five and sixty.[47] The *Baton Rouge States-Item* and the *Bogalusa Daily News* identified a core group of thirty women; the *New York Times* estimated the core group at twenty-five in number but reported of up to fifty women who participated in the protests at the schools. By mid-December, the *Louisiana Weekly* wrote that the cheerleaders' numerical strength had "dwindled to a mere handful" after the police had set up barricades in front of the schools and the boycott calls had shown overwhelming success.[48]

The Theatricalization of Protest

Segregationists had aimed their school boycott campaign at more pragmatic white parents like Arbon in an effort to bring attendance down further. Armand Duvio was one of many vocal segregationists resisting the integration of Frantz. Duvio, the father of a six-year-old first grader at the school (whom he withdrew), served as the president of the Dad's and Booster's Club of William Frantz and of the segregationist Frantz Cooperative Club. The latter club was later incorporated into the Ninth Ward Private School Association, a group chartered to set up a segregated, white private school. Duvio declared that education played a minimal role at the school at the moment and disseminated reports that the children were not being taught, claims that Redmond categorically denied. Calling on white parents of Frantz to not "resort to violence—that doesn't solve anything," Duvio announced that the school's parents would "plan" their "action" the following evening.[49]

On November 16, 1960, the meeting of the Frantz Cooperative Club and the White Educational Association, Inc., attracted a large crowd. Members of the audience dragged an effigy of Ruby Bridges into the Woodmen of the World Hall on Urquhart Street. Speakers urged the cheering crowd, made up of both McDonogh 19 and William Frantz Elementary parents, to donate, to petition, and to promote the two segregationist groups. When audience members asked Duvio what to "do with parents who send their children to integrated schools," he urged the audience not to "create violence," but advised to also not "associate" with these parents.[50]

Duvio and other speakers described plans for a private educational option for white children. Emphasizing the class component of New Orleans's school desegregation, Duvio criticized the Orleans Parish School Board for selecting the lower middle- and working-class Ninth Ward for integration. He stated that Judge Wright "couldn't force integration in the silk-stocking neighborhoods, but we're not going to stand for it. We're fighting." The meeting then proceeded to conjoin the two elementary school organizations into the Ninth Ward Private School Association, which subsequently worked to organize a private school for white pupils only.[51] Duvio used the same expression—"silk stocking"—for the city's wealthier district as the Capital Citizens' Council and the mothers' league had done in Little Rock. The Ninth Ward was as committed as they had been to put up a fight to preserve the cultural capital and spatialized power that white privilege were supposed to provide, even in the absence of economic capital.

Among the speakers at the Hall was also Mrs. A. F. Sedgebeer, president of the long-standing Frantz School Mothers' Club. She urged other mothers to "keep their children at home for their safety." Only two days earlier, Superintendent James Redmond had expressly distinguished William Frantz's "co-operative school club," headed by Sedgebeer, from Armand Duvio's newly established Co-operative Club, suggesting the two were not linked and that the mothers' club was not an active segregationist group. The two organizations were in fact closely cooperating, however, as Sedgebeer's participation in the meeting at the Hall suggests. Moreover, Sedgebeer provided evidence that she had a part in the plan to establish a private white school when on December 3, 1960, she responded to a press inquiry about the plans. The mothers' club's entanglements with the segregationist cause make it possible that cheerleaders were among its members. The club also may have unofficially cosponsored the November 16 mothers' march. In any case, Sedgebeer and the Frantz School Mothers' Club were active in white parents' resistance on a formal, organizational level, illustrating how everyday white supremacist culture motivated "ordinary" white women.[52]

Although during the following two school days bad weather reduced the crowds, protests continued at the desegregated schools, and jeering mobs reappeared. Adding to the carnival aspect of the protests that Steinbeck describes were two young female protesters at McDonogh who dressed up as stereotypes of Native Americans on November 17, wearing braids, bandanas, and costumes. The protesters smiled at the press cameras while holding two identical signs that read: "American Indians: We can't go to White Schools. Why should the Negro's [*sic*] go with White."[53] White protesters were not only invoking their perceived right to white privileges but insinuated that they were defending their indigenous territory from what they perceived as invading colonizers of color, appropriating the civil rights' struggles of marginalized groups.

Emerging for the first time after school desegregation had begun and the riots had broken out, the parents and other family members of Bridges as well as the other African American pupils Gail Etienne, Tessie Prevost, and Leona Tate gave press and television interviews about their experiences during the turmoil. Defiantly stating that they were "not afraid," that they were "determined to keep our children in school," and that they believed "our government will protect us," the parents had assembled in Alexander P. Tureaud's office, answering the questions of scores of local and national reporters. All of them reported that the children were doing well, although Ruby's mother, Lucille Bridges, admitted that her daughter had been frightened by "all that noise going on when we were going up the steps" at first. All of the parents assured the reporters that they had "sought the transfers of their own volition," as the schools "were closer to their homes." Despite the upbeat attitude that the parents and children conveyed, Bridges's father had already lost his job as a gas station attendant.[54]

In the meantime, the Louisiana legislature, Governor Jimmie Davis, and more than seven hundred state, parochial, and local officials were enjoined from interfering with the school board by New Orleans's three-judge federal court, which included Judge Wright. The state legislature was furious. Calling for continued resistance against integration, legislators yelled, "Hitler storm troopers" at the U.S. marshals and "Let's go to jail!" Democratic representative Wellborn Jack of Caddo questioned Judge Wright's mental health. The legislature expressly urged white parents of William Frantz and McDonogh 19 to keep their children out, thus aligning itself with the South Louisiana Citizens' Council, which praised the white boycotters. Historian Adam Fairclough remarks that the state legislators' belligerent rhetoric was mostly verbal radicalism: in the end, none of them had the courage to stand by their demands when threatened with jail.[55]

Grassroots segregationists also held protests in Baton Rouge in support of the aggressive rhetoric of the legislature. A photo in the *Alexandria Daily Town Talk* from November 18, 1960, shows a group of well-dressed, middle-aged and elderly men and women standing on the steps of the state legislature's building and carrying Confederate flags and protest signs that encouraged Davis to "Keep Fighting" and denounced the "Congolese Constitution," echoing Leander Perez's choice of words. The group from Louisiana's fourth congressional district (which includes Shreveport and surrounding northwestern areas) had come to the Pelican State's capital to display "their support of the legislature's battle against integration of New Orleans schools." A day later, a group of teenagers placed an effigy of Judge Wright, labeled "J. Wrong," at the state capitol's entrance and let reporters know that they planned on burning it. A swastika was painted on the effigy's back, a hammer and sickle on its front, and the puppet "held a small noose from which dangled a doll labeled 'States Rights.'"[56] The ideological confusion in segregationists' purported antiestablishment fight was not remarked on by the press.

A cooling-off period followed in the week after the downtown riots. Due to a three-day teachers' convention in Baton Rouge and the Thanksgiving holiday, the Crescent City's schools stayed closed for a week until November 28. Segregationists, however, did not rest. Absentee school board member Emile Wagner filed a suit that asked Redmond to turn over the names and addresses of all pupils who were still enrolled at William Frantz and McDonogh 19. Wagner declined to comment as to why he had asked for this information at first, but he later stated that "it's not the names of the four Negroes that I want—I know who they are. I want the names of the white children in those schools so I can make arrangements to get them in school, for their education."[57] White parents from both schools began to submit applications for their children to attend the neighboring St. Bernard Parish's public (and segregated) schools, assisted by Leander Perez. More than three hundred transfer applications were received by November 18. Joseph J. Davies Jr., St. Bernard Parish superintendent of schools, declared that the parish was ready to accommodate up to another five hundred student transfers from New Orleans. Furthermore, the parents' cooperative and segregationist supporters started to work out the details of setting up a segregated private school in St. Bernard Parish specifically for white William Frantz and McDonogh pupils of the first, second, and third grades. Operation Out was on its way.[58]

Louisiana's legislature remained defiant and made additional attempts to oust the Orleans Parish School Board, the board's lawyer Samuel Rosenberg, and Superintendent Redmond. It also passed a resolution that advised New Orleans's banks not to honor checks written by the school board and refused to release funds to pay William Frantz's and McDonogh 19's teachers' salaries. Not until February 1961, when the U.S. Justice Department, newly headed by Robert Kennedy, stepped in and Judge Wright finally ordered that the funds be released and that the banks honor school board checks did the board's financial crisis end.[59]

As of late November 1960, segregationists' spirits remained unbroken. Taking advantage of the school-free week, white parents and children from William Frantz and McDonogh 19, as well as other segregationist supporters and council officials, again flocked to the state capitol in Baton Rouge. The group was honored with a standing ovation and thundering applause by members of the state house as they carried a miniature, yard-long black coffin into the building.

The mock coffin contained a black-faced effigy that was wearing a black suit in the pocket of which was a small gavel and appeared to have a hole in its forehead. It represented Judge Wright. As the group entered the legislative chambers, one of several women in the crowd, some of whom were wearing black

Cheerleaders and fellow segregationists stage a mock funeral at the state capitol in Baton Rouge on November 23, 1960 (Alliance/Associated Press)

veils, shouted, "The judge is dead, we have slaughtered him." Her cry was echoed by other women, and several "feigned weeping and mourning," while others laughed. The group carried small black flags, Confederate emblems, and signs saying, "Thank God for the state legislature" and "Davis, our children's protector, thank God." Ruby Bridges remembered the "black doll in a coffin," which, she remarks in her memoir, "frightened me more than anything else," and a photo of protesting crowds of women, children, and a few men with the coffin is printed in the memoir.[60] Among the protesters at Baton Rouge was Dr. Emmett Irwin, president of the Citizens' Council of Greater New Orleans, who explained to the *Baton Rouge States-Item* that "the black flags were in mourning for federal usurpation of state sovereignty by 'judicial tyranny.'" A woman then told Irwin that "we need more doctors like you. . . . If we had them, we wouldn't have to fight."[61]

Some of the women protesters at the statehouse were cheerleaders.[62] According to the *Baton Rouge States-Item*, the "first bus load" of visitors had introduced themselves as parents of white William Frantz schoolchildren, and the mixture of women, children, and men was indeed characteristic of the protesting crowds in front of the school itself. The theatrical spectacle of a procession was, moreover, clearly carefully planned, reflecting the cheerleaders' basic strategy of putting on a show.[63] They claimed space on the streets and in the legislature through their performance. The brutality of the rhetoric, the "slaughtering" of Wright, echoed a white woman's earlier exclamation that the judge should be "hanged by his toes." It foreshadowed threats the cheerleaders would make against Ruby Bridges, Judge Wright, and white parents in the upcoming weeks. The fact that Irwin was among the protesters shows at least cooperation, even close ties, between protesters like the cheerleaders and the Citizens' Council of Greater New Orleans. Perhaps the cheerleaders were again taking advantage of the council's organizational experience and funds, as segregationist women had done before when they announced the march of the "Ladies of Frantz School" at the council's rally on November 15.

The cheerleaders routinely used belligerent rhetoric and violent imagery as a protest strategy. A picture taken by a *Paris Match* press photographer on December 1, 1960, depicts four young and middle-aged cheerful white women on their way to William Frantz school to continue their daily segregationist protest. A group of white men observes the scene in the background. The women carry several protest utensils, including a Confederate flag, what appears to be a black effigy, and a paper skull that makes an ominous threat to desegregation proponents. "Little Rock slowed you down, but New Orleans will stop you cold," reads one of their placards. "It once was when the big tough Federalmen were tracking the big bad outlaws. Now they keep occupied by playing nursemaids to four little Negers [*sic*]," said another. "Nursemaid," a supposedly insulting, effeminizing description, was a term the cheerleaders would frequently use.

The brutal imagery and rhetoric were followed by the physical harassment and violence on the part of the cheerleaders, a consciously transgressive strategy that the four black elementary school children experienced firsthand. Although reports by white-owned newspapers in the upcoming weeks focused primarily on the cheerleaders' actions toward white parents who still brought their children to William Frantz, the most imminent impact of the cheerleaders' protest was the distress they caused the four first graders at William Frantz and McDonogh 19. As white attendance dwindled to zero at McDonogh, "a mere handful of rowdy persons," among them cheerleaders, taunted the black pupils, yelling "you've got the whole school to yourself now." The white boycott was complete at McDonogh by November 21, 1960, the first week of desegregation. The school thus now drew few to no protesters, and so segregationists focused their protests on Frantz, where Bridges became the target.[64] After weeks of protests at William Frantz, during which the school still had three white students in attendance, the segregationist crowds shrunk. A core group of determined cheerleaders who would carry on the protest until the end of the school year came to the fore. In her memoir, Bridges remembers them as "angry, loud militants," whose "numbers were down" compared to the first two weeks of protests. The performative act that was cheerleading, however, would come into full force over the next few weeks.[65]

Bridges notes in her memoir that she had not been afraid at first because she did not understand that the crowds and the noise were directed at her. She thought that it might be carnival season's Mardi Gras, because Mardi Gras was "always noisy," a description that conveys the theatricality of segregationists' protests at the school and the festival-like character that can also be discerned in TV news reports and photos in newspapers.[66] Soon Ruby realized, however, that the crowds were hostile. They spat at her and her mother, threw various items at her, sang "Glory, glory, segregation," and shouted, "Go home, nigger" and "No niggers allowed here." Bridges distinctly remembers a woman in front of the school screaming at her, "I'm going to poison you. I'll find a way," and repeating the same threat every day.[67]

Psychiatrist Robert Coles observed Bridges and her parents and noted that Bridges did well at school and attended class regularly but had become "frightened and anxious" and lost her appetite. Bridges refused to eat her lunches or hid them in the school building, and she was "very careful about what she took to school to eat," refusing her favorite cookies, sandwiches, and freshly prepared food. Ruby opted for prepackaged food instead and only ate when others around her ate, too. She eventually confided in Coles that one of the cheerleaders had threatened to poison and kill her. Coles noted that "little nigger, we'll get you and kill you" and "we're going to poison you until you choke to death" were "commonplaces" among the insults and threats constantly directed at the six-year-old. Clearly, the mothers, as some newspapers called the group, and their behavior were anything but motherly toward a black child, and the only children worthy of protection to them were white children. Maternalism served as a white supremacist tool.[68] That the press referred to the cheerleaders' protests as "mothers'" activism further indicates that despite the absence of formal membership criteria the cheerleaders had developed a group identity through their actions and self-representations. Their group identity was not only grounded in their mutual segregationist activism but in their self-identity as an explicit women's group.

When classes resumed on November 28, 1960, more than four hundred former Frantz and McDonogh students in the fourth, fifth, and sixth grades had been transferred to segregated classes in several of the neighboring St. Bernard Parish's schools. Of these pupils, 183 were brought to Arabi, Carolyn Park, and St. Claude Heights schools every day for two weeks by two buses. The buses departed from the desegregated schools and had been chartered by Duvio and "a group of plumbers" (like Duvio himself) who jointly contributed $250 to cover the cost.[69] From the following week onward, the children were brought to St. Bernard Parish in two buses loaned to the segregationist parents by a local post of the Veterans of Foreign Wars Cadet Corps. This was a networking and organizational achievement that signified that the boycott's organizers had closer ties to political and civic groups than either side acknowledged. Although the Ninth Ward lacked economic, cultural, and social capital and thus influence with the city's elite, the working-class community was able to access resources by establishing ties with the city's broader community.[70]

As the white exodus from Frantz and McDonogh neared completion, the *Times Picayune* noted that the segregationist crowds at the schools were "the smallest and quietest since the desegregation." Perhaps thinking that by now the most ardently segregationist parents would have permanently withdrawn their children from the desegregated schools and that there would thus be less resistance to a countermove, Save Our Schools chose the third week of integration to initiate a concerted effort to bring the white children of moderate and liberal parents back to William Frantz School, where the segregationist boycott had not yet been completed.[71] Starting on December 1, 1960, Save Our Schools institutionalized a car lift service for white parents and their children. Save Our Schools introduced the carpool as a respectable and supposedly apolitical mothers' project. Stating that anyone who wanted a ride would be provided with one, Save Our Schools president Mary Sand's words and actions incensed the "boycott brigade," as the *Times Picayune* called the "hard core of women," the cheerleaders.[72]

On November 30, 1960, New Orleans's three-judge federal court declared the legislature's Interposition Act invalid, which "infuriated" the cheerleaders, the *Times Picayune* observed.[73] Despite the cheerleaders' claims that they would "keep fighting" and that "regardless of what they've decided, we will have segregated schools,"[74] the group was on the defensive. Even Thurgood Marshall was cautiously optimistic in a speech to the Oklahoma state NAACP convention in early December, stating that "we should see a considerable number of white children back in school with those four little colored girls. If only we can keep those crowds away from the schools."[75]

Faced with yet another lost legal battle and visible cracks in the segregationist front, the cheerleaders' response was immediate. Federal marshals had to be called in to escort the carpool after parents and Save Our Schools activists received threats. Cheerleaders and other segregationists damaged Save Our Schools members' cars and slashed their tires, after a list of the drivers was circulated.[76] A cheerleader complained that if it were not for the police protection that Save Our Schools had, "there would not be a growing number of pupils returning to the school."[77] The cheerleaders interpreted white parents' willingness to allow their children to attend desegregated Frantz with Bridges as treachery, since they believed united massive resistance would ultimately defeat desegregation. They began a violent intimidation campaign in late November and early December that would make national headlines, elevate their notoriety beyond the regional news, and permanently determine their public perception and image. The legislative strategy of Louisianan segregationists to circumvent desegregation had failed, and the "real battle was now being fought in the streets."[78] Drastic means were in order, and the cheerleaders became the primary women's group among New Orleans' segregationist street fighters who terrorized parents who continued to send their children to school.

Segregation's Street Fighters

Daisy Gabrielle was not easily intimidated. A native of Costa Rica and mother of six, she had served as a member of the Women's Army Corps in New Guinea during the Second World War. The domestic battle lines drawn at William Frantz initially did not deter the forty-two-year-old from continuing to send her children to school. She had grown up in New Orleans and had attended public school, although she did not finish her elementary education. Gabrielle's husband, James, a thirty-nine-year-old Rhode Island native whom Gabrielle called "Jerry" and whom she had met during her army service, worked as a gas- and water-meter reader for the city. Daisy Gabrielle was a housewife. The working-class family lived in an apartment in a Ninth Ward public housing unit.[79]

Two female neighbors approached Gabrielle on the first day of desegregation while she was playing with one of her children outside. The women said, "Daisy, you've got a child in Frantz, haven't you? You must be crazy! Don't you know there's niggers in there?" Gabrielle retorted that there was only one black girl in the school and did not react further. The women sneered at her and said, "Daisy, we didn't know you were a nigger lover," then walked off to congregate with other neighbors before rushing toward Frantz. Gabrielle had drawn the ire of her neighbors and would soon be confronted with the consequences that white parents had to face when they did not comply with the cheerleaders.[80]

Two days later, Gabrielle's ten-year-old son, Jimmy Jr., reported to his mother that "some women" had instructed him to tell her that she should stop taking Jimmy's little sister, Yolanda, to school unless she wanted to get beat up. Gabrielle continued to take her daughter to William Frantz. The school was located only three blocks from the family's home, and yet walking there quickly turned into running the gauntlet. The anonymous threats of physical violence against Gabrielle became more real, as a group of women and teenaged girls now trailed behind her and her daughter, snarling and cursing at them. Soon, the Gabrielles had to face a daily mob gathering outside their home. The mob was "armed with rocks and rotten eggs," *Good Housekeeping* wrote in a portrait of Daisy Gabrielle in 1961, aghast at the vulgarity of the cheerleaders, which did not accord with the magazine's ideas of femininity.[81]

Cheerleaders harass Daisy Gabrielle and her daughter Yolanda near William Frantz Elementary School (Alliance/Associated Press)

On the afternoon of November 29, 1960, when Gabrielle and a female neighbor who was originally from California picked their children up from Frantz, a mob of angry cheerleaders, thirty to forty women strong, began to follow and harass them. Having missed Gabrielle when she had brought Yolanda to school that morning, the cheerleaders showed up at her house later in the day, screamed insults, and threatened that they would "get that crumb" when she left.[82]

The cheerleaders' rhetoric became so vulgar that even whites sympathetic to their cause distanced themselves from them. The same day the cheerleaders chased Gabrielle and her daughter to the family's home, a white woman who owned property across from Frantz let the cheerleaders use her lawn to assemble. The homeowner withdrew her permission, however, when the women's shouts "grew profane." She "ordered them off," saying that she did not "want that kind of language used" in her yard. As the cheerleaders moved over to the next yard, they turned on the woman who had asked them to leave her property, calling her "nigger lover."[83] The cheerleaders' extreme stance did not allow for the slightest doubt or deviation. If people did not fully support their cause *and* their means of defending the white working-class community's central asset, access to white privilege, they instantly became the enemy.

The *New York Times* reported that four hundred people lined the streets when Gabrielle left the school building with Yolanda. According to the *Good Housekeeping* article, the atmosphere was carnival-like; the women, dressed "in bright, tight toreador pants, their hair done up in curlers, struck poses in front of the press cameras, kidding policemen and reporters." The magazine noted that the women were wearing "tight sweaters" to which they had pinned badges with segregationist slogans and insult. The magazine insinuated that the women's group was not only inappropriately and vulgarly dressed but dared to publicly parade their bodies for their political purposes—this, the magazine judged, amounted to a corporeality unbefitting for women in the public sphere in 1960. About two dozen of white women set on the mother and her neighbor as they made their way home.[84] This would be the first occasion on which the cheerleaders exercised physical violence toward white parents who did not comply with the segregationist boycott mandate. The *Times Picayune* wrote that when Gabrielle "tried to push through" the crowds of "cursing women, someone struck her from behind," while *Good Housekeeping* disclosed that Gabrielle was struck on the breast by a cheerleader described as "very large and very lusty." Gabrielle swung her purse in self-defense and struck a cheerleader on the head.[85]

Gabrielle later stated that her Californian neighbor and friend had left the school building first and had only attracted a little abuse and that the cheerleaders targeted her specifically: "They kept calling Yolanda 'poor little thing.' But they cursed me and called me 'nigger-lover' and told me they were going to beat the —— out of me."[86] *Southern School News* noted that Gabrielle was one of the parents who were "pushed around by screaming demonstrators—mostly women," whereas the *Chicago Daily Defender* was more explicit in estimating that about forty cheerleaders had first jeered Bridges when she left Frantz that afternoon. A dozen of these "snarling housewives, . . . howling curses and profanity," then attacked Gabrielle, who had tried to escape through a back door only to find the women waiting for her.[87] "You feel real brave in that crowd, you cowards," Gabrielle shouted at the cheerleaders. The group of women answered with repeated yells of "nigger lover!" Gabrielle was particularly dismayed that the women seemed to enjoy themselves while tormenting her.[88]

Confirming the cheerleaders' need for attention, the segregationist women became "more and more abusive" as Gabrielle "continued to disregard them," *Good Housekeeping* noted.[89] Gabrielle had to react to the group's theatrical performance because that reaction would generate the scandalized audience required to fulfill the group's purpose. Gabrielle's husband stepped up to the plate when he "came to the rescue and police broke up the crowd." *Good Housekeeping* reported that James Gabrielle had "stayed home from work in case of trouble," and hearing the commotion outside, he shoved his wife, the neighbor, and their children through the door and shouted at the mob, "Get out of here, you white scum. Leave us alone!"[90] The mob continued to knock on the Gabrielles' door and windows and yelled, "That's what we want. Keep your kid home."[91]

A few days earlier, Gabrielle had received another visit from a group of women who came to her home to try to persuade her to adhere to the boycott. When the *Times Picayune* asked who they were and what their purpose was, the women refused to elaborate. One member of the group declared, "All of us mothers are going to have to stick together, we're going to get the job done."[92] Their goal was not only to enforce a complete white boycott but to ensure that classes at the two desegregated schools would end. The boycotters eyed a 1922 state law that stated that "schools with an average attendance of 10 or less may not be kept open." Democratic state representative Wellborn Jack of Caddo Parish continued to push this tactic even after the three-judge federal court had rejected the Orleans Parish School Board's plea for a delay of integration on November 30. Jack told the segregationist protesters that the "city's schools could be segregated" despite this ruling, and that all they had to do was "keep those children out of those two schools."[93] The cheerleaders chose to take to the streets to try to do what the legislature and school board had been unable to.

Although the cheerleaders did not directly threaten her six-year-old daughter Yolanda, as this would have destroyed the group's credibility as white activist mothers, they still went beyond the mothers' league, which had no reservations about threatening the Little Rock Nine but had drawn the line at intimidating white children or physically attacking their parents at Central High School. Cheerleaders proclaimed they were protecting white children, including the white children who were, in their view, harmed by their own parents' insufficient devotion to white supremacy. The harm inflicted on these children whose parents the cheerleaders attacked in front of them or whom the cheerleaders instructed to deliver threats to can at best be seen as collateral damage the group had to assume for its tactics or at worst the result of a conscious strategy embraced by the group to make children afraid for their parents. It also served as a strategy to intimidate the parents of children who were directly addressed by the harassers and thus make them fearful for their own safety.

It might have been these types of transgressions that led James Gabrielle to call the cheerleaders white scum. His insult expressed the underlying attitude other whites had toward the women's group and was one of the first that was quoted publicly. They called the cheerleaders white trash. The Gabrielles explicitly distanced themselves from the kind of working-class identity that, grounded in racism, aspired to a higher social rank than black people, an identity that combined class consciousness with white supremacy.

The cheerleaders' description in *Good Housekeeping* echoes this sentiment, where they are portrayed as less than ladylike, vulgarly dressed, and badly behaved. The magazine depicts them as unkempt women who lacked public composure and basic manners, desperate to knock a reaction out of the classier Daisy Gabrielle and the public. Gabrielle's stated reason for enduring the harassment and continuing to take Yolanda to Frantz during late November and early December 1960 was that she was trying to take the moral high ground. The Gabrielles did not have a single black family friend; their objection to segregation stemmed, rather, from their Roman Catholicism, as Gabrielle noted in an interview with the *Pittsburgh Courier*.[94] But taking the moral high ground had consequences: "I think I lost 10 years of my life the night I made that final decision. . . . Whatever it was I heard an inner voice. And when I got up that morning, I told my husband Jerry, I'm taking Yolanda back. I don't hate any race or creed. I'm going to do what I think is the right thing. . . . Even when I walked past those screaming women, even when they shoved me, I closed myself in. I didn't hear their voices. I felt at peace with myself. You know, I'd rather take a beating from a mob than from my conscience."[95]

Gabrielle also acknowledged the cheerleaders' danger in a UPI interview published by the *Chicago Daily Defender*. She did not think that the women's group would physically hurt children, but she did believe that the women would break both of her legs "without thinking twice." Nevertheless, Gabrielle reiterated that she and her husband were determined not to give in to the mob. Her husband had "spent three years in a fox hole" during the Second World War, and they were therefore "not going to be told by a mob of women what to do and think." Gabrielle also expressed pity for the cheerleaders; she felt "very, very sorry for them," she said, and did not hate or dislike them but hoped that someday they would see her point of view. She knew that the cheerleaders' goal was to get Yolanda and every other white pupil out of Frantz in order to force the closing of the desegregated schools, and she thought that was a mistake: what "these women don't realize is that it would be a catastrophe" for the children to lose their public education system, she warned.[96] Gabrielle did not refer in either interview to the fact that she herself could be considered a woman of color as a Latina, nor did the cheerleaders. New Orleans's Hispanic residents had assimilated into the city's white society by the middle of the twentieth century, and so Gabrielle's origin read as a national, not a racial identity. The *Times Picayune* reported on the Costa Rica native's "slight Spanish accent," but, particularly in a state with a Spanish colonial history, Gabrielle's ethnic heritage passed as white.[97]

Beginning in December, the police erected barricades that kept the cheerleaders and other protesters a block away from Frantz. But cheerleaders regularly broke through police lines to strike Daisy Gabrielle and spit at her. Now estimated to be between fifteen and forty strong, they cursed and threatened to kill her. They threw rocks and rotten eggs. In one incident, the women were closing in on Gabrielle and one of the cheerleaders shoved her against a tree. In another, a female protester caught hold of Gabrielle's weapon of defense, a pocketbook that she would swing, and twisted it in a way that made the handle cut Gabrielle's arm until she bled. Again, the New Orleans Police Department made no arrests. Despite being in the same grade, Yolanda Gabrielle never attended class with Bridges but was taught in a separate classroom by herself. She began to have nightmares about the "ugly ladies; those ugly ladies who yell so ugly."[98]

After repeated death threats against the Gabrielles, physical attacks on Daisy Gabrielle, and attacks on their apartment, the police and Save Our Schools eventually intervened. Save Our Schools volunteers drove Daisy Gabrielle and Yolanda the few blocks to and from Frantz so they could avoid the hecklers, and the New Orleans Police Department stationed a police car outside their home on a twenty-four-hour-watch. The increased security measures did not deter the cheerleaders. According to Gabrielle, they were "led to the back by neighbors" living in the same housing unit as the Gabrielles and began to "race up and down like wild children on a spree, laughing and hooting and throwing stones and debris" through the family's kitchen window. Whenever Gabrielle and her daughter were brought to school in a car, the cheerleaders pelted the passing vehicle with various items, hit against the windows, and tried to kick the car.[99]

The *Bogalusa Daily News* reported that "someone in the 'Cheerleaders' threw a broken piece of brick, cracking the car window inches from the driver's head" one afternoon as the Save Our Schools driver, Gabrielle, and her daughter passed by. Police had been "unable to prevent the stoning of the car or other incidents," the newspaper continued, giving the impression the New Orleans Police Department had no other choice than to let the cheerleaders continue their terrorist attacks. One of the Save Our Schools members commented that she had "never felt so much hatred directed toward" her.[100]

As one of the two women who had driven Gabrielle and her daughter home from Frantz reported to Channel 6, one afternoon, they were faced with another car and a truck blocking the women's car one block away from the Gabrielles' home, while protesters rained rocks and eggs on them. Two policemen in plain clothes who had followed the Save Our Schools car got out of their vehicle, dispersed the crowd, and ordered the blockading car and truck to move. After the women had dropped off Gabrielle and her daughter, they reported that "the same truck started following the car," and that it was "driven by a woman accompanied by a small child." Afraid that the truck might ram them, the Save

Our Schools women sped at fifty miles an hour for several miles before the truck disappeared.[101]

Segregationist pressure was relentless. Save Our Schools drivers and families who did not comply with the segregationists' school boycott received threatening telephone calls. James Gabrielle, who technically could not be fired from his city job, accepted a pay cut, was denied promotion, and faced constant mobbing before he eventually quit his job, still convinced that he and his wife were "doing the right thing."[102] Two days before the Gabrielles finally left New Orleans after three weeks of constant threats and violence, thirty cheerleaders again marched on the Gabrielles' apartment and loudly picketed in front it. During the night, two bricks were hurled through the Gabrielles' kitchen window. The family announced that they were moving away from New Orleans and planned to resettle in James's hometown of North Providence, Rhode Island. Daisy Gabrielle insisted that her family did not leave "after trying to stir up trouble in the school." Rather, she noted that she had fought back against the cheerleaders because she was "look[ing] at this thing as a true Christian."[103]

By December 8, 1960, the family had left. Historian Morton Inger notes that the New Orleans Police Department's and Mayor Morrison's refusal to adequately protect the Gabrielles not only affected the family but also had consequences for the mindset of white New Orleanians who did not agree with the boycott. Officials' inertia "meant that men and women were free to act out their revengeful fantasies right in the streets" while "people whose support of open schools had been so carefully elicited were frightened back indoors." While the local cheerleaders harassed the four black schoolchildren and assaulted the Gabrielles, Mayor Morrison blamed the desegregation crisis on "outside agitators" and the press.[104]

Daisy Gabrielle was not the only parent who invoked their religion when explaining their decision to continue sending their white children to desegregated schools.[105] The white parents at Frantz who were committed to challenging Operation Out were devout Christians—both Catholic and Protestant—who understood desegregation to be a Christian principle. Some of these families had the advantage that their breadwinners could not be easily dismissed from their jobs in public service or in religious institutions—time and again, segregationists threatened parents who disregarded their boycott that they would put pressure on their employers to fire them. Three of the white parents who received less media coverage than the Gabrielles were Marvin Chandler, Marion L. McKinley, and Margaret Conner, whose children also continued to attend class at Frantz. Chandler and McKinley, both New Orleans Baptist Theological Seminary students, had begun to ignore the boycott by December. Soon thereafter, both families were faced with the cheerleaders' and other segregationists' harassment in person and on the telephone. Segregationists not only attacked McKinley's house but also his wife and a friend by throwing rocks during the day, and the family received death threats. At the same time, two other white parents of Frantz students, Delma Windham and Everett L. Poling, had been given twenty-four-hour police protection after their families' lives had been threatened and their car tires slashed.[106] Eventually, Marvin Chandler withdrew his children from Frantz, and the next day Marion McKinley followed suit.

Margaret Conner, a Catholic mother of nine, returned four of her children to Frantz after the initial commotion in November. Despite her run-ins with the cheerleaders, she would become the only white parent who did not withdraw her children, and she remained in New Orleans after the 1960–61 school year. Living only half a block from the school at the time, Conner stated in a 1985 interview that she "wasn't a crusader" in political terms. She stressed that her children attended a public school because the family could not afford parochial tuition fees and Frantz was the "neighborhood school." Two men, one of whom introduced himself as a citizens' council representative and the other of whom stated that he was "with the state," visited Conner's home in early December. Not only the cheerleaders made house calls, but as the *Chicago Daily Defender* speculated, "members of the political machine of Leander Perez."[107]

Reminiscent of a scene from a Mafia movie, the men visiting Conner offered the thirty-seven-year-old "protection" and urged her to let them transfer her children to segregated schools in St. Bernard Parish. "Our job is to help you," declared one of the men, adding that as long as there were integrated schools, "you will never have peace." Conner responded that she was neither for nor against integration, "just for education." The strangers asked for her name, which she gave to them, and then left. The New Orleans native was not a politically liberal woman, but she was a self-reflective one. Conner stated that she was "just as prejudiced as anyone," but that "all of a sudden, after all this," she was "losing some of it." Her children had attended parochial schools until 1958, when the family was no longer able to afford the tuition. During the 1960 crisis, Conner had kept the four children who attended Frantz out of school for two weeks until she realized that "the legislature didn't do one constructive thing" and sent them back. After the men's unannounced and unsuccessful visit, Conner received up to seventy-five anonymous phone calls a day. Although Mary Sand, the president of Save Our Schools, was a close friend and supported Conner, the harassment caused Conner a lot of emotional distress.[108]

Conner's actions, particularly her interactions with the cheerleaders, were much less publicized than the segregationists' attacks on Daisy Gabrielle. Her experiences shed another light on the cheerleaders' behavior—or on "the women," as Conner simply called them. In an interview with Alan Wieder twenty-five years after the desegregation crisis, Conner recalled some of her confrontations with the group. She, too, drew attention to the women's "showboating" for the press and the performative nature of their protests, although she remembered that the crowd had thinned out after a few weeks and only a core group of cheerleaders remained. Conner was astonished by the women's actions, reporting on an incident where she—visibly pregnant—was asked whether her baby was going to be black or white. Another time, cheerleaders harassed her, her children, and a priest while they were heading to a Catholic catechism class. Conner remembered that she, like Gabrielle, had to push her way through the crowd, eventually supported by two priests accompanying her and her children, and that the women's group picketed her house. Conner summarized her observations:

> There were a lot of women and they did things that were so unwomanly. We had a house that had a garage below it on one side. Of course, with all the kids we closed it in and made it into a long, big bedroom. It had a big window in front. I had a young black girl who would come iron for me. When all this started, I sat down with her and said, "You don't have to come. You might be in danger if you come. I won't be upset and we will still be friends if you don't want to come." And she said, "Oh no, I'll come." You know that kind of fight. So she would come on her day and one day we were downstairs making the beds and "the women" came and stood in front of my house. We went to the window and she said, "Look at that one, look at that one." Well, doggone it, the women saw us and they turned their backsides to us and shook their backsides. And she said, "Do you have a camera?" I said that I didn't have any film and she said, "That doesn't matter, pretend we are taking a picture." So I got the camera and the women were doing all kinds of nasty movements.[109]

The cheerleaders' behavior was unwomanly, unfeminine, and vulgar, as Conner saw it, a sight to behold in terms of never-witnessed-before behavior of heretofore unnoticed white neighborhood women in public. Conner concurred with Steinbeck regarding the cheerleaders' need for attention and an audience. The women started to do "nasty movements" when they thought Conner was taking their picture, aiming for maximum shock value and seeking to preserve their public and media reputation as a spectacle. Conner implied that the cheerleaders' movements had sexual undertones, which suggests that the women relished the shock value of what was perceived as vulgarity. The cheerleaders were putting on a show, both for their own attention-seeking gratification and as a way of ensuring their actions would stick in people's minds as a warning: if they behaved this way in public in defense of segregation, was there any outrageous action from which they would refrain?

The Reverend Lloyd Andrew Foreman, minister of the neighborhood's St. Mark's and Redeemer Methodist churches, soon found out. Foreman became another highly visible target of the cheerleaders' harassment campaign. The same day the cheerleaders physically attacked Daisy Gabrielle for the first time, they also tried to hinder Foreman and his five-year-old daughter Pamela Lynn from entering her kindergarten class at Frantz. The cheerleaders had already verbally abused Foreman each day previously. About fifty segregationist protesters, a majority of them "hopping-mad" women, the *Times Picayune* observed, set up a picket line on November 29, 1960. They tried to prevent Foreman and other white parents from crossing the street to reach the school entrance. Although police officers cleared a path for Foreman and his daughter, the cheerleaders closed in on Foreman and snarled at him. One of the cheerleaders eventually lunged past the police guard and shoved the minister, while other cheerleaders yelled, "White trash," "Nigger lover," and "He's got nigger blood!"[110]

After Foreman dropped his daughter off at Frantz, he was asked by a *Telenews* reporter why he continued to send her to school. Foreman calmly answered that he was simply acting on his privilege to do what he wanted to do, which was to take his child to school. "If others want to keep theirs out, that's their privilege," he explained. In the background, one can hear women booing and screaming, some of them yelling, "Niggers," and, directed at Foreman, "Every day you side with them."[111] In another interview, Foreman stressed that he and his wife were "native Louisianans" who were acting according to their conscience. Exposing the hypocrisy of the cheerleaders' actions, Foreman stated, "Everyone is talking about their rights, states' rights and rights to stay out of school. Yet dozens of white parents who have told me they really want to return their children to school are having their rights denied [to] them because of threats, intimidations and mob pressures. . . . We only want the privilege . . . to rear our children as we see fit. I felt, in making this decision, besides wanting Pamela to have respect for education, that I was simply trying to abide by the law of the land. It may be trite to say it, but I love this country, and I want to abide peacefully by the will of the majority and to teach my child to do so. . . . I felt that the city was being misrepresented, to the nation and the world, by these mobs, and I could not stand idly by and not take a stand."[112]

Bracing for another attack that day when he would go to pick up his daughter at noon, Foreman turned to Father Jerome Drolet, a Catholic priest who had also accompanied Foreman and his daughter to school the previous day. Drolet acted as a decoy, serving as a sacrificial target of the cheerleaders' wrath while Foreman came to meet his daughter at one of Frantz's back entrances. They made their way back safely to the Foreman's home. Drolet, meanwhile, elicited the cheerleaders' ire as he walked through the gathering in front of the school shortly before Pamela Lynn's kindergarten class ended. Holding up a Bible while making his way through the crowd, he smiled benignly as the women barked, "Communist," "Nigger lover," "You're some low man" at him.[113]

When the cheerleaders, about thirty in all, realized that they had missed

Foreman by focusing on Drolet, they marched to Foreman's house, one and a half blocks away from Frantz, and picketed in front of it. "Let's give the Reverend our blessings," one of them commented.[114] The cheerleaders insulted Foreman by calling him "white trash" and, without using the expression, similarly classified Drolet by calling him "some low man." The women were aware that national and some regional newspaper coverage implicitly framed them as white trash, and they had been directly insulted by James Gabrielle, who had called them white scum. By using the expression to slight their opponents, the cheerleaders turned around the term's meaning. "White trash," to them, did not refer to working-class whites exhibiting particularly vulgar behavior but described white people who ignored the white supremacist concept of white racial solidarity and, in their view, betrayed fellow whites. "Every day you side with them," one of the reproaches yelled at Foreman by cheerleaders, exemplified their notion that white trash were those who deserted the supposedly united white "us" for the black (and prointegration) "them."

That the women called the Catholic minister Drolet a "communist" indicates interest on the cheerleaders' side and again even direct ties with other Louisianan segregationist organizations. In a handwritten comment on a newspaper report about how the cheerleaders had harassed Drolet, Rainach wrote that there was a House Un-American Activities Committee report on Drolet concerning his relation to the "Citizens' Committee for Harry Bridges." The same information was later spread in a December 21, 1960, press release by Jackson Ricau, the director of the South Louisiana Citizens' Council. The press release indignantly noted that Drolet had "'decoyed' the people at Frantz school so a Methodist minister could unobtrusively escort his child into the school in defiance of Louisiana law" and also stated that Drolet was "the priest who in 1938 signed a petition to prevent deportation of Henry Bridges. Bridges is a notorious Communist."[115] Hence, that the cheerleaders recognized Jerome Drolet and associated him with "communist" activities, three weeks before the South Louisiana Citizens' Council sent off their press release, demonstrates their knowledge of segregationist propaganda and connections to the council movement.

When Foreman again outwitted about one hundred people the following day by taking Pamela Lynn in through the school's back door, about thirty women took their protest to Foreman's residence again. A procession of middle-aged and elderly women, and some men who stayed off to the side and observed and smiled at the women's actions, walked to Foreman's house. They stood in front of it, screaming. Most of the protesters, as the *Bogalusa Daily News* confirmed, were "members of the nucleus of hecklers, called by police 'the cheerleaders.'" The newspaper added that the cheerleaders "set up a doggerel chant outside the house which went: 'Nigger lover, nigger lover, nigger lover Jew; we hate niggers, we hate you.'"[116]

Cheerleaders jeer in front of the house of the Reverend Lloyd Foreman in New Orleans (Associated Press)

The cheerleaders continued to shout insults and also spat on the minister's lawn until the police ordered them off the sidewalk. A neighbor invited the group to continue the picket on his lawn. Daring Foreman to come out of his house, one of the women tied her scarf into a noose. Another cheerleader brandished a bandana and threatened to put it around Foreman's neck.[117] The cheerleaders harassed Foreman day in and day out, so that he eventually moved his family, not just once but several times to escape the women's group. The cheerleaders did not limit their attacks to his person and his house but also smashed his church's windows, threw red paint and tar on the porch to his house and the church walls, heckled Foreman during sermons, and distributed segregationist literature in front of the church.[118]

The cheerleaders favored violent imagery and death threats, and they put on an outrageous show. On December 2, 1960, *Telenews* showed a throng of about twenty young and middle-aged cheerleaders standing on the sidewalk. Confirming Steinbeck's description, the TV material shows how, as one cheerleader approaches, the rest of the group greets her cordially. Shortly thereafter, a procession of women and a few passive men in the background walk on the sidewalk toward an unknown destination. One of the cheerleaders holds up a "Remember Little Rock!" license plate while another ties an effigy of Mayor Morrison, whose name is scribbled on duct tape fastened to the doll, with a noose around its neck to it. They hold their work up to the camera while the group of women surrounding them laughs, cheers, and applauds.[119] The women's actions give the impression of being a rehearsed, theatrical stunt for the TV cameras. They sought to elicit as much shock value as possible while also still being genuine. The carnival-like character of the cheerleaders' behavior described by several eyewitnesses is also apparent in this newsreel.

Despite Foreman's comment that New Orleans was a "cosmopolitan city" and that the cheerleaders and other segregationist protesters did not "represent the total thinking of the community," the cheerleaders were a symptom of New Orleans's underlying problem. White supremacy and prosegregationist politics pervaded every social class in the city, and the continued inaction of the majority of the city's government, the police, the Catholic Church, and the business and civil community enabled the cheerleaders' reign of violence.[120]

The cheerleaders eventually crossed the line in early December 1960, however. Their physical attacks on white parents had reached a peak, and reporters remarked that the group's demonstrations "seemed to be the most bitter" since the downtown riots on November 16. Their protests had increased in number and intensity after white school attendance had risen for a week and the Orleans Parish School Board had been ordered to continue the desegregation process. "It doesn't make a damn," one of the cheerleaders shouted on December 1, 1960, "we are going to have segregated schools."[121] At this point, even sympathetic newspapers like the *Shreveport Journal* began to describe the cheerleaders as "fanatical." The cheerleaders had not only escalated the desegregation crisis with threats and physical attacks on people but, in what the *Pittsburgh Courier* deemed "downright ludicrous if the situation wasn't so tragic," some kicked and threw rocks at Foreman's dog. The pet's offense was its black and white fur, leading one of the cheerleaders to shout, "Look, he's even got an integrated dog."[122]

Some of the cheerleaders brought their children to their protests as well, and they can be frequently seen in press photographs of the cheerleaders. In one instance, one of them held her small child up to a TV camera, telling the boy to "tell them you hate niggers, say, I hate niggers," which the child refused to do. Children paraded up and down the street in front of Frantz with Confederate flags, recalling scenes at Little Rock's Central High School in early September 1957. A boy was trotting up and down the street wearing a sandwich board sign the front of which read "My daddy said no" and the back "Nigger, you'll never sit with me."[123] The cheerleaders incorporated children and teenagers into their performance in order to infuse it with the legitimacy of motherhood. The many young children present among the cheerleaders' protest gave the group the opportunity to raise the next generation of white supremacists. The group did not subdue its vulgarity in the children's presence, however, and sabotaged the image of maternalism with its own violence.

When Save Our Schools started its car lift service for white parents on December 1, 1960, the cheerleaders could see that the tide was turning against them. The women's group no longer directed its anger only at African Americans and white parents who defied the boycott but also turned onto reporters and bystanders at Frantz. The cheerleaders realized that George Dreyfous, an attorney and president of Louisiana's American Civil Liberties Union branch, was among them. Dreyfous had dropped off three elderly Save Our Schools members in his car. The cheerleaders began to chase Dreyfous and the women, who ran off in different directions. They had to be protected by a human police barrier from the segregationist women, who continued to curse at them. Seven policemen, the *Shreveport Journal* wrote, stood guard over the "three gray-haired ladies across the street from the howling 'cheerleaders.'"[124]

Times-Picayune reporter Jerry Hopkins had accidentally bumped into a cheerleader while taking notes on their attack on Dreyfous. Several cheerleaders then set on him and kicked, punched, and chased him, contending he had "struck one of them" with "a campstool," until police asked him to leave the scene. Two newsmen from *Time* and *Life* magazines, Ken Smelson and Greg Shukner, who were trying to film a television documentary about the city's school desegregation crisis, were also ordered to walk away. When Smelson asked one of the cheerleaders why she opposed interracial marriage, the cheerleader answered the question by whipping off her shoe and chasing the reporter down the street with it.[125]

The situation further escalated when some of the cheerleaders noted that Sydney Goldfinch was among the spectators. The white Tulane student was a member of the Congress of Racial Equality and had participated in sit-in demonstrations earlier that year. "That big gorilla," a Cheerleader shouted, "he was settin' in Woolworth's with them niggers." "That s.o.b.," another cheerleader exclaimed, and "the pack raced after him in full cry," the *New York Times* wrote.[126] The cheerleaders began to "manhandle" Goldfinch, shoving and kicking him and screaming "nigger lover" and "Jew bastard" at him until police freed him from the "pummeling by the irate women," as the *Times-Picayune* phrased it. One cheerleader screamed that she hoped Goldfinch would "have a bunch of mulatto grandchildren." Police escorted Goldfinch, who stated that he had not thought that the cheerleaders would recognize him, and three other young men who had accompanied him back to his car. As they drove off, the women thumped on the car roof.[127]

Goldfinch was the main target that morning. He was the symbol of a "race traitor." He had taken part in direct action with black civil rights activists and had, just like his fellow protesters, refused bail in service of their cause. The cheerleaders had "their people mixed up in terms of religion," the *Pittsburgh Courier* commented sarcastically, when they called Goldfinch a "Jew bastard," as Goldfinch was the son of a Protestant minister.[128] The women's choice of insult for a white student activist—whom they most likely perceived as an intellectual, given that Goldfinch was a philosophy student at Tulane University at the time—echoed the anti-Semitic, anti-intellectual, and racist views of Leander Perez and the Citizens' Council of Greater New Orleans.

The insult juxtaposed the women's and their neighborhood's working-class identity (emphasized by the *New York Times*'s verbatim quote of a cheerleader's unsophisticated accent) with the affluent, "silk-stocking" Garden District near Tulane University and its residents. By attacking Goldfinch, Dreyfous, and the Save Our Schools women, moreover, the cheerleaders prevented the establishment of a moderate, New Orleans counterpublic at the scene. They were defending their space, including the space of media representation they had created for themselves during the previous two weeks. The cheerleaders' violent strategy proved successful. After the group and fellow segregationists had escalated their protests in early December, exerting increasing economic and social pressure by harassing reluctant parents and supporters by telephone, in writing, in public, and at their homes, white attendance at Frantz again fell to single digits.

The increasingly cold weather, however, drastically reduced the number of protesters at Frantz. The police had begun to restrict the cheerleaders' and other segregationist protesters' access to the school area. A cheerleader core group, estimated by reporters to variously be "a handful," "two dozen," and frequently forty to sixty women continued their daily vigil at Frantz. They were less rowdy. They stopped their physical attacks on parents and bystanders. The *Alexandria Daily Town Talk* classified the remaining cheerleaders as a "band of bitter segregationist women" who were still determined to bully white parents who did not adhere to the school boycott.[129]

The smaller group abandoned its attempts to cover every entrance to Frantz. Instead of keeping up their shouting, most of the women calmly gathered around a parked car that displayed a sign saying, "Free Coffee for White Mothers" and shared a cup together.[130] The New Orleans Police Department's stricter interference thwarted new excesses of violence. Police moved the barricades further away from Frantz on all sides and thus kept most protesters away and out of earshot. Even the most determined cheerleaders could not come closer than standing across the street from the school's main entrance. Twenty women stood on a lawn across from Frantz, and police only allowed them to stay if they did not yell at the arrival of Ruby and the federal marshals. "We couldn't yell but we did give them the double-whammy," one cheerleader commented.[131]

The cheerleaders still taunted the federal marshals. Before police silenced them, they had repeatedly shouted, "Take care of her, you nurse-maids, . . . that's what we're paying you for," at the men. These taunts were more than an expression of white southern regional outrage at having their taxpayer dollars go to a federal institution that protected black people and enforced a verdict that was, in the cheerleaders' view, encroaching on Louisiana's states' rights. "Nursemaids" was a gendered insult that suggested that the federal marshals were emasculated by their desegregationist actions.[132]

Stymied in their physical street fight, segregationists turned to more indirect methods of intimidation. When citizen councils in New Orleans published the list of Save Our Schools drivers, which caused a wave of harassment directed at the activists, the carpool came to a halt. The number of white students who, with the support of the group, had reentered Frantz had peaked at twenty-three on December 6, 1960, but fell to seven pupils only three days later. President Mary Sand blamed this development on the harassment of her organization's volunteers and the children's parents. The number of white pupils never made it above ten again for the remainder of the school year. Meanwhile, white attendance at McDonogh was still at zero. Gail Etienne, Tessie Prevost, and Leona Tate were the only ones to remain in the building with eighteen white teachers, the principal, and administrative staff. About fifteen to twenty cheerleaders nevertheless continued to picket the school when it was in session.[133]

The Citizens' Council of Greater New Orleans did not give up either. It sponsored a rally on December 15, 1960, at the Municipal Auditorium, exactly one month after its successful rally in November. An estimated one thousand to twenty-five hundred accepted the council's invitation. The audience was thus a fourth of the size of that on November 15, which the council blamed on the cold and rainy weather. The crowd heard speeches from Superintendent Jackson and Frank R. Voelker, chairman of Louisiana's State Sovereignty Commission. Dr. Irwin, the chairman of the Citizens' Council of Greater New Orleans, brought a group of seven small white children to the stage, four of whom were in blackface. "On signal," the children kissed each other, upon which Irwin asked the audience: "That's just a little demonstration of what integration means. Is that what you want?" A unison yell of "No!" was the answer to his rhetorical question.[134]

The council urged its members to unify against desegregation and to encourage others to join the group. Speakers blasted New Orleans's city administration and the Orleans Parish School Board, which, in their view, had "adopted the 'inevitable' doctrine advanced by the socialists."[135] The council also insisted that the segregationist riot on November 15 had been a peaceful mothers' march that had been distorted by the press. Their bulletin made no mention of the "mothers'" violent behavior at the demonstration or in front of the two schools. On the contrary, the council used the fact that mothers took part in the downtown demonstrations as proof that the event could not have been violent. The bulletin then thanked the "dedicated and untiring work of many of its members" who had "substantially contributed to the successful boycott of the Frantz and McDonogh 19 Schools" and who had assisted parents who transferred their children to segregated schools.[136]

Similarly, the Association of Citizens' Councils of Louisiana benignly classified the cheerleaders' actions as "school mother pickets." Pretending that they were mere "mothers' pickets" served as an argumentative tool for organized segregationists to put pressure on New Orleans's city government and police department, while the cheerleaders' violence went consciously and self-servingly unmentioned in segregationist propaganda. The speaker for the association also noted that it had put its focus on hindering Save Our Schools' work.[137] On December 9, 1960, the association had asked the state's legislature to "investigate 12 persons whose automobiles are being used to take children to and from classes" at Frantz. Shreveport attorney and Association of Citizens' Councils of Louisiana's president Charles L. Barrett had sent the request to Joseph Thomas Jewell, speaker of the Louisiana House of Representatives. Barnett also sent a telegram to Morrison to inquire why he had used the "city police to thwart the school mother pickets of New Orleans and at the same time openly permit a notorious Communist-front organization to arrogantly promote integration and rile up racial trouble right under your nose."[138]

Despite most of the regional and national newspapers' and commenters' explicit or implicit consensus on the women's vulgarity and the subsequent message conveyed to their readership, not all readers agreed that the cheerleaders were terrorists. Readers of the conservative *Shreveport Journal*, for instance, continued to define the cheerleaders as mothers and praised the women's actions for their patriotic "bravery" and "spunk." Some of them criticized a perceived bias in media representations. Mrs. Roy Kinnaird of Springhill, Louisiana, wrote to the newspaper that the "determined mothers of New Orleans" who were leading the boycott against the schools "should be given medals for their bravery and fortitude instead of being castigated by the integrationist news services." She added that the cheerleaders were "patriots," and the nation depended on them to "remain free. . . . And to heck with such as J. Smelly Sight and his NAACP cheese-eating colleagues."[139]

M. C. Durr of Brookhaven, Mississippi, concurred and paid his compliments "to the finest group of loyal dedicated women at New Orleans I have ever read about in all the history books." Durr wrote that he had been moved to tears when reading about women's activities during religious persecutions in England

and of women's suffering during American wars, but, he explained, "at no time has there been shown a greater spirit of loyalty and devotion to country than is now being demonstrated by those New Orleans women."[140] John H. Mathews of Gibsland, Louisiana, wrote that the mother who said that November 30 court decision in favor of desegregation did not "make a damn," was a mother who was "putting the doctrine of 'interposition' into actual practice. She is practicing what she preaches. Her 'spunk' in the matter is admirable indeed."[141]

Giarrusso weighed in, too. He responded to an unfavorable *Shreveport Journal* editorial on December 9, 1960, which stated that the New Orleans Police Department's actions were aiding integrationists. In regard to the police's actions, Giarrusso wrote that "the white mothers" had been "allowed to demonstrate at will near and across" from Frantz "as long as their actions were confined to jeering." He boasted that not one of the mothers or other protesters had been arrested. Only after the cheerleaders, whom he referred to as "the mothers" throughout his letter, had thrown various items and physically attacked people did the police erect barriers. Giarrusso remarked that the women had "created conditions which could have easily led to the spilling of blood," a statement he evidently did not perceive as colliding with the pride he took in not making a single arrest. The police chief indignantly denied that the New Orleans Police Department was "aiding integration." In an editor's note to the letter, the *Shreveport Journal* then asked who the "outsiders" were who had "provoked the mothers."[142]

The women were more than just "concerned mothers," and what "provoked" them was the prospect of social equality with blacks. They embraced and acted on a virulent racist and anti-Semitic ideology. The group represented the aggressive and vulgar forefront of the city's massive resistance at the schools, a role not only unexpected but inaccessible to women before the crisis. The state of emergency that the cheerleaders' actions co-created not only invigorated massive resistance in the city but produced a performative space for them. As a result, certain gender-specific constraints regarding behavior public space were waived for them. Their performance extended the gendered frames in which the cheerleaders operated at the time. This was a reciprocal process. By taking actions that exacerbated the desegregation crisis, the women legitimized the actions they took in response to the desegregation crisis.

The language of local, regional, and national newspapers' coverage of the cheerleaders in November and early December was pointedly gendered. Repeatedly, newspapers wrote of "howling" and "screaming" women, and the *Shreveport Journal* called them "fanatical," insinuating that the cheerleaders were shrill and borderline hysterical.[143] Nonetheless, the cheerleaders were repeatedly referred to as "white mothers" in white-owned newspapers' coverage of the events, although the term was at times qualified when reporting on their most violent behavior.[144] News outlets with a less sympathetic disposition toward the cheerleaders (such as *Good Housekeeping* and, in particular, black-owned newspapers like the *Pittsburgh Courier*, the *New York Amsterdam News*, and the *Chicago Daily Defender*) expressed their opposition in equally gendered terms. "It is a reflection on Southern womanhood, and it's serious," wrote the *New York Amsterdam News* about the cheerleaders, with the *Pittsburgh Courier* chiming in that there were some "husky specimens of American 'white' womanhood" among the group.[145]

Several themes surface from the media's portrayal of the cheerleaders, and all of them illustrated gendered, racialized, and class-related perceptions and representations. First, the women were often described in a stereotypically feminine manner as mothers and housewives; indeed, some newspapers gave the impression that the group's behavior was close to hysteria by choosing dramatic and biased vocabulary for the women's protests. Second, newspapers and eyewitnesses who were critical toward the cheerleaders described the women as brute, unfeminine, and mannish, using that description as a way to express indignation at and signify the vulgarity of the cheerleaders. Finally, and closely linked to describing the cheerleaders as essentially unfeminine was the recurring emphasis on the women's bodily stature. Steinbeck, *Good Housekeeping*, the *Pittsburgh Courier*, and other outlets described the women as fat, chubby, or very large. Media outlets thus implied that the women lacked not only the genteel mannerisms but also the supposed physical delicacy of white southern belles. Photographs of the cheerleaders show a variety of body types, however. The repeated references to the supposedly large size of many cheerleaders reflected perceptions of their intimidating physical presence and the volume and intensity of their actions that were then projected on to their bodies. Not only were the women literally and figuratively taking up (public) space, but they were doing so without adhering to codes of conduct for white southern women in 1960.

The media also reported on cheerleaders' "bright, tight toreador pants," "tight sweaters," "multi-colored bandanas," and heavy makeup, or their "slacks," "tattered coats," headscarves, and "hair done up in curlers."[146] These descriptions portrayed the cheerleaders simultaneously as flamboyant and even sexually provocative, clad in form-fitting clothing, and as having an unkempt, lower-class, and vulgar appearance. The repeated focus on the women's appearances, both corporeal and sartorial, objectified the group. Some of the newspaper coverage was explicitly sexist, employing an essentialist and polarized understanding of womanhood (and manhood) and describing the women's behavior through disparaging comments about their physical appearance. The reports stressed the group's corporeality and lack of self-control.

In his account of his interviews with a cheerleader who had threatened to poison Bridges, psychiatrist Robert Coles repeatedly remarks on her physical appearance and eating behavior. The cheerleader in question—a mother of five—was, he writes, "an obese woman, plucking candy from cheap assortments during every visit I made." Coles then commented on the supposed irony that this woman, "who ate chocolates so passionately, . . . would poison a lonely chocolate-brown girl," thus employing the racist trope of black people as a commodity. His article pathologizes the woman's racism in terms of loneliness and the lack of prospects for her and her family. Coles also implies, however, that one of the attributes the woman lacked was self-control, both with respect to her eating habits and her emotions. She frequently became "weary" and then "surly," he notes, being a "very sad and very frightened" woman underneath.[147] Coles portrays the cheerleader as unable to adhere to moderation in any aspect of her life, be it nutrition, weight, language, emotions, or race relations. When Ruby entered Frantz, the cheerleader withdrew her son from third grade and left him without schooling for a whole year. Her son then attended a segregated private school, but by 1964 he was back at Frantz. His mother rationalized her reversal by stating that there were only few black students "in our schools now, anyway." Coles concluded that, in fact, abiding by her principles had cost her "more money than she could afford."[148]

For many observers, the cheerleaders were the epitome of white trash. The *Pittsburgh Courier* went as far as putting white in inverted commas when referring to the "specimen" of womanhood represented by the cheerleaders. Underlining this assessment, the *New York Amsterdam News* recounted an unconfirmed anecdote that one of the cheerleaders had asked her black next-door neighbor whether she could watch her children while she went to the school to protest. The newspaper also detailed how one of the women had offered to teach white children herself to make the boycott more efficient, although she had admitted that she never finished grammar school. Finally, the *New York Amsterdam News* paraphrased an unnamed social worker who had said that "a number of the jeering white women are on relief," and "the eggs they are tossing about so freely were purchased with welfare funds and would serve a better purpose in their refrigerators."[149] Newspapers did not have to use the expression "white trash." It was implied and clarified by the reporters' descriptions and choice of words. This marker of race and class was enhanced by gender. The cheerleaders, through their behavior and their appearance, performed a female white trash street politics. The Ninth Ward was their turf, and they sought to defend it by transgressive actions.

The Cheerleader Core Group

By December 9, 1960, the large crowds dispersed. It was at this time that a nucleus of cheerleaders became visible. This was a smaller group of women who were determined to continue their protest at Frantz. Notwithstanding their own, other segregationists', and media outlets' repeated emphasis that the cheerleaders were mothers of Frantz and McDonogh schoolchildren, not all of them had children at the schools or even children at all. The composition of the group was thus similar to that of the Mothers' League of Central High School on a smaller scale. In two interviews with the press in mid-December, this core group of cheerleaders gave insight into their social backgrounds, political beliefs, and daily actions. The *Alexandria Daily Town Talk* estimated that about forty to sixty women were now gathering daily at Frantz at this point, whereas the *UPI* interview that appeared in the *Chicago Defender* reported "about 40 regular members."[150] In total, the interviews introduced fourteen members of the cheerleaders' core group, ten of whom were identified by name or nickname. Both interviews featured a twenty-nine-year-old cheerleader named Mrs. Lee Hooks Jr. (identified as "Elsie" in the *Chicago Defender*), whom the rest of the group and police alike had baptized "the mother." Elsie Hooks was the cheerleaders' unofficial leader. She was a mother of two boys who did not attend either Frantz or McDonogh but an unidentified Catholic school. Hooks justified her participation in the protests by explaining that she was afraid that the parochial school system would be next if public school desegregation was successful. "I'll keep my kids at home ten years rather than send them to an integrated school. I didn't go to school with niggers and my kids aren't going to either," she proclaimed.[151]

Hooks was called "the mother" due to her perceived nurturing demeanor. She brought police officers on duty coffee in the mornings, stating that there was "nothing personal" about her opposition to the policemen. She hated "the job they are doing," though, and she was "bitter about the officials" who had sent the New Orleans Police Department. Hooks was a housewife and spouse to an electrician who, as she remarked, refused to work with black people. She declared that she admired Governor Jimmie Davis. "The governor is 100 percent on our side," she said. "I voted for him, and I bought every record he's got out. . . . Let him come down here with his guitar, and I'll sing along with him."[152]

Several other cheerleaders expressed a similar admiration for Davis. One of them was Antoinette Andrews, a forty-two-year-old mother of four grown-up children and grandmother to six school-aged grandchildren, who had participated in the mock funeral at the state capitol in November. In this interview, she agreed with Hooks: "We are going to win—we've got to. . . . Thank God we've got a governor who is sticking with us. . . . If all the governors were like him, we wouldn't have integration." Described as a "full-faced woman with streaks of gray in her black hair," the New Orleans native admitted that she had been a member of a local citizens' council since 1955. It is most likely that Andrews was a member of one of the local councils housed by the Citizens' Council of Greater New Orleans, either the St. Bernard Parish or the Metairie Citizens' Council of New Orleans, two of the councils founded that year.[153] At least to Andrews, the cheerleaders' activism was firmly based on a segregationist belief system that transcended the current crisis mode of Frantz's desegregation.

Neither Hooks's nor Andrews's children attended the schools, although the articles did not state whether one of Andrews's grandchildren previously had or not. To them, segregation was a matter of principle. Andrews was responsible for at least one attack on a passerby. When a black truck driver had stopped at a traffic light in front of the school three days prior to the interview, Andrews had thrown an egg at him. She had missed the driver's head, but the egg had smashed against the car's roof. The man glared at the women and drove off. Despite this incident, Andrews claimed that she knew what "most of the Negroes in this city" wanted, and, coincidentally, that was not to go to integrated schools. Other cheerleaders concurred. The people responsible for the escalation in their mind were the NAACP and New Orleans's city officials, in particular Mayor Morrison.

The sixty-year-old Vesta Alexander, one of the oldest cheerleaders, attended the demonstrations with her daughter and one of her grandchildren. Again, the defense of white supremacy was a multigenerational, family affair in New Orleans. Alexander remarked that Morrison was "not looking out for the interests" of white people: "We don't think we are getting a fair deal. We are not getting equal rights." That more than ninety police officers kept the cheerleaders and other protesters away from the school was one of the indicators, according to Alexander. Alexander's daughter, the thirty-one-year-old Marie Jenkins, claimed that her two children did not want to go to school with black pupils. The wife of a truck driver declared that her family was going to enroll nine-year-old Ray and eight-year-old Kathy, who were supposed to attend Frantz, in the white private school the segregationist Ninth Ward Private School Association established in St. Bernard Parish.[154]

The cheerleaders' reproaches and arguments, therefore, were quite similar to those of the Mothers' League of Central High School. The women blamed people whom they perceived as outside agitators or disloyal whites for the escalation of the crisis. Both groups believed the white elite had caved in to desegregationist pressure and had not properly supported Governor Orval Faubus in Arkansas or Governor Jimmie Davis in Louisiana, whom both groups admired for their (mostly verbal) radicalism.

Like the mothers' league, the cheerleaders claimed that they knew that local black residents did not want integration even as they harassed and intimidated them. The cheerleaders expressed a sense of loss of white entitlement and white privileges that the desegregation of "their" formerly white school gave rise to. They proclaimed that this was unfair toward working-class white people. The twenty-six-year-old "slim blonde" Betty J. Clement, a cheerleader who was single and had no children, told the *Alexandria Daily Town Talk* that "Negro schools are newer and prettier than the ones for white students, and they . . . will take over all the schools if we integrate."[155]

In contrast to the mothers' league, however, the cheerleaders had no interest in peaceful public principles. The women went on the offense whenever their protests were described as peaceful, and they complained about this demotion. "Peaceful?" one of them told the interviewer, "What do you want us to do, kill someone so you can say it's violent?" The cheerleaders' cursing, shoving, kicking, spitting, and hurling of various objects were deliberately violent means of protest. The group wanted to make headlines with their behavior—the more negative, the better. This not only ensured the kind of publicity that satisfied their attention seeking but had a political purpose: the cheerleaders created the impression that desegregation could not be achieved, at least not peacefully.

The cheerleaders made no attempt to mask their working-class background and to deny the white trash social status attributed to them. They exhibited a consciously vulgar and violent demeanor that would have been anathema to the mothers' league's effort to secure middle-class respectability. As reported in the *Chicago Defender*, one woman screamed, "They oughta lynch the dirty black dogs." A cheerleader named Ramona, described as a "thin redhead who wears thick glasses," said of Bridges that "every time I see that nigger come out of this school, I want to kill her."[156]

The cheerleaders did not discuss their attacks on Daisy Gabrielle in either interview, but when prompted about the Reverend Foreman, the "most consistent adversary" of Hooks according to the *Chicago Defender*, Hooks snarled that he was "a stupid, nigger-loving minister who is making trouble."[157] The cheerleaders admitted that the escalating violence and harassment toward Foreman resulted from his refusal to withdraw Pamela and the apparent futility of the group's prior protests. Responding to a question as to why the cheerleaders had smeared Foreman's porch with red paint, Marie Jenkins answered that the group was "booing and hollering, but it looks like the painting is the only thing left to do."[158]

Neither interview specified whether the women knew each other before they started demonstrating. The only reference to a friendship is to that between Ramona and her "freckle-faced friend Lil." That the cheerleaders employed nicknames for each other, however, demonstrates their group identity and a cordial relationship between the women. Indeed, one of the women's nicknames, "the Fullback," was a conscious play on the group's name. The Fullback was described as "tan" and "muscular" and as the tallest of the cheerleaders.[159] The cheerleaders played with both the pejorative media remarks about the physical appearance of some of their members and with the group's name by venturing into the same sports metaphors. The stature of the Fullback gave weight to the cheerleaders' protests and perceptions. The nickname was not deployed negatively, and the bearer of it did not object to it. On the contrary, the cheerleaders' nickname denoted the appreciation of an offensive asset.

The cheerleaders did not hesitate to express distinctly racist "reasons" for their activism. A fear of miscegenation was again at the top of the list. The Fullback declared that integration would "lead to intermarriage and result in murders and rapes." Cheerleader Betty Clement proclaimed that she opposed interracial marriage because mixing was "definitely wrong." Clement stated that she worked at an office where she ran a mimeograph machine (which perhaps answers the question as to how the group got the pamphlets they distributed). She did not talk to the three black delivery men who also worked at her place of employment. If all mothers withdrew their children from Frantz and McDonogh, Clement insisted, "we will win the battle." She omitted to mention that she had no children at either school; she was simply acting on her white supremacist convictions to justify her harassment of other parents.[160]

Lil maintained that she was "not mad at these four little girls" and was proud of the fact that she even had "taken milk to sick niggers" before. But she was worried "about four years from now," implying that the "real damage" of integration would become apparent when the children were teenagers and started dating.[161] In contrast, the unidentified cheerleader who regularly threatened to poison Bridges and later gave Coles an interview did not attempt to qualify her racism. She said that, in her view, black people were "lower than our dog in behavior. At least he knows his place and I can keep him clean. You can't even do that with them. . . . They're dirty and have you ever seen the food they eat? They eat pig food, and they eat just like them."[162]

The cheerleaders' white supremacist politics was clearly linked to an acute class consciousness. Most cheerleaders were housewives with no higher education and were married to working-class men. The mothers' league and other Little Rock segregationists resented that the "silk-stocking district" in Arkansas's capital had been spared, and the cheerleaders and New Orleans's grassroots segregationists felt the same. The cheerleader Coles analyzes told him that she had "enough to do just to keep going and to keep us alive without niggers coming around." This mother of five was poor, had not continued school after the eighth grade, and her husband—described as "wayward" and "fickly" by Coles—was an alcoholic who was only occasionally employed.[163]

Pathologizing the woman's racism, Coles concluded that this cheerleader projected her fear and anger about her husband's behavior and their family's situation onto Bridges, calling her viciousness toward Bridges a clear case of "scapegoating." As violent as her threats toward Bridges were, Coles noted that this cheerleader often made similar ones toward her own children, threatening to "choke them" if they misbehaved, a phrase uttered so regularly that the children did not seem "overly frightened" by it. Coles explains that the woman whose "life is cheated and impoverished" did not have "one reason" to join the cheerleaders. She was motivated by her hatred for black people, by the attitude of New Orleans's politicians and police, and by the fact "that there *was* a mob" that allowed her to join in and "express such despair and rage in public." This cheerleader had shouted at Bridges "because she was moved to cry out and protest her own fate."[164]

As apt as Cole's psychological assessment of this cheerleader may be, pathologizing her racism obscures the political motives of the group as a whole. It individualizes racism and removes her actions from their political context. Class-related deprivations were a pivotal factor in the women's motivation, but their race, gender, and performative actions were equally important and created a unique constellation. Segregationist women could be motivated by individual, class-related experiences of deprivation and a sense of entitlement that were fostered by everyday culture of white supremacy. In New Orleans, they were.

A closer examination of the women's social backgrounds, furthermore, reveals that the cheerleaders' core group was not uniform. At least two members of the group who were publicly known by name were unlikely cheerleaders: the housewife and self-taught Catholic Bible scholar Una Gaillot and Evelyn Jahncke, niece of Ernest Lee Jahncke, assistant secretary of the navy during Herbert Hoover's presidency. Neither of these women was an uneducated working-class white woman, and they were also both devout Catholics who interwove their segregationist resistance with their own religious reasoning. Religion was not a universally useful strategy for boosting segregationism, but lay people, including lay people in the Catholic Church, were able to utilize their religious beliefs for massive resistance. Their views were at odds with those of the church leadership that advocated for the desegregation of public and parochial schools.[165]

Una Gaillot identified herself as a cheerleader in the *Alexandria Daily Town Talk*'s interview in December 1960. She was not personally affected by the elementary schools' desegregation, as her three sons were older, but she was ideologically invested in the women's group's protests on a fundamental level. Gaillot saw herself as a Catholic (lay) scholar who was on a mission from God. She had founded her own segregationist organization, Save Our Nation, Inc., but refused to divulge its membership to the newspaper because "the NAACP will not do so" either.[166] Save Our Nation was a play on Save Our Schools, a name that indicated that in Gaillot's view, the question of desegregation was one of national importance and that desegregation could have catastrophic repercussions for American society as a whole. Whether Save Our Nation was ever more than a one-person committee, however, remains unclear. Echoing another cheerleader's statement of "I've been here from the start, and I'm staying to the finish," Gaillot took pride in the fact that she "had not missed a day" at Frantz since desegregation started.[167]

Gaillot became "one of New Orleans' most vocal militants," as historian Liva Baker notes. Gaillot was ultimately excommunicated by Archbishop Rummel in April 1962 alongside her fellow segregationist activists Jackson Ricau and Leander Perez.[168] Gaillot set her own segregationist biblical exegesis against Catholic doctrine, and Rummel justified her excommunication by stating that Gaillot was one of the segregationists who were "inciting others to rebel against church authority."[169] *Life* magazine captured Gaillot in a series of pictures taken shortly after her excommunication: Gaillot broke through a group of female visitors to the archbishop and approached Rummel on her knees. She asked him to "look up to heaven . . . and admit you know it's God's law to segregate." The eighty-five-year-old archbishop was unconvinced, and Gaillot's excommunication stood firm. A day later, Gaillot's husband, Bernard, asked Rummel to excommunicate him as well.[170]

The forty-year-old New Orleans native had self-published a twenty-two-page pamphlet in 1960, titled "God Gave The Law of Segregation (as well as the 10 Commandments) to Moses on Mount Sinai." In this pamphlet, Gaillot cited numerous examples of the Old Testament supposedly proving that segregation was God's will.[171] She argued that Adam had been white, that Jesus had therefore been white like his first ancestor, and that the Israelites, whom she equated with whites, were God's "chosen people."[172] Incessantly stating that her pamphlet was the ultimate "proof" of segregation's justice, Gaillot warned that God's wrath would be let loose on a desegregated nation.[173] In late August 1960, an anonymous letter reached Judge J. Skelly Wright that bore the hallmarks of Gaillot's rhetoric and included a photocopy of Save Our Nation's open letter to Archbishop Rummel, which the group (or one-woman venture) had published as an advertisement in a newspaper the same month. The open letter responded to Rummel's pastoral letter to the parish, which had been read at Sunday Mass on August 21. In his letter, Rummel declared his support for desegregation and urged fellow Catholics to pray for a just resolution to the impending desegregation crisis in New Orleans. In its lengthy reply, interspersed with bible citations, Save Our Nation sought to provide "proof that the Bible demands segregation!" The call by Sarah in Genesis for the separation of Isaac and Ishmael, according to Save Our Schools, meant that God wanted those "being of different stock or race" to separate. "Surely this must mean no playing together in schools also," the pamphlet stated, yanking the Old Testament to New Orleans's schools. Selectively quoting from Exodus, Esdras, and the Maccabees, Save Our Nation concluded that God did not create all men equal, that the devil was behind the integration efforts that divided the church, and that to integrate was "to refuse to obey" God's "law of segregation." The letter writer asked Wright to ask himself, "Since when does the minority rule? . . . Why is it, that the government officials send their children to private schools? . . . Do you believe in integrated marriages? Would you want your daughter married to a negro?"[174] Religious justifications for segregation were interwoven with worldly concerns, including those related to class, status, gender, and sexuality.

Massive resistance was a righteous task in Gaillot's view. The strife that had resulted from desegregation was not the result of segregationist resistance but, in her circular logic, proof of desegregation's sinfulness. Gaillot was an avid publicist for her cause; she sought to spread her message as far and wide and as often as possible. Even after the cheerleaders had stopped protesting in front of the schools, Gaillot continued her activism in the name of Catholicism interwoven with white supremacy. In an open letter to Cardinal Richard Cushing of Boston in December 1961, Gaillot charged that his recently announced lifetime membership in the NAACP was going against "God's chief law of segregation." Gaillot contended that the NAACP had been "organized by Anti-Christians" and that Cushing "should know that God curses all integrators."[175] Gaillot also contacted President John F. Kennedy by telegram and, echoing Cornelia Tucker's condescending tone in her letter to Robert Kennedy, advised him that if he complied with "Negro Martin Luther King" and the latter's supposed goal of a "Second Emancipation Proclamation," Kennedy would eliminate the separation of church and state. Gaillot addressed Kennedy as a fellow Catholic who should "know" to "uphold" segregation. "How can you grant this Negroes request and claim America is free?" she asked. "For further references check religions. All will not integrate because it is against their religious belief."[176]

Gaillot believed that governmental actions taken to assure the equal public treatment of all U.S. citizens in public institutions was tantamount to forcing a creed on its population, since, according to her, every religion on earth was opposed to desegregation. It was not she who was imposing her religious views on public institutions by opposing desegregation due to her religious convictions intermingled with white supremacy. Rather, by interfering with the imposition of her ideology on a public institution, the government was dissolving the separation of church and state. Carefully omitting that Dr. Martin Luther King Jr., was a pastor himself, Gaillot reduced him to "this Negro" and linked the continued oppression of black people to the nation's freedom. Her crude theses explain why a racist group like the cheerleaders would have appealed to her. Gaillot's exegesis served a white supremacist ideology. Never afraid of a theological argument, Gaillot challenged proponents of desegregation to show that her group Save Our Nation was wrong, stating that if her opponents had biblical proof, "we would be most happy to concede."[177] She asked the bishops of Atlanta, Savannah, and Charleston to meet her in New Orleans for a debate on Catholicism and racial justice in February 1961.[178] She concluded that "it was God's will that there be superiority and inferiority in more ways than one whether we like it or not. Will man go as far as demand equality even with God? Satan demanded equality."[179]

Gaillot did not mention whether she resorted to physical violence in her protests as part of the cheerleaders' core group—but it seems likely she did, as she herself stated that she had not missed a single day. Gaillot believed that the violent escalation of desegregation attempts across the South proved that God abhorred desegregation—a belief that could easily justify her own violent protest. When New Orleans's parochial schools set to desegregate in September 1962, she was one of the two picketers who carried protest signs in front of Archbishop Rummel's residence. The two middle-aged, elegantly dressed women held signs that read "Have Socialist Agents Infiltrated the Catholic Church? Integration Is Part of the International Communist Criminal Conspiracy."[180]

Even after the cheerleader core group dissolved before the start of the new school year, Gaillot continued to protest in front of public schools. On September 7, 1961, she picketed the token desegregation of Andrew Wilson Elementary School alongside fellow cheerleader Evelyn Jahncke. The women also returned to Frantz to register their opposition, carrying small protest signs that decried the "amalgamation of the races." Gaillot and Jahncke later sought a temporary injunction in civil district court to "restrain officials from interfering with peaceful assembly near public schools," alleging they had been "threatened" when picketing in front of Frantz. The case was dismissed.[181]

Gaillot would never abandon her belief that her biblical exegesis was the only true one, remarking that she "would be the biggest integrationist on the face of the earth" if she was "offered proof" that integration was morally valid. In 1965, Gaillot picketed against the appointment of black priests in the New Orleans archdiocese and, in the same year, protested her nineteen-year-old son's integrated army unit. "This is not Nazi Germany or a Communist country, but America," Gaillot stated, "and my son Kenneth must obey me under God and law." She said she would petition President Lyndon B. Johnson "to have her son guaranteed 'all white' military duty." Kenneth Gaillot did not comment but just said that he would let his mother "do the talking." Gaillot assured the media that her son's religious views mirrored her own. After Kenneth had to take the preintroductory army physical examination with black recruits present, Gaillot proclaimed that "the first amendment has been made void" and started to fly the United States flag at her home upside down.[182] In 1972, Gaillot went to court to insist on the racial labeling of blood in blood banks in state hospitals. In her petition, she stated that her "religious convictions do not permit her to accept a transfusion of blood from a person of another race." The federal appeals court dismissed her petition.[183]

Whereas Leander Perez was supposedly repentant, and the Church quietly readmitted him before his death, Gaillot had officially "renounced" the church in 1969. Nine years later, Gaillot watched her youngest son get married at the Mater Dolorosa Church from the family's car in the parking lot through the doors her nephews had propped open. She had done this twice before when her elder sons married in Catholic churches, and during several funeral services for relatives. The *Times Picayune* dedicated an entire page to Gaillot's story in 1978 after interviewing her at her house in Jefferson Parish, stating that the housewife had been called "witch, martyr, bigot, saint, racist, champion, 'screwball,' patriot, heretic, heroine . . . at one time or another" by both friends and foes. Gaillot continued to take pride in her defiance. She let *Life* readers know that she had "formally notified Archbishop Hannan, in a telegram shortly after Judge Perez' death, that, if she is in a hospital or in an unconscious state just prior to her death, she has renounced the Catholic Church." Gaillot also noted that according to her own research, "the last woman to be 'public[ally] excommunicated' before her was Joan of Arc," who had been known as "'Maid of Orleans,' while some people have referred to me as the 'Matron of New Orleans.'"[184]

In a 2005 interview, Gaillot reiterated her segregationist stance. She stated that there was "no way segregation is morally wrong and sinful. . . . The whole Bible from beginning to end is segregate, segregate, segregate!"[185] Gaillot also did not share the view that the cheerleaders were badly behaved. On the contrary, she stated in a 1987 interview that the protesting women were "ladies" and that they had "conducted themselves in a ladylike manner."[186] Gaillot did not acknowledge the cheerleaders' violent campaign, and neither did Evelyn Jahncke. Jahncke, another unlikely cheerleader, was a fifty-four-year-old New Orleanian at the time. As she emphasized in a letter to President Dwight D. Eisenhower, Jahncke was the niece of the former U.S. assistant secretary of the navy, Ernest Lee Jahncke. In 1936, Ernest Jahncke was expelled from the International Olympic Committee after he had objected to the games being held in Nazi Germany. Evelyn Jahncke referenced her uncle in the letter to Eisenhower, which reprimanded the former president for his public show of support for the Gabrielles in 1961 and insinuated that she was engaged in a righteous struggle. Like other massive resistance proponents, Jahncke suggested she saw "federal encroachment" as similar to the crimes of Nazi Germany.[187] Jahncke worked closely with Gaillot and continued to picket public schools with her. Jahncke's letter gives the lie to the idea that all cheerleaders were poorly educated. She delivered a lengthy statement that mocked James Gabrielle's supposed lack of professional skills, and she decried the alleged encroachment of the Supreme Court on Congress's legislative power, employing staples of conservative rhetoric.[188]

Eisenhower had expressed his dismay that James Gabrielle was forced out of his job as a water-meter reader. Jahncke advised Eisenhower that "the Mr. Gabrielle in question was not employed as a water-meter reader, as the local press would have all believe." She falsely charged that Gabrielle had been "tried for this position but made so many mistakes that he could not be used in this capacity."[189] Jahncke added that "municipal authorities" had divulged that they could not "understand why a man of two years of college cannot read a water meter." She suggested to Eisenhower that he had erred when he stated that the "government of laws, not of men" had to be supported by everyone in the case of desegregation. She wrote that he "surely must realize that the nine men of the Supreme Court are not the law making department of our nation" and that "Congress has never ratified the so-called 'law of the land,'" charging that the latter was "only the interpretation of the Supreme court and is contrary to all our history heretofore."

Jahncke thus employed a political argument prevalent in massive resistance: The Supreme Court encroached on the exclusive domain of the legislative branch by handing down a supposedly activist verdict. Challenging Eisenhower on a more personal level, she prompted him to "prove" his "sincerity and belief" and have his "grandchildren attend integrated schools as Mr. Gabrielle was doing, whom you compliment for his courage." She asked the former president if he had " the courage of the Gabrielle family." Finally, Jahncke implicitly dismissed James Gabrielle's actions as cowardly and unmanly, stating that if he "were a man of conviction and courage he would have stayed in New Orleans where," according to Jahncke, "there is not violence, as the press proclaims, but only peaceful picketing at the Frantz school in protest against the mixing of the races."[190]

In contrast to other cheerleaders, then, Jahncke was not explicitly proud of the violence the group was associated with. On the contrary, she refuted the suggestion that the group had ever been violent, and she charged that the newspaper reports were false. Jahncke outright denied any violence, echoing Gaillot's claim that the cheerleaders behaved like "ladies." Jahncke closed her letter by stating that she understood that Eisenhower attended church and was a Christian and asked whether he had "any respect for God's law of segregation." She advised Eisenhower to read Gaillot's pamphlet, which she enclosed with her letter. Jahncke concluded that she hoped that she, like the Gabrielles, would receive "a complimentary letter from you for taking a stand for individual rights for whites and constitutional rights as against the so-called law of the land."[191] Like Gaillot, Jahncke also established her own white supremacist group. She introduced the Southern Rescue Service as "a patriotic ladies' organization."[192] She had purposefully designed a badge for her organization that resembled a police badge, thus indicating the danger she believed desegregation represented, which she sold for $1.75 each.[193]

That at least some members of the cheerleaders' core group were not neighborhood women is also evidenced in one of the core group's last public protest performances in January 1961. Unlike at Frantz, the white boycott at McDonogh 19 had been complete since November 17, 1961. The cheerleaders were thus taken by surprise when the thirty-three-year-old father of six, John Thompson, sent his two sons, six-year-old Michael and nine-year-old Gregory, back to McDonogh. The children had attended a segregated school in St. Bernard Parish throughout the previous months, but Thompson stated that he felt that his children had not received "proper instruction" at their new school.[194] Thompson, an Alabama native, had moved to New Orleans the year before. He was an assistant fountain manager for the Walgreens drugstore company, and he had secured the support of federal marshals for his sons, who escorted the children to school.[195]

Word of the breached boycott quickly got around. Cheerleader Ethel Arieux, a neighborhood mother who had withdrawn her two children from the school in November 1960 and who had been arrested during the mothers' march, stated that she did not think there would be "many white children back in McDonogh." The thirty-three-year-old housewife continued, "I won't put mine back if I have to go to work to send them to private school." Arieux asserted that none of the white neighborhood families would follow Thompson's lead: "After all, that Thompson is an outsider. The boycott wasn't broken by one of us."[196]

On the next school day, two dozen cheerleaders waited for Gregory Thompson, who was the first of the Thompson children to reattend McDonogh. They yelled "traitor" when federal marshals accompanied the child into the school building.[197] The cheerleaders again set up a "schoolhour watch" on the scene to pressure the Thompsons into withdrawing their children.[198] Additionally, they announced a "mass demonstration" in protest of the Thompsons' school attendance. Yet even on their best picketing day, the group was incapable of rallying more than thirty-five to forty women.[199] Evidently, the majority of neighborhood women who were part of the performance of cheerleading were not part of the cheerleaders' core group. Their children now attended segregated schools in St. Bernard Parish. Only the most dedicated segregationist women continued the Operation Out in front of McDonogh.

The cheerleaders were still a force to be reckoned with, nonetheless, for the boycott breach had immediate repercussions for the Thompson family. The Thompsons were evicted from their four-room apartment by their landlady, Margaret Lezina, who evidently sympathized with the cheerleaders. The cheerleaders also expanded their protest by picketing a Walgreens store.[200] Between six and twelve white women picketed the parking lot of the Walgreens store in Arabi, a suburban neighborhood in St. Bernard Parish. The group vowed, "We'll get him fired if it takes a year." Wandering around the parking lot, the women carried protest signs that read "Walgreen's favor integration" and stated to the media that "they hoped their picketing would induce the national chain to fire Thompson."[201] Thompson, an ex-GI, was not fired by Walgreens, but the segregationist pressure drove his family out of New Orleans by February 1961.[202] "Jubilant segregationists," the *Shreveport Journal* reported, "whooped it up in front of the school when the news of Thompson's departure was learned."[203]

The women picketers' choice of location seems curious at first. Thompson was not employed at the Arabi store. The protesters stated that they were "mostly mothers of McDonogh 19 students" to the tipped-off press at first, but they later admitted that "they chose the Arabi store for picketing because it was near their homes."[204] As the *Alexandria Daily Town Talk* noted, the branch was "miles from the McDonogh 19 school district." The women then explained that they had picketed this particular store "because we can't do anything like this in the city. The police would arrest us—we know that."[205]

The women's actions and comments show that these segregationist women were not only capable of strategically planning protests but that other members of the cheerleaders' core group were not Frantz and McDonogh neighborhood residents. They were dedicated segregationist activists, perhaps even involved with the St. Bernard Citizens' Council that boasted a high female membership. That these women chose a store in Arabi—one of the citizens' council movement strongholds in which elementary schools now housed hundreds of former white Frantz and McDonogh students —further illustrates the ties between cheerleaders and the council movement. Either some of the cheerleaders were residents of St. Bernard's Parish or the cheerleaders had enough social capital within the area's segregationist movement to mobilize other women. One could further speculate whether the protesters at Walgreens were affiliated with the cheerleaders at all or might even have been financially compensated for their protests. The women picketing Walgreens effectively staged a publicity campaign through their performance. It would be one of the cheerleaders' last direct actions, staged on the last day of the 1960–61 school year. On June 9, 1961, a mere dozen white, young and middle-aged women picketed Frantz, sporting protest signs that stated, "It's Not an Old-Fashioned Idea to Fight for States Sovereignty" and "We're Mothers with Old-Fashioned Integrity and Pride in Our Race!"[206]

Although not all of the cheerleaders' core group can be subsumed under the assumed identity of white working-class neighborhood mothers, the lower social status of the majority of cheerleaders infused their activism, self-perception, and self-representation. The self-identification and external description as working-class people was equally present in the operations of the Ninth Ward Private School Association, which attached explicit class consciousness to its segregationist activism.

Class Consciousness and White Flight in the Ninth Ward

On December 8, 1960, the newly constructed Arabi Elementary School Annex in St. Bernard Parish opened its doors to 197 white students from New Orleans. Armand Duvio's Ninth Ward Private School Association kept its word. Two empty buildings in Arabi were converted into a private school for the white students of Frantz's and McDonogh 19's first three grades. C. E. Vetter, one of the initiative's spokespeople who was also a South Louisiana Citizens' Council official, declared that "so many volunteer workers" had shown up at the building, "some of them had to be turned away."[207] Louisiana's superintendent of education, Shelby M. Jackson, declared that children attending Arabi Annex would be provided with free textbooks by the state (as all other schools were), and Governor Davis signed a bill into law that provided grants to students "attending private, non-profit schools." By the end of the 1961–62 school year, Ninth Ward private school students had received over $100,000 through the grant-in-aid account of the state legislature. Armand Duvio explained that the facilities completed at Arabi Annex included eleven classrooms, a playground area, and a cafeteria "in which lunches will be prepared and served by mothers of the students."[208] Eight teachers stood at the ready.[209] Although none of the cheerleaders said so, it is possible that some of the neighborhood women might have been part of the group of mothers who now worked at the school.

Duvio and other spokespeople expressed pride in their accomplishment. In contrast to the women of the mothers' league, the cheerleaders and other segregationist parents of the Ninth Ward did not attempt to transcend their working-class identity in their rhetoric and behavior but instead relished in it. In a TV interview about the Arabi Annex, Duvio asserted that the school was an accomplishment by the people who were deemed a "low, poor class," who had no other choice after Judge Wright refused to "take the colored children out of the school." The only thing they could do, Duvio stated, was to provide their own, segregated facility. He claimed that "if Ms. Gabrielle and Reverend Foreman like their children to go to school with a colored child, . . . if they're doing it in good faith and not being paid off, . . . well, this is fine." Duvio suspected an integration lobby behind Gabrielles' and Foreman's actions that conspired against the Ninth Ward's common people. If Judge Wright

> wants to integrate his daughter with them [black pupils] instead of sending her to a big swanky private school, or Mayor Morrison, his children, or the rest of these people that's trying to push it, hooray! Let them go to Frantz school right now. But they're not doing it. They thought they had a low, poor class of people down here that they could push this on, and they found out that we were poor, most of us lack money, but these people don't lack any spirit, as you can see. These people are workers. And I mean, if only you could have shot this inside of our building down here that we put up, you'd have seen it. We may have a first-class system set up. Better, actually better, than what they had at William Frantz school.[210]

To Duvio, "they" were the political, judicial, and economic power structure of New Orleans who "pushed" integration on the "we" of the Ninth Ward's working class. What this "we" lacked in economic and cultural capital, Duvio stressed, they made up "in spirit." The white people of the Ninth Ward had inner-community social capital. They built their own white school through manual labor. Duvio's self-conscious defiance of the Ninth Ward's public perception was echoed in some of the cheerleaders' public statements. Equally protesting the perceived "push" on their neighborhood to integrate its schools by the city's elite, the cheerleaders displayed a sign at their pickets at William Frantz that stated "The law of the land is if you are poor, you mix. If you are rich, forget about it. Some law."[211] Cheerleaders also expressed a clear class consciousness in certain statements. The women approached their protest with a work ethos. Gaillot and Hooks took pride in not having missed more than two days of the group's picket in front of Frantz. When a reporter told one of the cheerleaders, who was complaining about the cold during their picket in early December, that she could "go home," she answered, "You don't think we have to stay? . . . We're working, too; we can't leave."[212]

In contrast to the mothers' league's two most prominent and self-identified "working mothers," Margaret Jackson and Mary Thomason, however, the members of the cheerleaders' core group were not referring to a profession but to their protest as their work. The majority of cheerleaders were introduced as housewives, but they went to work by organizing a disciplined, professional protest. They understood their performance as a job that had to yield media attention, thus keeping the crisis alive and proving that the spirit of the Ninth Ward could not be easily subdued by the city's elite and that integration could not be successfully accomplished in New Orleans. Creating publicity so as to unify the city's segregationist movement necessitated a particularly vicious campaign against white parents deemed traitors. Taking pride in their identity and not seeking to acquire cultural capital, the majority of the cheerleaders embraced their perceived vulgarity, which was closely tied to their exhibition of corporeality. The cheerleaders were doing their own form of manual labor.

By September 1961, the cheerleaders—with the exception of Una Gaillot and Evelyn Jahncke—had disappeared as suddenly as they had appeared the previous year, and token desegregation in New Orleans proceeded in four elementary schools. A cartoon in the *Southern School News* depicted two cheerleaders, drawn as stocky, middle-aged, poorly dressed women. Two small, well-dressed, and intimidated-looking black girls with books in their hands pass them by on their way to school when one of the cartoon cheerleaders tells the other, "This year I feel all screeched out."[213] The cheerleaders continued to be associated with the escalation of the New Orleans school desegregation crisis as well as with the figuratively and literally poor behavior of shabbily clad white working-class women.

Bridges continued to attend Frantz, and eventually other black pupils enrolled as well, but the Orleans Parish School Board decided to resegregate McDonogh 19 by turning it into a school for only black pupils. Gail Etienne's, Tessie Provost's and Leone Tate's parents protested with the help of Alexander P. Tureaud. The third graders were reassigned to the formerly all-white T. J. Semmes School in the fall of 1962. Once again, the three black girls had to desegregate a school. They experienced "the worst year of their lives," they later recalled, due to the constant racist harassment by white supremacist pupils and teachers.[214] At the start of the 1961–62 school year, fewer than ten other black pupils began to attend New Orleans's four desegregated elementary schools. Giarrusso deployed "60 uniformed and plainclothes officers" to each one, ordering them to arrest "any agitators" in order to avoid the violence of the previous year. School board president Riecke expressed his optimism that New Orleans's citizens would be "just as law-abiding as those in Atlanta" during the Crescent City's second year of token desegregation. In Louisiana, sixty-six of the sixty-seven school districts remained segregated.[215]

That the cheerleaders did not reappear after their initial protests in 1960 and 1961 can be explained by the fact that hundreds of Frantz's and McDonogh's former white students continued their education in the still segregated schools in St. Bernard Parish. The *Southern School News* reported that "some 325" of former Frantz and McDonogh students "went to the Arabi annex and another 200 were sprinkled around other St. Bernard schools."[216] Historian Juliette Landphair has shown that white flight played a significant role in the demise of segregationist protests in front of the Ninth Ward's desegregated schools. By 1970, the number of residents in the ward's Florida area, for example, had dramatically declined from 2,110 residents to 536, "a loss of over 77 percent of the white population." By September 1962, more than four thousand applicants had asked for a state tuition grant under the state legislature's "freedom of choice plan" to be able to attend segregated, private schools in New Orleans and its metropolitan area.[217] When the Archdiocese of New Orleans desegregated its elementary schools and high schools in September 1962, Gaillot and the Catholic Layman's League, headed up by the Citizens' Council of Greater New Orleans official and KKK member Jack Helm, asked fellow Catholics to "withhold church contributions" and to "establish more private schools. " Gaillot proclaimed that she would withdraw her sons from their Catholic high schools.[218]

That the cheerleaders could or would not rally for a second or third year of direct action in front of the schools did not mean that they had abandoned their white supremacist convictions. Despite their greatest efforts, token desegregation had become a fact, and the civil rights movement continued to make headway. The cheerleaders, along with many other white parents in the Ninth Ward, chose to evade desegregation rather than to violently (and ultimately unsuccessfully) confront it another year. The foundation for this evasion was built by the Ninth Ward Private School Cooperation and continued with further school privatizations.

Cheerleading was a performance, a display of a corporeality that women used to transgress gendered boundaries and thereby secure maximum public impact. This performance signified the cheerleaders' predominant working-class background and blue-collar ethics. The majority of cheerleaders were not interested in conveying sophisticated airs. The working-class neighborhood women expressed their opposition to desegregation, rooted in their awareness of a lack of economic capital (which significantly minimized their political influence, a long tradition in the Ninth Ward) and in white supremacist ideology as a belief system that underwrote the neighborhood's whites' few everyday privileges, a form of cultural capital distinguishing them from their black neighbors.

Just as in massive resistance writ large, the cheerleaders were not all the same; they were different ages, from different social backgrounds, and had different motivations, but they were still united by a shared cause. Their common denominator was the defense of white supremacy. The majority of the female protesters who identified as cheerleaders, both in performance and as a core group, were aware of their social status and linked it to their protest.

CHAPTER 4

Female Segregationists in Charleston

Cornelia Tucker's name had long been familiar to readers of South Carolina newspapers, as she had written numerous letters to the editor, particularly to the conservative Charleston newspaper the *News and Courier*, throughout the 1950s and 1960s. In late November 1957, two months after the Little Rock crisis had escalated, Tucker again took to her typewriter to craft a response to the Reverend James Vanwright, a letter from whom the *News and Courier* published a few days earlier. Vanwright, a black African Methodist Episcopal minister, had led the establishment of Dixie Training School, later called Berkeley Training School, the first public school for black pupils in Moncks Corner, South Carolina, in 1900.[1] Fifty-five years later, however, Bishop Frank Madison Reid suspended him from the church roll of elders, because in an article for the *News and Courier*, Vanwright advocated against racial integration. In November 1957, the reverend reiterated his stance in a letter to the editor. He argued that slavery in North America had made Christians out of heathens, and that since the Declaration of Independence, the United States had made citizens out of blacks, who now had to "learn the science of self-government" and "to live together as citizens and separately as a race."[2]

In her response, Cornelia Tucker thanked Vanwright in the name of Charleston. "Here," she wrote, "the white and the colored races have lived together in a relationship of affectionate interdependence based on mutual understanding." With familiar condescension, Tucker explained that white Charlestonians took "great pride in the advancement of our colored friends in education, in the professions and in business," adding that black people had "enriched our religion with their simple faith and emotional response." She praised what she saw as African Americans' special musical talent but warned that both black and white people should "bear in mind that all this did not come about by forced mixing of these races." Instead, white people's "intelligent appreciation" of black people's "best qualities" and the "active promotion" of black people's "efforts" had led to the latter's advancement. "White people of the South still have an innate sense of responsibility for the care of their colored friends," Tucker concluded, although "this relationship will inevitably be destroyed by forced mixing of the races."[3] Tucker's maternalism expressed a traditionalist, upper-class white Charlestonian attitude toward race relations. Charleston's elite eschewed open race baiting, instead making patronizing statements about how racial harmony had been achieved between the races. This chapter explores the massive resistance strategies of female grassroots agitators in Charleston and its surrounding Lowcountry from the early 1950s to 1963. Their stories serve as a contrast filter to the working- and lower middle-class performative strategies developed by the mothers' league in Little Rock and the cheerleaders in New Orleans. In Charleston, the most vocal and prominent female massive resistance proponents were middle and upper class and had previously been sociopolitically active; they relied on their economic, cultural, and social capital to successfully establish links to broader conservative networks in the region and the nation. The performative spaces created by these women, therefore, differed from those of their fellow white supremacist agitators in Little Rock and New Orleans. In short, the women of Charleston, too, used theatricalization and medialization as tools to legitimize their public activism, but as elite women, they did not need to use the strategies of escalation that working-class women relied on. In Charleston, hardline white supremacy was easily promoted in chiffon robes.

Grassroots activism played an important role in the Palmetto State's massive resistance campaign, and gender discourses and women's activities were a vital element. Little Rock's mothers' league and New Orleans' cheerleaders were women's groups that emerged from crises and helped to escalate them. These groups co-created and took advantage of a state of emergency. South Carolina's strategy, which circumvented a clearly localized desegregation crisis, not only allowed the state to evade token desegregation until after the zenith of the southern resistance movement but also resulted in a smaller and more scattered pattern of female segregationist activism. South Carolina politicians may have prided themselves on having avoided the violent escalations that took place in Little Rock and New Orleans, but Charleston emerged as a hub of white supremacist grassroots resistance nevertheless.

Opportunities for public transgression that had been afforded to more marginalized actors during localized crises in Little Rock and New Orleans, however, did not present themselves in Charleston or any other part of South Carolina. Put differently, the carnivalesque performative space created by working-class segregationist women in Little Rock and New Orleans, which allowed them to transgress public scripts, was unnecessary in Charleston. Segregationist women in the public eye in Charleston and in the Lowcountry, unlike their counterparts in Little Rock and in New Orleans, were predominantly middle-aged and senior, middle- to upper-class women. They had been active in conservative political causes before their involvement in massive resistance, and some of them had a meaningful standing in conservative club activism. Therefore, their approaches, their tactics, and their rhetoric differed, although women's massive resistance in South Carolina's Lowcountry, like that of women's activism in Little Rock and New Orleans, illustrates the links between segregationist resistance and broader conservative ideologies after the Second World War, which included social traditionalism, anticommunism, laissez-faire capitalism and opposition to governmental interventions, and freedom of choice.[4] Such ideologies comported with the beliefs of grassroots segregationists in South Carolina, justifying their defense of white supremacy and allowing them to transcend a southern sectional experience and enlist the support of whites across the nation. This chapter shows that, in contrast to the mothers' league and the cheerleaders, Charleston's segregationist women possessed the social and cultural capital to successfully establish lasting networks.

The Women of the Council

As in Arkansas and Louisiana, massive resistance in South Carolina was male dominated both from the top down and from the bottom up. The state's KKK experienced a revival after *Brown* and became the second-largest grassroots organization after the council. Although the Klan was universally condemned by politicians and the media, attendance at Klan rallies grew and was regularly estimated to be between "several hundred" to the Klan's exaggerated number of fifteen thousand people. An observer at a KKK rally in the town of Denmark noted his bemusement at the large "number of women in the procession." It had never occurred to him, he stated, "that females were in any way connected with the hooded order," let alone "would be parading in their own hooded robes."[5] The KKK was politically influential in a number of South Carolina counties, such as Greenville and Orangeburg. As membership in the state's council movement shrank in the mid- to late 1950s, rumors abounded that several chapters had been subverted by the Klan. This concern caused Baxter Graham, leader of the Association of Citizens' Councils of South Carolina, to issue an official council charter in 1958, obliging every member to adhere to the law.[6]

The Orangeburg Citizens' Council adopted a strategy that was successful in many southern states by employing a masculinist rhetoric of propaganda. The group frequently alluded to a sexualized discourse that spoke to the perceived dangers of miscegenation. Building on the traditional conception of southern white women as the gatekeepers of white racial purity and their need for protection, the Orangeburg Citizens' Council's publications routinely cast white women as victims of educational desegregation.[7] Claiming that the NAACP's secret aim was "intermarriage," in 1956 the Orangeburg Citizens' Council published an alleged report of two anonymous white female teachers at integrated schools in Washington, D.C., one of whom claimed that "her hardest job was to make the colored boys keep their trousers buttoned or zipped," an image that is reminiscent of the flyer distributed by Arkansas segregationists depicting a predatory "integration" demon chasing after southern white womanhood, his pants already undone. According to the Orangeburg Citizens' Council's pamphlet, another female teacher reported that "white girls" at her school were "afraid to lean over the drinking fountain to get a drink of water—because of the obscene actions of the milling negro boy in the halls." This depiction, effectively voiding white girls and women of agency, played into several aspects of massive resistance's propaganda and conservative fears. Segregationists tapped into a moral panic about potentially liberalizing sexual attitudes (tied to women's sexual agency), a fear of a loss of power and gendered and racialized entitlements inherent in white supremacy, and worries about juvenile delinquency.[8]

This public stylization of white female victimhood, however, was belied by the fact that white South Carolina women were vocal segregationists. Women across the South were members of local councils and affiliated their women's groups with councils. Some women even rose to the ranks of council officers. In Columbia's metropolitan area, Jesse Mathewes directed the St. Andrew's council with four other men. Charleston was an enclave of council activism, and copies of membership cards of the Charleston County Citizens' Council show that not only men but a number of their wives were members. Mrs. Earl R. Smith and Mrs. E. G. Dawson became directors of a Charleston council alongside six other men.[9]

The chapter at John's Island and Wadmalaw Island of the Charleston County Citizens' Council, which served as the umbrella organization for a number of local councils, was a hub of segregationist women's massive resistance. Located on the Lowcountry coastal line outside of Charleston, John's and Wadmalaw Islands belong to the Sea Islands that used to house many of the plantations that contributed to Charleston's antebellum status. Historian Steve Estes argues that the "geographic isolation of these islands and their large black majorities" not only allowed for the survival of creole cultures and languages, such as Gullah, but also contributed to the location's "extreme poverty" after the Civil War and to its "virulent racism." John's Island in particular had a reputation for racist violence in cases of the "smallest infractions of the social order."[10]

The Citizens' Council of John's and Wadmalaw Island was established in December 1955. According to a handwritten and perhaps only partial membership list of this council chapter's 250 members, 71 were women, often listed with their husbands. Hence, women constituted 28.4% of the members in this sample.[11] White women, however, were not mere appendices of their husbands. The minutes of the chapter's first organizational meeting in 1956 show that among the four officers elected, one was a woman, Margaret Beckett, who became the group's treasurer. The council's newly elected executive committee of twelve, moreover, had three women among its members. Elected for a three-year term was Mrs. C. B. Stevens, for a two-year term Mrs. Roger Robertson, and for a one-year term Mrs. N. F. Zittrauer. The executive committee invited Association of Citizens' Councils of South Carolina's executive secretary S. E. Rogers to "speak to the council" at the first meeting, which was held on February 3 and was "combined with a Fish supper given by the John's Island Civic Club." The choice of locale was not a coincidence. One of the council's executive officers, Mrs. N. F. Zittrauer, was listed as the John's Island Civic Club Ladies Auxiliary's head in August 1955. Zittrauer had been mentioned in the *News and Courier* when the civic club and its ladies' auxiliary adopted a resolution against school integration in John's Island.[12]

At least one of the council's female officers was thus no newcomer to local politics and segregationist activism. Zittrauer made use of her experiences as ladies' auxiliary executive to foster the connection between the John's Island Civic Club and the local citizens' council. She used her knowledge of group activism and leadership to expand her political action. Zittrauer's commitment to white supremacist politics exemplifies a trend among Charleston's female segregationists. Women who participated in massive resistance in the city and in a number of other locales in the state understood the movement as either a part or an extension of their previous conservative political activism. Not only did the John's Island and Wadmalaw Island Citizens' Council have a substantial female membership and a significant number of female elected officers, but there were women on all eight of its committees. Five of these committees were marked "regular" and three "special": four women, including the executive committee members Stevens, Zittrauer, Robertson, and Mrs. B. N. Hayes were members of the regular membership and finance committee. Margaret Beckett, the council's treasurer, was part of the regular legal advisory committee. Interestingly, although the membership of women in these committees suggests they were included in agendas regarding "everyday" concerns of the council, one could argue that both committees seem to have relegated women to supporting roles, as their jobs revolved around keeping track of members and membership dues, monitoring court orders, and taking care of other administrative work, and they seem to not have been part of the policy-making processes of the council in an official capacity.

One special committee solely comprised by women was the social affairs committee. Its members were Mrs. W. M. Hamilton (the council chairman's wife), executive committee members Robertson, Stevens, and Zittrauer, Mrs. Lee R. Fugiel, Mrs. Geo. W. Hills, and Mrs. Mary E. Fehbert.[13] Although the council's records do not state what type of activities the social affairs committee undertook, it seems reasonable to speculate that the women were responsible for social "outreach" or even in recruiting members from the white community. The branding of the majority of council women's activism thus accorded with typically gendered roles. Female activists' purpose was to communicate, to handle "social issues," to establish networks and secure participation from the community. All of these tasks, however, demonstrate segregationist women's crucial part in grassroots mobilization and their responsibility for organizing and policing white communities. Women also had a place in the council movement's formal power structure, as several women were among the group's executive committee and, therefore, jointly in charge of representing the council.

Elizabeth McRae describes women's prosegregation community work as that of "constant gardeners."[14] Indeed, women in South Carolina used the social networks they had built during years of community activism to defend segregation, the white supremacist hierarchization of society, and the everyday privileges it afforded to white people. Segregationist women, particularly the Lowcountry segregationist women who were well versed in community activism, had amassed social and cultural capital. They took on an intermediate leadership role that bridged the gap between the institutionalized leadership of segregationist organizations and the broad constituency of the prosegregation white community on a micromobilizational level.[15]

As Karen Cox shows in her study on the United Daughters of the Confederacy, elite southern women took leadership positions in the movement to memorialize and vindicate the Confederacy in the late nineteenth and early twentieth centuries. Members of the United Daughters of the Confederacy heralded the Lost Cause in order to defend white supremacy and states' rights, and they "sought to instill in white children a reverence for the political, social, and cultural traditions of the former Confederacy."[16] This new generation was, Cox notes, "actively engaged in massive resistance" in the mid-twentieth century and employed similar states' rights rhetoric.[17] Female activists in the massive resistance movement used the same tactics of the United Daughters of the Confederacy, moreover, when they demanded the screening of textbooks in public schools.[18] Conservative club women activists in South Carolina in the 1950s and 1960s constantly publicized the white southern cause, and monitoring public school education was one of their tools.

The John's Island and Wadmalaw Island chapter developed a practicable model of women's activism that made use of both women's supposed organizational and communicative abilities and white middle- and upper-class southern women's respectability to publicly further massive resistance. Electing women as executive officers simultaneously allowed for a subversion of the separation of the spheres. The small size of this council chapter encouraged women's participation and served as an opportunity structure that allowed them to take charge. The comparatively small size of South Carolina's citizens' council movement more generally, then, fostered women's prominence within it.

Geographically isolated from this Lowcountry network, one female segregationist in South Carolina formed her own group: Sara Sullivan Ervin of the northwestern mill town Ware Shoals, located in Abbeville, Greenwood, and Laurens Counties, founded the Women's States Rights Association in 1956. Ervin described her organization as a fraternal and patriotic association that pledged to promote "constitutional government, states' rights, individual liberties and freedom of choice" and "to combat socialism and communism." Whether Ervin, who resided on a cattle farm, recruited any other members to her association, however, remains unclear. Ervin carried out her work through "a large personal mailing list (people who have bought my book & friends)," to whom she sent segregationist material and her own writings. Ervin was no stranger to political and historical research and writing. She previously published a book titled *South Carolinians in the Revolution* in 1949 that listed the names of men and women who had fought in the Revolutionary War.[19]

Before founding the Women's States Rights Association, Ervin declared her interest in the segregationist Grassroots League in Charleston as well as in the state's citizens' council movement. Ervin stated that she "would like to help in any movement, backed by reputable and patriotic southerners, who believe in SEGREGATION, and States Right and who wish to fight Socialism & Communism." Her search for the appropriate organization, however, was unsuccessful. The mission of her own organization combined her segregationist core convictions with libertarian rhetoric—a conscious strategy Ervin outlined in a letter to Charleston segregationist Stanley Fletcher Morse. Ervin wrote that she had read about the Federation for Constitutional Government and sought to organize an affiliated group in the state, believing that "the people would more readily organize under some innocent sounding name." White people were too "AFRAID of this NAACP" to publicly organize otherwise. Ervin, nonetheless, continued that she was "sure that we have many patriotic South Carolinians who would 'dedicate their lives and fortunes' to save the white race and constitutional Government, if we can only FIND them, and USE them."[20]

Frequently using all capital letters for emphasis, Ervin started her segregationist activism as an avid letter writer to both segregationist groups, people in South Carolina, and Governor Timmerman shortly after the second *Brown* decision. In July 1955, Ervin beseeched Timmerman to intensify the state's resistance campaign, particularly regarding potentially moderate or integrationist public school teachers. Ervin was chiefly concerned with countering what she perceived as constant publicity campaigns by the NAACP in favor of school desegregation. To her, publicity was "the most potent weapon of all." In another letter to Timmerman, she asked him to appoint a segregationist publicity committee to work alongside the Gressette Committee and put "our side" in "EVERY ISSUE OF THE NEWSPAPERS." Ervin wrote that she had "been raising Cain in my own community about Integration, and dozens of people have complained to me, that they don't know what the Gressette Committee is DOING—that they don't like all this SECRECY—they feel NEGLECTED." Ervin also urged Timmerman to not rely solely on "a few prominent persons or Committees" and to not "ignore the people" but to take them into his confidence and thereby get their help for the segregationist cause.[21]

Ervin's letters show that she initially did not have any intention of forming a group herself. She was rather trying to learn more about existing segregationist organizations. Ervin saw herself as a grassroots member of massive resistance, not as a group leader. She thought that she could "contribute most by writing something along for the papers." She thus asked Morse whether he could provide her with a list of newspapers that covered the entire state and were willing to print regular segregationist contributors like herself. Ervin was in search of a leader for massive resistance in South Carolina, stating that "we need LEADERS. Let's pray for another WADE HAMPTON. THURMOND could have led us, before he went to the Senate. We need a man, UNAFRAID & competent & one the people KNOW & are willing to follow." Again, she asked Morse whether he could think of "such a man, we might DRAFT," proposing a "smart lawyer to lead our cause if we can get him."[22]

Her mention of the Confederate cavalry leader Wade Hampton and her reference to drafting a "leader" show that Ervin thought of massive resistance as a battle that had to be fought in order to avoid a second reconstruction. Ervin reported that she had tried her hardest to encourage white people in her small community. Now, she was in search of "a man," she wrote, to lead the fight for continued segregation, a leader who encouraged and made use of grassroots organizing. Ervin's Women's States Rights Association, therefore, followed in the tradition of Little Rock's Mothers' League of Central High School. Like the league, the Women's States Rights Association was founded only after Ervin failed to find a satisfactory outlet for her political activism in other established segregationist groups.

Ervin was not the only female segregationist grassroots activist who complained about the complacency of leading segregationists in the Palmetto State. Jessie Allison Butler, a former teacher and Charleston Citizens' Council member, reported that she, like Ervin, had written to "representatives in Washington time and time again, also the state and local leaders as well as letters to the editor" in pursuit of a stronger stance against desegregation. In Butler's opinion, "most of our men should have lace sewed on their trousers. They are afraid of their shadows, and most women! No comment." The bulk of Butler's letter was an appraisal of Cornelia Tucker. Butler lauded Tucker's perseverance "in spite of discouragement due to dealing with an apathetic people." She complimented Tucker for continuing with her work and for "endeavoring to enlighten" other people.[23]

The Grassroots League that Ervin had found intriguing was a segregationist group founded and led by Morse and had grown out of South Carolina's 1952 citizens' grassroots crusade in support of Dwight D. Eisenhower. Morse, born in Watertown, Massachusetts, in 1884, was a Harvard graduate who worked as an agricultural consultant in Mexico, Arizona, and Louisiana before settling his family in South Carolina in 1927.[24] His league entwined traditional conservatism (including appeals to transcendental virtues, freedom, and a mistrust of a centralized government), anticommunism, and white supremacy. He was active in conservative grassroots politics from the 1930s until his death in 1975 and was a citizens' council member, although he never held public office. His league circulated anticommunist and segregationist pamphlets (or "research bulletins," as the group called them) throughout the South. The Grassroots League established ties with other segregationist grassroots groups in Arkansas, Georgia, Louisiana, Mississippi, and Virginia, demonstrating the networks between segregationist grassroots groups across state lines.[25]

According to the *News and Courier*, Morse had been "termed by the House Un-American Activities Committee director the person best posted on Communist activities in South Carolina," and Morse regularly gave talks on the subject to audiences, including the Daughters of the American Revolution.[26] This broader anticommunist agenda drew the attention of Republican and antifeminist activist Phyllis Schlafly of Alton, Illinois, who contacted the Grassroots League in 1955. Schlafly thanked Morse for the group's "excellent pamphlet, 'Truth About Supreme Court's Segregation Ruling.'" She asked for additional information and material so that she might "aid" the league in "combatting this pro-Communist propaganda."[27] The intersection between anticommunism, white supremacy, and conservatism formed the groundwork for the New Right in the 1950s and early 1960s.[28]

The league had a comparatively high number of female members. Fifteen of the thirty-five applications on record came from women in 1955. Five years later, of the 216 listed members, 61 were women—a percentage of 28.2. Only 154 of the league's 1960 members were South Carolinians. Other members came from eighteen states across the country, illustrating the national appeal of the league's brand of white supremacy. In August 1962, its membership had increased to 224, 74 of whom were women. The overall membership numbers did not grow significantly, but the percentage of female members rose to 33 percent. As the prospect of the integration of South Carolina public educational facilities loomed larger—Charleston's public golf course and the public library had been desegregated in 1961—women became more active in the league.[29]

White Supremacy in Chiffon Robes

Signifying the ties between traditional conservative female activism in Charleston and massive resistance, Margaret Lipscomb, a native of Mullins in Marion County, who was still among the league's members in 1962, was elected its vice president in the spring of 1959. Lipscomb, born Margaret Smith, was a prominent figure in the women's club movement in South Carolina and belonged to numerous civic organizations. Her husband, Richard Edward Lipscomb, had served as Mullins's mayor. In 1950, Lipscomb was named Mullins's "Citizen of the Year." She had joined the Daughters of the American Revolution in 1926, and as a member of its governing board and its South Carolina state treasurer, Lipscomb later gave speeches on behalf of the group, for example about the Tamassee school that the organization had opened in 1919. In 1961, Lipscomb became one of the organization's six vice presidents general at its seventieth Continental Congress.

A year prior to her election as the Grassroots League's vice president, the South Carolina chapter of the Daughters of the American Revolution elected her as its new regent. Lipscomb had been the president of the state's American Legion Auxiliary, the state president of the Society of Colonial Dames of the Seventeenth Century, the chaplain general of the Dames of the Court of Honor, a member of the United Daughters of the Confederacy, and a member of the South Carolina Historical Society. In 1958, she became the only woman to sit on Marion County's planning board.[30] Lipscomb evidently saw her activism in the anticommunist, segregationist Grassroots League as being in line with her other work. For women's club activists like Lipscomb, white supremacy served as a tool of consolidation between conservative club activism and massive resistance. Lipscomb's accumulated organizational knowledge and her community standing, in turn, benefited small, white supremacist grassroots organizations like the Grassroots League.

Cornelia Tucker was also a member of the Grassroots League, having joined shortly after *Brown*, and she had made a name for herself in Charleston's public discourse.[31] Her incessant drumming up of segregationist publicity and the entanglement of anticommunism, states' rights, and white supremacy in her arguments, which she associated with the fight for a "constitutional form of government," with combating "creeping socialism," and with taking aim at what she saw as communist-led black civil rights activism, kept segregationist grassroots activism in the public eye throughout the 1950s and early 1960s.[32] Tucker associated white supremacy with the solemn causes of antiradicalism, freedom of choice, and the defense of middle-class white privileges, which appealed to a national audience. She repeatedly described the looming desegregation as a state of emergency.[33] Tucker's campaigns were not confined to Charleston or South

Carolina either but were national in scope. She undertook annual pilgrimages—or "crusades," as she also called them—from Charleston to Washington, D.C., in January to "picket the opening season" of Congress for her causes.[34]

"A militant grandmother" from Charleston, as the *Southern School News* described Tucker in 1955, Tucker was born in Charlotte, North Carolina, on October 15, 1881. Tucker had graduated from the Synodical College in Rogersville, Tennessee, and later taught French in Charleston. She had married Robert Pinckney Tucker in 1899 and had been living in their Charleston residence on Lamboll Street ever since. After her husband passed away in 1921, Tucker worked as a real estate agent and an antique dealer for several years. Although Tucker took an early interest in politics and advocated for women's suffrage, her political activism began in earnest only after the couple's four surviving children, two sons and two daughters, were grown. Beginning in the late 1930s, "the widow turned her attention to politics," the *News and Courier* reported in a birthday announcement in 1945.[35]

Initially, Tucker was a staunch supporter of the New Deal. She became disillusioned when Franklin D. Roosevelt advocated for the Judicial Procedures Reform Bill of 1937, known as the "court-packing plan" that would have allowed the president to appoint additional judges to the U.S. Supreme Court. Tucker founded the Supreme Court Security League of Charleston after discussing the issue at a dinner party at her house with a group of Charleston women. The group opposed Roosevelt's proposal, and it rapidly expanded its membership. Tucker organized membership drives to recruit additional women to the league. As its chairwoman, she initiated a letter writing campaign to Congress, and thousands of messages flowed to Washington, D.C., from across the nation in support of her mission. Tucker was also a sharp critic of federal social security measures, and she warned that welfare provisions posed the "danger" of "hocking" South Carolina to "the North or the Federal government" permanently.[36]

In 1938, Tucker withdrew from the Democratic Party. Tucker left because she thought that New Deal Democrats "were departing from all things southerners had cherished." She joined South Carolina's recently reorganized Republican Party and became its publicity director.[37] Throughout most of the twentieth century, the Republican Party in the state was powerless. Local Republican candidates received very few, if any, votes—the Democratic Party alone made political careers up until 1974, when Charles B. Edwards became the first Republican governor since Reconstruction.[38] One of the stumbling blocks for the South Carolina Republicans was the lack of a secret ballot until 1950. At the time, voters had to pick up their Democratic or Republican ballots and cast them in either the Democratic or the Republican voting box, thus revealing their preference. In her capacity as the South Carolina Republican Party's publicity director, Tucker pushed for a single ballot containing the names of all candidates for office to ensure that citizens' votes were in fact secret. Tucker not only picketed the South Carolina legislature over the lack of a secret ballot, but she also made waves in March 1940 when she took the speaker's stand in the state house of representatives, which had no Republican members. Tucker took the podium during the chamber's daily proceedings, "and that without invitation, permission or consent of any one," remarked the Columbia *State*.[39] She started to read out her speech shortly before the house was called to order, which interrupted the opening prayer—a faux-pas that Tucker reportedly did not notice. Tucker's twelve-minute speech in favor of the secret ballot was one stepping-stone to its introduction in the Palmetto State a decade later.[40]

Tucker framed her campaign for the secret ballot as being driven by female determination. She stated that she had the support of "club women throughout the state" and that if "the men of South Carolina are willing to leave me to fight the secret ballot battle single-handed, the women are not."[41] Tucker consciously transgressed gendered boundaries and presented fellow white club women as strong-minded, hands-on activists whose tenacity would "get the job done" even when white men's determination failed. The local press subsequently identified Tucker as "a leader in Republican circles in the state."[42] Tucker put on a performance with her transgressive actions in the state legislature, that of a concerned, politically engaged elderly lady with an eccentric edge.

Only four years after becoming a member of the GOP, Tucker withdrew from that party too and was henceforth an independent, although she still styled herself a "Dixie Republican."[43] Tucker's political activism was manifold throughout the 1940s and 1950s, but her penchant was for publicizing issues that she felt were vital to protecting her vision of freedom, democracy, and the proper ordering of American society. In 1943, Tucker served as the chairwoman of the National Defense Security League. In an open letter to President Roosevelt, she urged him to support binding antistrike legislation during the Second World War.[44]

After the Second World War, Tucker focused on her role as publicity chairwoman of Charleston's Business and Professional Women's Club. Leaving "ladylike gentility" and "the traditions of dignified Charleston behavior" behind, the *News and Courier*'s William Douglas Workman approvingly noted, Tucker became known as "the Resolute Lady" who fought for states' rights and segregation and defended anticommunism throughout the 1950s and 1960s.[45] Workman, an ardent segregationist who unsuccessfully ran for the U.S. Senate in 1962 on a Republican ticket, later wrote the foreword to Tucker's daughter Mary Badham Kittel's book about her mother, *The First Republican Belle*.

Tucker continued her avid letter writing to local and national politicians, urging them to investigate the alleged communist affiliations of authorities that the Supreme Court cited in *Brown*'s footnote 11, which Democratic Mississippi senator James O. Eastland had called for. She requested that every future Supreme Court appointee be "from a list prepared by the American Bar Association." Tucker later reversed her stance on the Bar Association and proposed that every state supreme court recommend candidates to the president and the senate.[46] Tucker also enlisted the help of tourists in Charleston. She conducted several "on-the-street" surveys, in which she approached visitors and read her Supreme Court reform proposals to them. If they indicated that they agreed with her, she asked them to send her message to the visitors' senators "along with their own opinion."[47]

Tucker campaigned for the introduction of textbooks "on democratic citizenship" for high school students in South Carolina. She was critical of the state of education and public affairs in the Palmetto State, again singling out "the men of this state": "Educators of Rock Hill, educators of Spartanburg, educators of Columbia—all women—have invited discussions, have started inquiries as to the alarming increase in our apathy toward the duties of citizenship at the polls. . . . Superintendent groups and boards of trustees for our high schools where this type of education must begin . . . are largely if not entirely composed of men."[48] Tucker added that women's civic club activism in Charleston had been "a pioneer in the field of civic education" and that she knew of no similar men's organization. Tucker, then, was tired of what she perceived as male apathy and framed women's civic activism not only as a citizen's duty but as a necessity.

Tucker repeatedly framed her decades-long campaign "for government and citizenship education" in high schools and colleges, requiring students to "have instruction in national and international political relations," as an anticommunist measure. In 1947, the South Carolina Board of Education not only accepted her recommendation for compulsory citizenship and government courses throughout the Palmetto State but also took Tucker's recommendation to develop a high school textbook on citizenship.[49] Twelve years later, C. Creighton Frampton, Charleston County Superintendent of Education, was still congratulating Tucker on having "worked diligently in having textbooks screened" for potentially subversive material. Due to her efforts, he claimed that "county and state officials" had "become keenly aware of the sinister schemes of those who would undermine our government through the medium of pernicious propaganda."[50]

Tucker used her perceived eccentricity as a performative tool to create a space in public political discourse for a senior segregationist, expanding the behavioral scripts accessible to her. Her transgressive actions could be justified by her age, experience, and the supposed state of emergency facing white supremacy that Tucker continued to warn the white community about. Tucker's activism provides insight into female segregationists' conscious efforts to bridge the divide between conservative female activism and the ideal of the gendered separation of the spheres, which was particularly pronounced in the 1950s era of domestic containment.[51]

Tucker and other female segregationists in the Lowcountry transcended supposedly ornamental southern white womanhood, creating a space for their public involvement by framing desegregation not as solely a matter of concern to children's education but also as a communist-inspired attack on constitutional government and on white privileges, an attack that in their view necessitated every white American's action. Tucker was willing to cross boundaries of supposedly acceptable behavior for southern white ladies in order to further her political goals. She once had believed that a woman's name should show up in the newspaper only twice in her life—"when she was born and when she died."[52] However, after she became active in politics, Tucker was the subject of numerous articles in the South Carolina papers, and she frequently contributed political commentary to the *News and Courier*. The newspaper, edited by the ardently segregationist Thomas Waring, regularly printed Tucker's letters to the editor and reported on her many segregationist initiatives.

A portrait by *News and Courier* author Otis Perkins mentioned early on that Tucker smoked cigarettes and, apparently, was also not opposed to the occasional glass of whiskey. In the late 1950s, Tucker recounted that she started typing and smoking "more than 20 years ago as part of her first crusade." Typing was a practical skill she relied on to ensure her letters were clear, but Tucker also believed that smoking would "lend a masculine quality" to her work, which was "mostly done by men," she stated.[53] Tucker herself, then, framed her activism as unusual for a woman and in need of a "masculine quality," of authority and credibility.

Using these performative actions and publicity stunts to attract media attention, voicing her opinions on controversial political matters in the press, and smoking cigarettes were three ways in which Tucker created a public political space for herself, but polite Charleston society did not necessarily approve of this less-than-ladylike behavior. The critics included her children and in-laws. From the start, the widow's family members frowned on her participation in politics as unbefitting for a lady. Tucker stated that it was her relatives, not the "government, political and civic leaders she approaches," who constituted the greatest oppositional force to her activism. She told the *Charleston Evening Post* that her family began to take a dim view of her activism after she "descended" into politics.[54] "That's why I changed my name to eliminate the Pinckney—so I'd at least not insult the Pinckneys," she quipped.[55]

Tucker acknowledged that it was difficult for a southern lady to be as expressive as she was. But her social status as a widow as well as her age were frequently mentioned as circumstances that authorized her outspokenness. Tucker's status lent legitimacy to her causes. Perkins's article referred to Tucker as a "venerable, white-haired grandmother" who "does her office work at a dining room table" and whose tenacity had at times been proven successful. The author noted that Tucker's mother had written for the *Atlantic Monthly* magazine, and that Tucker had developed an interest in public affairs early on in her life. Tucker was reading Shakespeare and Macaulay's essays at the age of nine, "instead of fairy tales." She also earned her college degree at the early age of sixteen. Despite her higher education and intellectual ability, Tucker simply described herself "as a housekeeper," the article added. Tucker stated that "gardening" was her hobby but admitted that she was "the worst housekeeper in the world," never having "anything to eat in the house" and always eating outside the home (although she deemed herself "a perfect cook").[56]

Tucker remarked that she liked "an occasional cocktail" and loved parties, playing cards, and the "intellectual stimulant" of personal contact with people. The *News and Courier* article portrayed Tucker as a sympathetic oddity. She presented herself as a mere "housekeeper" with a stereotypically feminine interest in social occasions and gardening, on the one hand, but in the recounting her political activism, however, she described herself as a woman with distinct stereotypically masculine qualities and habits. This juxtaposition allowed Tucker to engender an activist space that transcended the binarism of the separate spheres.

In sympathetic media portraits in local newspapers, journalists took great care to present Tucker as a woman who combined her household duties with a professional life. In 1960, for example, the *Charleston Evening Post* reported of a dinner party hosted by Tucker. Tucker was described as "elegant and charming" in her "champagne chiffon and a corsage of tawny pansies." Despite Tucker's depiction as a genteel southern belle, her dinner party was not merely a social call. Among the guests were a bishop, politicians, writers, artists, bankers, and military personal. Tucker not only entertained private friends but used her party for political networking. She was versed in employing her social status and capital to promote her causes.[57]

The article indicates that, unsurprisingly, Tucker was vehemently opposed to *Brown*. Whereas Tucker's political rhetoric predominantly focused on anticommunism, her writings became more explicitly racist when she took up the topic of the verdict and desegregation, and increasingly so, when massive resistance proved unequal to the task of preventing school desegregation in other states in the 1950s. In July 1954, Tucker wrote an open letter in connection to *Brown* in which she proclaimed that America had to wake up, as it was "embarking on a dangerous social experiment." She stated that all "this melodramatic harping on brotherly love and social equality of the races" was "a serious detriment" to the people who were trying to find a "realistic" solution to a "highly inflammable problem instigated by foreign propaganda," presenting herself as one of the rational southern thinkers among effeminate integrationists. A month later, Tucker wrote to then Lieutenant Governor Timmerman to say she was prepared to make "an earnest effort to help" him with "the tragic problem of race segregation." She attached a letter, "a result of many years of research," for his review, which she had also mailed to all members of the Supreme Court for their consideration before they rendered the verdict in *Brown II*.[58] A month earlier, Tucker had addressed Warren directly, interweaving constitutional arguments with racist diatribes. Echoing her response to James Vanwright, Tucker held that white people's "sense of responsibility" toward black Americans would be "destroyed" by compulsory desegregation. She sarcastically noted that she, too, was "a student of text books on sociology," alluding to segregationists' dismissal of Gunnar Myrdal's and Kenneth and Mamie Clark's studies that informed the *Brown* verdict, and that she had learned "that when social interrelationship is forced by law upon different races nothing can prevent amalgamation of these races."[59]

Tucker framed *Brown* as a crisis. She stated that the "status of the Supreme Court, composed of eminent jurists selected for experience and ability, has not been preserved." "Trained politicians," she observed, were "basing their decisions not on jurisprudence but on experimental ideologies." The *Charleston Evening Post* article not only introduced Tucker as an authority on the matter of "constitutional government" but also mentioned her previous activism against Roosevelt's "court packing" plan, thereby implying that the nation was yet again facing political upheaval due to factionist battles.[60] Tucker was one of the people capable of addressing this upheaval effectively, the article suggested, given her experience with publicity campaigns and grassroots activism.

After *Brown II* in 1955, Tucker maintained that segregation was "a matter of national security" in the defense against communism abroad and against infiltrated organizations and institutions at home. These included, in Tucker's view, the National Council of Churches, on whom she provided material to various segregationist groups.[61] During the 1950s, the National Council of Churches came to the fore as a supporter of the black freedom struggle, issuing a "Statement on the Churches and Segregation" in 1952, which called for the end of Protestant churches' complicity in racial segregation and discrimination.[62]

The council's promotion of civil rights and advocacy for social equality irked Tucker. "From its very inception the National Council of Churches has acted as an agency for promoting leniency toward communism," she wrote in 1961, charging that the council had been "exposed as such" in the conservative *U.S. News & World Report*. Tucker lamented the clergy's complacency and the fact that the "few laymen" who had sought to withdraw their church from the National Council of Churches had been voted down. It was an "accepted fact that Christianity is now engaged in a conflict for survival against godless communism," Tucker continued. In her view, the National Council of Churches actively promoted communism, with, for example, its book recommendation lists for church members, which included authors Langston Hughes and W. E. B. Du Bois. Tucker deemed these authors "notorious" and charged that they were "celebrating the success of communism's war against religion." The book list recommended "authors of blasphemy, communist propaganda and filth," Tucker complained. Only the laity had "protested to the bishops" that these recommendations were "an offense to our Christian faith and our sense of moral decency."[63]

While Tucker's name is not listed on the extant membership rolls of South Carolina's citizens' councils, Tucker supported them and was quick to endorse their mission publicly. After attending a large citizens' council meeting in early October 1955, she praised the organization and its leader. "Hats off to the North Charleston Citizens' Council and Mr. Micah Jenkins for an inspiring rally," Tucker exclaimed. She found kindred spirits among the council members. "Here are people," she said, "who instead of spending time over their tea cups and cocktails indignantly condemning the Supreme Court racial order get up and . . . [do] something about this usurpation of our rights." Tucker also applauded the two guest speakers. William J. Simmons, a leader of the Mississippi citizens' council movement, "held us spellbound as he explained the origin and purpose of Citizens' Councils with responsibility for maintaining the American way of life." Democratic governor S. Marvin Griffin of Georgia followed, giving a talk that "was like a shot in the arm of the liberty-loving—and fighting—spirit of our forebears." The council meeting instilled "a renewal of courage" in her and showed her "a means through which to channel this courage." Tucker endeavored to advance the council movement in Charleston County.[64]

An admirer of Democratic Mississippi senator James O. Eastland, Tucker was in frequent contact with him. In fact, Tucker could be described as the ardent segregationist's unofficial publicist in South Carolina. Eastland sent her hundreds of copies of his speeches on the alleged communist conspiracy behind the Supreme Court's ruling. Tucker shared the senator's suspicions of a Russian plot involving *Brown*. She joined him in calling for Congress and "members of patriotic organizations" to investigate the matter fully. Eastland acknowledged Tucker's tenacity and wrote that he knew of "no one in the South" who was "doing more hard and efficient work" than Tucker. "You may be assured that I approve of your method 100%," Eastland concluded.[65]

In August 1955, Tucker again contacted South Carolina's new governor Timmerman as well as South Carolina state and U. S. senators to protest the *Brown* ruling. Adding her own typewritten handbill made up of rhetorical questions and statements about *Brown* to each letter, Tucker charged that the Supreme Court was "dissatisfied with our constitution" and that this "questioning of the wisdom" of the U.S. Constitution had to be investigated.[66] Tucker argued that if a probe of the Supreme Court's sources proved that the "authorities" cited by it were "in any way connected with Communist-front movements, no iron curtain should hide this fact from the American people." Tucker's use of ironic quotation marks when referring to authorities on which the Supreme Court relied conveys the disgust people and writings she deemed communist elicited from her. Her letter initiative again echoed the most prominent political themes of massive resistance's countercampaign to *Brown* that eschewed explicitly racist rhetoric: anticommunism and the defense of states' rights.[67]

Throughout her activist years, Tucker had been able to adapt her rhetoric to different audiences. Increasingly, however, she abandoned her emphasis on desegregation arguments that centered on constitutional government. She became more candid in her disapproval of integration out of her contempt for "miscegenation," and she stirred fears of black and communist conspiracies. Race mixing would, in her view, eventually cause white people's doom. These views permeated her letters to both media outlets and politicians in the late 1950s and 1960s. Tucker did not mince words depending on who her listeners were anymore. She publicly and repeatedly propagated racism. Linking anticommunism with white supremacist doctrine, Tucker stated, "Profound thinkers, the world over, warn that Caucasian civilization is at stake in this communist plan to mongrelize all nations—except Russia." In her view, the Supreme Court, organized labor, clergy, politicians, and mass media in the northern, eastern, and western parts of the country were accomplices in this plan "to sacrifice civilization on the communist altar of mongrelization." Only southern segregationists stood in the way of "irrevocable disaster," asserted Tucker. "Are we to become a mulatto nation in preparation for Russian conquest?" she asked. The alarming prospect of widespread race mixing was, in her view, "the real reason" the South had to "do battle in every field against the 'subtle tactics of the Communists.'"[68]

In December 1960, that is, in the midst of the school desegregation crisis in New Orleans, Tucker wrote a letter to the *Times Picayune*. Tucker charged, "Let us stop that beating around the bush with 'Southern tradition,' 'states [*sic*] rights,' etc., and get down to the basic reason for intelligent opposition to forced race mixing." Desegregation would lead to a biracial society, and this would mean "the downfall of this established culture." If "white American culture ceased to exist within a generation or two, then apathetic whites who had allowed the Supreme Court's desegregation rulings to stand unchallenged would have no one to blame but themselves," Tucker charged. She criticized the media organizations by stating that "their representatives are students of history. They, of all people, should recognize this mongrelization plan as a backward step from a civilization cherished and nurtured for many centuries." She warned that the "civilization of ancient Greece died and suffered oblivion, but not through their own willful self-destruction."[69]

The clergy, Democrats and Republicans, and organized labor were all dupes to the communist conspiracy, according to Tucker. Yet they should all "recognize this mongrelization plan as a backward step from a civilization cherished and nurtured for many centuries." Finally, Tucker turned to a national audience. She criticized what she saw as other regions' complacency in the battle for white supremacy: "In the North, East and West, a vast majority of the people are opposed to forced mixing of the races—for themselves. What are they doing to save their country from this irrevocable disaster? Exactly nothing. As of today, the South stands as our nation's sole bastion of defense against communist plans for world conquest.[70]

The grandmother's prior public expressions of supposedly benevolent maternalism and "sincere interest in the progress of all" had given way to outright racism. Tucker abandoned all pretense that opposition to school desegregation was not rooted in racism. She asked fellow segregationists in New Orleans to unmask the actual, underlying issue, which she found not only reasonable but also worthy of publicity, and to rally round white supremacy.[71]

The New Orleans desegregation crisis alarmed citizens' council members in South Carolina's Lowcountry. The Deep South had another chink in its armor. The Citizens' Council of Sumter, a city one hundred miles northeast of Charleston, asked the Democratic South Carolina governor and native Charlestonian Ernest Hollings to intervene. "In view of the disturbing situation in New Orleans and the apparent weakening of the Louisiana Governor," wrote council chairman Ralph B. Kolb, "we urge you . . . to take the lead in getting the Governors of the other three southern states that have not yet yielded and offer to the Governor of Louisiana our full support." The South had reached its Rubicon. In the name of all council officers, Kolb urged Hollings to persuade Governor Davis of Louisiana to execute the "police powers of the state," seize the four black first graders from Frantz and McDonogh elementary schools, and "take them into protective custody for their own protection and/or to restore order in the city. This would bring the sovereignty of the state versus federal government into direct issue which would have to be adjudicated in the courts." When Hollings simply responded that he had already offered Davis his "sympathy and support," the Citizens' Council of Sumter stated that it realized that its suggestion called for a "drastic procedure" that may have "unpleasant consequences" but that Hollings and other southern governors had given their "solemn pledge" to circumvent desegregation.[72]

New Orleans's desegregation crisis gave another boost to council publicity in the Lowcountry. The Charleston County Citizens' Council published pamphlets and ran advertisements that attempted to scare fellow white citizens into joining: "Today it is the Louisiana Story! The NAACP promises that South Carolina is next!" The council was quick to point out that the $5 annual membership fee for joining one of the councils in St. Andrews, James Island, Mount Pleasant, the city of Charleston, North Charleston, St. Pauls/Edisto and John's Island/Wadmalaw Island covered "both husband and wife in the case of married couples."[73] Shortly thereafter, the Charleston County Citizens' Council director, Charlestonian Thomas H. Carter, and the newly formed Coastal Carolina Citizens' Council, headed by Charlestonian Charles Cotesworth Pinckney, chartered the Foundation of Independent Schools, Inc. The nonprofit organization, modeled after the Prince Edward School Foundation in Virginia, planned to institutionalize a private school system "in any or all counties in the state of South Carolina." The Lowcountry's councils thus implemented parallel campaigns of defiance against and evasion of the prospect of school desegregation, setting up their own preparedness measures.[74]

Convergences with Conservatism

The color-blind rhetoric of school choice and school education was a line of argument that linked grassroots white supremacists to a wider network of conservative activists and organizations. In Tucker's case, it was not just her anticommunist and states' rights campaigns but her activism on behalf of citizenship education in high schools that connected her to a national grassroots network of conservatives in the 1950s. In the fall of 1959, Tucker was invited to be a speaker at the We the People Convention in Chicago. Tucker had addressed the convention before in 1957. Two years later, Thomas Parker, a member of the national advisory committee of the Coalition of Conservative Voters, arranged for her to deliver a featured speech in Chicago. Tucker's "Education for World Peace" resolution, which she presented in a forty-five-minute speech, was unanimously adopted by the six hundred delegates. The plan called for instruction on "the free enterprise system as a part of public school education" and for the anticommunist screening of all textbooks used to teach students about government. The *News and Courier* congratulated Tucker and stated that she was "familiar" to the newspaper's readers "as a stalwart defender of the rights of American citizens." Her "talents" had now also been "recognized" in Chicago.[75] At the September 19, 1959, convention, speakers included members of the Washington, D.C., and Chicago chapters of the Daughters of the American Revolution. Barry Goldwater gave the keynote address, titled "How to Win a Non-Partisan Victory for Freedom." We the People described itself as a group of "conservative citizens opposed to socialism and world government." The group was affiliated with the Congress of Freedom, a conservative conglomerate of politicians, media people, and constituents who lobbied for the abolition of the federal income tax and a drastic reduction of the welfare state, were ardent anticommunists, and opposed federal desegregation legislation as well as the United Nations.[76]

At its 1959 convention, We the People charged that Chief Justice Earl Warren had "seriously jeopardized the security of our beloved nation" without explicitly mentioning the *Brown* decisions. We the People's board of directors then elected Billy James Hargis as its new president. The Oklahoma evangelist had been broadcasting his *Christian Crusade* program on radio and television for years, promoting an anticommunist, segregationist, and Christian fundamentalist agenda and claiming that the civil rights movement was a communist plot.[77] The organization's president also rallied against the perceived communist infiltration of the National Council of Churches, one of Tucker's causes. White supremacy, anticommunism, and antistatism served as the common denominators of We the People's alliances with different strands of the conservative movement. Tucker and other segregationists used white supremacy to consolidate diverging views across right-wing grassroots organizations.[78]

At the September 1959 convention, Tucker led a demonstration in support of Goldwater for president after the senator's keynote. Nine months later, Tucker discovered that Barry Goldwater had returned her campaign contribution with a note of thanks, as he was not (yet) running for office. Tucker continued to root for a Nixon-Goldwater ticket.[79] In a letter to the editor, published a month before the We the People convention, Tucker wrote that the upcoming presidential election did not "present an insoluble problem for Southern conservatives." Their "fate" now rested "in the hands of their heretofore none too highly esteemed state Republican parties." If southern delegates backed Goldwater, she continued, he could, "with his Midwest following, . . . defeat Rockefeller and give us a Nixon-Goldwater ticket."[80]

During Goldwater's presidential bid five years later, Tucker reminded the public that her "proposal for Goldwater for President" had been "the first one of record" as far as she was aware. Tucker proclaimed that due to "the Republican reconstruction period," southerners had "quite reasonably stuck with the national Democratic party for years," but that Roosevelt's "post-war agreements" looked "like surrender to Russia." Ever since, southerners had been "looking around for some means of freedom from the Democrat yoke of 'tax and tax, spend and spend, elect and elect.'" Tucker concluded that in her "crystal ball, I now see in the making, a Dixie for Goldwater with no circumlocution of the two-party system."[81] Tucker was invested in building solid and lasting political coalitions for the defense of white supremacy and conservative policies in the South and across the nation.

Although Tucker was by then registered as an independent, circumventing southern segregationists' turn to a third party was an important issue on her agenda. "For many years this third party business has been a stumbling block in the South's political progress," she wrote in 1959. "By all means, let's have a 'Solid South,'" she continued, but she advised that the South "have it the Cotton Smith way." Ellison Durant "Cotton Ed" Smith, who represented South Carolina in the U.S. Senate from 1909 until his death in 1944, had proposed "a Southern convention with duly elected delegates to attend both Democratic and Republican" meetings, according to Tucker. These delegates would then report back to the southern convention as to who was more sympathetic to the white supremacist cause.[82]

Tucker imagined eventually expanding this strategy past the South: "There are plenty of conservatives both, Democrat and Republican, north of the Mason and Dixon line." We the People was one organization in which, she noted, these conservatives were "well organized"; indeed, the organization had already sent conservative delegates to both Republican and Democratic conventions who then reported back to the group.[83]

Tucker called for a united conservative front in the face of what she perceived as the erosion of states' rights and white supremacy. She complained that "Tennessee, Georgia, Louisiana, Texas and other Southern states already have 'Conservative,' 'States Rights,' 'Constitutional,' 'Jeffersonian' conservative parties of their own, but they get nowhere. Why? Instead of getting on one band wagon, each trundles his own wheelbarrow loaded with plans of political advancement for their own leaders. Why not merge with such organizations as We The People . . . and get some results? . . . Left-wingers have indeed taken over because conservatives will not work together."[84] Notwithstanding George Wallace's presidential bid for the American Independent Party in 1968, South Carolina's conservative politicians shared Tucker's skepticism of third-party politics. Strom Thurmond had been the States' Rights Party's presidential candidate in 1948, and the Dixiecrats carried Alabama, Louisiana, Mississippi and South Carolina. In 1964, however, Strom Thurmond was among the first southern Democrats to leave the party and join the Republicans in support of Goldwater.[85] Goldwater appealed to southern conservatives for many reasons, and the Arizona senator courted their vote with his early iteration of the Republicans' southern strategy.[86] Whereas Goldwater had voted in favor of federal civil rights legislation in 1957 and 1960, he opposed the Democrats' comprehensive Civil Rights Act in 1964. Goldwater painted this decision as taking a stand for states' rights, property rights, and "freedom of association."[87] Goldwater presented the federal government as a corrupted cesspool that wielded unconstitutional power over the free market and curbed individual rights, that redistributed wealth through high taxes, and that was willing to compromise with communism abroad instead of terminating it.[88] He combined his economic and political critiques with forceful rhetoric on increasing "immorality," "rising crime" and the need for "law and order" in the country, tapping into moral panic about social liberalism.[89] Goldwater conservatism attracted white women, and women's organizations; the Goldwater Gals and Mothers for Moral America supported him for the same reasons conservative men did.[90]

Cornelia Tucker based her support for Goldwater on his categorical opposition to federal intervention on the state level, his advocacy for limited government, his hawkish foreign policy propositions in the battle against communism, and his message of normative conservatism. These stances mirrored her own beliefs. The self-proclaimed Dixie Republican's support for Goldwater illustrates the success of fusionism. By using the common denominators of anticommunism and opposition to the New Deal, particularly to the expansion of the welfare state and big government, right-wing activists fused moral traditionalism and libertarianism into a conservative movement that stepped onto the national stage in the late 1950s.[91]

In 1964, Tucker set to work to prevent the Republican National Convention from nominating New York governor Nelson Rockefeller. Indeed, Goldwater could count on a conservative grassroots network throughout the Sunbelt that ensured his nomination at the convention, and his supporters also voted down several moderate platform amendments.[92] Despite her personal interest, Tucker did not attend the 1964 Republican National Convention. In an interview with the *Atlanta Times*, Tucker remarked that she had instead been "busy writing people about making the platform one that was consistent with the principles" of Goldwater. Tucker and Goldwater had become "friends" during Tucker's annual visit to the capital to picket Congress for her causes, according to the newspaper. Tucker claimed that she and her helpers had sent out five hundred telegrams that stated that "the people" had "spoken loudly for Barry Goldwater and the principles for which he stands." Tucker credited her message to Wisconsin congressman Melvin B. Laird, who was the Republican platform committee chair and would later become secretary of defense, with getting "the ball rolling to make the platform what it is today."[93] Tucker thus contributed to the 1964 Republican platform's focus on limited government, anticommunism, and—notwithstanding the GOP's support for a civil rights bill—opposition to what the party called "inverse discrimination." The Republican Party's stance on "inverse discrimination" was an early expression of the ideology of "reverse racism," and the party opposed proactive measures that combated public school segregation, for example, busing.[94] In October 1964, Goldwater stated that the Constitution was color blind and that compelling children to attend certain schools was as wrong as preventing others from attending certain schools because of their skin color. This freedom of choice rhetoric effectively appropriated the language of civil rights activism and social justice, and Goldwater thus appealed to voters who sought to defend white privileges.[95]

Although Goldwater carried South Carolina, Louisiana, his home state of Arizona, and three other southern states, he was soundly defeated by Lyndon B. Johnson, who amassed over 60 percent of the popular vote. One of the reasons for Goldwater's loss was the fact that he was unable to dissociate himself from his image as an extremist. The support Goldwater received from the John Birch Society, for example, did not help his case. Founded by the retired candy manufacturer Robert Welch in 1958, the right-wing fringe organization promoted vast, anticommunist conspiracy theories, implicating the highest circles of U.S. politics, including President Eisenhower and Supreme Court chief justice Earl Warren.[96]

Its right-wing, conspiratorial ideology was the center of controversy a few years earlier when U.S. Army officer Edwin Anderson Walker was ousted from his post in 1961. Walker, who had been the federal troops' commander during Central High's desegregation crisis, was stationed in Augsburg, Germany, at the time. The *Overseas Weekly* charged that the general had used the society's propaganda material in army training sessions that accused Presidents Roosevelt, Truman, and Eisenhower of participating in a vast communist conspiracy. Walker also gave an interview in which he called Eleanor Roosevelt and President Truman "definitely pink," a statement condemned by President Kennedy. Edwin Walker resigned in November 1961. Less than a year later he was arrested for his role in the mob violence at Ole Miss.[97]

Tucker not only reprimanded Robert Kennedy for his intervention in Mississippi in 1962, but she had also commented on the administration's repudiation of the John Birch Society the year before. In May 1961 Tucker again wrote to the *News and Courier*. She defended the society's dissemination of its publications: "Diligent search for the cause of President Kennedy's defamatory outburst reveals nothing detrimental to the organization. It was guilty of sending out tracts on Mr. Robert Welch's personal opinion that 'Without precautionary measures democracy leads to mobocracy.' So what? Ever since ancient Greece learned this truth from her own bitter experience, every intelligent writer on comparative government has been expounding on this fact."[98] Tucker reduced the society's mass propaganda to the "personal opinion" by its leader, exonerating Welch at the same time by stating that his thinking was in line with every "intelligent" political scientist and historian.

Tucker added that, given the accuracy of the Birch Society's analysis in her view, the armed forces should not be "deprived of such knowledge." Tucker also found the reproaches against President Eisenhower reasonable: "So Mr. Welch said President Eisenhower and members of his State Department had been 'acting like knowing communist agents in their policy of concession and leniency to Russia.' Ever since World War II, when we began underwriting the Russian Empire, historians of integrity have been exposing similar courses taken by our

Presidents and State Departments. Because Gen. Eisenhower is a 'popular hero' is he exempt from similar criticism heaped upon Truman and Roosevelt?[99]

Tucker sought to shift the controversy from the John Birch Society to the National Council of Churches. She wrote that the "public is apparently more scandalized by what Robert Welch . . . has to say about Dwight Eisenhower than in what the National Council of Churches had to say in its recommended church literature of blasphemy, filth and Communist propaganda."[100] Not only did Tucker condemn the March on Washington as mob rule two years later, she also implicated the National Council of Churches in it when she stated that it was "promoting and financing this admittedly dangerous procedure" and that "every citizen whose church is affiliated with the National Council of Churches is giving this mob march his own individual moral and financial support."[101] In 1965, Tucker complained that the United States, "a so-called Christian nation," still gave "moral and financial support" to the National Council of Churches, which, in her view, used churches "for the evil purposes of promoters of the Communist conspiracy."[102] Tucker shared at least aspects of the John Birch Society's conspiratorial worldview and entertained the possibility that highest-ranking members of the federal government were part of a communist plot. At the same time, Tucker warned against what she termed a "mobocracy," in which the demands of social movements influenced policy, and she portrayed the civil rights movement as a threat to democracy.

On the day of the March on Washington for Jobs and Freedom in 1963, *The State* printed Tucker's comment: "So this widely published 'Exposition of National Insanity' is really coming off in the capital of the United States of America. . . . A mob of 'around a quarter of a million' will march on Washington demanding additional 'civil rights' be enacted into federal law. The White House will be opened in their honor. The President and the Vice President will be on hand to welcome them and to encourage this form of mob rule."[103] Tucker never saw mob rule as a way of describing southern segregationists' defiance of existing civil rights legislation, of course. To Tucker, the "mob" were marginalized groups and social liberals who countered her elitist and white supremacist views. In Tucker's view, they were intruding on white spaces and threatening white privileges.

Tucker linked her opinions on the fate of white supremacy to international politics not only in relation to anticommunism but also to South African apartheid. Tucker was a derisive commentator of the Sharpeville Massacre in the eponymous township south of Johannesburg. On March 21, 1960, seven thousand black South Africans had assembled to protest the state's pass laws, which controlled their movements and ensured racial segregation. The demonstrators moved on to a police station and held a rally outside. White police officers opened fire and killed sixty-nine people. The officers also wounded over 180 other protestors, many of whom were shot in the back as they fled. The following days saw protests, strikes, and marches across the country. South Africa's government declared a state of emergency and jailed thousands of anti-apartheid activists. A protest ban remained in place for half a year, and the government outlawed anti-apartheid organizations, including the Pan Africanist Congress and the African National Congress.[104]

Tucker rebuked an editorial in the *News and Courier* that had condemned the Sharpeville massacre as a "return to barbarism." Tucker begged to differ: "Anglo-Saxon civilization is at stake throughout the entire world," she wrote, and the communist plan "to mongrelize" the United States was under way. Tucker also denounced solidarity protests by U. S. university students. She stated that Princeton University had already "desecrate[ed] the chapel pulpit with a preaching invitation for Martin Luther King Jr., foremost leader of the cause [of mongrelization]!"[105] Tucker was not alone in portraying black people in South Africa and in the United States as a threat to white (supremacist) civilization. White supremacist responses in South Africa evoked colonialist language and framed the Sharpeville protests as a threat to white masculinity. "If we did not act," one South African constable stated, "the blacks would have killed us—and then gone on to slaughter our women and children."[106] Tucker echoed this colonialist sentiment.

Segregationists, particularly the citizens' council movement in Mississippi, reiterated Tucker's defense of South African apartheid. Rhodesia's Unilateral Declaration of Independence in 1965 was supported by segregationists, John Birch Society members, and Goldwater Republicans alike.[107] Indeed, this renewed emphasis on transnational white supremacy allowed southern segregationists to shift their focus from sectional issues to a global outlook, thereby laying the groundwork for their ideology's continued relevance in the latter half of the 1960s.[108]

In April 1960, Tucker again wrote to the *News and Courier*. She criticized the fact that the federal government condemned state violence in South Africa while failing to denounce Russia and Cuba. Tucker was referring to the violent suppression of the Hungarian Revolution in 1956 and the guerilla warfare in the Cuban Revolution in 1959. Tucker blamed this perceived disparity on the victims' skin color and the federal government's concessions to black people's demands and its international reputation:

> According to the prevailing fad, [the] butcher of Budapest must not be censured by white men as long as his victims are white people. When Cuba's tyrant Castro butchers all those who dare oppose him we must bear in mind that Castro, a white man, butchers his own race. Now those high ranking United States government officials who failed to censure Russia and Cuba but who 'have the colos-

sal gall to censure the government of South Africa' are white men and among the South African casualties were Negroes. It is expedient that United States government officials confrom [*sic*] with prevailing public opinion as to what is expected of them in racial matters.[109]

According to Tucker, the civil rights movement, which she equated with "mongrelization," could not be "defended as 'progressive.' It is as reactionary as anything in the whole field of social evolution. We Americans are on the backward road from a civilization cherished for more than 2,000 years."[110] Tucker understood domestic and foreign policy through the lenses of conspiratorial anticommunism and antiblack racism. White supremacy consolidated the conglomerate of simultaneous anti-intellectualism and elitism, anticommunism and traditionalist morality, and free market advocacy and social antiliberalism that made up Tucker's worldview.

Tucker was vehemently opposed to the United States Supreme Court's 1962 *Engel v. Vitale* decision, in which the court struck down compulsory school prayers and Bible study in public schools. Tucker started a petition on the Fourth of July in 1962. According to her estimations, she collected fifteen hundred signatures within eleven days, which she sent off to Associate Justice Potter Stewart, the lone dissenter.[111] Tucker added that she had collected signatures from people "from 16 states" and that her petitions were to be presented to Earl Warren along with a letter she authored. In this letter, Tucker asked the court to reconsider the verdict and to show where in the constitution the Supreme Court was given "power to rule on religious issues."[112]

Tucker continued to weigh in on current policy issues, including the death penalty and the ERA. In 1961, Tucker mocked clergymen and religious laity for participating in death penalty debates. She wrote that she doubted their wisdom unless they were "thoroughly conversant with the psychological effect of capital punishment on the criminally inclined." She added that "criminal laws are enacted for one purpose only. That purpose is to prevent crime."[113] Tucker was also no stranger to the ERA debate. Long before the amendment passed Congress in 1972 and failed to meet the ratification deadline ten years later, Tucker publicly contested an equal rights bill. In the early 1940s, Tucker expressed her opposition to the proposed amendment, which she based on both states' rights and gendered ideas. Tucker sarcastically stated that it had taken "over sixteen years of unremitting effort" until "the women of America have at last succeeded in getting a bill introduced requiring that 'Men and women shall have equal rights throughout the United States.'" This was not praise, however. Tucker noted that South Carolina already had laws in place that protected women's agency, property, and welfare. ERA proponents' examples of sexist discrimination, including the barring of women from jury duty and the refusal to grant women legal business status, reminded her of the comedian Dooley's quip that "man has the rights and woman has the privileges, for instance, a man has the right to a trial by a jury of his peers while a woman has the privilege of a trial by her admiring inferiors."[114]

Tucker dismissed the "many pronouncements from leading club women" on the proposed amendment, suggesting that they were "replete with high sounding phrases" about women's independence and individual choice. "Now I have lived to a ripe old age in South Carolina," Tucker claimed, but she noted that she had "yet to see a woman prevented by the men of the Palmetto State from living her own life, from developing her own personality or from expressing her own convictions when, where, and to whom she pleases." Tucker warned that South Carolina's women must not lose "their allegiance to States Rights," and if they were dissatisfied with the state's laws, they should appeal to the state's assembly, not the U.S. Congress. In the early 1940s, then, Tucker had already expressed central themes of Phyllis Schlafly's and other female anti-ERA activists' campaigns against "big government" and intrusive legislation.[115]

Additionally, Tucker appealed to conservative gender ideals when she reminded her readers that "once there throbbed in the bosom of American manhood, a vibrant chivalry, a sense of protectiveness for women which prompted the making of many of our laws. Slowly but surely this tribute to womanhood is disappearing. In the battle for our rights, do we not run the risk of loosing [*sic*] something we have hitherto cherished, something of infinite value?"[116]

Tucker opposed the ERA in 1943 because of her reactionary political and social perspective, which included biologist gender essentialism. Tucker did not see her own political activism as clashing with these sentiments because she was campaigning in support of reactionary politics and tried to stir men into action. Twenty years later, her views on women's equality had further regressed. In a letter to *The State* in July 1963, Tucker blamed the state of the union, which she described as a "dangerous situation," on the voters. Tucker wrote: "Our forefathers denied the ballot to paupers, married women and idiots. The taxpayer took care of the paupers and idiots. The menfolk took care of their respective women folk." She added that if today every person who was "'on relief' were denied the ballot, if only those who could prove that they knew what they were voting about participated in elections, if women were no longer allowed to cancel or double the vote of their [husbands]," the electorate would be based on "ability rather than in numbers."[117] Tucker thus advocated for the disfranchisement of those she saw as undeserving of the vote. Two years before the 1965 Voting Rights Act, by suggesting that certain groups of people should not be allowed to vote, Tucker insinuated that striking down states' voting restrictions was a mistake.

In his farewell address to the state legislature on January 9, 1963, outgoing governor Hollings admitted that the state was "running out of courts" in its decade-long quest to circumvent public school desegregation. Although directly challenged by a red-faced Gressette who proclaimed that there would be "no surrender," South Carolina's political establishment enacted further measures to limit desegregation to a minimum during the following months. By June, the legislature had enacted a tuition grants plan for private schools, whose proponents barely mentioned race but clouded its purpose in the colorblind rhetoric of "healthy competition between public and private schools" to "upgrade education." Union County senator John D. Long had also proposed an amendment to segregate pupils by sex, in order to "place a barrier between our white women and colored men. . . . The Federal Government has not yet pre-empted sex, thank God." The amendment was voted down after the Gressette Committee announced that it was not yet needed.[118] When Charleston's schools were ordered to desegregate in September 1963, a white supremacist safety net had already been put in place.

Tucker, too, continued her activism after Charleston began to desegregate. She proceeded to contact libraries and asked them to purge their shelves of "un-American" literature."[119] At the same time, Tucker sought to establish a legislative council on textbooks in South Carolina, which failed to materialize. Tucker complained that she did not receive sufficient support from like-minded organizations: "Where were the D.A.R.s and the American Legion?" she asked. "Where were all these people who clutter up the mail with tracts on insidious propaganda and lack of Americanism in our public school textbooks?" She added that without these groups' lobbying power, the legislature was "not likely to expediate [*sic*] legislation on any issue just because one lone greatgrandmother [*sic*] wants it."[120]

In 1964, Tucker had toyed with the idea of reestablishing her National Defense Security League, stating that there was "public interest concerning our seemingly vacillating policy in Viet Nam."[121] The idea never came to fruition. Tucker passed away on October 28, 1970, at her son Thomas's home in Atlanta, where she had moved a few years earlier.[122] Throughout the 1960s, she had continued her campaigns against what she perceived as creeping communism and against the "mongrelization" of the United States through desegregation. Tucker was an active proponent of massive resistance for over a decade. Her tenacity tells the story of segregationist women who were not pawns of the segregationist movement but committed ideologues in their own right. The Charleston segregationists Tucker, Lipscomb, and Zittrauer had amassed experience in conservative club activism prior to massive resistance's emergence in the 1950s and employed it in their grassroots activism. They focused on publicity for the segregationist movement and continuously kept segregation on the radar by framing desegregation as a national emergency. Tucker smoothed out white supremacy with broader conservative politics. She attempted to transcend a southern sectional experience by emphasizing national questions of constitutional government, anticommunism, and states' rights and thus aligned herself with new conservatism.

The strategic quality of top-down preparedness and countermeasures against desegregation in South Carolina are crucial to understanding the state's underestimated role in massive resistance. Grassroots activism played more than a complementary role in mobilizing the state's white population, however. Grassroots activists were responsible for implementing a steady stream of propagandistic publicity measures in an attempt to rally both a Solid South and a conservative nation. Tucker was a woman at the forefront of these efforts in the 1950s and 1960s. Her story and the stories of other female grassroots activists in Charleston's massive resistance movement exemplify white segregationist women's vital role in establishing legitimacy for the movement as well as their personal, ideological investment in white supremacy.

Eventually, a number of male fellow activists recognized the role of women not only as tools for achieving respectability for their causes but also as agents on the political stage. The Hartville Citizens' Council explicitly extended "a special invitation to ladies and teen-agers," and the Orangeburg Citizens' Council claimed that it was "imperative that women also realize the value of being able to vote. They will realize the importance when we point out that when a great number of Negroes registered in Orangeburg this month, Negro women outnumbered the men three to one." In a letter addressing the Daughters of the American Revolution in 1966, Grassroots League's leader Morse reflected on his experiences with like-minded female activists and declared that women "are the best fighters against any menace to their homes, children or freedom. Like a lioness or a she-bear, a woman attacks violently, recklessly, without fear of consequences, anything which threatens her family."[123]

Women played an ideological and practical part in the defense of segregation, linking their activism in massive resistance to their participation in traditional women's groups such as the Daughters of the American Revolution and the United Daughters of the Confederacy. Finally, segregationist women's activism was not solely confined to questions of education. Women took part in conservative politics on a broader scale, arguing for their idea of the "constitutional form of government," anticommunism and the "integrity" of the "white race." In contrast to the mothers' league and the cheerleaders, women in South Carolina were more disposed toward activism in established groups, and they could rely on the social and cultural capital amassed by decades of conservative activism and a higher education.

Whereas the crisis in Little and New Orleans gave way to the rise of protests by women who had otherwise not had a voice in their cities' politics, Charleston and the Lowcountry never developed such localized, crisis-related opportunity structures. Thus, women's segregationist activism in massive resistance there followed the more traditional route of broader social activism in the area, which linked conservative ideals with white supremacy. White supremacist female activists in the Lowcountry, however, were versed in performing motherhood and grandmotherhood as means of gaining access to public discourse and wielding influence in local, regional, and national politics. They incorporated agitation for massive resistance with prior conservative activism and profited from their middle- and upper-class backgrounds, their age, and their organizational experience when it came to shaping grassroots white resistance in the Lowcountry and conservative discourses across state and regional lines.

CONCLUSION

White Women and Everyday White Supremacy

New Orleans did not become another Little Rock. By 1960, the Southern Christian Leadership Conference, the NAACP, the Student Nonviolent Coordinating Committee, the Congress of Racial Equality, and other grassroots organizations active in the civil rights movement challenged Jim Crow on a fundamental level. The election of John F. Kennedy heralded the dawn of a new generation of politicians. Although the Kennedy administration did not want the federal government to insert itself into the altercations between civil rights activists and massive resistance supporters, activists in the civil rights movement succeeded in making it a part of a national agenda. The U.S. Supreme Court's verdict in *Cooper v. Aaron* in 1958 clarified that violent resistance to a verdict by the nation's highest court could not be used as a justification to ignore or directly defy *Brown* and other desegregation verdicts. By 1960, five years had passed since the *Brown II* decision, and federal district courts began to ask for school boards' desegregation plans. In 1963, almost a decade after *Brown*, South Carolina became the last state to finally admit African Americans to a previously lily-white public educational institution.

It is within this evolving national context that the Mothers' League of Central High School, the cheerleaders of New Orleans, and female segregationists in Charleston staged their protests against school desegregation in particular and against the attack on racial discrimination and white supremacy more broadly. Their examples show that women's activism and massive resistance's campaigns more generally were strongly influenced by socioeconomic and cultural factors, local conditions, and the spatialization of power, expressed in class and social status, educational backgrounds, racial composition of neighborhoods and school districts, community networks, and local and regional politics. These local and regional conditions, in turn, were connected to the national stages of civil rights protests, federal legislation, and court verdicts. Massive resistance, then, was determined by a multitude of factors. The female agitators examined in this book led particular campaigns within this segregationist, white supremacist movement.

There is an immediate connection between the mothers' league and the cheerleaders, as both women's groups membership was primarily constituted by women of comparable social backgrounds. The majority of the members of both groups were white working- to lower middle-class women, frequently homemakers, who lacked the economic and social capital that their cities' political, economic, and social elite possessed. Mothers' league members and cheerleaders decried what they perceived as an attack on the only form of capital at their disposal, which promised access to spatialized power, the potential to acquire cultural capital through education, and an everyday culture of white privilege that was supposed to afford them preferential treatment. Both groups understood whiteness as property and exhibited a class-related fear of being further displaced. Black pupils in New Orleans and Little Rock alike drew the ire of female segregationists, who falsely stated that black schools were not only equal to white ones, but even better than "theirs," thus depicting the black pupils as intruders who sought to encroach on supposedly white-owned spaces and eventually overthrow what segregationist women perceived as the natural social order. The motivational force of everyday white supremacist culture that promised preferential treatment and spatialized power for whites across the socioeconomic spectrum spurred these "ordinary" women into action, to defend what they thought was rightfully theirs.

The rhetorical choices of the cheerleaders and mothers' league, as well as the council groups to which the women had a close relationship, were similar when referring to upper-class whites. Both groups referred to their cities' affluent and nondesegregated neighborhoods as silk-stocking districts, voicing an explicit class consciousness in relation to desegregation. Both groups expressed their dismay at seemingly having been chosen as the objects of a social experiment or as the ones to be sacrificed. The segregationist women perceived the rhetoric of tolerance propagated by whites in Little Rock's Pulaski Heights and New Orleans's Garden District as nothing more than hypocrisy and performative acceptance without real-life consequences. To them, middle- and upper-class whites in affluent city districts and in suburbia had created their own performative spaces of verbal liberalism but physical spatial segregation.

The basic common denominator for female segregationists, as for their male counterparts, was a belief in white supremacy. The women cherished the one systemic privilege they had while being considered economic and cultural inferiors: they were *white* trash. Both groups were acutely concerned about what they perceived as the inevitable consequence of "race mixing." Whereas the mothers' league was more careful in its public statements and often only alluded to miscegenation through its insistence on preserving the "integrity of the races," the cheerleaders' core group was explicit in its opposition to "interracial marriage." There were members of both the core group of cheerleaders and members of the mothers' league who were not mothers of schoolchildren attending the affected schools but mothers and grandmothers to children whom they feared would eventually have to attend desegregated schools. These mothers and grandmothers as well as women without children were there on principle, defending segregation out of deeply held white supremacist convictions and a sense that they were entitled to white privileges and preferential treatment.

Some of the women were closely affiliated with citizens' councils. They had previously been active in the grassroots, segregationist resistance movement. In contrast to their counterparts in the Women's Emergency Committee to Open Our Schools and Save Our Schools, however, these women were predominantly unknowns in their cities' civic societies. They were, therefore, outside of established social networks and cut off from the traditional routes of political influence through economic and social capital. Although the mothers' league claimed it had received many pleas to help organize other mothers' leagues from across the country, and Little Rock's mothers' league indeed attempted a national campaign with Strike Back, neither the mothers' league nor the cheerleaders ultimately possessed the social capital to institutionalize a substantial and permanent women's group or form a national network of organizations. The cheerleaders' and mothers' league's organizational efforts remained limited to local and regional networking with individuals and groups that closely matched their ideology. The Women's Emergency Committee to Open Our Schools and Save Our Schools, in contrast, were in contact with each other, and these middle- and upper-class women were adept at forming social networks.[1]

Both the cheerleaders and the mothers' league framed their activism as that of concerned mothers. Both groups announced mothers' marches. In both cities, male-dominated segregationist groups, including the Capital Citizens' Council and the Citizens' Council of Greater New Orleans, repeatedly referred to them as mothers, thereby providing a justification for the women's behavior. The citizens' councils omitted to mention the women's transgressive actions, particularly the violence exhibited by cheerleaders. Just like their counterparts in the Women's Emergency Committee to Open Our Schools and Save Our Schools, the members of the mothers' league and the cheerleaders ranged from single women in their twenties without children to young and middle-aged mothers and homemakers to divorcées and grandmothers or elderly women without children. The composition of these groups was heterogeneous yet still lily white.

In terms of religious beliefs, a paradox emerges. Although the mothers' league officially stated that the group was a gathering of Christian mothers, it subsequently made only a few references to its religious convictions.[2] Its circular letter to parents, nevertheless, certainly made use of religious rhetoric. In this letter the group claimed that the current crisis was a divine test of segregationists' moral strength. The league's then vice president, Margaret Jackson, moreover, declared in September 1957 that while she "held no personal animosity" toward African Americans, "God himself" had set white and black people "apart by boundaries and language." Religion was a factor for at least some of the mothers' league members, who were primarily Protestant, including Mary Thomason, a congregant at the Reverend Wesley Pruden's Broadmoor Baptist Church. Members of the cheerleaders' core group, particularly Una Gaillot and Evelyn Jahncke, more explicitly grounded their segregationist activism in their religion. Gaillot employed her own biblical exegesis to justify her white supremacist worldview. Although she was excommunicated in 1962 for violating Catholic Church doctrine and inciting segregationist resistance to parochial school desegregation, she continued to affirm her religious belief in segregation as late as 2005 and renounced the Catholic Church for what she saw as heresy.

Both women's groups created a space for their activism in public through performative actions. Bystanders and the media noted that the women enjoyed the attention afforded to them through their actions. Both groups had exhibitionist tendencies, and their performances enabled them to expand the gendered and racialized frames of their public activism. They created performative spaces in which they could operate more freely, constructing carnival-like public displays of racism. The creation of a carnival-like atmosphere, at times exuberant, at times sinister, allowed for gender-specific transgressions. The women were able to slip into bolder roles. They actively sought and used media exposure and public attention—this extraordinary public state was co-created by segregationist women and in turn conducive to the women's continued activism.

The groups' structures, strategies, self-representations, and actions can, however, be clearly distinguished from one another. Whereas the mothers' league's officers were on a quest for middle-class respectability and stressed that their protests were nonviolent, the majority of cheerleaders made no attempt to hide their predominantly working-class background or to object to the public perception of them as white trash. Instead, they took distinctive pride in their social status and in the transgressive vulgarity and violence of their actions. At times, they even bemoaned the newspapers' failure to report on their most outrageous behavior.

Mothers' league members carefully composed themselves, appearing in their best clothes, with dressed hair, and wearing supposedly sophisticated hats.[3] The mothers' league was in pursuit of cultural and social capital and the socially upward mobility that would come with that capital. The cheerleaders, in contrast, were described as women in vulgarly tight clothing and with curlers in their hair. They consciously employed a distinct corporeality in their protests, which transgressed gender- and class-related expectations of how white women's bodies ought to appear in public.[4] The outrageousness of the cheerleaders' behavior was rooted not only in the fact that they did not act like stereotypical women but also in the fact that they did not act like "proper" white women. The cheerleaders' behavior exposed their exclusion from the white southern belle ideal. They played into stereotypes about blue-collar women's lack of femininity. Despite the citizens' councils' and other segregationists' description of the cheerleaders as mothers, they were masculinized in their portrayal by the press and eyewitnesses, to the point that Steinbeck suggests that the group of women were "not mothers, not even women."

The mothers' league attempted to eschew such vulgar and corporeal transgressions. It resorted to the appeal of segregationism as a test of true masculinity, while often exhibiting a behavior that was subsequently described as hysterical. This gendered behavior not only served as a publicly accessible expression of anger for these women but also as a strategy through which they could be absolved of accountability for violence.[5] Furthermore, the mothers' league adhered to the unspoken rules of motherly behavior and gendered passivity only in theory during the September riot.

While both the mothers' league and the cheerleaders stepped into local power vacuums that served as opportunity structures, the groups pursued different political and legal strategies. Whereas the cheerleaders were the street fighters of New Orleans's segregationist movement, which had failed in its political and legal attempts to block desegregation, the mothers' league was more diverse and dynamic with its activism, employing a variety of approaches to expand its influence beyond its immediate campaign to keep Central High School segregated. Even as it failed to keep the Little Rock Nine out, the league attempted to spur a movement toward the resegregation of the school through sabotage campaigns inside the school, legal action, lobbying work, and election campaigns. The mothers' league thus not only sustained its activism over a much longer period than the cheerleaders but was more versed in cloaking its ultimately similar goal of maintaining a white supremacist hierarchy in the rhetoric of states' rights, anticommunism, freedom of association, and good government.

That the cheerleaders were protesting the desegregation of two elementary schools necessitated a different approach, however. Unlike the mothers' league, the cheerleaders could not agitate teenaged students, and so they opted for a complete boycott. In addition, because the Louisiana State legislature was unsuccessful in its various attempts to circumvent desegregation, the cheerleaders' actions had to be more radical than the mothers' league's in order to stir media attention and create the state of emergency that the women's activism critically depended on. The actions, self-representations, and public perceptions of both the mothers' league and the cheerleaders, nevertheless, were determined at the intersection of the different forms of capital, race, gender, and region that the women occupied and the attention that media afforded them.

Mothers' league members and cheerleaders alike questioned the whiteness of parents who continued to send their children to desegregated schools. They turned the common meaning of the term "white trash" on its head so that instead of its marking a lack of economic and cultural capital it signified a perceived lack of racial loyalty and racist solidarity. This reproach was most violently followed up by the cheerleaders in their constant effort to produce a white segregationist front and achieve the schools' resegregation or closure.

Whereas New Orleans did not become another Little Rock, historian Ronald Formisano has argued that Boston, Massachusetts, became another New Orleans, fourteen years after the Crescent City's school desegregation crisis. In June 1974, federal district court judge W. Arthur Garrity Jr. ruled against the Boston School Committee in *Morgan v. Hennigan*, a class-action lawsuit brought by the NAACP two years earlier. Garrity found that public schools in Boston showed systematic patterns of racial segregation, despite the school committee's persistent denials of such segregation. In fact, Boston had a long history of residential and educational segregation. When the NAACP founded its local chapter in the city in 1950, it took on the issue right away, and black Bostonians initiated several protest campaigns against customary segregation in the city and the state.[6] Deliberately misrepresented as a southern issue by politicians and the media alike, segregation was prevalent in the North and in the West, and civil rights activists from San Francisco to Chicago to Detroit and to Boston rallied against it. Historians have thus criticized appeals to the idea of de facto segregation as disingenuous, arguing that the racial segregation produced by supposedly colorblind pupil placement plans, residential zoning laws, housing policies, and white flight was hardly coincidental.[7]

In Boston, Judge Garrity issued a variety of orders to end educational segregation, including the busing of schoolchildren to achieve integration.[8] South Boston's white working class erupted. Northern segregationists resorted to mob violence that recalled the violent clashes in Little Rock, Oxford, and Clinton, and female-led, segregationist grassroots groups, particularly Louise Day Hick's Restore Our Alienated Rights, organized forceful resistance against desegregation. The violent escalations came after years of segregationist agitation in Boston. Having observed civil rights protestors and their segregationist counterparts a decade earlier, segregationist agitators in Boston took a page from them and borrowed their protest strategies for their cause; some even copied southern segregationists by establishing "alternative," segregated white schools outside Boston's public school system.[9]

In 1966, Robert Coles, the psychiatrist who had interviewed a cheerleader in 1960, published an article in the *Atlantic Monthly* that reported on his interviews with working-class segregationist women in South Boston. Although the interviewees denied racist intent behind their opposition to desegregation measures, their reasoning for springing into action was strikingly similar to that of the cheerleaders. An Irish mother of six and a devout Catholic whose husband worked in a utility company's repair shop expressed resentment against both black people and "the rich out there in the suburbs, who keep on telling us what we should do." Another working-class mother echoed these sentiments, criticizing the media, the Catholic Church, and affluent suburbia for its newly found support for black civil rights. In contrast to the cheerleaders, the Boston women tacitly acknowledged black people's historic plight, but expressing what Coles identified as envy, they charged that their own white working-class communities had it just as bad and that nobody payed attention to their struggles. Coles concluded that the segregationist agitators in Boston were "stymied at the complexity" of the modern "social and economic system" and therefore resorted to hate rather than making a show of solidarity for equally better circumstances.[10]

Formisano identifies working-class Bostonians' actions as a form of reactionary populism, an iteration of a long history of movements by working- and lower middle-class people who have felt wronged by the establishment, even though they accepted, even advocated for, discrimination against other social groups and did not pose challenges to established sociopolitical and economic power structures that led to perceived injustices against working-class communities.[11] Neither liberal nor conservative per se, Formisano argues, reactionary populism characterizes a variety of grassroots movements throughout the history the United States, including the "white backlash" against desegregation that had been brewing in Boston since the early 1960s. Boston's anti-desegregation riots sprang from "rampant citizen alienation from impersonal government, drawing on an ingrained, deeply felt sense of injustice, unfairness, and deprivation of rights.[12]

Were the Little Rock's mothers' league's and New Orleans's cheerleaders' working-class segregationist actions also a case of reactionary populism then? In part they were. Like their Bostonian working-class sisters, the women in Little Rock and New Orleans felt belittled and mistreated by established political and economic forces, including the respective city's elites and the federal government. In Little Rock and New Orleans, female grassroots segregationist resistance grew out of their feeling that working-class communities had been slighted by affluent white elites, who preached moderation but practiced segregation in their separate spaces in suburbia and affluent city neighborhoods where there was little residential integration. In Little Rock and New Orleans, officials claimed that a bureaucratic procedure had been followed in choosing which schools to desegregate, and pleas to transfer white children out of these schools went unheeded. Like the women in South Boston, the women in Little Rock and New Orleans felt they had been deprived of their rights. This sentiment, however, was rooted in everyday white supremacy and the belief that a white establishment owed solidarity to fellow white people across all classes. A white supremacist sense of entitlement underlay the women's perception that they were being deprived of a natural right. As Kevin Kruse has shown for the desegregation of public facilities in Atlanta, white working-class whites felt that public spaces "had been 'stolen' from them," because they believed that these public spaces were rightfully theirs on account of their race.[13] The material circumstances and low social status of working-class and middle-class whites, their lack of economic, cultural, and social capital, and the subsequent lack of political influence that would have enabled them to redirect desegregation away from their communities were entangled with a belief in white supremacy that eradicated every chance for interracial working-class solidarity and reformist action. Reactionary populism in the case of Little Rock, New Orleans, and Boston was thus underwritten by the civil rights movement's fundamental challenge to white supremacy that motivated these segregationists to act against desegregation and black people's battle for social and economic equality across the nation. Although the Boston women may have claimed they were not, in fact, racist, there was little ideological difference between segregationist agitators in the Deep South and in the Northeast. Massive resistance could clearly branch out nationally.[14] These violent clashes against desegregation measures in the early 1970s, however, were massive resistance's last hurrah as an organized countermovement to *Brown* and the national civil rights movement's fundamental challenge of white supremacy. A strategic adaptation was in order after almost two decades of offensive and at times violent resistance had failed to overpower the federal government and intimidate black civil rights activists. Historian Matthew Lassiter argues that in the increasingly metropolitan Sunbelt South, economic and demographic changes displaced massive resistance's open defiance and gave way to "suburban identity politics based on consumer status, taxpayer rights, and meritocratic individualism" that could maintain segregation with the help of the colorblind rhetoric of antibusing and freedom of choice.[15]

Whereas working- and lower middle-class grassroots segregationists in Arkansas and in Louisiana placed their hopes on former Democratic Alabama governor and arch-segregationist George Wallace and his American Independent Party in the presidential elections of 1968 and 1972, South Carolina notably went down a different path, and segregationist grassroots agitators like Cornelia Tucker laid the groundwork for this route. After leaving the Democrats in 1964 and switching to the Republican Party, Strom Thurmond vigorously campaigned for Richard Nixon in the 1968 presidential election. Nixon carried the state and the nation.[16] Segregationists in the Palmetto State, whether inside political institutions or at the grass roots, were not in the business of reactionary populism. Although white supremacists in the state terrorized black activists and condemned the Washington, D.C., establishment, including the Supreme Court, the grassroots agitators who rose to prominence in the state, particularly in Charleston and the Lowcountry, were upper- and middle-class networkers with considerable social capital, and they certainly were not opposed to elitism. Charleston and the state of South Carolina generally, moreover, eschewed the kinds of localized school desegregation crises that erupted in Little Rock, New Orleans, and Boston and that had enabled working-class segregationist women (and men) to become politically influential. By institutionalizing so-called preparedness measures early on and implementing various top-down and bottom-up measures to circumvent *Brown*'s implementation, South Carolina's communities were able to avoid the notoriety of Little Rock or New Orleans during the 1950s and 1960s.

Segregationist politicians and grassroots activists in South Carolina were no less determined to preserve white supremacy, however. Segregationist female activists across the state helped to police white communities' commitment to the defense of white supremacy. Particularly in Charleston and the Lowcountry, they formed strong networks. Female segregationists' prior experience in broader social and club activism brought organizational experience to the state's grassroots massive resistance campaign, and segregationist female agitators in Charleston portrayed their involvement in massive resistance as a natural extension of their prior conservative activism for patriotic organizations and women's clubs, including the Daughters of the American Revolution and the United Daughters of the Confederacy. These women introduced different arguments white supremacist could draw on in defense of their worldview, and they initiated and supported strategic coalitions with conservative grassroots groups.

In contrast to their working-class fellow segregationists in other locales, the segregationist women in Charleston, most notably Cornelia Tucker and Margaret Lipscomb, had enough social capital not only to seek alliances with the New Right and modern conservative organizations but to establish lasting links. The changing social and political landscape in the mid- to late 1960s forced white supremacy to change its strategies. Middle- and upper-class segregationist women played an integral part in the successful permutation of openly racist politics into supposedly colorblind conservative policies in the service of white supremacy during the 1960s. They interwove traditional conservative themes like anticommunism and antistatism with white supremacist ideology, thereby forging a colorblind rhetoric that transcended narrow topical and sectional battles. Upper- and middle-class women did not have to resort to creating scandals and states of emergency to gain political influence—they relied on decades of organizational experience and networking skills, as well as the resources that attended those skills and experience. They, too, however, created performative spaces in order to transgress gendered expectations—Tucker relied on her eccentricity, for example, as a means of justifying what polite Charleston society regarded as unusual behavior.

Lending a sense of respectability and maternal gravitas to prominent social causes, women not only spearheaded organizational efforts but served as devoted activists and as at least symbolic leaders. In Little Rock, New Orleans, and Charleston, white women mobilized segregationists and independents in the defense of white supremacy. White women were far from mere passive observers. They led the way. Their actions illustrate the significance of both grassroots activism in massive resistance more broadly and segregationist women's activism more specifically, both of which contributed vitally to the white supremacist backlash against the black freedom struggle and its quest for legal, social, and economic equality.

While white women challenged white segregationist men to live up to gendered expectations of segregationist chivalry, they took decisive action themselves, mostly under the socially acceptable cover of motherhood. The gendered media portrayal of segregationist women as "hysterical" and thus irrational added to the idea of female fragility that was belied by segregationist aggressiveness in practice. The mothers' league's activism was not irrational but fluid, dynamic, and adaptable. It included political lobbying and legal action, direct action in front of the school and at rallies, sabotage of Central High's daily routine, and eventually participation in the formal political process. Ultimately, the league attempted to appeal to a national audience and transcend a southern sectional struggle by camouflaging the white supremacist baseline of their activism and trying to align themselves within a broad conservative spectrum by incorporating rhetoric that focused on freedom of choice, states' rights, anticommunism, and religion. In the end, the league failed in this endeavor owing to its lack of economic and social capital and the transparency of its own racism that could only be masked by colorblind rhetoric for so long.

The cheerleaders of New Orleans were predominantly women of lower social strata in the Crescent City. In contrast to the mothers' league, however, they and their fellow Ninth Ward segregationists took pride in their working-class roots and derived a sense of achievement from their form of protest. Perhaps taking advantage of the heightened attention threshold of a bigger city, the cheerleaders chose to engage in a verbally and physically violent form of activism. Their actions were both unusual for female activists and for organized segregationists in general, given the increasing attempts to appeal to national audiences by masking the centrality of racism in their cause. The cheerleaders, portrayed as unfashionable, unattractive, uneducated, and vulgar, consciously courted the negative media coverage as a means to secure personal, narcissistic self-gratification and attention. They also used this media coverage to ensure the dissemination of segregationist propaganda and to intimidate black citizens and white citizens alike, who, in their view, sabotaged white supremacist unity.

Some of the cheerleaders were already members of citizens' councils prior to their first protest at Frantz and McDonogh 19 elementary schools. Steinbeck's assertion that the women were performing a rehearsed play for the spectators and were decidedly vulgar and aggressive is accurate. The assumption that the cheerleaders were thus irrational or the equivalent of "demented children" is untenable and implicitly sexist.

The women transgressed boundaries through their rhetorical vulgarity, physical expressions, and violence. Their segregationist and reactionary political convictions were just as firm as that of male segregationists, as the statements of several of their members make clear. While their form of protest underlines the self-centeredness of some segregationist women's public activism and illustrates how they consciously attempted to ensure maximum impact through maximum outrageousness, the cheerleaders also clearly had a goal that was deeply rooted in their worldview. Their actions helped to further and keep the topic of segregation alive in a massive resistance phase (after Little Rock) and place (the cosmopolitan New Orleans), where such resistance seemed ultimately futile.

Charleston's most prominent women segregationists, in turn, refrained from any display of verbal or physical violence. The absence of localized desegregation shaped the kind of activism women segregationists took up. Their activism was scattered, apart from its focal point in Charleston. The absence of formal leadership was the decisive opportunity structure that enabled the rise to prominence and influence of segregationist women's groups, as evidenced in the strong showing of both the mothers' league and the cheerleaders. South Carolina, in contrast, never provided this opportunity. But the absence of a concrete (school) desegregation crisis neither circumvented female activism in South Carolina nor prevented female segregationists from entering the public sphere. As the membership rolls of John's Island and Wadmalaw Island Citizens' Council and the Charleston Grassroots League indicate and as Cornelia Dabney Tucker's activism shows, a number of women took active part in the leadership structure of the segregationist grassroots movement in the state.

Female activists were agents with their own segregationist convictions, who had the will to defy the *Brown* decision. White supremacist women mobilized and policed white communities. Their activism manifested through public, stylized resistance performances and through community-oriented, disciplinary actions toward white parents who, in the women's view, subverted a white supremacist front. These women filled the spaces of power that the wrestle between local, regional, and federal powers had left unattended. White women shaped white community responses to desegregation. Their white supremacist ideology informed their identities and their fight for everyday white privilege.

NOTES

Short Forms and Abbreviations

Bates Papers	Daisy Bates Papers
Blossom Papers	Virgil T. Blossom Papers
Brown Papers	J. Arthur Brown Papers
Faubus Papers	Orval Eugene Faubus Papers
Gamble Papers	Harry Pollard Gamble Sr. Papers
George Papers	Wesley Critz George Papers
Gremillion Papers	Jack P. F. Gremillion Papers
Hollings Papers	Ernest F. Hollings Papers
Huckaby Papers	Elizabeth Paisley Huckaby Papers
Johnson Collection	Justice Jim Johnson Collection
Lehmann Papers	Jane T. Lehmann Papers
Midlo Collection	Natalie Midlo Collection
Morse Papers	Stanley Fletcher Morse Papers
Murphy Papers	Sara Alderman Murphy Papers
Perez Papers	Leander Henry Perez Papers
Rousseve Papers	Charles B. Rousseve Papers
Rainach Papers	William M. Rainach Papers
Rogers–Stevens Collection	Kim Lacy Rogers–Glenda Stevens Collection
Stockley Papers	Grif Stockley Papers
Sutherland Collection	Matthew R. Sutherland Collection
Timmerman Papers	George Bell Timmerman Jr. Papers
Touchstone Papers	Ned Touchstone Papers
Tucker Papers	Cornelia Dabney Ramseur Tucker Papers
Tureaud Papers	Alexander Pierre Tureaud Papers
Waring Papers	Thomas R. Waring Jr. Papers
Wright Papers	J. Skelly Wright Papers
Workman Papers	William D. Workman Jr. Papers

ASA	Arkansas State Archives, Little Rock
COC-ARC	College of Charleston, Avery Research Center for African American History and Culture
COC-SC	College of Charleston, Special Collections
LOC	Library of Congress, Manuscript Division
LSU-SC	Louisiana State University, Baton Rouge, Louisiana and Lower Mississippi Valley Collections, Special Collections
LSUS-NWLA	Louisiana State University Shreveport, Northwest Louisiana Archives
NOPL-SC	New Orleans Public Library, Special Collections
SCDAH	South Carolina Department of Archives and History
SCHS	South Carolina Historical Society, Charleston
SCL	South Caroliniana Library, University of South Carolina, Columbia
TU-ARC	Tulane University, Amistad Research Center
TU-LRC	Tulane University, Louisiana Research Collection
UALR-ASI	University of Arkansas, Little Rock, Arkansas Studies Institute
UALR-BC	University of Arkansas, Little Rock, Butler Center for Arkansas Studies
UALR-SC	University of Arkansas, Fayetteville, Special Collections
UCLA	University of California, Los Angeles, Television and Film Archive, Hollywood
UNC-SHC	University of North Carolina, Chapel Hill, Southern Historical Collection
UNC-SOHC	University of North Carolina, Chapel Hill, Southern Oral History Collection
UNO-LSC	University of New Orleans, Louisiana and Special Collections
UOG-CRDL	Digital Library of Georgia and Walter J. Brown media Archives and Peabody Awards Collection
USC-SCPC	University of South Carolina, South Carolina Political Collections

Introduction. White Supremacy, White Women, and Desegregation

1. Crespino, *In Search of Another Country*, 15–17, 41–43; Lewis, *Massive Resistance*, 150; Newman, *The Civil Rights Movement*, 84. Parts of this introduction have been published in the *South Carolina Historical Magazine*; see Brückmann, "'Work . . . Done Mostly by Men.'"

2. "South Carolina Officials Stand Firm against Court Decree," *Southern School News*, July 1955, 14; Tucker to Kennedy, October 31, 1962, Tucker Papers, box 2, folder 23, SCL.

3. Tucker to Kennedy, October 31, 1962, Tucker Papers, box 2, folder 23, SCL.

4. Tucker to Kennedy, October 31, 1962, Tucker Papers, box 2, folder 23, SCL.

5. Lewis, *Massive Resistance*, 4; see also Bartley, *The Rise of Massive Resistance*.

6. See McRae, *Mothers of Massive Resistance*, 9–19.

7. Jones-Rogers, *They Were Her Property*, 202–5.

8. Apple and Golden, introduction, xiii–xvii, xv; Kerber, *Women of the Republic*, 283–87.

9. Feldstein, "'I Wanted the Whole World to See,'" 133. Also see Feldstein, *Motherhood in Black and White*.

10. Feldstein, "'I Wanted the Whole World to See,'" 134.

11. Roy, *Bitters in the Honey*, 173.

12. McRae, *Mothers of Massive Resistance*, 19. On new cultural history, see Fass, "Cultural History/Social History," 39–46, Hunt, *The New Cultural History*, 5, and Mallon, "Time on the Wheel," 735. On the history of whiteness, see Brattain, *The Politics of Whiteness*, Ignatiev, *How the Irish Became White*, Frankenberg, *Displacing Whiteness*, Harris, "Whiteness as Property," 1707–91, Kolchin, "Whiteness Studies," Roediger, *Towards the Abolition of Whiteness*, Roediger, *The Wages of Whiteness*, and Wray, *Not Quite White*. Crucial studies include Arnesen, "Whiteness and the Historians' Imagination," and Wickberg, "Heterosexual White Male." On gender, race, and discourse, see Foucault, "Prisons et asiles dans le mécanisme du pouvoir," Foucault and Gordon, *Power/Knowledge*, Scott, "Gender," Oakley, *Sex, Gender, and Society*, Hawkesworth, "Confounding Gender," Butler, *Gender Trouble*, Mouffe, "Feminism, Citizenship, and Radical Democratic Politics," and Fields, "Ideology and Race in American History." On class, forms of capital, and intersectionality, see Bourdieu, "The Forms of Capital," Crenshaw, Gotanda, Peller, and Thomas, *Critical Race Theory*, and MacKinnon, "Intersectionality as Method."

13. McMillen, *The Citizens' Council*.

14. The contrast to the now manifold studies on women in the civil rights movement is remarkable. See, for example, Barnett, "Invisible Southern Black Women Leaders in the Civil Rights Movement," Crawford, *Women in the Civil Rights Movement*, Collier-Thomas, *Sisters in the Struggle*, Hall, *Revolt against Chivalry*, Ling and Monteith, *Gender and the Civil Rights Movement*, Little, *You Must Be from the North*, Murray, *Throwing Off the Cloak of Privilege*, and Robnett, *How Long? How Long?* On masculinity and ultraconservative movements, including massive resistance, see Frederickson, "'As a Man, I Am Interested in States' Rights,'" and Cuordileone, "'Politics in an Age of Anxiety.'" On women in massive resistance, see Anderson, *Beyond Little Rock*, Jacoway, *Turn Away Thy Son*, and McRae, *Mothers of Massive Resistance*.

15. Ruoff, "Southern Womanhood," especially 38–39, 84–85, 185–86; Jacoway, "Down from the Pedestal," 348–50; Hall, *Revolt against Chivalry*, xx–xxii, 151–53. Also see Cash, *The Mind of the South*.

16. See Schechner, *Performance Theory*, 15, 68, Butler, "Performative Acts and Gender Constitution," 519–21, and de Certeau, *The Practice of Everyday Life*, xxii, 43.

17. Guard, *Radical Housewives*, 12.

18. Guard, *Radical Housewives*, 12, 15.

19. Nickerson, *Mothers of Conservatism*, xiv, xv.

20. Nickerson, *Mothers of Conservatism*, xx–xxi, 3.

21. Isenberg, *White Trash*; Merritt, *Masterless Men*, 5.

22. Harris, "Whiteness as Property," 1713.

23. Isenberg, *White Trash*, 1; Fields, "Ideology and Race in American History," 150.

24. Bourdieu, "Symbolic Capital and Social Classes," 294–96; Bourdieu, *Outline of a Theory of Practice*, 78–81.

25. Bourdieu, "What Makes a Social Class," 3–4.

26. Bourdieu, "The Forms of Capital," 46–48. All forms of capital transform into symbolic capital, Bourdieu argues, "once they are perceived and recognized as legitimate." See Bourdieu, "What Makes a Social Class?," 4.

27. Bourdieu, "The Forms of Capital," 44–51.

28. Bourdieu, "What Makes a Social Class?," 5, 13.

29. Soja, *Postmodern Geographies*, 79–91.

30. Adolphine Terry, quoted in Murphy, *Breaking the Silence*, 46.

31. "Angry Women Set upon White Mother of Pupil," *Times Picayune*, November 30, 1960, 3; "Housewives Try to Block Minister from Taking Child to Frantz School," *Bogalusa Daily News*, November 29, 1960, 1; "Rowdyism Haunts Integrated Schools," *Louisiana Weekly*, December 3, 1960, 1, 7; "Priest Defies Mob," *Chicago Daily Defender*, November 29, 1960, 1.

32. See Isenberg, *White Trash*, Wray and Newitz, *White Trash*, and Wray, *Not Quite White*.

33. Isenberg, *White Trash*, 150–51, 176–80; Wray and Newitz, *White Trash*, 4.

34. Isenberg, *White Trash*, 249–52; see, for example, White America, Inc., Capital City Chapter, pamphlet, September 28, 1955, Johnson Collection, box 2, folder 23, ASA. On the origin of the term "hillbilly," see Isenberg, *White Trash*, 256.

35. Isenberg, *White Trash*, 250–51, 257–58.

36. Roediger, *Towards the Abolition of Whiteness*; see also Brattain, *The Politics of Whiteness*, Kelley, *Race Rebels*, and Merritt, *Masterless Men*.

37. Bourdieu, "Symbolic Capital and Social Classes," 300.

38. de Certeau, *The Practice of Everyday Life*, 117.

39. See, for example, Parkinson, *Democracy and Public Space*, 50–61; Kelley, *Race Rebels*, 56–59.

40. Kelley, *Race Rebels*, 59.

41. Goffman, *The Presentation of Self in Everyday Life*, 22.

42. Goffman, *The Presentation of Self in Everyday Life*, 104.

43. Schechner, *Performance Theory*, 131.

44. Butler, "Performative Acts and Gender Constitution," 520–28. Butler contradicts Goffman regarding roles and the ascription of identity (528).

45. See photograph and caption, "Encouragement for the Governor," *Arkansas Gazette*, September 29, 1957, 1, Steinbeck, *Travels with Charley*, 258–59, and Charlotte Walker, "By the Way," *Charleston Evening Post*, May 7, 1960, 2–A.

46. Martin, *The Theater Is in the Street*, 4–6.

47. Schechner, *Performance Theory*, 15, 192; Scott, *Domination and the Arts of Resistance*, 3–29; Glass, introduction, 16; Gregson and Rose, "Taking Butler Elsewhere," 38.

48. See Jacoway, *Turn Away Thy Son*, 7; Bridges, *Through My Eyes*, 15–16; Scott, *Domination and the Arts of Resistance*, 173.

49. Scott, *Domination and the Arts of Resistance*, 173.

50. Meyer and Minkoff, "Conceptualizing Political Opportunity," 1458. See also McCammon, Campbell, Granberg, and Mowery, "How Movements Win," and Meyer and Staggenborg, "Movements, Countermovements, and the Structure of Political Opportunity."

51. Neidhardt and Rucht, "The Analysis of Social Movements," 450. See also Rucht and Neidhardt, "Towards a 'Movement Society?,'" 9.

52. See Hall, "The Long Civil Rights Movement," 1233–63, Arnesen, "Reconsidering the 'Long Civil Rights Movement,'" 34, and Cha-Jua, Keita, and Lang, "The 'Long Movement' as Vampire."

53. See Frederickson, "'As A Man, I Am Interested in States' Rights.'"

54. Lewis, *Massive Resistance*, 7.

55. McRae, *Mothers of Massive Resistance*, 10.

56. See Brückmann, "Citizens' Councils, Conservatism, and White Supremacy," and Rolph, *Resisting Equality*, 3.

57. On the historiographical debate regarding the emergence of twentieth-century conservatism, see Phillips-Fein, "Conservatism," and Durham, "On American Conservatism and Kim Phillips-Fein's Survey of the Field."

58. Durham, "On American Conservatism and Kim Phillips-Fein's Survey of the Field," 757–759; Kruse, *White Flight*, 7–11; Lassiter, *The Silent Majority*, 2–16. See more generally Lewis, "Virginia's Northern Strategy," McGirr, *Suburban Warriors*, Noble, "Conservatism in the USA," Phillips-Fein, "Conservatism," and Zelizer, "Rethinking the History of American Conservatism." See also Brückmann, "Citizens' Councils, Conservatism, and White Supremacy."

59. See Gross, Medvetz, and Russell, "The Contemporary American Conservative Movement," 330.

60. Lewis, *Massive Resistance*, 7.

Chapter 1. Massive Resistance in Arkansas, Louisiana, and South Carolina

1. *Brown v. Board of Education of Topeka*, 347 U.S. 483 (1954).

2. Bates, *The Long Shadow of Little Rock*, 47–48; see also Patterson, *Brown v. Board of Education*, 71.

3. *Brown v. Board of Education*, 349 U.S. 294 (1955). See, for example, Brown and Webb, *Race in the American South*, 274–75, Patterson, *Brown v. Board of Education*, 84–85, and Peltason, *Fifty-Eight Lonely Men*, 13. For a critical account, see Klarman, "How Brown Changed Race Relations."

4. John Bell Williams to the House of Representatives, May 19, 1954, *Congressional Record*, 83rd Congress, 6857; see also McMillen, *The Citizens' Council*, 15–92.

5. "Georgia," *New York Times*, May 18, 1954, 20; John Bell Williams to the House of Representatives, May 19, 1954, *Congressional Record*, 83rd Congress, 6857. See also Katagiri, *The Mississippi State Sovereignty Commission*, xxvii; "Georgia," *Southern School News*, September 1954, 8; Brown and Webb, *Race in the American South*, 274; "Arkansas," *Southern School News*, September 1954, 2.

6. "Arkansas," *Southern School News*, September 1954, 2.

7. Bartley, *The Rise of Massive Resistance*, 116–17; Day, *The Southern Manifesto*, 64, 72–107.

8. Day, *The Southern Manifesto*, 26–27; see Bartley, *The Rise of Massive Resistance*, 116–17; Declaration of Constitutional Principles, March 12, 1956, *Congressional Record*, 84th Congress.

9. Lewis, *Massive Resistance*, 1, 3–5.

10. See McMillen, *The Citizens' Council*, xii, Brown and Webb, *Race in the American South*, 275–76, and Lewis, *Massive Resistance*, 10. On massive resistance more generally, see Bartley, *The Rise of Massive Resistance*, Wilhoit, *The Politics of Massive Resistance*, and Lewis, *Massive Resistance*.

11. "Conquer and Breed," 1958, Johnson Collection, ASA, https://digitalcollections.uark.edu/digital/collection/Civilrights/id/231.

12. See Fredrickson, *The Black Image in the White Mind*, 275–82.

13. See Ruoff, "Southern Womanhood," 38–39, Hodes, "The Sexualization of Reconstruction Politics," and Godfrey, "'Sweet Little Girls'?," 61.

14. Painter, *Southern History across the Color Line*, 118.

15. Connell, *Masculinities*, 37; also see Kimmel, *Manhood in America*, 49–52.

16. Cited in Heale, *McCarthy's Americans*, 245.

17. Baton Rouge Southern Gentlemen's Organization, "White Man Of Today," George Papers, #3822, series 1.3, box 3, folder 21, UNC-SHC.

18. "A Southern Gentleman" to Wright, June 2, 1958, Wright Papers, 308, box 12, folder "Unfavorable, 1958–1959"; "A New Orleans Segregationist" to Wright, June 30, 1959, Wright Papers, box 12, folder "Unfavorable, 1958–1959"; "Grandma" to Wright, date-stamped December 7, 1960, Wright Papers, box 13, folder "Unfavorable, Dec. 1960," Library of Congress, Manuscript Division.

19. On behavioral scripts and performance, see Berrey, *The Jim Crow Routine*, 4.

20. Lewis, *Massive Resistance*, 185.

21. Blossom, *It Has Happened Here*, 2; McMillen, "White Citizens' Council and Resistance to School Desegregation in Arkansas," 95; Bartley, "Looking Back at Little Rock," 116; "Has Arkansas Gone Liberal?," *Chicago Defender*, May 7, 1955, quoted in McMillen, *The Citizens' Council*, 94.

22. Freyer, *The Little Rock Crisis*, 20; Kirk, *Redefining the Color Line*, 21; Blee, *Women of the Klan*, 28; Murphy, *Breaking the Silence*, 14.

23. "Arkansas," *Southern School News*, September 1954, 2; Freyer, *The Little Rock Crisis*, 19; Jacoway, *Southern Businessmen and Desegregation*, 12. See also Kirk, *Beyond Little Rock*.

24. "Arkansas," *Southern School News*, September 1954, 2; Kirk, *Redefining the Color Line*, 63–64; Kirk, "'A Study in Second Class Citizenship.'"

25. See Freyer, *The Little Rock Crisis*, 19, 23, Godfrey, "'Sweet Little Girls'?," 106–7, Kirk, "Arkansas, the Brown Decision, and the 1957 Little Rock School Crisis," 67–70, Kirk, *Redefining the Color Line*, 4–5, and McMillen, "White Citizens' Council and Resistance to School Desegregation in Arkansas," 95–99.

26. See Kirk, "Arkansas, the Brown Decision, and the 1957 Little Rock School Crisis," 69–70, and "Arkansas," *Southern School News*, April 1955, 3.

27. See Reeves, "Board Orders All Dollarway District Schools to Open Friday on Segregated Basis," *Arkansas Democrat*, September 23, 1959, 1, and John L. Ward, "NAACP Leader Promises Attack on Placement Law," *Arkansas Democrat*, November 9, 1959, 1.

28. "Arkansas," *Southern School News*, April 1955, 3; see Kirk, "Arkansas, the Brown Decision, and the 1957 Little Rock School Crisis," 70.

29. Stockley, *Ruled by Race*, 235–39; see also Kirk, *Redefining the Color Line*, 40–42. Bates became one of Arkansas's civil rights movement's leaders, and she persistently fought for the Little Rock Nine at Central High School and racial equality nationwide.

30. "Arkansas," *Southern School News*, September 1954, 2.

31. "Arkansas," *Southern School News*, February 1955, 2; Kirk, *Redefining the Color Line*, 87–88.

32. Iggers, "The Race Question in Little Rock's Schools before 1956." Iggers, who was forced to emigrate to the United States during the reign of National Socialism in Germany, was an active member of the Little Rock NAACP.

33. Freyer, *The Little Rock Crisis*, 16–18; Kirk, *Redefining the Color Line*, 93, 96; Kirk,

"Massive Resistance and Minimum Compliance," 81–94; also see Iggers, "The Race Question in Little Rock's Schools before 1956," 287, and Bartley, *The Rise of Massive Resistance*, 253.

34. Cooper to Bates, August 3, 1955, Blossom Papers, MC 1364, box 3, folder 1, UALR-SC; Iggers, "The Race Question in Little Rock's Schools before 1956," 289–90; Jacoway, *Turn Away Thy Son*, 53–54; Kirk, *Redefining the Color Line*, 98.

35. *Aaron v. Cooper*, August 18, 1956, Civ. no. 3113, U.S. Dist. Ct. E. Ark. *Cooper v. Aaron* was ultimately decided by the U.S. Supreme Court in September 1958.

36. See Jacoway, *Turn Away Thy Son*, 44; "Arkansas," *Southern School News*, June 1957, 9.

37. See Godfrey, "'Sweet Little Girls'?," iii; Lewis, *Massive Resistance*, 14, 83, 88; see also Painter, *Southern History across the Color Line*, 117–19.

38. Vervack, "The Hoxie Imbroglio," 25; Godfrey, "'Sweet Little Girls'?," 133–38; Jacoway, *Turn Away Thy Son*, 44–45; McMillen, *The Citizens' Council*, 95–96; David Appleby, "Hoxie: The First Stand," http://newsreel.org/transcripts/Hoxie-Transcript.html. L. D. Poynter of Pine Bluff, a chief clerk at the St. Louis Southwestern Railway Company and founder of White America, was elected president of the Association of Citizens' Councils of Arkansas in 1956; see Poynter, FBI interview report, September 9, 1957, 331, Little Rock Central High Integration Crisis, FBI Records, box 1, folder 937 (3), UALR-SC, Godfrey, "'Sweet Little Girls'?," 22, 78–91, 143, and McMillen, "White Citizens' Council and Resistance to School Desegregation in Arkansas," 100.

39. Jacoway, *Turn Away Thy Son*, 56.

40. Murphy, *Breaking the Silence*, 124. Also see Bartley, *The Rise of Massive Resistance*, 253–54, Cope, "'Honest White People of the Middle and Lower Classes'?," 49, Godfrey, "'Sweet Little Girls'?," 187, Freyer, *The Little Rock Crisis*, 17, Jacoway, *Turn Away Thy Son*, 56–57, and Peltason, *Fifty-Eight Lonely Men*, 34–35.

41. See Central High School special bulletin, September 4, 1957, Huckaby Papers, MC 428, box 1, folder 2, UALR-SC, Godfrey, "'Sweet Little Girls'?," 126–28, Murphy, *Breaking the Silence*, 35, 124–25, Roy, *Bitters in the Honey*, 3, and Williams, "Class."

42. Bartley, *The Rise of Massive Resistance*, 254–55; Jacoway, *Turn Away Thy Son*, 57; Central High School Board of Education to Guthridge, July 26, 1957, Blossom Papers, box 4, folder 3, UALR-SC. The letter was signed by all six board members, and copies were sent to the *Arkansas Democrat* and *Arizona Gazette*.

43. See Association of Citizens' Councils of Arkansas, "Fabalouse Promises," *Arkansas Faith*, November 1955, 19–21, Johnson Collection, box 2, folder 22, ASA, "Segregation: The Issue," *Arkansas Faith*, May 1956, 3, Bates Papers, MC 582, box 4, folder 1, UALR-SC, Merrill B. Taylor, letter to the editor, *Arkansas Gazette*, July 18, 1957, newspaper clipping, Blossom Papers, box 20, folder 9, UALR-SC, and Capital Citizens' Council, advertisement, *Arkansas Recorder*, July 12, 1957, 8. In this advertisement, the Capital Citizens' Council asked Faubus to appoint his three members to the Arkansas State Sovereignty Commission and take steps toward interposition.

44. Capital Citizens' Council advertisement, "Race-Mixing in Little Rock, North Little Rock, Ft. Smith and All Arkansas Schools Can Be Stopped by the Governor," *Arkansas Record*, July 5, 1957, newspaper clipping, Blossom Papers, box 21, folder 1, UALR-SC; Capital Citizens' Council, advertisement, *Arkansas Record*, July 12, 1957, 8.

45. On Wesley Pruden's family background, ministerial career and political affiliations, see Goddard, "Race, Religion, and Politics," and Blossom, *It Has Happened Here*, 39–40, 47.

46. Pruden to the Little Rock School Board, July 6, 1957, Blossom Papers, box 7, folder 2, 1–2; "Board Asked to Provide Segregation," *Arkansas Democrat*, June 28, 1957, newspaper clipping, Blossom Papers, box 20, folder 9, UALR-SC. Also see Capital Citizens' Council, advertisement, *Arkansas Recorder*, July 19, 1957, 8. For a detailed discussion of these tactics, see Godfrey, "'Sweet Little Girls'?," 138, 197–99, and Anderson, "Massive Resistance, Violence, and Southern Social Relations," 206–9, 213.

47. Iggers, "The Race Question in Little Rock's Schools before 1956," 291; Kirk, *Redefining the Color Line*, 106–7; Kirk, "Arkansas, the Brown Decision, and the 1957 Little Rock School Crisis," 73–74.

48. Fairclough, *Race and Democracy*, 2, 5–6. Also see Taylor, *Louisiana*, 42, 57–59, 143–44, and Goldstone, *Inherently Unequal*, 153–59.

49. U.S. Bureau of the Census, "Population of the 100 Largest Urban Places: 1960," table 19, www.census.gov/population/www/documentation/twps0027/tab19.txt; Baker, *The Second Battle of New Orleans*, 3–4; Fairclough, *Race and Democracy*, 8.

50. Inger, *Politics and Reality in an American City*, 39; Baker, *The Second Battle of New Orleans*, 4. See Fairclough, *Race and Democracy*, 9, 18–20; Hirsch, "Simply a Matter of Black and White," 266–72; Devore and Logsdon, *Crescent City Schools*, 208–10.

51. Fairclough, *Race and Democracy*, 9; see also McMillen, *The Citizens' Council*, 66.

52. Fairclough, *Race and Democracy*, 7–9.

53. Baker, *The Second Battle of New Orleans*, 8; Hirsch, "Simply a Matter of Black and White," 268.

54. See Moore, *Black Rage in New Orleans*, 21–23, and Hirsch, "Simply a Matter of Black and White," 274–83; also see Inger, *Politics and Reality in an American City*, 10.

55. Baker, *The Second Battle of New Orleans*, 283; Inger, *Politics and Reality in an American City*, 18–19; see Chapital to Morrison, April 11, 1960, NAACP Papers, New Orleans branch, mss 28, box 28-70, topical folder "Correspondence Incoming—Outgoing April 1–15, 1960," UNO-LSC. On segregationist propaganda, see undated and untitled note, Perez Papers, 1954–69, box 1, topical folder "Segregation General," NOPL. See also Moore, *Black Rage in New Orleans*, 19, 29, and White League of Louisiana, "Morrison Betrays White Race," undated pamphlet, ca. 1946, Tureaud Papers, reel 15, box 18, frames 1122–23, TU-ARC.

56. See Devore and Logsdon, *Crescent City Schools*, 179–225.

57. Baker, *The Second Battle of New Orleans*, 3; Douglas, "*Bush v. Orleans Parish School Board* and the Desegregation of New Orleans Schools," 2, 56–57; New Orleans Improvement League, "A Study of Some Tangible Inequalities in the New Orleans Public Schools," ca. 1957, 2, Tureaud Papers, reel 11, box 13, frame 392, TU-ARC; "Louisiana," *Southern School News*, December 1954, 6.

58. Devore and Logsdon, *Crescent City Schools*, 225, 232–34.

59. Devore and Logsdon, *Crescent City Schools*, 232; Baker, *The Second Battle of New Orleans*, 3; Douglas, "*Bush v. Orleans Parish School Board* and the Desegregation of New Orleans Schools," 3.

60. Jeansonne, *Leander Perez*, 253; Baker, *The Second Battle of New Orleans*, 265; Inger, *Politics and Reality in an American City*, 18; also see Douglas, "*Bush v. Orleans Parish School Board* and the Desegregation of New Orleans Schools," 3.

61. Baker, *The Second Battle of New Orleans*, 223–25. See also Frystak, *Our Minds on Freedom*, 76; "Segregation Void in Public Schools," *Times Picayune*, May 18, 1954, 1–2.

62. "Segregation Void in Public Schools," 2; "The U.S. Supreme Court Decision," editorial, *Louisiana Weekly*, May 29, 1954, 4–B. For a prosegregationist piece, see "Segregation Decision," editorial, *Times Picayune*, May 18, 1954, 8.

63. "Louisiana," *Southern School News*, September 1954, 13; Fairclough, *Race and Democracy*, 169; Baker, *The Second Battle of New Orleans*, 225–26.

64. "Louisiana," *Southern School News*, September 1954, 13; see also Mark Newman, "The Catholic Church and Desegregation in the Diocese of Baton Rouge."

65. McMillen, *The Citizens' Council*, 59; Baker, *The Second Battle of New Orleans*, 226; Devore and Logsdon, *Crescent City Schools*, 235; also see "Louisiana," *Southern School News*, September 1954, 6, Baker, *The Second Battle of New Orleans*, 227, Fairclough, *Race and Democracy*, 170, and Jeansonne, *Leander Perez*, 225.

66. Tureaud to the Orleans Parish School Board, June 16, 1955, Orleans Parish School Board Collection, mss 147, box 1, folder 3, UNO-LSC; Devore and Logsdon, *Crescent City Schools*, 237; Baker, *The Second Battle of New Orleans*, 248; see also Inger, *Politics and Reality in an American City*, 18.

67. Baker, *The Second Battle of New Orleans*, 259–65, 286; Inger, *Politics and Reality in an American City*, 17.

68. Archbishop Francis Rummel, "The Morality Of Racial Segregation," February 11, 1956, 1, 3, Sutherland Collection, mss 230, box 1, folder 1, UNO-LSC. This letter was circulated "to the clergy, religious and laity, Archdiocese of New Orleans."

69. See Inger, *Politics and Reality in an American City*, 18, 22–23, Baker, *The Second Battle of New Orleans*, 283.

70. McMillen, *The Citizens' Council*, 61–63; Baker, *The Second Battle of New Orleans*, 230; The Association of Citizens' Councils of Louisiana, Inc., Homer, citizens' council member list, December 19, 1956, Touchstone Papers, #392, 1900–1985, box 5, folder 71, LSUS-NWLA. Ned Touchstone was the editor of the Association of Citizens' Councils of Louisiana's propaganda magazine the *Councilor*.

71. McMillen, *The Citizens' Council*, 63.

72. McMillen, *The Citizens' Council*, 67; see also Devore and Logsdon, *Crescent City Schools*, 239.

73. McMillen, *The Citizens' Council*, 66. McMillen questions this number.

74. See Brückmann, "Citizens' Councils, Conservatism, and White Supremacy in Louisiana," 3–4; see also Jackson Ricau, "How to Preserve Segregated Schooling in Louisiana," South Louisiana Citizens' Council, July 8, 1960, Rogers–Stevens Collection, 317, box 2, folder 15, TU-ARC.

75. McMillen, *The Citizens' Council*, 69–70. On Louisiana citizens' councils' development until 1972, see Brückmann, "Citizens' Councils, Conservatism, and White Supremacy in Louisiana."

76. Association of Citizens' Councils of Louisiana mailing list, January 30, 1957, Touchstone Papers, box 7, folder 88, LSUS-NWLA; council membership list, December 30, 1958, Touchstone Papers, box 7, folder 93, LSUS-NWLA.

77. Council officer list, undated, Touchstone Papers, box 6, folder 84, LSUS-NWLA.

78. Perez to Martin, November 18, 1955, articles of incorporation of the St. Bernard Citizens' Council, November 18, 1955, certificate of incorporation, November 21, 1955, and membership list of the St. Bernard Citizens' Council, undated carbon copy, Perez Papers, box 1, topical folder "St. Bernard Citizens' Council," NOPL-SC.

79. Paul R. Davis to the superintendents of all parishes, March 1, 1958, Rainach Papers, #077, box 5, topical folder: "Citizens' Councils, 1956–1960," LSUS-NWLA; Frances P. Sims to Leroy Allen West, August 12, 1958, Rainach Papers, box 5, topical folder "Citizens' Councils, 1956–1960," LSUS-NWLA.

80. Baker, *The Second Battle of New Orleans*, 328–29; Devore and Logsdon, *Crescent City Schools*, 240–41.

81. See Baker, *The Second Battle of New Orleans*, 279–96, McMillen, *The Citizens' Council*, 67, and "Louisiana," *Southern School News*, July 1960, 12.

82. See Baker, *The Second Battle of New Orleans*, 331–32, Orleans Parish School Board, minutes, May 24, 1960, 98, Orleans Parish Desegregation Files, minutes, part 41, UNO-LSC, and Fairclough, *Race and Democracy*, 237.

83. Cited in Baker, *The Second Battle of New Orleans*, 333.

84. South Louisiana Citizens' Council, *Citizens' Report*, 2, no. 5 (1960): 1–2, Sutherland Collection, box 1, folder 9, UNO-LSC; "Louisiana," *Southern School News*, July 1960, 12; Baker, *The Second Battle of New Orleans*, 310–14; Fairclough, *Race and Democracy*, 236–42.

85. "Louisiana," *Southern School News*, July 1960, 12; Baker, *The Second Battle of New Orleans*, 310–14; Fairclough, *Race and Democracy*, 236–42.

86. Save Our Schools, "Our Stake in New Orleans Schools: A Study in Education and Economics," August 1, 1960, Sutherland Collection, box 1, folder 9, UNO-LSC.

87. Fairclough, *Race and Democracy*, 236–237; Inger, *Politics and Reality in an American City*, 25; Citizens' Council of Greater New Orleans, bulletin, July 1, 1960, Lehmann Papers, #214, box 1, folder 9, TU-ARC; Ricau to Rainach, June 29, 1960, Rainach Papers, box 5, topical folder "Citizens' Councils, 1956–1960," LSUS-NWLA. See Tyler, *Silk Stockings and Ballot Boxes*, 203–28. Another organization working for continuing public education, the Committee for Public Education, formed in June 1960. Similarly lobbying to keep the city's schools open and drawing its membership from the upper and middle classes, the committee dissociated itself from the liberal Save Our Schools. Members described their group as consisting of "segregationist but law-abiding" parents and sought to avoid being branded as integrationists or communists. This tactic, however, worked only to a limited extent. The same Citizens' Council of Greater New Orleans bulletin that labeled Save Our Schools an "integration front" named the Committee for Public Education a "related" organization and stated that both groups were "agitating for integration." See Fairclough, *Race and Democracy*, 237, Inger, *Politics and Reality in an American City*, 28–29, and Citizens' Council of Greater New Orleans, bulletin, July 1960, Lehmann Papers, box 1, folder 9, TU-ARC.

88. Viguerie to Davis, September 29, 1960, Rainach Papers, box 5, topical folder "Citizens' Councils, 1956–1960," LSUS-NWLA; Baker, *The Second Battle of New Orleans*, 314–24.

89. South Louisiana Citizens' Council, "The Citizens' Report," vol. 2, no. 6, June–July 1960, Sutherland Collection, mss 230, box 1, folder 9, UNO-LSC.

90. Louisiana State Advisory Committee to the United States Commission on Civil Rights, *The New Orleans School Crisis* (Washington, D.C.: U.S. Government Printing Office, 1961), 6; Orleans Parish School Board, minutes, June 20, 1960, 117–18, Orleans Parish Desegregation Files, minutes, part 41, UNO-LSC; "Louisiana State Officials Resist Desegregation Order," *Southern School News*, September 1960, 1.

91. "Louisiana State Officials Resist Desegregation Order," *Southern School News*, September 1960, 1, 15.

92. Inger, *Politics and Reality in an American City*, 30–32. Governor Davis, *Southern School News* reported, failed to follow up on his pledge that he "would go to jail before any integration would take place." He was made a party to the Williams suit alongside state attorney Jack Gremillion, and the lengths he went to to avoid being served with papers by U.S. marshals proved to be a source of comic relief: "In highlights of the summons chase, marshals placed one summons on the coffee table in the governor's office after tapping a secretary on the shoulder with the papers. Immediately state employes [*sic*] cut a glass top for the table and screwed it into place over the federal summons as all employes [*sic*] avoided touching the documents. Another summons was left on the doorstep of the governor's mansion. The papers were weighted down with two cement blocks and a note was placed over them saying: 'Do Not Touch'" ("Louisiana State Officials Resist Desegregation Order," 15).

93. Frystak, "'Ain't Gonna Let Nobody Turn Me Around,'" 308–10; also see Baker, *The Second Battle of New Orleans*, 325–30, and Fairclough, *Race and Democracy*, 265–96.

94. Orleans Parish School Board, minutes, October 10, 1960, 332, Orleans Parish Desegregation Files, minutes, part 41, UNO-LSC; Matthew R. Sutherland, letter to the editor, *Times Picayune*, November 4, 1960, 12.

95. Orleans Parish School Board, minutes, November 10, 1960, special meeting, 391–96, Orleans Parish Desegregation Files, minutes, part 41, UNO-LSC; Baker, *The Second Battle of New Orleans*, 2–3, 399; Fairclough, *Race and Democracy*, 239–40; Inger, *Politics and Reality in an American City*, 36.

96. Inger, *Politics and Reality in an American City*, 37.

97. Inger, *Politics and Reality in an American City*, 37–38; Baker, *The Second Battle of New Orleans*, 398; Fairclough, *Race and Democracy*, 250–51. On the history of New Orleans's Ninth Ward, see Landphair, "Sewerage, Sidewalks, and Schools."

98. "Interposition Bill Approved by House," *Times Picayune*, November 7, 1960, 1, 22; Shelby M. Jackson, "state-wide television broadcast" transcript, November 1, 1960, Gremillion Papers, #772, box 1, folder 27, TU-LRC; "Bills' Passage Will Keep," 19, and "Monday Declared 'School Holiday,'" *Times Picayune*, November 13, 1960, 1, 26; "U.S. Judge Enjoins Legislature," *Times Picayune*, November 14, 1960, 1; Lee Callaway, "Orleans Board Standing Firm," *Times Picayune*, November 14, 1960, 1; "Louisiana," *Southern School News*, December 1960, 1; Fairclough, *Race and Democracy*, 242–43.

99. Bartley, *The Rise of Massive Resistance*, 46.

100. Cox, "'Integration with [Relative] Dignity,'"; see also Tony Badger, "From Defiance to Moderation," Newby, *Black Carolinians*, 288, and White, "Managed Compliance," 405.

101. Thurmond, interview with Bass and DeVries, February 1, 1974, 15–16, UNC-SOHC. Strom Thurmond's black daughter, Essie Mae Washington-Williams, whom he fathered at the age of twenty-two with the family's sixteen-year-old black housemaid and never publicly acknowledged, passed away in 2013 at the age of eighty-seven.

102. Bartley, *The Rise of Massive Resistance*, 30; Farmer, "Memories and Forebodings"; Lau, *Democracy Rising*, 7, 177; Quint, *Profile in Black and White*, 2–6.

103. See the handbill dated ca. May 1955, Brown Papers, box 5, folder 5, COC-ARC. See also "Citizens' Council Movement Is Spurred in South Carolina," *Southern School News*, October 1955, 3, "S.C. Legislature Plans Resolution to Reaffirm Sovereignty," *Southern*

School News, January 1956, 5, White, "Managed Compliance," 201–6, and Quint, *Profile in Black and White*, 104.

104. See Burton, Burton, and Appleford, "Seeds in Unlikely Soil," 177–87, Lau, *Democracy Rising*, 191–96, Lau, "Mr. NAACP," and Quint, *Profile in Black and White*, 6–12.

105. Quint, *Profile in Black and White*, 13.

106. Lau, *Democracy Rising*, 193–95; Burton, Burton, and Appleford, "Seeds in Unlikely Soil," 177; Quint, *Profile in Black and White*, 12.

107. Lau, *Democracy Rising*, 194–204; Burton, Burton, and Appleford, "Seeds in Unlikely Soil," 186–87; Quint, *Profile in Black and White*, 36; White, "Managed Compliance," 28–29.

108. Burton, Burton, and Appleford, "Seeds in Unlikely Soil," 188; Quint, *Profile in Black and White*, 13.

109. Burton, Burton, and Appleford, "Seeds in Unlikely Soil," 188–91; Quint, *Profile in Black and White*, 14–18.

110. Bartley, *The Rise of Massive Resistance*, 44–50, 70; "Address by Governor James F. Byrnes at Rally of South Carolinians for Eisenhower, in Charleston, S.C., October 21, 1952," South Carolinians for Eisenhower, box 1, folder 1, USC-SCPC.

111. Bartley, *The Rise of Massive Resistance*, 44–45; Burton, Burton, and Appleford, "Seeds in Unlikely Soil," 15–16; "South Carolina," *Southern School News*, September 1954, 12. Also see Badger, *From Defiance to Moderation*, 7–8, Quint, *Profile in Black and White*, 15–18, and White, "Managed Compliance," 43–44.

112. Baker, *Paradoxes of Desegregation*, 112-113; "South Carolina," *Southern School News*, September 1954, 12.

113. Badger, *From Defiance to Moderation*, 11; Bartley, *The Rise of Massive Resistance*, 45–46; Burton, Burton, and Appleford, "Seeds in Unlikely Soil," 16–17; Catsam, "Into the Maw of Dixie," 2; Quint, *Profile in Black and White*, 17; White, "Managed Compliance," 55–59.

114. "Supreme Court Outlaws School Segregation," *The State*, May 18, 1954, 1; "SC Leaders Adopt 'Wait-See' Attitude on Court Decision," *The State*, May 18, 1954, 1; "South Carolina," *Southern School News*, September 1954, 12.

115. "South Carolina," *Southern School News*, September 1954, 12; Timmerman, quoted in "S.C. Politics Overshadow School Issue during July," *Southern School News*, August 1956, 9; Bartley, *The Rise of Massive Resistance*, 75–76; Quint, *Profile in Black and White*, 93–95.

116. "South Carolina," *Southern School News*, September 1954, 12.

117. Bartley, *The Rise of Massive Resistance*, 75–76; Catsam, "Into the Maw of Dixie," 2; Quint, *Profile in Black and White*, 104; "New Legislation on Schools," *Southern School News*, February 1957, 10; "S.C. Legislature Passes New Act Aimed at NAACP," *Southern School News*, March 1957, 6; "S.C. Legislature Weighs More School Bills," *Southern School News*, May 1957, 3. Also see Bartley, *The Rise of Massive Resistance*, 217–18, and White, "Managed Compliance," 241.

118. "Lower Court Decrees Mark Busy Month," *Southern School News*, August 1955, 1; "S.C., Va. Decrees," *Southern School News*, August 1955, 1; Baker, *Paradoxes of Desegregation*, 128–29.

119. Baker, *Paradoxes of Desegregation*, 136.

120. Bartley, *The Rise of Massive Resistance*, 93; Quint, *Profile in Black and White*, 28.

121. Charleston *News and Courier*, editorial, July 14, 1958, 12.

122. See McMillen, *The Citizens' Council*, 76. See also William D. Workman Jr., "Citizens Councils Grow at Rate of One a Week," *News and Courier*, July 1, 1955, 14-C, and White, "Managed Compliance," 184.

123. Association of Citizens' Councils of South Carolina, "The First Half-Year," June 14, 1956, Workman Papers, box 31, integration/civil rights folder, Citizens' Councils, South Carolina 1955–56, USC-SCPC.

124. White, "The White Citizens' Council of Orangeburg County, South Carolina," 261–62; "Resistance to Desegregation Is Increasing in South Carolina," *Southern School News*, September 1955, 6; Association of Citizens' Councils of South Carolina, "The First Half-Year," June 14, 1956, 1, Workman Papers, box 31, topical folder "Integration/Civil Rights, Citizens' Councils, South Carolina 1955–56," USC-SCPC; "Organization of a Local Citizens' Council," typewritten manuscript, date-stamped October 7, 1955, Timmerman Papers, #S548004, box 5, topical folder "Misc. Segregation," SCDAH.

125. O'Brien, "'The South Considers Her The Most Peculiar,'" 127–32; Smyth, "Segregation in Charleston in the 1950s," 100.

126. Korstad, "Could History Repeat Itself?," 255.

127. Hart, *Building Charleston*, 4.

128. Holden, "'The Public Business Is Ours,'" 125–27; Baker, *Paradoxes of Desegregation*, 22.

129. Fraser, *Charleston! Charleston!*, 336–38, 387–92; Estes, *Charleston in Black and White*, 14; Smyth, "Segregation in Charleston," 99–101.

130. Estes, *Charleston in Black and White*, 43.

131. Baker, *Paradoxes of Desegregation*, 144.

132. Hale, "'The Fight Was Instilled in Us,'" 4–5, 21–26.

133. Baker, *Paradoxes of Desegregation*, 144–45; "NAACP Counsel Says State to Become Next Legal Front," *Southern School News*, October 1962, 18.

134. Robert McHugh, "Charleston Schools Ordered to Admit 13: District 20 Must Enroll All in '64," *The State*, August 23, 1963, 1; Baker, *Paradoxes of Desegregation*, 23; Smyth, "Segregation in Charleston in the 1950s," 106–12; Hale, "'The Fight Was Instilled in Us,'" 4–5, 21–26. The original lawsuit named Minerva Brown as the lead plaintiff. Minerva graduated high school while her case was pending, so her younger sister Millicent took her place in the lawsuit.

135. "Charleston Group Set '64 Date For Opening New Private School," *Southern School News*, October 1963, 16. In 1963, the University of South Carolina at Columbia admitted its first black student since Reconstruction, the eighteen-year-old Henri Monteith, niece of Columbia civil rights activist Modjeska Simkins. Segregationists planted a bomb near her home. See "Dynamite Explosion Rips Ground Near Monteith Residence," *Southern School News*, September 1963, 23.

136. Baker, *Paradoxes of Desegregation*, 147; "Gov. Hollings Fields Questions Asked by European Press," *Southern School News*, November 1962, 14.

137. Cited in "Gov. Hollings Fields Questions Asked by European Press," *Southern School News*, November 1962, 14; "Courts Criticized: Compliance Plan Has Opposition," *Southern School News*, February 1963, 8; "South Carolina," *Southern School News*, June 1963, 14.

Chapter 2. The Mother's League of Central High School

1. "High Schools Are Reopened at Little Rock," *Southern School News*, September 1959, 1–2; "Two Negroes Quietly Enter CHS after Police Fight with Marchers," *Arkansas Democrat*, August 12, 1959, 1; "One Year Later," *Arkansas Gazette*, August 12, 1960, 11A.

2. "High Schools Are Reopened at Little Rock," 1.

3. A total of six African American students were admitted to Central High School and Hall High School, the latter desegregated for the first time: Carlotta Walls, Jefferson Thomas, Elizabeth Eckford, Effie Jones, Elsie Robinson, and Estella Thompson ("High Schools Are Reopened at Little Rock," 2; Chappell, "Diversity within a Racial Group," 191; Williams, introduction, viii).

4. The Labor Day bombings, perpetrated by KKK members and Capital Citizens' Council member E. A. Lauderdale, would be the last act of offensive resistance against desegregation. See Cope, "'The Master Conspirator' and His Henchmen."

5. Martin Holmer, "Segregationists Win 3–1," *Arkansas Democrat*, September 28, 1958, 1.

6. Bartley, *The Rise of Massive Resistance*, 252.

7. Lewis, *Massive Resistance*, 88; Drews, Gerhard, and Link, "Moderne Kollektivsymbolik."

8. "Legal Action Promised in Interference with Opening of Little Rock's Schools," *Arkansas Democrat*, August 11, 1959, 1.

9. "High Schools Are Reopened at Little Rock," 1. Amis Guthridge had worked for the States' Rights Party campaign in 1948 and unsuccessfully run for Congress against Representative Brooks Hays in 1952; see Jacoway, *Turn Away Thy Son*, 66.

10. "Legal Action Promised in Interference with Opening of Little Rock's Schools," 2.

11. "Two Negroes Quietly Enter CHS after Police Fight with Marchers," 2; "Legal Action Promised in Interference with Opening of Little Rock's Schools," 2.

12. On the political and constitutional aspects of the crisis, see Bartley, *The Rise of Massive Resistance*, McMillen, "White Citizens' Council and Organized Resistance to Desegregation in Arkansas," Peltason, *Fifty-Eight Lonely Men*, Spitzberg, *Racial Politics in Little Rock*, Reed, "Orval E. Faubus," and Wallace, "Orval Faubus." On the social and cultural history of the crisis, see Anderson, "Massive Resistance, Violence, and Southern Social Relations," Anderson, *Little Rock*, Baer, *Resistance to Public School Desegregation*, Beals, *Warriors Don't Cry*, Branton, "Little Rock Revisited" (Branton was the NAACP's local attorney from Pine Bluff, Arkansas), Campbell and Pettigrew, "Racial and Moral Crisis," Chappell, "Diversity within a Racial Group," Cope, "'Honest White People of the Middle and Lower Classes'?," Cope, "'A Thorn in the Side'?," Cope, "'Everybody Says All Those People . . . Were from out of Town but They Weren't,'" Cope, "'Marginal Youngsters' and Hoodlums of Both Sexes?," Cope, "'The Workingest, Fightingest Band of Patriots in the South'?," Gates, "Power from The Pedestal," Godfrey, "'Sweet Little Girls'?," Godfrey, "'It's Time for the Mothers to Take Over,'" Jacoway, "Down from the Pedestal," Jacoway, *Turn Away Thy Son*, Kirk, *Redefining the Color Line*, Kirk, *Beyond Little Rock*, Lewis, *Massive Resistance*, 84–89, and Roy, *Bitters in the Honey*.

13. Bates, press conference statement, November 1, 1957, NAACP Papers, part 20, "White Resistance and Reprisals," reel 6, group 3, box A-274, frames 00498–00499. See also Kirk, "Daisy Bates, the National Association for the Advancement of Colored People, and the 1957 Little Rock School Crisis," and Woods, "'Designed to Harass.'" Origi-

nally filed as *Aaron v. Cooper*, U.S. the Supreme Court issued its ruling in September 1958 as *Cooper v. Aaron* because the school district had previously appealed. See https://encyclopediaofarkansas.net/entries/aaron-v-cooper-741.

14. See Huckaby, *Crisis at Central High*, Brewer, *The Embattled Ladies of Little Rock*, and Murphy, *Breaking the Silence*. Brewer and Murphy were members of the Women's Emergency Committee to Open Our Schools.

15. Foucault and Gordon, *Power/Knowledge*, 98; Soja, *Postmodern Geographies*, 11, 21.

16. Butler, "Performative Acts and Gender Constitution," 519–20.

17. Guthridge, interview with Luther, 6, Murphy Papers, box 1, folder 26, UALR-SC. See also Godfrey, "'Sweet Little Girls'?," 154.

18. Cope, "'The Workingest, Fightingest, Band of Patriots in the South,'" 141.

19. See Cope, "'A Thorn in the Side'?," 164–65, and director's brief (2673), 69B, FBI Little Rock School Crisis Report, box 1, file 5, UALR-ASI.

20. Cope, "'A Thorn in the Side'?," 163–65; see also Chappell, *Inside Agitators*, 103.

21. Bartley, *The Rise of Massive Resistance*, 257; Godfrey, "'Sweet Little Girls'?," 130.

22. Bates, *The Long Shadow of Little Rock*, 3–4.

23. Blossom, *It Has Happened Here*, 54.

24. "Griffin Guest at Citizens Council Meet," *Arkansas Gazette*, August 22, 1957, 1; Jerry Dhonau, "Griffin Vows to Maintain Segregation," *Arkansas Gazette*, August 23, 1957, 1–2A; "Arkansas Segregationists Gain, Then Lose, Victory to Bar Negro Entries," *Southern School News*, September 1957, 6–7.

25. "Integration Resistance Is Urged," *Arkansas Democrat*, August 23, 1957, 2.

26. "Integration Resistance Is Urged," 2; Dhonau, "Griffin Vows to Maintain Segregation," 2A.

27. "Arkansas Segregationists Gain, Then Lose, Victory to Bar Negro Entries," 6; "Gay Council Throng Applauds Griffin for Speech Flaying Integration," *Arkansas Gazette*, August 23, 1957, 2A; Aaron, FBI interview report, September 5, 1957, 364, FBI Little Rock School Crisis Report, box 2, file 8, UALR-ASI. On Mary Opal Foreman's membership in the Mothers' League of Central High School and the council, see also Mother's League of Central High School membership list, October 31, 1957, Murphy Papers, box 11, folder 5, UALR-SC, Cope, "'A Thorn in the Side'?,"164. On her personal life, see Mary Opal Foreman, obituary, www.rollerfuneralhomes.com/services.asp?page=odetail&id=3766&locid=#.

28. Aaron, FBI interview report, September 5, 1957, 364, FBI Little Rock School Crisis Report, box 2, file 8, UALR-ASI; "Gay Council Throng Applauds Griffin for Speech Flaying Integration," 2A. See also Murphy, *Breaking the Silence*, 125, and Godfrey, "'Sweet Little Girls'?," 14, 42–43, 230–33. On the importance of public attire and behavior in the civil rights movement more generally, see Chappell, Hutchinson, and Ward, "'Dress Modestly, Neatly . . . As If You Were Going to Church.'"

29. Douglas, FBI interview report, September 10, 1957, 275, FBI Little Rock School Crisis Report, box 2, file 14, UALR-ASI.

30. "Gay Council Throng Applauds Griffin for Speech Flaying Integration," 2A; "Little Rock Students Register," *Arkansas Democrat*, August 23, 1957, 1.

31. "Mothers' League Has Open Meeting," *Arkansas Gazette*, August 24, 1957, 7A; "Gay Council Throng Applauds Griffin for Speech Flaying Integration," 2A; "Little Rock Students Register," 1.

32. "Little Rock Students Register," 1.

33. "Mothers League Has Open Meeting," 7A; Jamison, FBI interview report, September 9, 1957, 273, FBI Little Rock School Crisis Report, box 2, file 14, UALR-ASI. Jamison, catering manager at the Lafayette Hotel, stated that Ted Dillaha Sr., owner of Dillaha Fruit Company and the Capital Citizens' Council 's vice president in 1957, had arranged the room at the hotel for the first public meeting of the league and that the bill had been sent to the Capital Citizens' Council. The Skyway Room at Lafayette Hotel was the Capital Citizens' Council's regular meeting venue; see Guthridge, interview with Luther, 6, Murphy Papers, box 1, folder 26, UALR-SC, and Shelly, FBI interview report, September 11, 1957, 276, Murphy Papers, box 9, folder 5, UALR-SC.

34. Bickle, FBI interview report, September 9, 1957, 151, Little Rock Central High Integration Crisis, FBI Records, box 1, folder 933 (1), UALR-SC. The close relationship between the Capital Citizens' Council and the Mothers' League of Central High School, particularly when the league was just forming, is undeniable. According to Graeme Cope, at least twenty-one league members or their partners, that is, 12.7 percent of the group's total membership, were also members of the Capital Citizens' Council. See Cope, "'A Thorn in the Side'?," 164–65. See also director's brief (2673), 68, FBI Little Rock School Crisis Report, box 1, file 5, UALR-ASI, Jamison, FBI interview report, September 9, 1957, 273, FBI Little Rock School Crisis Report, box 2, file 14, UALR-ASI, Aaron, FBI interview report, September 5, 1957, 364, FBI Little Rock School Crisis Report, box 2, file 8, UALR-ASI, and McMullins, FBI interview report, September 9, 1957, 274, FBI Little Rock School Crisis Report, box 2, file 14, UALR-ASI. Nadine Aaron later denied knowing "anyone by the name of TED BILLAHA [*sic*] or similar name," despite the fact that Ted Dillaha had arranged the room for the meeting.

35. Webb, FBI interview report, September 10, 1957, 252, and Webb, FBI interview report, September 10, 1957, 253, FBI Little Rock School Crisis Report, box 2, file 14, UALR-ASI; Mother's League of Central High School membership list, Murphy Papers, box 11, folder 5, UALR-SC. See also Button, FBI interview report, September 7, 1957, 373, FBI Little Rock School Crisis Report, box 2, file 8, UALR-SC, "Governor Says He Probably Will Call Meeting of Sovereignty Board on Suits," *Arkansas Gazette*, August 21, 1957, 2A, "Mothers League Has Open Meeting," 7A, and "Arkansas Segregationists Gain, Then Lose, Victory to Bar Negro Entries," 6.

36. "Arkansas Segregationists Gain, Then Lose, Victory to Bar Negro Entries," 6.

37. "Arkansas Segregationists Gain, Then Lose, Victory to Bar Negro Entries," 6; Bates to Carter, August 31, 1957, Stockley Papers, box 2, folder 9, UALR-BC. Carter was an NAACP special counsel. See also Kirk, *Redefining the Color Line*, 112.

38. "Mothers League Has Open Meeting," 7A.

39. Taylor, letter to the editor, *Arkansas Gazette*, July 18, 1957, Blossom Papers, MC 1364, box 20, folder 9, UALR-SC; Godfrey, "'Sweet Little Girls'?," 22, 78–91, 143. See Goddard, "Race, Religion, and Politics" for information about Wes Pruden.

40. Blossom, *It Has Happened Here*, 39–40, 47. The record of some of the forty-two external attendees of the school board meeting on July 25, 1957, lists Ted Dillaha and Wes Pruden of the Capital Citizens' Council and L. D. Poynter, founder of White America, Inc. Two of the six female attendees listed might have been women who later became members of the Mothers League of Central High School: Mrs. Robert Mitchell and Mrs. Ottie Bennett (a "Mrs. Eva Mitchell" and a "Mrs. Mary Evelyn Bennett" are reg-

istered on the Mothers' League's membership list ("Minutes of the L.R. Board of Education Meeting," July 25, 1957, Blossom Papers, box 18, folder 18, UALR-SC; Mother's League of Central High School membership list, October 31, 1957, Murphy Papers, box 11, folder 5, UALR-SC). See also Poynter, FBI interview report, September 9, 1957, 331, Little Rock Central High Integration Crisis, FBI Records, box 1, folder 937 (3), UALR-SC, and McMillen, "The White Citizens' Council and Resistance to School Desegregation in Arkansas."

41. See Lewis, *Massive Resistance*, 10.

42. Fitzhugh, FBI interview report, September 8, 1957, 262, FBI Little Rock School Crisis Report, box 2, file 14, UALR-ASI; Douglas, FBI interview report, September 10, 1957, 275, FBI Little Rock School Crisis Report, box 2, file 14, UALR-ASI; "4th Woman Files for House Post," *Arkansas Democrat*, April 18, 1958, 2. Douglas, an FBI special agent, had checked the records of Little Rock's Credit Bureau to gather information about the league's officials.

43. Harden, FBI interview report, September 8, 1957, 384, Little Rock Central High Integration Crisis, FBI Records, MC 1027, box 1, folder 933 (3), UALR-SC.

44. Thomason, FBI interview report, September 4, 1957, page number illegible, Little Rock Central High Integration Crisis, FBI Records, MC 1027, box 1, folder 933 (1), UALR-SC and Jackson, FBI interview report, September 6, 1957, 350, FBI Little Rock School Crisis Report, box 2, file 8, UALR-ASI. See also Fitzhugh, FBI interview report, FBI Little Rock School Crisis Report, box 2, file 14, UALR-ASI September 8, 1957, 262, Jackson, FBI interview report, September 6, 1957, 350, box 2, file 14, UALR-ASI, and Harden, FBI interview report, September 8, 1957, 384–86, Little Rock Central High Integration Crisis, FBI Records, box 1, folder 933 (3), UALR-SC.

45. Thomason, FBI interview report, September 4, 1957, page number illegible, Little Rock Central High Integration Crisis, FBI Records, box 1, folder 933 (1), UALR-SC, and Stephens, FBI interview report, September 5, 1957, 367, FBI Little Rock School Crisis Report, box 2, file 8, UALR-ASI.

46. Fitzhugh, FBI interview report, 262, FBI Little Rock School Crisis Report, box 2, file 14, UALR-ASI; Aaron, FBI interview report, September 5, 1957, 364, FBI Little Rock School Crisis Report, box 2, file 8, UALR-ASI.

47. Thomason, FBI interview report, September 4, 1957, page number illegible, Little Rock Central High Integration Crisis, FBI box 1, folder 933 (1), UALR-SC.

48. Godfrey, "'Sweet Little Girls'?," 128.

49. Huckaby to Paisley, August 25, 1957, Huckaby Papers, MC 428, box 1, folder 3, UALR-SC. See Jackson, FBI interview report, September 6, 1957, 350, FBI Little Rock School Crisis Report, box 2, folder 8, Forbess, FBI interview report, September 7, 1957, 258, FBI Little Rock School Crisis Report, box 2, file 14, UALR-ASI, and Mother's League of Central High School membership list, Murphy Papers, box 11, folder 5, UALR-SC.

50. Blossom, FBI interview report, September 7, 1957, 2–3, Blossom Papers, box 4, folder 10, UALR-SC.

51. See, for example, Jim Johnson, "What Are the States Rights?" *Arkansas Faith* 1, no. 2 (1955), 7, NAACP Papers, part 20, "White Resistance and Reprisals, 1956–65," reel 13, group 3, box A-282. See also Kruse, "The Fight for 'Freedom of Association,'" 101–2, and Kruse, *White Flight*.

52. Aaron, FBI interview report, September 5, 1957, 364, FBI Little Rock School Cri-

sis Report, box 2, file 8, UALR-ASI; Jackson, FBI interview report, September 6, 1957, 350, FBI Little Rock School Crisis Report, box 2, file 8, UALR-ASI; Fletcher Knebel, "The Real Little Rock Story," *Look Magazine*, November 12, 1957, 32.

53. Aaron, FBI interview report, September 5, 1957, 364, FBI Little Rock School Crisis Report, box 2, file 8, UALR-ASI; see also Jackson, FBI interview report, September 6, 1957, 350, FBI Little Rock School Crisis Report, box 2, file 8, UALR-ASI, Bill Lewis, "Ike Says Mob Encouraged by Faubus," *Arkansas Gazette*, September 29, 1957, 2A, and Cope, "'A Thorn in the Side'?," 185. Graeme Cope has noted that at least 18.8 percent of the league had children at Central High School and that most were girls. Although the exact number of Central High parents among the league is unknown, a significant number, then, did not have children at Central High School at the time. The number of parents whose children might not have reached high school age yet (such as the children of Nadine Aaron, the league's first president) or who were attending different white high schools (which parents might have feared would be integrated next) could explain the membership composition ("'Everybody Says All Those People . . . Were from out of Town, but They Weren't,'" 254; "'A Thorn in the Side'?," 171).

54. Wilson, letter to the editor, North Little Rock, *Arkansas Gazette*, October 11, 1957, 4A.

55. Terry, quoted in Murphy, *Breaking the Silence*, 46.

56. Harden, FBI interview report, September 8, 1957, 384–85, Little Rock Central High Integration Crisis, FBI Records, box 1, folder 933 (3), UALR-SC.

57. Mothers League of Central High School, statement of purpose ("D"), October 31, 1957, Murphy Papers, box 11, folder 5, UALR-SC.

58. Mothers' League of Central High School, open letter, *Arkansas Democrat*, October 7, 1957, newspaper clipping, Blossom Papers, box 24, folder 1, UALR-SC; Capital Citizens' Council, advertisement, newspaper clipping, Blossom Papers, box 24, folder 1, UALR-SC. Julian Miller paid for the Capital Citizens' Council ad.

59. Mothers' League of Central High School, open letter.

60. Claude Sitton, "Troubled Actors in the Little Rock Drama," *New York Times*, October 5, 1957, 11, 21. No woman with the surname Jones appears on the league's official membership list. Jones, nonetheless, claimed that she was "a charter member" of the women's group, suggesting that the membership was still in flux or the membership list from October 1957 was incomplete.

61. "Troubled Actors in the Little Rock Drama," 21.

62. Aaron, FBI interview report, September 5, 1957, 365, FBI Little Rock School Crisis Report, box 2, file 8, UALR-ASI.

63. Mothers' League of Central High School, advertisement, *Arkansas Gazette*, August 27, 1957, newspaper clipping, Blossom Papers, folder 21, box 5, UALR-SC. The ad was paid for by Mary Thomason.

64. "Segregation Leaders Urge Non-Violence," *Arkansas Democrat*, August 28, 1957, 1; "Petition Adopted at 'Mothers League' Meeting Asks Faubus to Prevent Integration of Schools," *Arkansas Gazette*, August 28, 1957, 1B.

65. Harden, FBI interview report, September 8, 1957, 384–385, Little Rock Central High Integration Crisis, FBI Records, box 1, folder 933 (3), UALR-SC ; "Petition Adopted at 'Mothers League' Meeting Asks Faubus to Prevent Integration of Schools," 1B. See also

Lewis, FBI interview report, September 7, 1957, 377–78, FBI Little Rock School Crisis Report, box 2, file 8, UALR-ASI. Lewis was a reporter for the *Arkansas Gazette*.

66. Lewis, FBI interview report, September 7, 1957, FBI Little Rock School Crisis Report, box 2, file 8, UALR-ASI; Hightower, FBI interview report, September 8, 1957, 272, FBI Little Rock School Crisis Report, box 2, file 14, UALR-ASI. See also Sample, FBI interview report, September 8, 1957, 381, Little Rock Central High Integration Crisis, box 1, folder 933 (3), UALR-SC.

67. "Petition Adopted at 'Mothers League' Meeting Asks Faubus to Prevent Integration of Schools," 1B.

68. Harden, FBI interview report, September 8, 1957, 386, Little Rock Central High Integration Crisis, FBI Records, box 1, folder 933 (3), UALR-SC.

69. Forbess, FBI interview report, September 7, 1957, 258–59, FBI Little Rock School Crisis Report, box 2, file 14, UALR-ASI.

70. Murphy, *Breaking the Silence*, 41. The league's disdain was aimed at the Little Rock School Board, particularly Superintendent Blossom, and the group started to circulate petitions calling for his dismissal in early September. See Dyer, FBI interview report, September 6, 1957, and Lightcap, FBI interview report, September 6, 1957, FBI Little Rock School Crisis Report, box 2, file 14, UALR-ASI.

71. "Petition Adopted at 'Mothers League' Meeting Asks Faubus to Prevent Integration of Schools," 1B.

72. "Mother's League Is Organized," *Arkansas Gazette*, August 27, 1957, newspaper clipping, Blossom Papers, box 5, folder 21; see also "Gay Council Throng Applauds Griffin for Speech Flaying Integration," 2A.

73. Miller, "North Little Rock Six"; "Mother's League Is Organized."

74. Jerry Dhonau, "Daily Crowds at School Scene," *Arkansas Gazette*, September 8, 1957, 6A; Capital Citizens' Council, advertisement, *Arkansas Democrat*, September 23, 1957, 9. See also Mother's League of Central High School membership list, Murphy Papers, box 11, folder 5, UALR-SC, and Ernest Valachovic, "Mann Asks Race Groups for Records," *Arkansas Gazette*, October 16, 1957, 1.

75. "Petition Adopted at 'Mothers League' Meeting Asks Faubus to Prevent Integration of Schools," 1B.

76. "Segregation Leaders Urge Non-Violence"; "Petition Adopted at Mothers' League Meeting Asks Faubus to Prevent Integration of Schools." See also Hightower, FBI interview report, September 8, 1957, 271, FBI Little Rock School Crisis Report, box 2, file 14, UALR-ASI, and Sample, FBI interview report, September 8, 1957, 381, Little Rock Central High Integration Crisis, FBI Records, box 1, folder 933 (3), UALR-SC.

77. "Petition Adopted at 'Mothers League' Meeting Asks Faubus to Prevent Integration of Schools," 1B. See also Dhonau, FBI interview report, September 11, 1957, 278, FBI Little Rock School Crisis Report, box 2, file 14, UALR-ASI.

78. "Segregation Leaders Urge Non-Violence," 1. When questioned by the *Arkansas Gazette* about right-wing activist John Kasper's desire to visit Little Rock, Thomason said, "I wish John Kasper would stay out of Arkansas. We are a group of Christian mothers opposed to violence and Kasper certainly would not be welcomed by anyone I know" ("Guthridge Says Kasper Not Welcome," *Arkansas Gazette*, August 29, 1957, 2A). See also Webb, *Rabble Rousers*, 39–71.

79. Cope, "'A Thorn in the Side'?," 163; see also Lewis, *Massive Resistance*, 84.

80. "Anti-Integration Order Asked in Chancery Suit," *Arkansas Gazette*, August 28, 1957, 1; "Court Bars School Integration Here," *Arkansas Democrat*, August 29, 1957, 1. See also Jacoway, *Turn Away Thy Son*, 96.

81. Kirk, *Redefining the Color Line*, 113; "Court Bars School Integration Here," 1.

82. *Thomason v. Cooper*, 254 F.2d 808, no. 15915, U.S. Court of Appeals Eighth Circuit, April 28, 1958; Jacoway, *Turn Away Thy Son*, 95. See also "Senate Passes Rights Bill," *Arkansas Gazette*, August 30, 1957, 1.

83. FBI, "Events, Information, Statements, ETC, prior to September 3, 1957," 28–29, Little Rock Central High Integration Crisis, FBI Records, box 1, folder 933 (1), UALR-SC.

84. See Murphy, *Breaking the Silence*, 41.

85. Thomason, quoted in Jacoway, *Turn Away Thy Son*, 96.

86. George Bentley and Ernest Valachovic, "State Court Rules against Integration," *Arkansas Gazette*, August 30, 1957, 1–2A.

87. Thomason, FBI interview report, September 4, 1957, page number illegible, FBI Little Rock Central High Integration Crisis, FBI Records, box 1, folder 933 (1), UALR-SC.

88. Huckaby, *Crisis at Central High*, 70; Thevenet, FBI interview report, September 7, 1957, 269, FBI Little Rock School Crisis Report, box 2, file 14, UALR-ASI.

89. "State Court Rules against Integration," 1; Blossom, *It Has Happened Here*, 60.

90. FBI, "Events, Information, Statements, ETC, prior to September 3, 1957," 28, Little Rock Central High Integration Crisis, FBI Records, box 1, folder 933 (1), UALR-SC. Thomason's estimate of three hundred members was not made up whole cloth. At the league rally two days earlier, *Arkansas Gazette*'s photographer Larry Obsitnik observed that attendees "wrote their names on a register" (FBI interview report, September 7, 1957, 312, Little Rock Central High Integration Crisis, FBI Records, box 1, folder 933 (2), UALR-SC). Mrs. Alton C. Hightower, a housewife whose daughter attended Central High School, claimed that there were between 250 to 300 women and men present. Hightower told the FBI that the attendees "registered as attending guests to reflect the number at the meeting"; apparently, this was the action Obsitnik had observed (FBI interview report, September 8, 1957, 271, Little Rock Central High Integration Crisis, FBI Records, box 1, folder 933 (3), UALR-SC). The league's recording secretary Mary Thomason, in charge of keeping track of the group's membership, either conflated this attendance list with a membership list or consciously used an attendance list as an alleged membership register. Another possibility is that Hightower had been mistaken in (or tricked into) assuming that she was signing an attendance list while she was actually registering for the league. In her FBI interview, Hightower denied membership, and indeed, she is not listed on the league's official membership list of October 1957 (Mother's League of Central High School membership list, Murphy Papers, box 11, folder 5, UALR-SC). Thomason was not the only league officer who believed Hightower to be a member, however. In her second September interview with the FBI, the league's vice president Margaret Jackson furnished several names of members and mentioned Hightower (FBI interview report, September 7, 1957, 354, FBI Little Rock School Crisis Report, box 2, file 8, UALR-ASI). At best, then, Thomason's claim that the league had three hundred members and the mention of Hightower as a member was a misunderstanding and indicative of a rushed and chaotic organization process (or Hightower had lied to the FBI about her membership and left the

group before October, when the league's membership list was filed); at worst, officers of the league deliberately tricked rally attendees into signing an attendance register that the group then used as a de facto membership list to boost its size and thus legitimacy as a white mothers' spokesgroup for the court hearing and the general public.

91. "State Court Rules against Integration," 1–2A.

92. Blossom, *It Has Happened Here*, 60; Jacoway, *Turn Away Thy Son*, 95–97; "State Court Rules against Integration," 1.

93. "Arkansas Segregationists Gain, Then Lose, Victory to Bar Negro Entries," 6; Blossom, *It Has Happened Here*, 60; "State Court Rules against Integration," 1.

94. "Arkansas Segregationists Gain, Then Lose, Victory to Bar Negro Entries," 6; "State Court Rules against Integration," 2A.

95. "Congratulations on Victory," *Arkansas Democrat*, August 29, 1957, 1, photograph by Gunter; see also "Court Bars School Integration Here," 1.

96. Cope, "'A Thorn in the Side'?," 161, 178–79.

97. On the origin of Thomason's lawsuit and whether Orval Faubus himself instigated it, see Thomason, FBI interview report, September 4, 1957 page number illegible, FBI Little Rock Central High Integration Crisis, FBI Records, box 1, folder 933 (1), UALR-SC, Faubus, *Down from the Hills*, 197–201, and Pagan, interview with Upton, August 22, 1972, 2, Murphy Papers, box 5, folder 3, UALR-SC. See also Bartley, *The Rise of Massive Resistance*, 264, Cope, "'A Thorn in the Side'?," 178, Freyer, *The Little Rock Crisis*, 101, Godfrey, "'It's Time for the Mothers to Take Over,'" 12–13, and Jacoway, *Turn Away Thy Son*, 110–12.

98. Faubus, speech, September 2, 1957, 9–12, Faubus Papers, MC F27301, box 496, folder 1, UALR-SC.

99. On the desegregation struggle in Clinton, Tennessee, see van West, "Clinton Desegregation Crisis."

100. See Thevenet, FBI interview report, 270, FBI Little Rock School Crisis Report, box 2, file 14, UALR-ASI.

101. Bates, *The Long Shadow of Little Rock*, 57.

102. Ernest Valachnovic, "U.S. Judge Rejects Chancery Injunction," *Arkansas Gazette*, August 31, 1957, 1–2A; Bobbie Forster, "Court Rules Out Changes on Integration," *Arkansas Democrat*, August 31, 1957, 1. According to Daisy Bates, it had actually been NAACP attorney Wiley Branton who had "placed the matter before" Judge Davies and had asked for a "federal injunction" (Bates to Carter, August 31, 1957, Stockley Papers, box 2, folder 9, UALR-BC).

103. "Court Rules Out Changes on Integration."

104. "The Little Rock Story," *Southern School News*, October 1957, 1; Ray Moseley, "Faubus Calls National Guard to Keep Schools Segregated," *Arkansas Gazette*, September 3, 1957, 1; Faubus, interview with DeVries and Bass, June 14, 1974, 29–33, UNC-SOHC; "What They're Saying About Little Rock," *Arkansas Gazette*, September 5, 1B. Other citizens' councils and other segregationist groups interpreted Faubus's move as support for their cause. In a telegram to Faubus, the Citizens' Council of Greater New Orleans stated that if "all chief executives in the southern states take your courageous stand there would never be any racial strife in the South. We urge you to stand firm and to keep faith so that you may serve as an example for others to do likewise." ("What They're Saying About Little Rock," *Arkansas Gazette*, September 5, 1B) Three years later, several New

Orleans politicians cited Little Rock as an example of the lengths to which they were willing to go in their protest against William Frantz and McDonogh 19 elementary schools' desegregation.

105. "Little Rock Quiet on Eve of Opening Integrated Schools," *Arkansas Gazette*, September 2, 1957, 1–2A.

106. Alves, FBI interview report, September 4, 1957, 359, Little Rock Central High Integration Crisis, FBI Records, box 1, folder 933 (2), UALR-SC; Brooks, FBI interview report, September 6, 1967, 355–56, FBI Little Rock School Crisis Report, box 2, file 8, UALR-ASI; Thevenet, FBI interview report, September 7, 1957, 269, FBI Little Rock School Crisis Report, box 2, file 14, UALR-ASI; Mother's League of Central High School membership list, Murphy Papers, box 11, folder 5, UALR-SC.

107. Alves, FBI interview report, September 5, 1957, 359, Little Rock Central High Integration Crisis, FBI Records, box 1, folder 933 (2).

108. Jackson, FBI interview report, September 6, 1957, 351, FBI Little Rock School Crisis Report, box 2, file 8, UALR-ASI; Sedberry, FBI interview report, September 7, 1957, 375, Little Rock Central High Integration Crisis, FBI Records, box 1, folder 933 (3), UALR-SC; Huckaby, *Crisis at Central High*, 70.

109. Aaron, FBI interview report, September 5, 1957, 364–65, FBI Little Rock School Crisis Report, box 2, file 8, UALR-ASI.

110. Gay, FBI interview report, September 5, 1957, page number illegible, Little Rock Central High Integration Crisis, FBI *Records*, box 1, folder 933 (2), UALR-SC; Heitmann, FBI interview report, September 8, 1957, 256, and Huff, FBI interview report, September 7, 1957, 261, FBI Little Rock School Crisis Report, box 2, folder 14, UALR-ASI.

111. Alves, FBI interview report, September 4, 1957, 359, Little Rock Central High Integration Crisis, FBI Records, box 1, folder 933 (2); Godfrey, "'It's Time for the Mothers to Take Over,'" 21–23; Godfrey, "'Sweet Little Girls'?," 149. At this point, the *Arkansas Gazette* reported of "some 15" eligible black pupils who could enter Central High School on September 3, 1957. Sandusky thus at least doubled the number of black students when talking to Alves. See "A Time of Testing," 1.

112. Cope, "'A Thorn in the Side'?," 171.

113. Anderson, "Massive Resistance, Violence, and Southern Social Relations," 212.

114. Miller, FBI interview report, September 8, 1957, 246, FBI Little Rock School Crisis Report, box 2, file 14, UALR-ASI.

115. Jacoway, *Turn Away Thy Son*, 7. The "carnival atmosphere" outside Central High parallels the contemporary descriptions of segregationist crowds, particularly the cheerleaders, in New Orleans three years later in 1960. Preceding the New Orleans' cheerleaders on a smaller scale, the crowd's actions were consciously performative, aiming at creating publicity for both the desegregation crisis and the women themselves.

116. Jerry Dhonau, "Crowd of 400 Watches White Students Enroll," *Arkansas Gazette*, September 4, 1957, 1 and 1B.

117. "In the Crowd," *Arkansas Democrat*, September 3, 1957, 2–A.

118. Dhonau, "Crowd of 400 Watches White Students Enroll," 1B.

119. Jackson, FBI interview report, September 6, 1957, 351, FBI Little Rock School Crisis Report, box 2, file 8, UALR-ASI; Cope, "'A Thorn in the Side'?," 179.

120. Stephens, FBI interview report, September 5, 1957, 367–68, FBI Little Rock School Crisis Report, box 2, file 8, UALR-ASI.

121. Stephens, FBI interview report, September 5, 1957, 367–68, FBI Little Rock School Crisis Report, box 2, file 8, UALR-ASI. See also Cope, "'A Thorn in the Side'?," 179.

122. Stephens, FBI interview report, September 5, 1957, 368, FBI Little Rock School Crisis Report, box 2, file 8, UALR-ASI.

123. Ernest Valachovic, "Judge Orders Start of Integration Today," *Arkansas Gazette*, September 4, 1957, 1; Ray Moseley, "National Guard to Stay," *Arkansas Gazette*, September 4, 1957, 1; Leslie Carpenter, "Brownell Studying Whether to Move against Faubus," *Arkansas Gazette*, September 4, 1957, 1. On the front page, a *Gazette* editorial scolded Faubus for the crisis he had created, which "the rest of us must now suffer" ("The Crisis Mr. Faubus Made," *Arkansas Gazette*, September 4, 1957, 1).

124. Miller, FBI interview report, September 8, 1957, 246, FBI Little Rock School Crisis Report, box 2, file 14, UALR-ASI; Robert Troutt, "Crowd Jeers as Negro Students Attempt to Enter Central High," *Arkansas Democrat*, September 4, 1957, 1–2A; Jacoway, *Turn Away Thy Son*, 3–8. See also Anderson, *Little Rock*, 1–4, and Margolick, *Elizabeth and Hazel*. On Hazel Bryan and her social background, see Isenberg, *White Trash*, 247–49.

125. Jacoway, *Turn Away Thy Son*, 4–5; Kirk, *Redefining The Color Line*, 116–17; Ray Moseley, "9 Negroes Barred on Faubus Order," *Arkansas Gazette*, September 5, 1957, 1–2A; George Douthit, "Armed Troops Turn Back 9 Negroes at Central High School," *Arkansas Democrat*, September 4, 1957, 1–2; Jerry Dhonau, "Negro Girl Turned Back," *Arkansas Gazette*, September 5, 1957, 1–2A; Johnson, FBI interview report, September 6, 1957, 45, Little Rock Central High Integration Crisis, FBI Records, box 1, folder 933 (1), UALR-SC. Terrence Roberts, another pupil of the Little Rock Nine, had arrived shortly after Eckford and was turned away by the guards as well. After briefly greeting Eckford, Roberts walked away to the hooting of the crowd (Dhonau, "Negro Girl Turned Back," 2A; Adren Cooper, "'Didn't Think It Would Go This Far,'" *Arkansas Democrat*, September 5, 1957, 7).

126. See Godfrey, "'Sweet Little Girls'?," iii, 199, Bates, *The Long Shadow of Little Rock*, 69–71, Jacoway, *Turn Away Thy Son*, 5, Dhonau, "Negro Girl Turned Back," 1–2A, and Dhonau, "Daily Crowds at School Scene," 6A.

127. Dhonau, "Daily Crowds at School Scene," 6A.

128. Dhonau, "Crowd of Curious Continue to Mill," 1. See also Oberste, FBI interview report, September 5, 1957, 317–18, Little Rock Central High Integration Crisis, FBI Records, box 1, folder 933 (3), UALR-SC, Button, FBI interview report, 373, FBI Little Rock School Crisis Report, box 2, file 8, UALR-ASI, and Bickle, FBI interview report, September 9, 1957, 151, Little Rock Central High Integration Crisis, FBI Records, box 1, folder 933 (1), UALR-SC. Oberste was the photographer for KATV; Button was chief photographer for KARK-TV.

129. Sedberry, FBI interview report, September 7, 1957, 375, Little Rock Central High Integration Crisis, FBI Records, MC 1027, box 1, folder 933 (3), UALR-SC.

130. Aaron, FBI interview report, September 5, 1957, 364, FBI Little Rock School Crisis Report, box 2, file 8, UALR-ASI; Jackson, FBI interview reports, September 6 and September 7, 1957, 350, 354, FBI Little Rock School Crisis Report, box 2, file 8, UALR-ASI; Thomason, FBI interview report, September 4, 1957, page number illegible, Little Rock Central High Integration Crisis, FBI Records, box 1, folder 933 (1), UALR-SC; Forbess, FBI interview report, September 7, 1957, 258–59, FBI Little Rock School Crisis Report, box 2, file 14, UALR-ASI; Sedberry, FBI interview report, September 7, 1957, 375, Little Rock

Central High Integration Crisis, FBI Records, box 1, folder 933 (3), UALR-SC; Shatzer, FBI interview report, September 8, 1957, 388, FBI Little Rock School Crisis Report, box 2, file 8, UALR-ASI; Thevenet, FBI interview report, September 7, 1957, 269, FBI Little Rock School Crisis Report, box 2, file 14, UALR-ASI; Mother's League of Central High School membership list, Murphy Papers, box 11, folder 5, UALR-SC.

131. Lightcap, FBI interview report, September 6, 1967, 371–72, Little Rock Central High Integration Crisis, FBI Records, box 1, folder 933 (1), UALR-SC; Sandusky, FBI interview report, September 6, 1957, 357, and Elrod, FBI interview report, September 7, 1957, 374, FBI Little Rock School Crisis Report, box 2, file 8, UALR-ASI; Webb, FBI interview report, September 10, 1957, 253, FBI Little Rock School Crisis Report, box 2, file 14, UALR-ASI; Foreman, FBI interview report, September 8, 1957, 255, FBI Little Rock School Crisis Report, box 2, file 14, UALR-ASI; Mother's League of Central High School membership list, Murphy Papers, box 11, folder 5, UALR-SC.

132. Foreman, FBI interview report, September 8, 1957, 255, FBI Little Rock School Crisis Report, box 2, file 14, UALR-ASI; Thomason, FBI interview report, September 4, 1957, page number illegible, FBI Little Rock School Crisis Report, box 2, file 8, UALR-ASI; Jacoway, *Turn Away Thy Son*, 95.

133. Ray Moseley, "Faubus Withdraws Guard after Court Enjoins Him," *Arkansas Gazette*, September 21, 1957, 1.

134. Robert Troutt, "Situation Calm on Two Fronts," *Arkansas Democrat*, September 1, 1957, 1; "Tension Easing," photograph, *Arkansas Democrat*, September 1, 1957, 1; Huckaby, *Crisis at Central High*, 27; Huckaby to Paisley, September 8, 1957, Huckaby Papers, box 1, folder 3, UALR-SC; Kirk, *Redefining the Color Line*, 118; Ray Moseley, "Judge Refuses Delay in School Integration," *Arkansas Gazette*, September 8, 1957, 1. Also see "Chief Counsel of NAACP Now on Scene," *Arkansas Gazette*, September 7, 1957, 1, and "School Board Stymied by Troops," *Arkansas Democrat*, September 5, 1957, 1–2.

135. "School Board Stymied by Troops," 2; Miller, FBI interview report, September 12, 1957, page number illegible, and Hugh Lynn Adams, FBI interview report, September 13, 1957, page number illegible, Little Rock Central High Integration Crisis, FBI Records, box 1, folder 855, UALR-SC. Miller, of West Memphis, Arkansas, was president of the Crittenden County White Citizens' Council; Adams, of Bassett, Arkansas, was president of the Mississippi County Citizens' Council.

136. "Guthridge Talks Dis-integration in Alabama," *Arkansas Gazette*, September 17, 1957, 2A.

137. See Lewis, *Massive Resistance*, 12, 87.

138. Note about Katherine Dame's phone call, September 17, 1957, Faubus Papers, box 498, folder 4, UALR-SC.

139. Troutt, "Negroes to Enter Central Monday," 1; "City and State Police to Be There Today," 1.

140. Thomason, quoted in Cope, "'A Thorn in the Side'?," 169; "City and State Police to Be There Today," 1.

141. Mosley, "Faubus Withdraws Guard after Court Enjoins Him," 1; Robert McCord, "Faubus Says 'Now Begins Crucifixion,'" *Arkansas Democrat*, September 20, 1957, 1; Robert Troutt, "Negroes to Enter Central Monday," *Arkansas Democrat*, September 22, 1957, 1; Bartley, *The Rise of Massive Resistance*, 267–68; Kirk, *Redefining the Color Line*, 118; see also "City and State Police to Be There Today," *Arkansas Gazette*, September 23, 1957, 1.

142. Cope, "'Everybody Says All Those People . . . Were from out of Town, but They Weren't,'" 254.

143. Director's brief (2673), 54, 43–44, FBI Little Rock School Crisis Report, box 1, file 5, UALR-ASI.

144. Director's brief (2673), 46, FBI Little Rock School Crisis Report, box 1, file 5, UALR-ASI; Hilda Thevenet, FBI interview report, September 7, 1957, 269, FBI Little Rock School Crisis Report, box 2, file 14, UALR-ASI; Huckaby, *Crisis at Central High*, 70.

145. Ramsey, FBI interview report, September 28, 1957, page number illegible, Little Rock Central High Integration Crisis, FBI Records, box 2, folder 971 (1), UALR-SC.

146. Jerry Dhonau, "Mobs at Both Ends of School Kick, Beat, Chase and Yell," *Arkansas Gazette*, September 24, 1957, 1–2A.

147. Director's brief (2673), 43–44, 53, FBI Little Rock School Crisis Report, box 1, file 5, UALR-ASI.

148. Phyllis Dillaha, "Wails, Threats," *Arkansas Democrat*, September 23, 1957, 1; Dhonau, "Mobs at Both Ends of School, Kick, Beat, Chase, and Yell," 2A; director's brief (2673), 44, FBI Little Rock School Crisis Report, box 1, file 5, UALR-ASI; "Collection for Policeman," photograph, *Arkansas Gazette*, September 24, 1957, 1B.

149. Dhonau, "Mobs at Both Ends of School, Kick, Beat, Chase, and Yell," 2A; director's brief (2673), 43–44, 53, FBI Little Rock School Crisis Report, box 1, file 5, UALR-ASI; Jacoway, *Turn Away Thy Son*, 170.

150. Godfrey, "'Sweet Little Girls'?," 177; Dhonau, "Mobs at Both Ends of School, Kick, Beat, Chase, and Yell," 2A; Dillaha, "Wails, Threats," 1; Benjamin Fine, "President Threatens to Use U.S. Troops," *New York Times*, September 24, 1957, 18.

151. Dhonau, "Mobs at Both Ends of School, Kick, Beat, Chase, and Yell," 2A; Troutt, "Growing Violence Forces Withdrawal of 8 Negro Students at Central High," 2.

152. Lewis, *Massive Resistance*, 84.

153. Alex Wilson, "Defender Reporter Beaten by Mob Tells His Story," *Chicago Daily Defender*, September 25, 1957, 22; Dhonau, "Mobs at Both Ends of School Kick, Beat, Chase, and Yell," 1–2A; Jacoway, *Turn Away Thy Son*, 172. The journalists were L. A. Wilson of Memphis's *Tri-State Defender*, James L. Hicks of New York *Amsterdam News*, Moses J. Newson of the *Baltimore Afro-American*, and Little Rock photographer Earl Davy.

154. Dhonau, "Mobs at Both Ends of School Kick, Beat, Chase, and Yell," 2A.

155. Dhonau, "Mobs at Both Ends of School, Kick, Beat, Chase, and Yell," 2A; Troutt, "Growing Violence Forces Withdrawal of 8 Negro Students at Central High," 1–2. At the time, there was confusion as to how many of the Little Rock Nine attended school on September 23, 1957. Evidently, the mob's information was that only eight students had entered Central High, a number that both the *Arkansas Gazette* and *Arkansas Democrat* reported. Daisy Bates, on the other hand, states in *The Long Shadow of Little Rock* that all nine students were at Central High that day (88–89). Similarly, Central High's vice president Elizabeth Huckaby confirmed that all of the Little Rock Nine attended school that day (Huckaby Papers, box 1, folder 3, UALR-SC).

156. Dhonau, "Mobs at Both Ends of School, Kick, Beat, Chase, and Yell," 2A; director's brief (2673, 53–54, FBI Little Rock School Crisis Report, box 1, file 5, UALR-ASI. Thevenet's statement was confirmed by the school registrar Earnestine Opie, whom Thevenet said she "trusted" and who announced that the Little Rock Nine had been "withdrawn

from School" as far as she knew. See Dhonau, "Mobs at Both Ends of School, Kick, Beat, Chase, and Yell," 2A.

157. Patillo, quoted in Jacoway, *Turn Away Thy Son*, 171; conversation between Current and Bates, transcript, September 23, 1957, 1–2, Stockley Papers, box 2, folder 7, UALR-BC; director's brief (2673), 54, FBI Little Rock School Crisis Report, box 1, file 5, UALR-ASI; Bates, *The Long Shadow of Little Rock*, 93–94.

158. Robert Troutt, "Growing Violence Forces Withdrawal of 8 Negro Students at Central High," *Arkansas Democrat*, September 23, 1957, 1; conversation between Current and Bates, transcript, September 23, 1957, 1–2, Stockley Papers, box 2, folder 7, UALR-BC; Kirk, *Redefining the Color Line*, 119; Bartley, *The Rise of Massive Resistance*, 268.

159. Capital Citizens' Council, advertisement, *Arkansas Democrat*, September 23, 1957, 9. The advertisement was paid for by a "Group of Patriotic Christians," which included Julian Miller, the husband of a league member.

160. "Troops Scarcely Mentioned at Citizens' Council Meeting," *Arkansas Gazette*, September 25, 1957, 2A; "Council for Abolishing All Schools," *Arkansas Democrat*, September 25, 1957, 4.

161. The group's official financial statement of October 31, 1957, showed a balance of only $240.52. As the group never collected membership dues (and apparently did not receive any substantial financial support from the Capital Citizens' Council apart from its footing of the league's first rallies' and hotel room bills), its only sources of income up to that point were two collections taken up on August 23, 1957, and September 24, 1957, as well as the proceeds from a cake sale the group had held on October 26, 1957. A total of $365.02 was collected, of which $124.50 was spent on newspaper advertisements. By January of the next year, Margaret Jackson admitted at a league meeting that the group "was broke," and a collection was taken up again. See Mothers League of Central High School, financial statement, October 31, 1957, Murphy Papers, box 11, folder 5, UALR-SC, and "Clashes Mark Little Rock Month," *Southern School News*, February 1958, 12–13.

162. "Troops Scarcely Mentioned," 2A; "Council for Abolishing All Schools," 4; George Douthit, "Faubus under Fire to Call Legislature," *Arkansas Democrat*, September 27, 1957, 1.

163. Faubus, speech, September 26, 1975, WSB-TV news film, clip 39763, UOG-CRDL, http://dlg.galileo.usg.edu/crdl/id:ugabma_wsbn_39763; "Governor Calls for Calm, Order," *Arkansas Gazette*, September 27, 1957, 1.

164. Godfrey, "Bayonets, Brainwashing, and Bathrooms," 50–56.

165. "Governor Calls for Calm, Order" 1–2A; Godfrey, "'Sweet Little Girls'?," 186.

166. "FBI Agent Denies Report Girls Detained," *Arkansas Gazette*, October 4, 1957, 1–2A.

167. Mother's League of Central High School membership list, Murphy Papers, box 11, folder 5, UALR-SC; "FBI Agent Denies Report Girls Detained," *Arkansas Gazette*, October 4, 1957, 1.

168. Ray Moseley, "Boycott Chiefs Disappointed as 50 Students Walk Out," *Arkansas Gazette*, October 4, 1957, 1.

169. George Douthit, "New State Laws to Deal with CHS Considered," *Arkansas Democrat*, September 28, 1957, 1; Lewis, "Ike Says Mob Encouraged by Faubus," 1–2A; "Little Rock's Situation in Arkansas' Spotlight," *Southern School News*, November 1957, 6; Homer Bigart, "Faubus Is Defiant," *New York Times*, September 29, 1957, 1, 56.

170. Bigart, "Faubus Is Defiant," 56.

171. Jones, letter to the editor, Little Rock, *Arkansas Gazette*, October 3, 1957, 4.

172. Jackson and Thomason, petition to Faubus, September 28, 1957, Faubus Papers, box 499, folder 10, UALR-SC.

173. Lewis, "Ike Says Mob Encouraged by Faubus," 2A.

174. Wyllie, "Conversations in the South," 2, March 3, 1959, Faubus Papers, box 498, folder 6, UALR-SC.

175. Despite Jackson's proclamation, her daughter Sandra started to reattend Central High School in early October, a development indicative of the league's change in strategy. See Lewis, "Ike Says Mob Encouraged by Faubus," 2A, and Cope, "'A Thorn in the Side'?," 163, 185.

176. Lewis, "Ike Says Mob Encouraged by Faubus," 2A.

177. Lewis, "Ike Says Mob Encouraged by Faubus," 2A; Jackson and Thomason, petition to Orval Faubus, September 28, 1957, Faubus Papers, box 499, folder 10, UALR-SC. See also Douthit, "New State Laws to Deal with CHS Considered," 1, Bigart, "Faubus Is Defiant," 56, and "Little Rock's Situation in Arkansas' Spotlight," 6.

178. Jackson and Thomason, petition to Orval Faubus, September 28, 1957, Faubus Papers, box 499, folder 10, UALR-SC; see also Jacoway, *Turn Away Thy Son*, 198.

179. "A Mother," letter to the editor, *Arkansas Democrat*, September 30, 1957, 10.

180. See Accapadi, "When White Women Cry," 209.

181. Lewis, "Ike Says Mob Encouraged by Faubus," 2A; Bigart, "Faubus Is Defiant," 56; "Encouragement for the Governor," photograph, *Arkansas Gazette*, September 29, 1957, 1. Although Sammie Dean Parker refused to give her name to the reporters that day, her identity as the girl hugging Faubus is later confirmed in "Two Pupils Tell of Change in Attitude towards Segregation," *Arkansas Gazette*, October 15, 1957, 7A. See also "Delay of Pine Bluff, Ark., Plans Linked to Segregation Events at Little Rock," *Southern School News*, April 1958, 12.

182. Schechner, *Performance Theory*, 15, 68; de Certeau, *The Practice of Everyday Life*, 43.

183. Soja, *Postmodern Geographies*, 21.

184. Douthit, "New State Laws to Deal with CHS Considered," 1.

185. "Little Rock's Situation in Arkansas' Spotlight," 6; *Jackson v. Kuhn*, 254 F. 2d 555, no. 15889, U.S. Court of Appeals Eighth Circuit, April 28, 1958; "Little Rock's Situation in Arkansas' Spotlight," 6; "Mother Sues for Removal of Soldiers," *Arkansas Gazette*, October 3, 1957, 1.

186. Director's brief (2673), 38, 38A, FBI Little Rock School Crisis Report, box 1, file 5, UALR-ASI.

187. Relman Morin, "Both Sides Remain Adamant in Central High Stalemate," *Arkansas Gazette*, November 24, 1957, 2A.

188. Mr. and Mrs. O. Childers, white citizens' council applications, Little Rock, 1956, Johnson Collection, box 3, folder 16, ASA. Childers's husband, Robert, was a pest control operator.

189. "Mothers League Changes Leaders," *Arkansas Gazette*, October 25, 1957, 2A.

190. "Mothers League Changes Leaders," 2A.

191. "Central Figures in Crisis Vary in Their Reactions," *Arkansas Gazette*, October 2, 1957, 1, 2A.

192. "Central Figures in Crisis Vary in Their Reactions," 1.

193. Huckaby, *Crisis at Central High*, 61–62. Cope notes that "Charlene . . . may have turned up specifically to join an organized walk-out on October 3" ("'A Thorn in the Side'?," 185).

194. Moseley, "Boycott Chiefs Disappointed as 50 Students Walk Out," 1.

195. Director's brief (2673), 57, FBI Little Rock School Crisis Report, box 1, file 5, UALR-ASI; "Reader, Little Rock," letter to the editor, *Arkansas Gazette*, October 19, 1957, 4.

196. See Isenberg, *White Trash*, 180, 198. On momism, see Evans, *Born For Liberty*, 234–36.

197. "White Native, Little Rock," letter to the editor, *Arkansas Gazette*, October 10, 1957, 2A.

198. Godfrey, "'Sweet Little Girls'?," 126; see also Roy, *Bitters in the Honey*, 3.

199. Jackson to Matthews, December 13, 1957, and December 21, 1957, Blossom Papers, box 7, folder 8, UALR-SC; Edward Martin, "Mothers League Recites Charges in 2-Page Letter," *Arkansas Gazette*, December 15, 1957, 14A; Freedom Fund for Little Rock, advertisement, *Arkansas Democrat*, December 23, 1957, 2. Margaret Jackson paid for this ad. The Freedom Fund for Little Rock was another segregationist group founded by Capital Citizens' Council official Malcolm Taylor; see director's brief (2673), 71, FBI Little Rock School Crisis Report, box 1, file 5, UALR-ASI.

200. Jackson to Matthews, December 13, 1957; Blossom Papers, box 7, folder 8, UALR-SC; Blossom, *It Has Happened Here*, 162–64.

201. "White Trash Matthews," Murphy Papers, box 9, folder 5, UALR-SC.

202. Jackson to Matthews, December 21, 1957, Blossom Papers, box 7, folder 8, UALR-SC.

203. Freedom Fund for Little Rock, advertisement, *Arkansas Democrat*, September 23, 1957.

204. Huckaby, *Crisis at Central High*, 111.

205. Director's brief (2673), 26B, FBI Little Rock School Crisis Report, box 1, file 5, UALR-ASI.

206. Cope, "'A Thorn in the Side'?," 187; Godfrey, "Bayonets, Brainwashing, and Bathrooms," 63–64; Godfrey, "'Sweet Little Girls'?," 189–90.

207. Huckaby, *Crisis at Central High*, 61–63; Ray Moseley, "Girl 'Source' Says Charge against Soldiers Isn't True," *Arkansas Gazette*, October 9, 1957, 1–2A. Craighead told the *Gazette* that the account given by Orval Faubus and others was "an 'exaggerated' version of something she had said to other students: 'The soldiers do not go into the girls' dressing room,' she said" (2A).

208. Faubus to Walker, October 7, 1957, Faubus Papers, box 496, folder 8, UALR-SC.

209. Moseley, "Girl 'Source' Says Charge against Soldiers Isn't True," 2A.

210. Huckaby, *Crisis at Central High*, 62; "GIs in Girls Dressing Rooms," *Arkansas Gazette*, October 8, 1957, 1.

211. See Godfrey, "Bayonets, Brainwashing, and Bathrooms," 43–45.

212. See Bates, *The Long Shadow of Little Rock*, 115–21. The remaining four hundred National Guardsmen stationed at Central High were defederalized and withdrawn in May 1958, and Jackson announced a party at her home for the occasion ("Guardsmen Sent Home," *New York Times*, May 30, 1958, 40).

213. Huckaby, *Crisis at Central High*, 70–71.
214. Huckaby, *Crisis at Central High*, 74.
215. Typewritten note on January attendance, Huckaby Papers, box 2, folder 18, UALR-SC; Anderson, *Little Rock*, 113.
216. Huckaby, *Crisis at Central High*, 131.
217. Segregationist flyer, undated, Murphy Papers, box 9, folder 5, UALR-SC.
218. Note, April 10, 1958, Huckaby Papers, box 2, folder 18, UALR-SC. Also see Godfrey, "'Sweet Little Girls'?," 220–21.
219. "Ouster of Pupil Is Laid to Attack," *New York Times*, March 5, 1958, 28.
220. Moseley, "Boycott Chiefs Disappointed as 50 Students Walk Out," 1; "Report to Mr. Blossom on Darlene Holloway," Huckaby Papers, box 2, folder 18, UALR-SC.
221. Blossom, *It Has Happened Here*, 135–36; "Little Rock's Situation in Arkansas' Spotlight," 6; Templeton, investigation report, Arkansas State Police, 5, Faubus Papers, box 498, folder 2, UALR-SC.
222. Director's brief (2673), 69B, FBI Little Rock School Crisis Report, box 1, file 5, UALR-ASI. Repeated bomb scares in the winter of 1958 further destabilized the school's daily routine. See "Stick of Dynamite Found in CHS," *Arkansas Democrat*, January 20, 1958, 1.
223. Bobbie Foster, "Police Again Search CHS for 'Bomb,'" *Arkansas Democrat*, January 21, 1958, 1–2.
224. Huckaby, *Crisis at Central High*, 89–90.
225. Huckaby, *Crisis at Central High*, 89–90.
226. Hofstadter, *The Paranoid Style in American Politics*, 6, 25–39.
227. See also advertisement, *Arkansas Democrat*, January 25, 1958, 3.
228. On Thomason's election, see "Pruden New Head of Council," *Arkansas Democrat*, December 18, 1957, 12.
229. "Fuss over Integration Injected into Campaign for City Board Posts," *Arkansas Gazette*, September 29, 1957, 4A. Capital Citizens' Council official E. A. Lauderdale also entered the race.
230. "Fuss over Integration Injected into Campaign for City Board Posts," 4A; Ernest Valachovic, "Little Rock Board Candidates Face 'Moneyless' Campaigns," *Arkansas Gazette*, October 9, 1957, 1B.
231. Advertisement, *Arkansas Democrat*, November 4, 1957, 4, emphasis in the original. See also Capital Citizens' Council, advertisement, *Arkansas Democrat*, November 4, 1957, 14.
232. "A Neighbor," letter to the editor, *Arkansas Gazette*, November 5, 1957, 4A.
233. Bill Lewis, "Spirits of Segregationists Rise and Fall with Returns," *Arkansas Gazette*, November 6, 1957, 1–2A.
234. "Near Stalemate Reported at Arkansas High School," *Southern School News*, December 1957, 2; "Little Rock Voters Choose Directors to Run City Today," *Arkansas Gazette*, November 5, 1957, 1B; "Segregationist Vote Strength Surprises," *Arkansas Gazette*, November 7, 1957, 1.
235. Lewis, "Spirits of Segregationists Rise and Fall with Returns," 1–2A.
236. George Bentley, "Griffin, Mrs. Dixon Lose Some Votes but Keep Victories," *Arkansas Gazette*, November 9, 1957, 1.

237. "Pruden New Head of Council," 12.

238. "4th Woman Files for House Post," 2.

239. "4th Woman Files for House Post," 2.

240. "L. C. Young Choice for Sheriff," *Arkansas Democrat*, August 13, 1958; "Incumbent Legislators, Mrs. Oates Win Races," *Arkansas Gazette*, August 13, 1958, 1.

241. *Arkansas Democrat*, advertisement, August 7, 1958, 5A, emphasis in original. Mary Thomason paid for the ad.

242. See "Incumbent Legislators, Mrs. Oates Win Races," 1. On the links between racially reactionary politics and emerging conservative policies, see Lewis, "Virginia's Northern Strategy," 145, McGirr, *Suburban Warriors*, and Noble, "Conservatism in the USA."

243. *Arkansas Democrat*, advertisement, August 7, 1958, 5A, emphasis in original.

244. "Mothers' League Plans Expansion in State, Nation," *Arkansas Gazette*, October 23, 1957, 2A; "League of Mothers Eyes North," *Arkansas Democrat*, October 13, 1957, newspaper clipping, Blossom Papers, box 24, folder 4, UALR-SC.

245. "South Not Dead, Johnson Says," *Arkansas Democrat*, March 21, 1958, 4.

246. Mothers League of America, advertisement, *Arkansas Democrat*, October 16, 1957, newspaper clipping, Blossom Papers, box 24, folder 4, UALR-SC. Margaret Jackson paid for this ad.

247. "League of Mothers Eyes North."

248. "Mothers League Changes Leaders, Plans Expansion," *Arkansas Gazette*, October 25, 1957, newspaper clipping, Blossom Papers, box 24, folder 6, UALR-SC.

249. "CHS Mothers' League Plans Meeting Tonight," *Arkansas Gazette*, November 7, 1960, 1B.

250. "League of Mothers Eyes North."

251. "School Board Cites Inability to Enforce Compliance," *Arkansas Democrat*, February 21, 1958, 1; "Board Decision Was Made 2 Weeks Ago," *Arkansas Democrat*, February 21, 1958, 1.

252. "Ruling Hailed, Criticized," *Arkansas Democrat*, June 21, 1958, 1.

253. "City's High Schools Closed by Governor," *Arkansas Democrat*, September 13, 1958, 1.

254. George Douthit, "Governor Elated by Decision, Sees Opening of Schools Coming Quickly," *Arkansas Democrat*, September 28, 1958, 1.

255. "Louisiana Ad 'Salutes Little Rock,'" *Arkansas Democrat*, September 24, 1958, 1.

256. Cope, "'The Workingest, Fightingest, Band of Patriots in the South'?," 142; "Louisiana Ad 'Salutes Little Rock,'" 1; Bobbie Forster, "Petitions to Recall Four on School Board Circulated by Mothers,'" *Arkansas Democrat*, September 20, 1958, 1.

257. *Arkansas Democrat*, advertisement, September 24, 1958, 6. The ad was paid for by Pauline McLenden.

258. Bobbie Forster, "TV Schooling Starts Monday," *Arkansas Democrat*, September 18, 1958, 1; George Douthit, "Group to Operate School Chartered," *Arkansas Democrat*, September 17, 1958, 1.

259. Cope, "'The Workingest, Fightingest, Band of Patriots in the South'?," 146–47; "Rebel Rouser," Thomas J. Raney High School, January 18, 1959, vol. 1, no. 1, Women's Emergency Committee Collection, reel MG 00499, box 6, folder 11, ASA; Robert Troutt, "Ex-Raney Pupils Stage Rally," *Arkansas Democrat*, August 10, 1959, 1.

260. Save Our Schools, Inc., Women's Emergency Committee Records, reel MG00499, box 6, folder 11, ASA.

261. Gates, "Down from the Pedestal," 218–19; Godfrey, "'Sweet Little Girls'?," 230–50; Jacoway, introduction, 11–13.

262. Murphy, *Breaking the Silence*, 125.

263. Mothers' League of Central High School, advertisement, *Arkansas Democrat*, May 23, 1959, 4.

264. Mothers' League of Central High School, advertisement, newspaper clipping, undated, ca. 1959, Women's Emergency Committee Records, reel MG 00504, box 16, folder 1, ASA; John L. Ward, "Mothers League Seeks Recall of Matson, Lamb, Tucker," *Arkansas Democrat*, May 10, 1959, 1; Mothers' League of Central of High School, advertisement, *Arkansas Democrat*, May 24, 1959, 10A.

265. Gates, "Power from the Pedestal," 220–21.

266. "School Election Lacked Issues," *Arkansas Gazette*, December 5, 1959, 1; Murphy, *Breaking the Silence*, 153–54.

267. "Segregationists Seek to File Additional Signatures," photograph, *Arkansas Democrat*, May 13, 1959, 1; Bobbie Forster, "Early Check Reflects Signatures Sufficient For Vote on Each Slate," *Arkansas Democrat*, May 13, 1959, 1; Murphy, *Breaking the Silence*, 154; "School Election Lacked Issues," 1.

268. "Two 'Moderates' Are Re-Elected to Little Rock's School Board," *Southern School News*, January 1960, 5; advertisement, *Arkansas Gazette*, December 1, 1959, 14A.

269. "Moderates Retain School Board Posts," *Arkansas Gazette*, December 2, 1959, 1.

270. "Two 'Moderates' Are Re-Elected to Little Rock's School Board," 5.

271. "Dollarway's Statement Is Approved by Federal Judge," *Southern School News*, June 1960, 6.

272. Cope, "'The Master Conspirator' and His Henchmen," 52.

Chapter 3. The Cheerleaders of New Orleans

1. Steinbeck, *Travels with Charley*, 249–53, 255.

2. Steinbeck, *Travels with Charley*, 256, 256–57.

3. Steinbeck, *Travels with Charley*, 257–59, 258.

4. Steinbeck, *Travels with Charley*, 258–59.

5. Several literary works have thematized the cheerleaders; see, for example, Coles and Ford, *The Story of Ruby Bridges*, and Sharenow, *My Mother the Cheerleader*.

6. See Wieder, "One Who Stayed," 195.

7. Baker, *The Second Battle of New Orleans*, 394–95; Fairclough, *Race and Democracy*, 244; Jeansonne, *Leander Perez*, 258; Lee Callaway, "Orleans Board Standing Firm," *Times Picayune*, November 14, 1960, 1; Fritz Harsdorff, "Desegregation of Public Schools Is Carried Out without Violence," *Times Picayune*, November 15, 1960, 1–2; "Louisiana," *Southern School News*, December 1960, 1. Also see "The Battle of New Orleans," *New York Times*, November 15, 1960, 38.

8. Harsdorff, "Desegregation of Public Schools Is Carried Out without Violence," 2; "Mayor Praises Orleans Public," *Times Picayune*, November 15, 1960, 13.

9. "Two Little Rock White Schools with 11 Negroes Reportedly Quiet," *Times Picayune*, November 16, 1960, 9; "Faubus Scores Orleans Mixing," *Alexandria Daily Town Talk*,

November 16, 1960, 11. Faubus, too, asserted that the black students were merely being used as pawns.

10. "U.S. Power Grab Seen in Mixing," *Times Picayune*, November 15, 1960, 4.

11. Although newspapers mostly used the term "Negro" when they quoted segregationist women, the women themselves used the word "nigger." The *Times Picayune* and other papers avoided printing the slur, but they also eliminated the rabidly racist language underlining the women's statements.

12. "New Orleans Schools Integrated," *Alexandria Daily Town Talk*, November 14, 1960, 1; "N.O. Schools Are Integrated," *Baton Rouge States-Item*, November 14, 1960, 1; "N.O. Schools Integrated; No Violence," *Louisiana Weekly*, November 18, 1960, 1, 8; Walter Goodstein, "Police-Guarded Negro Pupils Jeered," *Times Picayune*, November 15, 1960, 8; Jerry Hopkins, "Frantz School Crowd Noisy," *Times Picayune*, November 15, 1960, 9; Charles C. Phillips, "Whites Protest with Boos as School 'Mixes,'" *Shreveport Journal*, November 14, 1960, 1. See also Baker, *The Second Battle of New Orleans*, 400. The *Shreveport Journal* was edited by segregationist George Shannon, who officially joined the Citizens' Councils of America in 1971 ("Shannon Joins Citizens' Council," *Shreveport Times*, September 21, 1971, 26).

13. Hopkins, "Frantz School Crowd Noisy," 9; Phillips, "Whites Protest with Boos as School 'Mixes,'" 1.

14. Hopkins, "Frantz School Crowd Noisy," 9; John E. Rousseau, "6-Year-Old Negro Girl Mob Targets," *Pittsburgh Courier*, November 16, 1960, 2. See also Wilhoit, *The Politics of Massive Resistance*, 187–88.

15. "New Orleans Schools Integrated," 1.

16. Goodstein, "Police-Guarded Negro Pupils Jeered," 8.

17. "Orleans Police Break Up Crowds," *Alexandria Daily Town Talk*, November 15, 1960, 7.

18. Harry P. Gamble Sr., letter to the editor, *Shreveport Journal*, November 14, 1960, 8–A. Gamble, an attorney, was state representative for Winn Parish in 1904 and 1906 and state assistant attorney general in 1912. He also joined the segregationist Society for the Preservation of State Government and Racial Integrity in 1955 (see McMillen, *The Citizens' Council*, 62). On September 27, 1957, the *Times Picayune* published a piece by Gamble in which he condemned the "invasion of Arkansas by federal troops" (Gamble Papers, mss. 4054, box 1, folder 4, LSU-SC).

19. "Rowdiness Marks Mixing," *Times Picayune*, November 16, 2; "Orleans Police Break Up Crowd," *Alexandria Daily Town Talk*, November 15, 1960, 7.

20. "School Attendance Rises," *Times Picayune*, November 16, 1960, 14; see Fairclough, *Race and Democracy*, 250–51, and Inger, *Politics and Reality in an American City*, 38.

21. "Rowdiness Marks Mixing at Schools," 1–2; "Little Teaching Being Done at New Orleans School," *Shreveport Journal*, November 15, 1960, 1; Claude Sitton, "Tension Rising in New Orleans as Result of School Integration," *New York Times*, November 16, 1960, 1.

22. "Rowdiness Marks Mixing at Schools," 2; "Orleans Police Break Up Crowd," 7. See also "New Orleans, Recess Expected to Ease Tensions in School Integration Dispute," Telenews, November 16, 1960, vol. 13, issue 233, roll no. 2451, SG 10874, Hearst Metrotone News Collection, UCLA.

23. "New Orleans, White Schools in New Orleans Integrated," *Telenews*, November

15, 1960, vol. 13, issue 232, roll no. 2246, SG 11436, Hearst Metrotone News Collection, UCLA.

24. "New Orleans, White Schools in New Orleans Integrated," *Telenews*, November 15, 1960, vol. 13, issue 232, roll no. 2246, SG 11436, Hearst Metrotone News Collection, UCLA.

25. "Rowdiness Marks Mixing at Schools," 2.

26. "Rowdiness Marks Mixing at Schools," 2; Ben Thomas, "New Orleans Mothers Say They Will Continue Boycott," *Alexandria Daily Town Talk*, January 20, 1961, 8; "Violence, Jeers, and Boos Mark Second Day of School Integration in N.O. Today," *Baton Rouge States-Item*, November 15, 1960, 1.

27. Rousseau, "6-Year-Old Negro Girl Mob Targets," 2; "Citizens Group to Hear Talks," *Times Picayune*, November 13, 1960, 18; "Arrests of Marshals," *Times Picayune*, November 16, 1960, 1, 19; "Segregationists Ask People to Back Showdown," *Shreveport Journal*, November 16, 1960, 1; Fairclough, *Race and Democracy*, 244; Jeansonne, *Leander Perez*, 259.

28. "Arrests of Marshals," 1, 19; "Segregationists Ask People to Back Showdown," 1; "Petition for Impeachment against J. Skelly Wright, Federal Judge, to the House of Representatives of the United States Congress," undated, Touchstone Papers, box 7, folder 97, LSUS-NWLA.

29. Rousseau, "6-Year-Old Negro Girl Mob Targets," 2.

30. "Arrests of Marshals," 19; Carlton F. Wilson, "Women 'Cheerleaders' Tell Why They Fight Integration," *Alexandria Daily Town Talk*, December 9, 28.

31. "Arrests of Marshals," 19; "Orleans Police Break Up Crowd," 7.

32. "Arrests of Marshals," 19. See also Rousseau, "6-Year-Old Negro Girl Mob Targets," 2.

33. On U.S. opposition to Congo's Prime Minister Patrice Lumumba and the military intervention in the Congo in the context of the Cold War, see Nolan, *The Transatlantic Century*, 226.

34. "Congo Cannibals Rite Reviving," *Times Picayune*, November 27, 1960, 28. The article stated that "U.N. officials were convinced that one of the eight Irish soldiers killed in a recent Balubaö ambush in northern Katanga was eaten in a cannibal ritual."

35. Gordon, "'Midnight Scenes and Orgies,'" 769, 782.

36. "Segregation," *Southern School News*, December 1960, 1.

37. "Jeers, Violence Mark March," *Times Picayune*, November 17, 1960, 6; "Arrests of Marshals," 1; "Teenager Thrust Stymied by Hoses," *Times Picayune*, November 17, 1960, 1 and 22. See also "Hoses Turned on Marches," *Bogalusa Daily News*, November 16, 1960, 1.

38. "Jeers, Violence Mark March," 6.

39. "Jeers, Violence Mark March," 6; "Teenager Thrust Stymied by Hoses," 1; Claude Sitton, "2,000 Youths Riot in New Orleans," *New York Times*, November 17, 1960, 1, 30; "Mob Violence Disgraces City before Whole World," *Louisiana Weekly*, November 16, 1960, 1, 7; "Racists Go Mad in New Orleans," Chicago Daily Defender, November 17, 1960, 1; "Hoses Turned on Marchers," 1; "Louisiana," *Southern School News*, December 1960, 9.

40. "N.O. Police Clash with Irate Mob," *Baton Rouge States-Item*, November 16, 1960, 1; "Teenager Thrust Stymied by Hoses," 1; "Jeers, Violence Mark March," 6.

41. “New Orleans,” *Telenews*, November 17, 1960, vol. 13, issue 234, roll no. 2464, SG 1490, Hearst Metrotone News Collection, UCLA.

42. “New Orleans,” *Telenews*, November 17, 1960, vol. 13, issue 234, roll no. 2464, SG 1490, Hearst Metrotone News Collection, UCLA.

43. “Federal Court Overrules Interposition,” *Bogalusa Daily News*, November 30, 1960, 1.

44. “Federal Court Overrules Interposition,” 1; “White Women Battle,” *Bogalusa Daily News*, December 2, 1960, 1; “At Orleans School, Women Manhandle University Student,” *Shreveport Journal*, December 1, 1960, 1; Warner, “Housewives Ignore U.S. Judges' Edict,” 1; “Legislature Ignores U.S. Supreme Court,” *Louisiana Weekly*, December 10, 1960, 1; “Black-White Dog in N.O. Finds Color against Him,” *Pittsburgh Courier*, December 10, 1960, 2; “La. Jeerleaders Rage 2nd Week,” *Chicago Defender*, December 10, 1960, 2; “The South,” *Time*, December 12, 1960, 20. The *Chicago Daily Defender*—as the name indicates, a daily newspaper—was an addition to the *Chicago Defender*, which appeared and continues to appear weekly.

45. James F. Moldenhauer, letter to the editor, *Times Picayune*, December 7, 1960, Section 1, 12.

46. Wihstutz, introduction, 2–4.

47. Warner, “Housewives Ignore U.S. Judges Edict,” 1; Wilson, “Women 'Cheerleaders' Tell Why They Fight Integration,” 28; Ed Clinton, “N.O. Integration Situation Still Tense,” *Baton Rouge States-Item*, November 29, 1960, 1; “Violence Still Plagues N.O.,” *Baton Rouge States-Item*, December 7, 1960, 1; “Federal Court Overrules Interposition,” 1; “White Women Battle,” 1; Claude Sitton, “Angry Scuffles Mar Integration,” *New York Times*, November 30, 1960, 1; “Legislature Ignores U.S. Supreme Court,” 1.

48. Clinton, “N.O. Integration Situation Still Tense,” 1; “Violence Still Plagues N.O.,” 1; “Federal Court Overrules Interposition,” 1; “White Women Battle,” 1; Sitton, “Angry Scuffles Mar Integration,” 1; “Legislature Ignores U.S. Supreme Court,” 1.

49. “No Instruction for Negro Girl,” *Times Picayune*, November 15, 1960, 1; “School Attendance Rises,” 14; “Little Teaching Being Done at New Orleans School,” 1.

50. “Bid for Private Schools Heard,” *Times Picayune*, November 17, 1960, 2–9.

51. “Bid for Private Schools Heard,” 2–9; “Parents Urged to Fight Mixing,” *Alexandria Daily Town Talk*, November 17, 1960, 13.

52. “Bid for Private Schools Heard,” 2–9; “School Attendance Rises,” 14; “Private School Facilities Aim,” *Times Picayune*, December 3, 1960, 1.

53. “School Mix Issues Face Court Today,” *Times Picayune*, November 18, 1960, 1 and 6.

54. “Jeers, Taunts Ignored By 4 Little Girls,” *Louisiana Weekly*, November 26, 1960, 1, 3; “Pupil Parents Are Unafraid,” *Times Picayune*, November 18, 1960, 13; Coles, “Racial Conflict and a Child's Question,” 164. Two other black fathers were federal employees, which provided them job security.

55. “N.O. Schools Are Integrated,” *Baton Rouge States-Item*, November 14, 1960, 1; “Louisiana,” *Southern School News*, December 1960, 9; “Solons Urge School Boycott,” *Times Picayune*, November 17, 1960, 33; “Citizens Council Praises Parents,” *Times Picayune*, November 18, 1960, 22; Fairclough, *Race and Democracy*, 247.

56. *Alexandria Daily Town Talk*, photograph, November 18, 1960, 1; “Orleans Is Calm As Court Studies Integration Case,” *Baton Rouge States-Item*, November 19, 1960, 1; “Wright Says Duty Forces His Actions,” *Baton Rouge States-Item*, November 21, 1960, 1.

57. "Identities of White Pupils in Schools Held Suit's Aim," *Times Picayune*, November 27, 1960, 1.

58. "La. Solons OK Teachers' Pay, *Times Picayune*, November 24, 1960, 1, 6; "Redmond Target of Wagner Action," *Times Picayune*, November 26, 1960, 1, 24; "Identities of White Pupils in Schools Held Suit's Aim," 1.

59. "Redmond Target of Wagner Action," 1; "Identities of White Pupils in Schools Held Suit's Aim," 1; Fairclough, *Race and Democracy*, 244–47.

60. Bridges, *Through My Eyes*, 16, 19–21.

61. "Parents, Children 'Mourn' at Capitol," *Baton Rouge States-Item*, November 23, 1960, 1, 6–A; "Parents Stage Demonstration," *Times Picayune*, November 24, 1960, 22.

62. One of the cheerleaders present in Baton Rouge was Antoinette Andrews (Wilson, "Women 'Cheerleaders' Tell Why They Fight Integration," 28).

63. "Parents, Children 'Mourn' at Capitol," 1, 6–A.

64. "Rowdyism Haunts Integrated Schools," 1, 7.

65. "Louisiana," *Southern School News*, December 1960, 9; Bridges, *Through My Eyes*, 38; Inger, *Politics and Reality in an American City*, 55–56; see also Lewis, *Massive Resistance*, 118.

66. Bridges, *Through My Eyes*, 15–16.

67. Bridges, *Through My Eyes*, 16, 20–22; Coles, "Racial Conflict and a Child's Question," 164–65.

68. Coles, "Racial Conflict and a Child's Question," 164–65; see also Fairclough, *Race and Democracy*, 248–49.

69. "Boycott Total in McDonogh 19," *Times Picayune*, November 29, 1960, 1, 13.

70. "Angry Women Set upon White Mother of Pupil," *Times Picayune*, November 30, 1960, 1, 3.

71. "Boycott Total in McDonogh 19," 1.

72. "Writ May Open School Cash," *Times Picayune*, December 3, 1960, 1, 21.

73. "School Case Going to U.S. High Court," *Times Picayune*, December 1, 1960, 1.

74. Interview with two unidentified female segregationist protesters, December 1960, WSB-TV news film, clip 42576, UOG-CRDL, http://dlg.galileo.usg.edu/crdl/id:ugabma_wsbn_42576.

75. "Hecklers Gather Outside Church to Jeer Minister," *Times Picayune*, December 5, 1960, 1, 26.

76. "Louisiana," *Southern School News*, January 1961, 1; Save Our Schools, Inc. script, undated, Women's Emergency Committee Papers, reel MG 00499, box 6, folder 11, ASA; Fairclough, *Race and Democracy*, 249; see also Inger, *Politics and Reality in an American City*, 55.

77. "Writ May Open School Cash," 21.

78. Inger, *Politics and Reality in an American City*, 56; see also Lewis, *Massive Resistance*, 118.

79. Davin Zinman, "Friends Change, but Not Principles," *Times Picayune*, December 3, 1960, 8; Baker, *The Second Battle of New Orleans*, 417; Fairclough, *Race and Democracy*, 250.

80. Isabella Taves, "The Mother Who Stood Alone," *Good Housekeeping*, April 1961, 30.

81. Taves, "The Mother Who Stood Alone," 30.

82. "Two White Parents Slip Children into School," *Shreveport Journal*, November

30, 1960, 1; Claude Sitton, "U.S. Court Voids Louisiana's Ban on Integration," *New York Times*, December 1, 1960, 1, 26; "Angry Women Set upon White Mother of Pupil," 1, 3.

83. "Two White Parents Slip Children into School," 1.

84. Sitton, "Angry Scuffles Mar Integration," 32; Clinton, "N.O. Integration Situation Still Tense," 1, 4A. See also Sitton, "U.S. Court Voids Louisiana's Ban on Integration," 26, and "Police Force Path through Angry Orleans Mothers," *Shreveport Journal*, November 29, 1960, 1.

85. "Angry Women Set upon White Mother of Pupil," 3; Taves, "The Mother Who Stood Alone," 34.

86. Taves, "The Mother Who Stood Alone," 32.

87. "Louisiana," *Southern School News*, January 1961, 1, 10; "Snarling New Orleans Mob Attacks Mother," *Chicago Daily Defender*, November 30, 1960, 2.

88. Sitton, "Angry Scuffles Mar Integration," 32; Taves, "The Mother Who Stood Alone," 34. See also Sitton, "U.S. Court Voids Louisiana's Ban on Integration," 26, "Angry Women Set upon White Mother of Pupil," 1, 3, "Two White Parents Slip Children into School," 1, 16A, and Inger, *Politics and Reality in an American City*, 52.

89. Taves, "The Mother Who Stood Alone," 32.

90. "Angry Women Set upon White Mother of Pupil," 3; Taves, "The Mother Who Stood Alone," 32.

91. "Two White Parents Slip Children into School," 16A. See also "Louisiana," *Southern School News*, January 1961, 10, and "Snarling New Orleans Mob Attacks Mother," 2.

92. "Angry Women Set upon White Mother of Pupil," 3.

93. Warner, "Housewives Ignore U.S. Judges' Edict," 1.

94. "Gabrielles Hope to Return to N.O. despite Bigots," *Pittsburgh Courier*, May 27, 1961, 15.

95. Zinman, "Friends Change, but not Principles," 8.

96. Carlton Wilson, "No Mob Thinks for Me," *Chicago Defender*, December 10, 1960, 1.

97. Weise, *Corazón De Dixie*, 16, 35; Zinman, "Friends Change, but not Principles," 8.

98. "Crowd Attacks Four at School," *Times Picayune*, December 2, 1960, 1; "Demonstrators Kept Block away from Integrated School," *Times Picayune*, December 7, 1960, 23; Taves, "The Mother Who Stood Alone," 30, 34, 36.

99. Taves, "The Mother Who Stood Alone," 30– 34.

100. Taves, "The Mother Who Stood Alone," 34; "Demonstrators Kept Block Away from Integrated School," 23; "White Women Battle," 1.

101. "Esso Reporter," December 5, 1960, Midlo Collection, box 1, folder 10, TU-ARC. See Inger, *Politics and Reality in an American City*, 57.

102. Taves, "The Mother Who Stood Alone," 36, 121; "Threats Slash Pupil Numbers," *Times Picayune*, December 10, 1960, 1. See Baker, *The Second Battle of New Orleans*, 417.

103. "Two New Orleans Parents Become Heroes and Villains in School Crisis," *Southern School News*, January 1961, 10.

104. "State Takes N.O. Case to Supreme Court," *Alexandria Daily Town Talk*, December 7, 1960, 2; "Violence Still Plagues N.O.," 1; "School Blockade Is Likely to Continue," *Baton Rouge States-Item*, December 8, 1960, 1, 12–A; "Two New Orleans Parents Become Heroes and Villains in School Crisis," 10; Inger, *Politics and Reality in an American City*, 52–53, 58.

105. See Chappell, *A Stone of Hope*.

106. "U.S. Marshals Escort Whites to N.O. Classes," *Alexandria Daily Town Talk*, December 9, 1960, 1; "Pressure Threatens N.O. School Mixing," *Baton Rouge States-Item*, December 10, 1960, 1, 5–A; "Threats Slash Pupil Numbers," 1, 16; "Louisiana," *Southern School News*, January 1961, 10. Although Louisianan newspapers wrote of only two incidents, Inger states that the McKinleys had reported that their windows had been smashed nine separate times (Inger, *Politics and Reality in an American City*, 56).

107. "Pressure Threatens N.O. School Mixing," 1, 5–A; "Threats Slash Pupil Numbers," 16; John Payton, "Valiant La. Mother Won't Bow to Racists," *Chicago Daily Defender*, December 15, 1960, 5.

108. Wieder, "One Who Stayed," 194–95, 197–98; Blue, *St. Mark's and the Social Gospel*, 164.

109. Wieder, "One Who Stayed," 196, 197.

110. "Angry Women Set upon White Mother of Pupil," 3; "Housewives Try to Block Minister from Taking Child to Frantz School," 1; "Rowdyism Haunts Integrated Schools," 1, 7; "Priest Defies Mob," *Chicago Daily Defender*, November 29, 1960, 1; Martha Wilson, "Minister Taunted by N.O. Boycotters," *Baton Rouge States-Item*, November 30, 1960, 11–C.

111. "New Orleans Integration Troubles Continue," Telenews, November 30, 1960, vol. 13, issue 243, roll no. 2564, SG 1492, Hearst Metrotone News Collection, UCLA.

112. "Minister Taunted by N.O. Boycotters," 11–C.

113. "Louisiana," *Southern School News*, January 1961, 10; Sitton, "Angry Scuffles Mar Integration," 1, 32.

114. "Two White Parents Slip Children into School," 1, 16–A.

115. Handwritten comment on a newspaper clipping, December 5, 1960, Rainach Papers, box 44, topical Folder "Miscellaneous October 1, 1960–December 31, 1960," LSUS-NWLA; Jack Ricau, South Louisiana Citizens' Council press release, December 21, 1960, Rogers–Stevens Collection, box 2, folder 5, TU-ARC.

116. "Federal Court Overrules Interposition," 1; "At Orleans School, Women Manhandle University Student," 1, 8–A.

117. "Housewives Demonstrations Continue in New Orleans," Telenews, December 1, 1960, vol. 13, issue 224, roll No. 2566, SG 10879, Hearst Metrotone News Collection, UCLA. The *Baton Rouge States-Item* wrote that the cheerleaders did not say "Jew," but "boo." Even if the cheerleaders did not try to "insult" (in their view) Foreman by calling him a Jew and thus show their anti-Semitism in this instance, however, they did call Sydney Goldfinch, a Tulane student and a white civil rights supporter who was the son of a Protestant minister, a "Jew bastard." See "Women Picketing Integrated School Kick Tulane Student," *Baton Rouge States-Item*, December 1, 1960, 1, 12–A, "At Orleans School, Women Manhandle University Student," 1, "Black-White Dog in N.O. Finds Color against Him," 2, and "Court Says Interposition Not Valid Theory," *Shreveport Journal*, November 30, 1960, 1.

118. "17 Whites Enter Frantz School," *Alexandria Daily Town Talk*, December 5, 1960, 1; see also Baker, *The Second Battle of New Orleans*, 416–17.

119. "Housewives' White Boycott Foiled," Telenews, December 2, 1960, vol. 13, issue no. 245, roll no. 2588, SG 10880, Hearst Metrotone News Collection, UCLA.

120. Wilson, "Minister Taunted by N.O. Boycotters," 11-C; Fairclough, *Race and Democracy*, 261; Inger, *Politics and Reality in an American City*, 52–53.

121. "Women Picketing Integrated School Kick Tulane Student," 1, 12–A.

122. "At Orleans School, Women Manhandle University Student," 1; "Black-White Dog In N.O. Finds Color against Him," 2.

123. "Black-White Dog In N.O. Finds Color against Him," 2; see also "At Orleans School, Women Manhandle University Student," 1, "Crowd Attacks Four At School," 1, 17, "New Orleans Fiasco Has Its Lighter Side," *New York Amsterdam News*, December 17, 1960, 11, and Taves, "The Mother Who Stood Alone," 34.

124. "Women Picketing Integrated School Kick Tulane Student," 1, 12–A; "At Orleans School, Women Manhandle University Student" 1.

125. "Women Picketing Integrated School Kick Tulane Student," 1; "Integrationists Flee Crowds at New Orleans," *Alexandria Daily Town Talk*, December 1, 1960, 1–2.

126. Claude Sitton, "Boycott Weaker in New Orleans," *New York Times*, December 2, 1960, 2, 14.

127. Sitton, "Boycott Weaker in New Orleans," 2, 14; "Crowd Attacks Four At School," 1, 17.

128. "Black-White Dog in N.O. Finds Color against Him," 2.

129. "Black-White Dog in N.O. Finds Color against Him," 2; "Women Picketing Integrated School Kick Tulane Student," 1, 12–A; "U.S. Marshals Escort Whites," 1; "Threats Slash Pupil Numbers," 1; "Court Blocks Plan for New School Board," 1, 14; "17 Whites Enter Frantz School," 1.

130. "17 Whites Enter Frantz School," 1.

131. "17 White Children Attend Frantz," *Bogalusa Daily News*, December 5, 1960, 1; "White Attendance Drops at Frantz," *Bogalusa Daily News*, December 7, 1960, 1.

132. "17 White Children Attend Frantz," 1.

133. Sitton, "Boycott Weaker in New Orleans," 2, 14; "Black-White Dog in N.O. Finds Color against Him," 2; "Women Picketing Integrated School Kick Tulane Student," 1, 12–A; "U.S. Marshals Escort Whites," 1; "Threats Slash Pupil Numbers," 1; "Court Blocks Plan for New School Board," 1, 14; "White Attendance Drops at Frantz," *Bogalusa Daily News*, December 7, 1960, 1; "SOS Reveals Its Motives," *Shreveport Journal*, editorial, December 12, 1960, 8A; "Louisiana," *Southern School News*, January 1961, 10; Frystak, "'Ain't Gonna Let Nobody Turn Me Around,'" 309; Inger, *Politics and Reality in an American City*, 56–61.

134. "Louisiana," *Southern School News*, January 1961, 11.

135. Citizens' Council of Greater New Orleans, bulletin, December 1960, Midlo Collection, box 1, folder 5, TU-ARC.

136. Citizens' Council of Greater New Orleans, bulletin, December 1960, Midlo Collection, box 1, folder 5, TU-ARC.

137. Citizens' Council of Greater New Orleans, bulletin, December 1960, Midlo Collection, box 1, folder 5, TU-ARC.

138. "Citizens Council Demands Probe," *Times Picayune*, December 10, 1960, 4.

139. Kinnaird, letter to the editor, *Shreveport Journal*, December 14, 1960, 14–A.

140. Durr, letter to the editor, *Shreveport Journal*, December 12, 1960, 8–A.

141. Mathews, letter to the editor, *Shreveport Journal*, December 3, 1960, 2–A.

142. Giarrusso, letter to the editor, *Shreveport Journal*, December 12, 1960, 8–A.

143. "At Orleans School, Women Manhandle University Student," 1. See also Sitton, "Boycott Weaker in New Orleans," 14, "10 White Children Enter N.O. School," *Alexandria Daily Town Talk*, December 2, 1960, 1, 2, "Crowd Attacks Four At School," 1, and Fairclough, *Race and Democracy*, 247.

144. See "At Orleans School, Women Manhandle University Student," 1, Sitton, "Boycott Weaker in New Orleans," 14, "10 White Children Enter N.O. School," 2, "Crowd Attacks Four At School," 1, Sitton, "U.S. Court Voids Louisiana's Ban," 26, Clinton, "N.O. Integration Situation Still Tense," 1, Wilson, "Minister Taunted by N.O. Boycotters," 11–C, "Hoses Turned on Marchers," 1, "Housewives Try to Block Minister from Taking Child to Frantz School," 1, Mathews, letter to the editor, 2–A, "SOS Reveals Its Motives," 8A, and Kinnaird, letter to the editor, 14–A. These media outlets assumed that the cheerleaders were all mothers of Frantz and McDonogh schoolchildren. However, although most of the protesting women in November and early December who were interviewed by the media stated that they had children at one of the two schools, the nucleus of cheerleaders who continued the women's protest after police had restricted protesters' access to Frantz's school grounds did not necessarily, as a detailed interview in the local *Alexandria Daily Town Talk* and a UPI interview reveal (Wilson, "Women 'Cheerleaders' Tell Why They Fight Integration," 28).

145. "New Orleans Fiasco Has Its Lighter Side," 11; "Black-White Dog in N.O. Finds Color against Him," 2; Taves, "The Mother Who Stood Alone," 34; Steinbeck, *Travels with Charley*, 258.

146. Taves, "The Mother Who Stood Alone," 34; "La. Jeerleaders Rage 2nd Week," 2; Steinbeck, *Travels with Charley*, 257–59; Hopkins, "Frantz School Crowd Noisy," 9; "Black-White Dog in N.O. Finds Color against Him," 2.

147. Coles, "Racial Conflict and a Child's Question," 168.

148. Coles, "Racial Conflict and a Child's Question," 167.

149. "Black-White Dog in N.O. Finds Color against Him," 2; "New Orleans Fiasco Has Its Lighter Side," 11.

150. Wilson, "Women 'Cheerleaders' Tell Why They Fight Integration," 28; "La. Jeerleaders Rage 2nd Week," 2.

151. Wilson, "Women 'Cheerleaders' Tell Why They Fight Integration," 28; "La. Jeerleaders Rage 2nd Week," 2.

152. Wilson, "Women 'Cheerleaders' Tell Why They Fight Integration," 28; "La. Jeerleaders Rage 2nd Week," 2.

153. Wilson, "Women 'Cheerleaders' Tell Why They Fight Integration," 28; New Orleans citizens' councils' charters, Perez Papers, box 1, topical folder "Citizens' Councils of New Orleans," NOPL.

154. Wilson, "Women 'Cheerleaders' Tell Why They Fight Integration," 28.

155. Wilson, "Women 'Cheerleaders' Tell Why They Fight Integration," 28.

156. "La. Jeerleaders Rage 2nd Week," 2.

157. "La. Jeerleaders Rage 2nd Week," 2.

158. Wilson, "Women 'Cheerleaders' Tell Why They Fight Integration," 28.

159. "La. Jeerleaders Rage 2nd Week," 2.

160. "La. Jeerleaders Rage 2nd Week," 2; Wilson, "Women 'Cheerleaders' Tell Why They Fight Integration," 28.

161. “La Jeerleaders Rage 2nd Week,” 2.

162. Bridges, quoted in Coles, “Racial Conflict and a Child's Question,” 168.

163. Coles, “Racial Conflict and a Child's Question,” 167–68.

164. Coles, “Racial Conflict and a Child's Question,” 167–69.

165. See Dailey, “The Theology of Massive Resistance.”

166. Wilson, “Women ‘Cheerleaders’ Tell Why They Fight Integration,” 28.

167. Wilson, “Women ‘Cheerleaders’ Tell Why They Fight Integration,” 28.

168. Baker, *The Second Battle of New Orleans*, 343.

169. Newspaper clipping, undated (ca. 1962), Catholic Council on Human Relations Records, box 1, folder 7, TU-ARC.

170. “A Kneeling Racist and an Upright Bishop,” *Life Magazine*, April 27, 1962, 44. Leander Perez and Jackson Ricau were also excommunicated. They were later reinstated. On Perez's quiet readmission to the church, see Brückmann, “Citizens' Councils, Conservatism, and White Supremacy in Louisiana,” 13.

171. Gaillot, *God Gave the Law of Segregation (as well as the 10 Commandments) to Moses on Mount Sinai*, 1960, University of Southern Mississippi, Digital Collections, https://digitalcollections.usm.edu/uncategorized/digitalFile_157cbc66-1bc3-41b6-92cd-cd1c2287524f/.

172. Gaillot, *God Gave the Law of Segregation (as well as the 10 Commandments) to Moses on Mount Sinai*, 3, 18–19.

173. Gaillot, *God Gave the Law of Segregation (as well as the 10 Commandments) to Moses on Mount Sinai*, 15–16.

174. Save Our Nation, “Reply to Archbishop Rummel: Proof That the Bible Demands Segregation!,” August 29, 1960, attached as a photocopy to an anonymous letter by “A True Segregationist” to J. Skelly Wright, August 29, 1960, Wright Papers, box 12, folder “Unfavorable, Aug. 1960,” Library of Congress, Manuscript Division.

175. Gaillot to Cushing, December 4, 1961, Catholic Council of Human Relations Records, box 1, folder 7, TU-ARC.

176. Gaillot to Kennedy, telegram, Catholic Council of Human Relations Records, box 1, folder 7, TU-ARC.

177. Save Our Nation, Inc., advertisement, newspaper clipping, February 13, 1961, Save Our Schools Records, box 4, folder 11, TU-ARC.

178. “Segregationist Scores Bishop,” newspaper clipping, February 22, 1961, Save Our Schools Records, box 4, folder 13, TU-ARC.

179. Gaillot, letter to the editor, *New Orleans States-Item*, April 12, 1961, 8.

180. Undated newspaper clipping (ca. 1962), Catholic Council on Human Relations Records, box 1, folder 7, TU-ARC.

181. “New Orleans Admits 12 Negroes without Disturbances,” *Southern School News*, October 1961, 2.

182. “Woman Ousted by Church Renounces It,” *Shreveport Times*, December 23, 1969, 2–A; “New Archbishop Accepts Pastoral Staff in Orleans,” *Shreveport Times*, October 14, 1965, 15–A; John Lang, “Mrs. Gaillot Fights to Keep Son out of Integrated Unit,” *Alexandria Daily Town Talk*, September 4, 1965, 4–B; “Mrs. Gaillot Flying Flag Upside Down,” *Shreveport Times*, September 7, 1965, 4–A.

183. “N.O. Woman Loses Bid to Label Blood,” *Shreveport Times*, July 28, 1972, 36.

184. "Woman Ousted by Church Renounces It," 2–A; Wesley Jackson, "Excommunicate Holds to Her Views," *Times Picayune*, September 24, 1978, 16. On Perez's readmission, which only came to be known to the public at his funeral, evoking protests, see "Priests Object to Perez Rites," undated newspaper clipping, ca. March 1969, and "Bishop Perry Defends Rites," *Times Picayune*, March 26, 1969, newspaper clipping, Rousseve Papers, box 4, folder 17, TU-ARC.

185. Poché, "Religion, Race, and Rights," 187. Poché interviewed Gaillot on February 14, 2005.

186. Blue, *St. Mark's and the Social Gospel*, 165; Poché, "Religion, Race, and Rights," 189.

187. See "Faubus Scores Orleans Mixing," 11, and "U.S. Power Grab Seen in Mixing," 4.

188. Jahncke, letter to the editor, *Shreveport Journal*, January 2, 1961, 6–A.

189. Jahncke, letter to the editor, *Shreveport Journal*, January 2, 1961, 6–A.

190. Jahncke, letter to the editor, *Shreveport Journal*, January 2, 1961, 6–A.

191. Jahncke, letter to the editor, *Shreveport Journal*, January 2, 1961, 6–A.

192. Wilson, "Women 'Cheerleaders' Tell Why They Fight Integration," 28.

193. Wilson, "Women 'Cheerleaders' Tell Why They Fight Integration," 28.

194. Thomas, "New Orleans Mothers Say They Will Continue Boycott," 8; "Two White Children Attend Integrated School in New Orleans," *Alexandria Daily Town Talk*, January 21, 1961, 4; "Nine-Year-Old's Return Sets Off New Flurry," *Southern School News*, March 1961, 9; see also Fairclough, *Race and Democracy*, 250.

195. "New Orleans Mothers Say They Will Continue Boycott," 8; "Two Brothers Enter School," *Shreveport Journal*, January 31, 1961, 1.

196. "New Orleans Mothers Say They Will Continue Boycott," 8.

197. "Nine-Year-Old's Return Sets Off New Flurry," 9; "Two White Children Attend Integrated School in New Orleans," 4.

198. "Nine-Year Old's Return Sets Off New Flurry," 9; "Two White Children Attend Integrated School in New Orleans," 4.

199. "Two White Children Attend Integrated School in New Orleans," 4; "Pupil Is Jeered at M'Donogh 19," *Times Picayune*, January 30, 1961, 1.

200. "Pupil Is Jeered at M'Donogh 19," 1.

201. William Cook, "Women Picket Drug Firm in School Boycott," *Alexandria Daily Town Talk*, February 1, 1961, 24; for photographs of the women, see Catholic Council on Human Relations Records, box 1, folder 7, TU-ARC.

202. "McDonogh School Boycott Restored," *New Orleans States-Item*, February 1, 1961, 1; William Cook, "Thompsons Leave Town," *Shreveport Journal*, February 1, 1961, 1.

203. Cook, "Thompsons Leave Town," 1–2–A.

204. Cook, "Women Picket Drug Firm in School Boycott," 24.

205. "McDonogh School Boycott Restored," 4.

206. *Southern School News*, photograph, July 1961, 8.

207. "Private School Facilities Aim," 1; "Arabi School Annex Gleams," *Times Picayune*, December 9, 1960, sec. 2, 5; "School Readied for 400 Pupils," *Times Picayune*, December 7, 1960, sect. 2, 2; "Hecklers Gather Outside Church to Jeer Minister," *Times Picayune*, December 5, 1960, 1, 26.

208. "School Readied for 400 Pupils," sec. 2, 2; "Orleans Parish Board Members Rate New Decision 'Lenient,'" *Southern School News*, June 1962, 9.

209. "Arabi School Annex Gleams," sec. 2, 5; see Fairclough, *Race and Democracy*, 251.

210. Armand Duvio, interview, WSB-TV news film, clip 44811, December 1, 1960, UOG-CRDL, http://dlg.galileo.usg.edu/crdl/id:ugabma_wsbn_44811, my emphasis.

211. *Shreveport Journal*, photograph, December 5, 1960, 1.

212. "10 White Children Enter N.O. School," 1.

213. "New Orleans Admits 12 Negroes without Disturbance," 2.

214. Kathy Reckdahl, "'The McDonogh 3' Help Unveil Historical Marker at their 1960 School," *Times Picayune*, November 14, 2010, https://www.nola.com/news/education/article_c10b1497-3208-5b6b-89d3-3e5aaf418503.html.

215. "Louisiana," *Southern School News*, September 1961, 1; "Four More Schools in New Orleans to Become Biracical," *Southern School News*, September 1961, 8. On Atlanta, see Bayor, *Race and the Shaping of Twentieth Century Atlanta*, and Lassiter, *The Silent Majority*, 94–118.

216. "New Orleans Admits 12 Negroes without Disturbance," 2.

217. Landphair, "Sewerage, Sidewalks, and Schools," 62; "Over 4,000 Ask for Tuition Grants," *Southern School News*, September 1962, 7. In April 1962, Judge Skelly Wright left the state to take up a position at the U.S. Court of Appeals in Washington, D.C. His successor Judge Frank B. Ellis then reversed Wright's ruling that all first six grades of New Orleans's public schools were to be desegregated in September 1962. Ellis ordered that all first graders should be able to attend the school of their choice without a pupil placement procedure. The Orleans Parish School Board welcomed this decision. See "Louisiana," *Southern School News*, June 1962, 1, and "Orleans Parish Board Members Rate New Decision 'Lenient,' *Southern School News*, June 1962, 9.

218. "Coadjutor Granted Leadership Power Over Archdiocese," *Southern School News*, June 1962, 9; on Jack Helm, see Brückmann, "Citizens' Councils, Conservatism, and White Supremacy in Louisiana."

Chapter 4. Female Segregationists in Charleston

1. James E. Clyburn, speech, House of Representatives, July 27, 2010, *Congressional Record, Extensions of Remarks*, vol. 156, part 10, 14236–37.

2. James Vanwright, "Not All Want Integration," *News and Courier*, September 4, 1955, 14; "AME Church Suspends Pro-Jim Crow S.C. Elder," *Jet*, November 3, 1955, 24; Vanwright, letter to the editor, "Citizens Made in America," *News and Courier*, November 22, 1957, 12-A.

3. Tucker, letter to the editor, *News and Courier*, November 28, 1957, newspaper clipping, Tucker Papers, roll R174, SCL.

4. On grassroots conservatism after the Second World War, see McGirr, *Suburban Warriors*, Noble, "Conservatism in the USA," Phillips-Fein, "Conservatism," and Zelizer, "Rethinking the History of American Conservatism." On links between massive resistance and conservatism, see Brückmann, "Citizens' Councils, Conservatism and White Supremacy," and Lewis, "Virginia's Northern Strategy."

5. Undated and anonymous script on a Ku Klux Klan parade in Denmark, South Carolina, Workman Papers, box 32, topical folder "Integration/Civil Rights/Ku Klux Klan," USC-SCPC.

6. Quint, *Profile in Black and White*, 38–41; McMillen, *The Citizens' Council*, 78–79.

Also see "South Carolina Officials Stand Firm against Court Decree," *Southern School News*, July 1955, 14, "Resistance to Desegregation Is Increasing in South Carolina," *Southern School News*, September 1955, 6–7, and "Roster of Citizens' Councils," February 15, 1956, John's Island/Wadmalaw Island Citizens' Council, 1 folder, MSS 34–9, COC-SC.

7. Orangeburg Citizens' Council, February 13, 1956, vol. 1, no. 1, SCL; Orangeburg Citizens' Council, April 2, 1956, vol. 2, no. 2, #322.43 Orl, SCL.

8. "Integration Almost Ruins D.C.," Orangeburg Citizens' Council, February 13, 1956, 4, SCL.

9. Copies of membership cards of the Charleston County Citizens' Council, undated, and handwritten membership list, undated, John's Island/Wadmalaw Island Citizens' Council, 1 folder, COC-SC; "Association of Seven Citizens' Councils of Charleston County," Waring Papers, #1207.00, series 23, box 393, folder 4, SCHS.

10. Estes, *Charleston in Black and White*, 15–17. The civil rights activist Septima Clark started her teaching career on John's Island.

11. Grimball to Hamilton, December 10, 1955, copies of membership cards of the Charleston County Citizens' Council, undated, and handwritten membership list, undated, John's Island/Wadmalaw Island Citizens' Council, 1 folder, COC-SC.

12. Charleston County Citizens' Council, School District 9, John's Island, minutes, undated, ca. January 1956, John's Island/Wadmalaw Island Citizens' Council, 1 folder, COC-SC; "John's Islanders Will Reject Integration," *News and Courier*, August 23, 1955, 16–A; see also "Association of Seven Citizens' Councils of Charleston County," Waring Papers, box 393, folder 4, COC-SC.

13. "Roster of Citizens' Councils," February 15, 1956, John's Island/Wadmalaw Island Citizens' Council, 1 folder, COC-SC.

14. McRae, *Mothers of Massive Resistance*, 19.

15. On the role of bridge leaders, see Robnett, "African-American Women in the Civil Rights Movement," 1661.

16. Cox, *Dixie's Daughters*, 2, 1–5.

17. Cox, *Dixie's Daughters*, 161.

18. Cox, *Dixie's Daughters*, 161–162.

19. "S.C. Legislature Weighs New Bills to Back Up Segregation," *Southern School News*, February 1956, 16; Ervin to Morse, March 9, 1955, Morse Papers, box 8, folder 583, SCL; Ervin, *South Carolinians in the Revolution*.

20. Ervin to Morse, March 9, 1955, Morse Papers, box 8, folder 583, SCL; Ervin to Morse, August 8, 1955, Morse Papers, box 8, folder 588, SCL.

21. Ervin to Timmerman, July 27, 1955, Timmerman Papers, box 2, topical folder "Education Committee on Segregation," SCDAH. See also Ervin to Morse, August 8, 1955, Morse Papers, box 8, folder 588, SCL.

22. Ervin to Morse, August 8, 1955, Morse Papers, box 8, folder 588. SCL; see also Andrew, *Wade Hampton*.

23. Butler to Tucker, July 13, 1961, Tucker Papers, box 2, folder 20, SCL.

24. See Richards, "The Political Life of Stanley Fletcher Morse."

25. Richards, "The Political Life of Stanley Fletcher Morse," 1–6; Morse to Jenkins, September 11, 1954, Morse Papers, box 6, folder 432, SCL; "Grassroots League—Administrative, 1955," undated, Morse Papers, box 5, folder 401, SCL; Grassroots League, press release, August 11, 1955, Morse Papers, box 5, folder 401, SCL; Grassroots League, undated

advertisement, Morse Papers, box 5, folder 383, SCL; Morse to Poynter, July 24, 1957, Morse Papers, annex, box 8, folder 608, SCL.

26. "Women's News," *News and Courier*, October 15, 1959, 1–C.

27. Schlafly to the Grassroots League, May 20, 1955, Morse Papers, annex, box 8, folder 584, SCL.

28. See Lee, *Creating Conservatism*, especially 197–99.

29. "Members of the Grassroots League, Inc.," September 1, 1960, and August, 1962, Morse Papers, box 6, folder 436, SCL. On the desegregation of public facilities in Charleston, see Richards, "The Political Life of Stanley Fletcher Morse," 6.

30. Newspaper clipping dated 1957, Morse Papers, box 5, folder 406, SCL; newspaper clipping dated 1959, Morse Papers, box 5, folder 408, SCL; "General Assembly Completes Session without Enacting New School Laws," *Southern School News*, June, 1959, 9; "State Officer to Address DAR Chapter," *News and Courier*, September 24, 1953, B-1; "Legion Auxiliary Installs Officers," *News and Courier*, June 24, 1956, 12–A; "State DAR Names Mrs. Lipscomb Head," *News and Courier*, March 18, 1958, 7–A; "DAR Urges U.S. Step Up Support of China in U.N.," *News and Courier*, April 12, 1961, 10–B.

31. Morse described her as an "outstanding member" (Morse to Cook, September 23, 1955, Tucker Papers, box 1, folder 6, SCL).

32. Tucker, "Education for National Security," April 1963, Tucker Papers, box 2, folder 24, SCL. Tucker sent this document to the South Carolina legislature.

33. See Brückmann, "'Work . . . Done Mostly By Men.'"

34. "Charlestonians Inaugurate Movement to Bombard Congressmen Daily," *Greenville News*, February 11, 1940, newspaper clipping, Tucker Papers, roll R174, SCL. See also Kittel, *The First Republican Southern Belle*, 13–14.

35. "South Carolina Officials Stand Firm against Court Decree," *Southern School News*, July 1955, 14; R. E. Grier, "Around the State House," *The State*, undated newspaper clipping, and "S.C. Birthday," October 15, 1947, *News and Courier*, newspaper clipping, Tucker Papers, roll R174, SCL; "Mrs. Cornelia D. Tucker, Political Petrel, Dies," *Charleston Evening Post*, October 28, 1970, 11–A; see also McRae, *Mothers of Massive Resistance*, 75–77.

36. "Women Starting Court Protests:," *Greenville News*, February 11, 1940, newspaper clipping, Tucker Papers, roll R174, SCL; "South Carolina Officials Stand Firm against Court Decree"; "S.C. Birthday," newspaper clipping, October 15, 1947, *News and Courier*, *Tucker*, roll R174, SCL; McRae, *Mothers of Massive Resistance*, 76; note signed by Tucker, May 2, 1939, Tucker Papers, roll R174, SCL; see also Kittel, *The First Republican Belle*, 14. Mary Badham Kittel, who made a name for herself as an expert on flower arrangements, was one of Tucker's two daughters.

37. "Woman Who Defied Assembly of South Carolina Is Visitor," *Greenville News*, February 9, 1941, newspaper clipping, Tucker Papers, roll R174, SCL.

38. Fraser, *Charleston! Charleston!*, 346.

39. "Woman Gives Speech to House in Spite Gavel," *The State*, March 16, 1940, 1.

40. "Woman Gives Speech to House in spite Gavel," 1; McRae, *Mothers of Massive Resistance*, 77–79.

41. "Mrs. Tucker Says Women Will Fight for Secret Ballot," *The State*, March 18, 1941, 1.

42. "Mrs. Tucker Says Women Will Fight for Secret Ballot;" see also Brückmann, "Work . . . Done Mostly by Men," and McRae, *Mothers of Massive Resistance*, 78–79.

43. "Mrs. Tucker Says Women Will Fight for Secret Ballot"; "S.C. Birthday"; "Mrs. Tucker's Plan Approved by Governor," *News and Courier*, September 26, 1956, newspaper clipping, Tucker Papers, roll R174, SCL.

44. "Letter to the President," May 3, 1943, newspaper clipping, *Tucker*, roll R174, SCL.

45. Kittel, *The First Republican Belle*, 22; "Mrs. Tucker Says Women Will Fight"; Workman, introduction, xi–xii; "Mrs. Cornelia Tucker Boards Plane," *News and Courier*, January 3, 1956, 8–B; "Mrs. Tucker's Plan Approved by Governor," *News and Courier*, September 26, 1956, newspaper clipping, Tucker Papers, roll R174, SCL; "Mrs. Tucker, SC Crusader, Leaves for Washington," *The State*, January 3, 1957, 1; "Mrs. Tucker Again," *Greenville News*, June 14, 1954, 4.

46. Tucker to Congress, January 1956, Tucker Papers, box 1, folder 2, SCL; Otis Perkins, "Mrs. Cornelia Dabney Tucker," *News and Courier*, May 4, 1958, 5–C.

47. "Tourists Surveyed on Court Proposal," *News and Courier*, March 31, 1958, newspaper clipping, Tucker Papers, roll R174, SCL.

48. "Citizenship Texts to Be Urged in Business Women's Week," *Charleston Evening Post*, 8–D, ca. 1947–48, newspaper clipping, Tucker Papers, roll R174, SCL; letter to the editor, undated, ca. 1948–50, *News and Courier*, newspaper clipping, Tucker Papers, roll R174, SCL.

49. "Education Board to Use Book Recommended by Mrs. Tucker," September 6, 1947, *Charleston Evening Post*, newspaper clipping, Tucker Papers, roll R174, SCL.

50. Frampton to Tucker, August 10, 1959, Tucker Papers, roll R174, SCL.

51. See May, *Homeward Bound*.

52. Kittel, *The First Republican Southern Belle*, 22.

53. Perkins, " Mrs. Cornelia Dabney Tucker," 5–C; McRae, *Mothers of Massive Resistance*, 77.

54. Charlotte Walker, "By the Way," *Charleston Evening Post*, May 7, 1960, 2–A.

55. Perkins, " Mrs. Cornelia Dabney Tucker," 5–C. See also Kittel, *The First Republican Southern Belle*, 16–17, 22–23.

56. Perkins, " Mrs. Cornelia Dabney Tucker," 5–C.

57. Walker, "By the Way," 2–A.

58. Tucker to Timmerman, August 12, 1954, Timmerman Papers, box 1, topical folder "Timmerman General 1954 Campaign Segregation 1 of 2," USC-SCPC.

59. Tucker to Warren, July 23, 1954, Timmerman Papers, box 1, topical folder "Timmerman General 1954 Campaign Segregation 1 of 2," USC-SCPC.

60. "Mrs. Tucker Says Court's Stand Aims at Amalgamation," July 26, 1954, *News and Courier*, newspaper clipping, Tucker Papers, roll R174, SCL.

61. Tucker, letter to the editor, "Satisfying Moscow," *News and Courier*, July 5, 1954, newspaper clipping, Tucker Papers, roll R174, SCL; "South Carolina Officials Stand Firm against Court Decree," *Southern School News*, July 1955, 14; Ricau to Tucker, May 7, 1961, Tucker Papers, box 2, folder 20, SCL.

62. Findlay, *Church People in the Struggle*, 14.

63. Letters to the editor by Tucker, *News and Courier*, February 4, 1961 and December 17, 1961, Tucker Papers, roll R174, SCL.

64. Tucker, letter to the editor, "Citizens' Rally," *News and Courier*, October 7, 1955, newspaper clipping, Tucker Papers, roll R174, SCL.

65. Eastland to Tucker, June 16, 1955, Tucker Papers, box 1, folder 4, SCL.

66. Tucker to Timmerman, date-stamped August 2, 1955, Timmerman Papers, box 5, topical folder "Misc. Segregation," SCDAH.

67. Eastland to Tucker, June 16, 1955, Tucker Papers, box 1, folder 4, SCL.

68. Tucker, letter to the editor, *News and Courier*, April 25, 1959, newspaper clipping, Tucker Papers, roll R174, SCL.

69. Tucker, letter to the editor, *Times-Picayune*, December 16, 1960, 12, sec. 1. A longer version of the letter was also printed the *Montgomery Advertiser*, December 8, 1960; see Tucker Papers, roll R174, SCL.

70. Tucker, letter to the editor, *Montgomery Advertiser*, December 8, 1960, newspaper clipping, Tucker Papers, microfilm, roll R174, SCL.

71. See Tucker, letter to the editor, *News and Courier*, April 25, 1959, newspaper clipping, Tucker Papers, microfilm, roll R174, SCL.

72. Kolb to Hollings, December 2, 1960, and December 5, 1960, and Hollings to Kolb, December 3, 1960, Hollings Papers, box 14, folder "Citizens' Council, c. 1959–1963," USC-SCPC. On Hollings's role in South Carolina's desegregation battle, see Badger, "From Defiance to Moderation."

73. Charleston County Citizens' Council pamphlet and application form, December 28, 1960, Workman Papers, box 47, folder "Civil Rights, Citizens Councils, 1960–1962," USC-SCPC.

74. William D. Workman, "To Maintain Segregation," newspaper clipping, March 21, 1961, Workman Papers, box 47, folder "Civil Rights, Citizens Councils, 1960–1962," USC-SCPC.

75. "We The People," *News and Courier*, September 21, 1959, Tucker, letter to the editor, *News and Courier*, December 17, 1958, and editorial, *News and Courier*, September 22, 1959, newspaper clippings, Tucker Papers, roll R174, SCL.

76. McRae, *Mothers of Massive Resistance*, 204–5.

77. "Highlights of Program," handbill, September 19, 1959, Chicago, and "Supreme Court Draws Blast at Convention," undated newspaper clipping, ca. September 1959, Tucker Papers, roll R174, SCL. See Hendershot, *What's Fair on the Air*, 170–205.

78. "Woman Seeks Required Political Economics Study," *Greenville News*, newspaper clipping, 1959, Tucker Papers, roll R174, SCL; "We The People" September 21, 1959, *News and Courier*, newspaper clipping, Tucker Papers, roll R174, SCL.

79. Goldwater to Tucker, June 14, 1960, Tucker Papers, box 1,folder 18, SCL; Lee, *Creating Conservatism*, 92–102.

80. Newspaper clipping, *News and Courier*, August 13, 1959, Tucker Papers, roll R174, SCL.

81. Sharon Brown, "'Lone Crusader' Here for Goldwater Visit," *Atlanta Times*, September 15, 1964, newspaper clipping, Tucker Papers, roll R174, SCL; Tucker, letter to the editor, *Greenville News*, July 25, 1964, 2.

82. Tucker, letter to the editor, *Times Picayune*, June 29, 1959, newspaper clipping, Tucker Papers, roll R174, SCL.

83. Tucker, letter to the editor, *News and Courier*, December 17, 1958, newspaper clipping, Tucker Papers, roll R174, SCL.

84. Tucker, letter to the editor, *News and Courier*, December 17, 1958, newspaper clipping, Tucker Papers, roll R174, SCL.

85. See Diamond, *Roads to Dominion*, 62.

86. López, *Dog Whistle Politics*, 18.

87. López, *Dog Whistle Politics*, 19; McGirr, *Suburban Warriors*, 133.

88. López, *Dog Whistle Politics*, 18.

89. See McGirr, *Suburban Warriors*, 132–34, 188.

90. See Nickerson, *Mothers of Conservatism*, xiii, 137–58, McGirr, *Suburban Warriors*, especially 140–41, and Diamond, *Roads to Dominion*, 29–64.

91. Diamond, *Roads to Dominion*, 29–31. See also Lee, *Creating Conservatism*.

92. Diamond, *Roads to Dominion*, 62–64; McGirr, *Suburban Warriors*, 140–141.

93. Brown, "'Lone Crusader' Here for Goldwater Visit," *Atlanta Times*, September 15, 1964, newspaper clipping, Tucker Papers, roll R174, SCL.

94. "1964 G.O.P. Platform To Support Rights Bill," *New York Times*, June 2, 1964; Diamond, *Roads to Dominion*, 62.

95. López, *Dog Whistle Politics*, 84.

96. Diamond, *Roads to Dominion*, 12, 62–64.

97. Diamond, *Roads to Dominion*, 12; Eric Pace, "Gen. Edwin Walker, 83, Is Dead; Promoted Rightist Causes in 60's," *New York Times*, November 2, 1993, B-10.

98. Tucker, letter to the editor, *News and Courier*, May 4, 1961, newspaper clipping, Tucker Papers, roll R174, SCL.

99. Tucker, letter to the editor, *News and Courier*, May 4, 1961, newspaper clipping, Tucker Papers, roll R174, SCL.

100. Tucker, letter to the editor, *News and Courier*, April 7, 1961, 6–A.

101. Tucker, letter to the editor, *The State*, August 28, 1963, newspaper clipping, Tucker Papers, roll R263, SCL.

102. Tucker, letter to the editor, *The State*, April 17, 1965, newspaper clipping, Tucker Papers, roll R174, SCL.

103. Tucker, letter to the editor, *The State*, August 28, 1963, newspaper clipping, Tucker Papers, roll R263, SCL. The same letter was printed that day in the *News and Courier* and the *Charleston Evening Post*; see Tucker Papers, roll R263, SCL.

104. Frankel, *An Ordinary Atrocity*, 51–67; Lodge, *Sharpeville*, 87–109. On the history of the apartheid regime, see Clark and Worger, *South Africa*, 35–72. On the relationship between black civil rights activists and South African antiapartheid activists, see Grant, *Winning Our Freedoms Together*. On the implications of the Sharpeville Massacre for South African apartheid, see Lodge, *Sharpeville*, 167, and Frankel, *An Ordinary Atrocity*, 5–7.

105. Tucker, letter to the editor, *News and Courier*, March 30, 1960, Tucker papers, roll R174, SCL.

106. Frankel, *An Ordinary Atrocity*, 122.

107. Rolph, "The Citizens' Council and Africa," 642.

108. Rolph, "The Citizens' Council and Africa," 649; Rolph, *Resisting Equality*, 3; also see Brückmann, "Citizens' Councils, Conservatism, and White Supremacy," 2–3.

109. Tucker, letter to the editor, *News and Courier*, April 13, 1960, Tucker Papers, roll R174, SCL. See also her letter to the editor, *News and Courier*, April 6, 1960.

110. Tucker, letter to the editor, *News and Courier*, March 30, 1960, Tucker Papers, roll R174, SCL.

111. "Petition Signatures Total 1,500," *Charleston Evening Post*, July 16, 1962, newspaper clipping, Tucker Papers, roll R174, SCL.

112. "Petition Signatures Total 1,500," *Charleston Evening Post*, July 16, 1962, newspaper clipping, Tucker Papers, roll R174, SCL See also "Petition Asks for Change of Supreme Court Ruling," *News and Courier*, July 6, 1962, 7–A.

113. Tucker, letter to the editor, *News and Courier*, March 30, 1961, 6–A.

114. Tucker, letter to the editor, News and Courier, ca. 1943, newspaper clipping, Tucker Papers, roll R174, SCL.

115. See Diamond, *Roads to Dominion*, 168–69.

116. Tucker, letter to the editor, *News and Courier*, ca. 1943, newspaper clipping, Tucker Papers, roll R174, SCL.

117. Tucker, letter to the editor, *The State*, July 18, 1963, 10–A.

118. "Courts Criticized," *Southern School News*, February 1963, 8; "Segregation-by-Sex Proposal Voted Down by State Senate," *Southern School News*, May 1963, 14; "South Carolina," *Southern School News*, June 1963, 14.

119. "UNICORN—A Project of the Information and Education Committee, Citizens' Council Of Greater Charleston," November 1965, Morse Papers, box 3, folder 388, SCL; Temple to Tucker, February 21, 1962, Tucker Papers, box 2, folder 23, SCL.

120. Tucker, letter to the editor, *News and Courier*, November 8, 1963, newspaper clipping, Tucker Papers, roll R263, SCL.

121. Tucker, letter to the editor, *Charleston Evening Post*, August 25, 1964, newspaper clipping, Tucker Papers, roll R263, SCL.

122. "Mrs. Cornelia D. Tucker, Political Petrel, Dies," 11–A.

123. Hartsville, South Carolina, Citizens' Council, flyer, Workman Papers, box 32, topical file "Integration/Civil Rights/Citizens Councils, 1957–1959," SCMPC; Orangeburg Citizen' Council, February 13, 1956, 2, SCL; Morse to the DAR, November 1, 1966, Morse Papers, box 5, folder 413, SCL.

Conclusion. White Women and Everyday White Supremacy

1. See Save Our Schools, Inc., script, Women's Emergency Committee Records, reel MG 00499, box 6, folder 1, ASA.

2. Cope, "'The Workingest, Fightingest, Band of Patriots in the South'?" 151.

3. Women's Emergency Committee to Open Our Schools member Sara Murphy observed, however, that their attempts to appear just as elegant as their affluent Pulaski Heights counterparts when lobbying the state legislature were ultimately futile (Murphy, *Breaking the Silence*, 125).

4. Reagon, "Gender & Race," 127; Spelman, "Woman as Body": 109–31.

5. See Accapadi, "When White Women Cry," 208–15.

6. Delmont and Theoharis, introduction, 192–94; Miletsky, "Before Busing," 207–15.

7. Kruse, *White Flight*, 7–11; Lassiter, "De Jure/De Facto Segregation," 25–33; Lassiter, *The Silent Majority*, 16; Miletsky, "Before Busing."

8. Formisano, *Boston against Busing*, 1–2, 20.

9. Formisano, *Boston against Busing*, 1–16, and 139–40. As Formisano notes, Bostonian segregationists, just like southern segregationists a decade earlier, observed the strategies

and tactics of civil rights activists and appropriated their forms of direct action as well as the civil rights movement's "freedom schools" (139–40).

10. Coles, "The White Northerner."

11. Formisano, *Boston against Busing*, 3–4 and 172.

12. Formisano, *Boston against Busing*, 3 and 10.

13. Kruse, *White Flight*, 125.

14. Lewis, *Massive Resistance*, 126–28; McRae, *Mothers of Massive Resistance*, 234–40.

15. Lassiter, *The Silent Majority*, 30, 198.

16. See Kruse, *White Flight*, 253.

BIBLIOGRAPHY

Arkansas

UNIVERSITY OF ARKANSAS, FAYETTEVILLE, SPECIAL COLLECTIONS

Arkansas Council on Human Relations Records, ms Ar4,
Daisy Bates Papers, MC 582
Elizabeth Huckaby Papers, MC 428
Little Rock Central High Integration Crisis, FBI Records, MC 1027
Orval Eugene Faubus Papers, MC F27301
Sara Alderman Murphy Papers, MC 1321
Virgil T. Blossom Papers, MC 1364

UNIVERSITY OF ARKANSAS, LITTLE ROCK, ARKANSAS STUDIES INSTITUTE

FBI Little Rock School Crisis Reports, 0044
Hugh Patterson Collection

BUTLER CENTER FOR ARKANSAS STUDIES, CENTRAL ARKANSAS LIBRARY SYSTEM

Grif Stockley Papers, BC.MSS.01.01

ARKANSAS STATE ARCHIVES, LITTLE ROCK

Justice Jim John Collection
Women's Emergency Committee Records

NEWSPAPERS

Arkansas Democrat
Arkansas Gazette
Arkansas Recorder

Louisiana

LOUISIANA STATE UNIVERSITY, BATON ROUGE, LOUISIANA AND LOWER MISSISSIPPI VALLEY COLLECTIONS, SPECIAL COLLECTIONS

Harry Pollard Gamble Sr., Papers, mss 4054

LOUISIANA STATE UNIVERSITY SHREVEPORT, NORTHWEST LOUISIANA ARCHIVES, SPECIAL COLLECTIONS

Ned Touchstone Papers #392
William M. Rainach Papers, #077

NEW ORLEANS PUBLIC LIBRARY, SPECIAL COLLECTIONS

Leander Henry Perez Papers

TULANE UNIVERSITY, NEW ORLEANS

Louisiana Research Collection

Jack P. F. Gremillion Papers, #772

Amistad Research Center

Catholic Council on Human Relations Records, #077
Jane T. Lemann Papers, #241
Natalie Midlo Collection #254
Kim Lacy Rogers–Glenda Stevens Collection, #317
Charles B. Rousseve Papers
Save Our Schools Records
Alexander Pierre Tureaud Papers, microfilm

UNIVERSITY OF NEW ORLEANS, LOUISIANA, SPECIAL COLLECTIONS

Matthew R. Sutherland Collection, mss 230
NAACP Papers, New Orleans Branch, mss 28
Orleans Parish School Board Collection, mss 147

NEWSPAPERS

Alexandria Daily Town Talk
Baton Rouge States-Item
Bogalusa Daily News
Louisiana Weekly
New Orleans States-Item
Shreveport Journal
Times Picayune

South Carolina

COLLEGE OF CHARLESTON

Avery Research Center

J. Arthur Brown Papers

Special Collections

John's Island/Wadmalaw Island Citizens' Council

SOUTH CAROLINA DEPARTMENT OF ARCHIVES AND HISTORY

George Bell Timmerman Jr., Papers, Series #S548004
Thomas R. Waring Jr. Papers, #1207.00, Series 23

UNIVERSITY OF SOUTH CAROLINA, COLUMBIA

South Caroliniana Library

Cornelia Dabney Ramseur Tucker Papers, P.Plb
Cornelia Dabney Tucker Papers, Scrapbooks, microfilm, R174 and R263.
Stanley Fletcher Morse Papers
Orangeburg Citizens' Council, #322.43 Orl

South Carolina Political Collections

South Carolinians for Eisenhower Papers
William D. Workman Jr. Papers

NEWSPAPERS

Charleston Evening News
Greenville News
News and Courier
The State

Other Primary Source Collections

LIBRARY OF CONGRESS, MANUSCRIPT DIVISION, WASHINGTON, D.C.

J. Skelly Wright Papers, 308.
NAACP Papers, part 20, "White Resistance and Reprisals," reel 6, group 3, box A-274, microfilm.

UNIVERSITY OF CALIFORNIA, LOS ANGELES, TELEVISION AND FILM ARCHIVE

Hearst Metrotone News Collection

UNIVERSITY OF NORTH CAROLINA, CHAPEL HILL, SOUTHERN ORAL HISTORY COLLECTION

Published Primary Sources

Bates, Daisy. *The Long Shadow of Little Rock: A Memoir*. New York: David McKay, 1962.
Beals, Melba. *Warriors Don't Cry: A Searing Memory of the Battle to Integrate Little Rock's Central High*. New York: Washington Square Press, 1995.
Blossom, Virgil T. *It Has Happened Here*. New York: Harper, 1959.
Bridges, Ruby. *Through My Eyes*. New York: Scholastic, 1999.
"*Brown v. Board of Education, et al.*, 347 U.S. 483 (1954)." In *Little Rock U.S.A.: Materials for Analysis*. Edited by Wilson Record and Jane Cassels Record, 3–6. San Francisco: Chandler, 1960.
Coles, Robert. "The White Northerner: Pride and Prejudice." *Atlantic Monthly*, June 1966. https://www.theatlantic.com/past/docs/politics/race/whitenor.htm.
Ervin, Sara S. *South Carolinians in the Revolution: With Service Records and Miscellaneous Data, also Abstracts of Wills, Laurens County (Ninety-Six District), 1775–1855*. Baltimore, MD: Genealogical Publishing Company, 1949.
Faubus, Orval Eugene. *Down from the Hills*. Little Rock, AR: Pioneer Press, 1980.
Huckaby, Elizabeth. *Crisis at Central High: Little Rock, 1957–58*. Baton Rouge: Louisiana State University Press, 1980.

Iggers, Georg C. "The Race Question in Little Rock's Schools before 1956." In *Little Rock U.S.A.: Materials for Analysis*. Edited by Wilson Record and Jane Cassels Record, 283–91. San Francisco: Chandler, 1960.
Kittel, Mary B. *The First Republican Belle*. Columbia, SC: R. L. Bryan, 1969.
Louisiana State Advisory Committee to the United States Commission on Civil Rights. *The New Orleans School Crisis*. Washington, DC: U.S. Government Printing Office, 1961.
Murphy, Sara A. *Breaking the Silence: Little Rock's Women's Emergency Committee to Open Our Schools, 1958–1963*. Fayetteville: University of Arkansas Press, 1999.
Myrdal, Gunnar. *An American Dilemma: The Negro Problem and Modern Democracy*. New York: Harper and Row, [1944] 1962.
Steinbeck, John. *Travels with Charley: In Search of America*. 3rd ed. London: Penguin, 1988.

OTHER NEWSPAPERS AND MAGAZINES

Chicago Daily Defender
Chicago Defender
Good Housekeeping
Jet Magazine
Life Magazine
New York Amsterdam News
New York Times
Pittsburgh Courier
Southern School News
Time Magazine

Secondary Sources

Accapadi, Mamta M. "When White Women Cry: How White Women's Tears Oppress Women of Color." *College Student Affairs Journal* 26, no. 2 (2007): 208–15.
Anderson, Karen. *Little Rock: Race and Resistance at Central High School*. Princeton, NJ: Princeton University Press, 2010.
———. "Massive Resistance, Violence, and Southern Social Relations: The Little Rock, Arkansas, School Integration Crisis, 1954–1960." In *Massive Resistance: Southern Opposition to the Second Reconstruction*. Edited by Clive Webb, 203–20. Oxford: Oxford University Press, 2005.
Anderson, Peggy. *The Daughters: An Unconventional Look at America's Fan Club—the DAR*. New York: St. Martin's Press, 1974.
Andrew, Rod. *Wade Hampton: Confederate Warrior to Southern Redeemer*. Chapel Hill: University of North Carolina Press, 2008.
Apple, Rima D., and Janet L. Golden. Introduction to *Mothers and Motherhood: Readings in American History*. Edited by Rima D. Apple and Janet L. Golden, xiii–xvii. Columbus: Ohio State University Press, 1997.
Arnesen, Eric. "Reconsidering the "Long Civil Rights Movement." *Historically Speaking* 10, no. 2 (2009): 31–34.

———. "Whiteness and the Historians' Imagination." *International Labor and Working-Class History 60 (Fall 2001)*: 3–32.
Badger, Tony. "From Defiance to Moderation: South Carolina Governors and Racial Change." In *Toward The Meeting of the Waters: Currents in the Civil Rights Movement of South Carolina during the Twentieth Century*. Edited by Winfred B. Moore Jr. and Orville V. Burton, 3–21. Columbia: University of South Carolina Press, 2008.
Baer, Frances L. *Resistance to Public School Desegregation: Little Rock, Arkansas, and Beyond*. El Paso: LFB Scholarly Publishing, 2008.
Baker, Liva. *The Second Battle of New Orleans: The Hundred-Year Struggle to Integrate the Schools*. New York: Harper Collins, 1996.
Baker, R. Scott. *Paradoxes of Desegregation: African American Struggles for Educational Equity in Charleston, South Carolina, 1926–1972*. Columbia: University of South Carolina Press, 2006.
Barnett, Bernice M. "Invisible Southern Black Women Leaders in the Civil Rights Movement: The Triple Constraints of Gender, Race, and Class." *Gender and Society*, no. 7 (1993): 162–82.
Bartley, Numan V. "Looking Back at Little Rock." *Arkansas Historical Quarterly* 25, no. 2 (1966): 101–16.
———. *The Rise of Massive Resistance: Race and Politics in the South during the 1950s*. 2nd ed. Baton Rouge: Louisiana State University Press, 1997.
Bayor, Ronald H. *Race and the Shaping of Twentieth-Century Atlanta*. Chapel Hill: University of North Carolina Press, 1996.
Berg, Manfred. *"The Ticket to Freedom": The NAACP and the Struggle for Black Political Integration*. Gainesville: University of Florida Press, 2007.
Bernhard, Virginia, Betty Brandon, Elizabeth Fox-Genovese, and Theda Purdue, eds. *Southern Women: Histories and Identities*. Columbia: University of Missouri Press, 1992.
Berrey, Stephen A. *The Jim Crow Routine: Everyday Performances of Race, Civil Rights, and Segregation in Mississippi*. Chapel Hill: University of North Carolina Press, 2015.
Binder, Arnold, Gilbert Geis, and Dickson D. Bruce. *Juvenile Delinquency: Historical, Cultural, and Legal Perspectives*. 3rd ed. Cincinnati, OH: Anderson, 2001.
Blee, Kathleen M. *Women of the Klan: Racism and Gender in the 1920s*. Berkeley: University of California Press, 1992.
Blue, Ellen. *St. Mark's and the Social Gospel: Methodist Women and Civil Rights in New Orleans, 1895–1965*. Knoxville: University of Tennessee Press, 2011.
Borstelmann, Thomas. *The Cold War and the Color Line: American Race Relations in the Global Arena*. Cambridge, MA: Harvard University Press, 2003.
Bourdieu, Pierre. *Distinction: A Social Critique of the Judgement of Taste*. Translated by Richard Nice. Oxford, UK: Routledge, [1984] 2010.
———. "The Forms of Capital." In *Education: Culture, Economy and Society*. Edited by A. H. Halsey, Hugh Lauder, Phillip Brown, and Amy Stuart Wells, 46–58. Oxford: Oxford University Press, 1997.
———. *Outline of a Theory of Practice*. Translated by Richard Nice. Cambridge: Cambridge University Press, 1977.
———. "Symbolic Capital and Social Classes." Translated by Loïc Wacquant. *Journal of Classical Sociology* 13, no. 2 (2013): 292–302.

———. "What Makes a Social Class? On the Theoretical and Practical Existence of Groups." *Berkeley Journal of Sociology* 32 (1987): 1–17.

Branton, Wiley A. "Little Rock Revisited: Desegregation to Resegregation." *Journal of Negro Education* 52, no. 3 (1983): 250–69.

Brattain, Michelle. *The Politics of Whiteness: Race, Workers, and Culture in the Modern South*. Princeton, NJ: Princeton University Press, 2001.

Brewer, Vivion L. *The Embattled Ladies of Little Rock, 1958–1963: The Struggle to Save Public Education at Central High*. Fort Bragg, CA: Lost Coast Press, 1999.

Brown, David, and Clive Webb. *Race in the American South: From Slavery to Civil Rights*. Edinburgh: Edinburgh University Press, 2007.

Brown, Sarah H. "Congressional Anti-Communism and the Segregationist South: From New Orleans to Atlanta, 1954–1958." *Georgia Historical Quarterly* 180, no. 4 (1996): 785–816.

Brown Givens, Sonja M., and Jennifer L. Monahan. "Priming Mammies, Jezebels, and Other Controlling Images: An Examination of the Influence of Mediated Stereotypes on Perceptions of an African American Woman." *Media Psychology* 7, no. 1 (2005): 87–106.

Brückmann, Rebecca. "Citizens' Councils, Conservatism, and White Supremacy in Louisiana, 1964–1972." *European Journal of American Studies* 14, no. 1 (2019): 1–25.

———. "'Work . . . Done Mostly by Men': Cornelia Dabney Tucker and Female Grassroots Activism in Massive Resistance in South Carolina, 1950–1963." *South Carolina Historical Magazine* 117, no. 2 (2016): 96–120.

Burton, Orville V., Beatrice Burton, and Simon Appleford. "Seeds in Unlikely Soil: The Briggs v. Elliott School Segregation Case." In *Toward The Meeting Of The Waters: Currents in the Civil Rights Movement of South Carolina during the Twentieth Century*. Edited by Moore, Winfred B. Jr. and Orville V. Burton, 176–200. Columbia: University of South Carolina Press, 2008.

Butler, Judith. "Contingent Foundations: Feminism and the Question of 'Postmodernism.'" In *Feminists Theorize the Political*. Edited by Judith Butler and Joan W. Scott, 3–21. New York: Routledge, 1992.

———. *Gender Trouble: Feminism and the Subversion of Identity*. 2nd ed. New York: Routledge, 1999.

———. "Performative Acts and Gender Constitution: An Essay in Phenomenology and Feminist Theory." *Theatre Journal* 40, no. 4 (1988): 519–31.

Butler, Judith, and Joan W. Scott, eds. *Feminists Theorize the Political*. New York: Routledge, 1992.

Campbell, Ernest Q., and Thomas F. Pettigrew. "Racial and Moral Crisis: The Role of Little Rock Ministers." *American Journal of Sociology* 64, no. 5 (1959): 509–16.

Cash, W. J. *The Mind of the South*. New York: Knopf, 1941.

Catsam, Derek C. "Into the Maw of Dixie: The Freedom Rides, the Civil Rights Movement, and the Politics of Race in South Carolina." *The Proceedings of the South Carolina Historical Association*. Columbia: South Carolina Historical Association, 2005, 1–20.

Censer, Jane T. *The Reconstruction of White Southern Womanhood, 1865–1895*. Baton Rouge: Louisiana State University Press, 2003.

Certeau, Michel de. *The Practice of Everyday Life*. Translated by Steven Rendall. Berkeley: University of California Press, 1988.

Chafe, William H. *The Paradox of Change: American Women in the 20th Century*. Oxford: Oxford University Press, 1991.

Chafe, William, Harvard Sitkoff, and Beth Bailey, eds. *A History of Our Time: Readings on Postwar America*. 6th ed. Oxford: Oxford University Press, 2006.

Cha-Jua, Sundiata Keita, and Clarence Lang. "The 'Long Movement' as Vampire: Temporal and Spatial Fallacies in Recent Black Freedom Studies." *Journal of African American History* 92, no. 2 (2007): 265–88.

Chappell, David L. "Disunity and Religious Institutions in the White South." In *Massive Resistance: Southern Opposition to the Second Reconstruction*. Edited by Clive Webb, 136–50. Oxford: Oxford University Press, 2005.

———. "Diversity within a Racial Group: White People in Little Rock, 1957–1959." *Arkansas Historical Quarterly* 64, Summer (2007): 181–93.

———. *Inside Agitators: White Southerners in the Civil Rights Movement*. Baltimore, MD: John Hopkins University Press, 1994.

———. "Religious Ideas of the Segregationists." *Journal of American Studies* 32, no. 2 (1998): 237–62.

———. *A Stone of Hope: Prophetic Religion and the Death of Jim Crow*. Chapel Hill: University of North Carolina Press, 2004.

Chappell, Marisa, Jenny Hutchinson, and Brian Ward. "'Dress Modestly, Neatly . . . As If You Were Going to Church': Respectability, Class, and Gender in the Montgomery Bus Boycott and the Early Civil Rights Movement." In *Gender and the Civil Rights Movement*. Edited by Peter J. Ling and Sharon Monteith, 69–100. New Brunswick, NJ: Rutgers University Press, 2004.

Cho, Sumi, Kimberlé W. Crenshaw, and Leslie McCall. "Toward a Field of Intersectionality Studies: Theory, Applications, and Praxis." *Signs* 38, no. 4 (2013): 785–810.

Clark, Nancy, and William H. Worger, *South Africa: The Rise and Fall of Apartheid*. New York: Longman, 2004.

Clinton, Catherine. *The Plantation Mistress: Woman's World in the Old South*. New York: Pantheon, 1982.

Coles, Robert. "Racial Conflict and a Child's Question." *Journal of Nervous and Mental Disease* 140, no. 2 (1965): 162–70.

Coles, Robert, and George Ford. *The Story of Ruby Bridges*. Special anniversary ed. New York: Scholastic, 2010.

Collier-Thomas, Bettye, ed. *Sisters in the Struggle: African American Women in the Civil Rights–Black Power Movement*. New York: New York University Press, 2001.

Connell, R. W. *Masculinities*. 2nd ed. Berkeley: University of California Press, 2005.

Connolly, Nathan, ed. *Know Your Place: Essays on the Working Class by the Working Class*. Liverpool, UK: dead ink, 2017.

Cope, Graeme. "'Everybody Says All Those People . . . Were from out of Town, but They Weren't': A Note on Crowds during the Little Rock Crisis." *Arkansas Historical Quarterly* 67, no. 3 (2008): 245–67.

———. "'Honest White People of the Middle and Lower Classes'? A Profile of the Capital Citizens' Council during the Little Rock Crisis of 1957." *Arkansas Historical Quarterly* 61, no. 1 (2002): 37–58.

———. "'Marginal Youngsters' and 'Hoodlums of Both Sexes'? Student Segregationists during the Little Rock School Crisis." *Arkansas Historical Quarterly* 63, no. 4 (2004): 380–403.
———. "'The Master Conspirator' and His Henchmen: The KKK and the Labor Day Bombings of 1959." *Arkansas Historical Quarterly* 76, no. 1 (2017): 49–67.
———. "'A Thorn in the Side'? The Mothers' League of Central High School and the Little Rock Desegregation Crisis of 1957." *Arkansas Historical Quarterly* 52, no. 2 (1998): 160–90.
———. "'The Workingest, Fightingest, Band of Patriots in the South'? The Mothers' League of Central High School during the Lost Year, 1958–1959." *Arkansas Historical Quarterly* 72, no. 2 (2013): 139–57.
Cox, Karen. *Dixie's Daughters: The United Daughters of the Confederacy and the Preservation of Confederate Culture*. Gainesville: University Press of Florida, 2003.
Cox, Ron M., Jr. "'Integration with [Relative] Dignity': The Desegregation of Clemson College and George McMillan's Article at Forty." In *Toward the Meeting of the Waters: Currents in the Civil Rights Movement of South Carolina during the Twentieth Century*. Edited by Winfred B. Moore Jr. and Orville V. Burton, 274–85. Columbia: University of South Carolina Press, 2008.
Crawford, Vicki L., ed. *Women in the Civil Rights Movement: Trailblazers and Torchbearers, 1941–1965*. Bloomington: Indiana University Press, 1990.
Crenshaw, Kimberlé. "Mapping the Margins: Intersectionality, Identity Politics, and Violence against Women of Color." *Stanford Law Review* 43, no. 6 (1991): 1241–99.
Crenshaw, Kimberlé, Neil Gotanda, Gary Peller, and Kendall Thomas, eds. *Critical Race Theory: The Key Writings That Formed the Movement*. New York: New Press, 1995.
Crespino, Joseph. *In Search of Another Country: Mississippi and the Conservative Counterrevolution*. Princeton, NJ: Princeton University Press, 2007.
Critchlow, Donald T. *Phyllis Schlafly and Grassroots Conservatism: A Woman's Crusade*. Princeton, NJ: Princeton University Press, 2005.
Crutcher, Michael E., Jr. *Tremé: Race and Place in a New Orleans Neighborhood*. Athens: University of Georgia Press, 2010.
Cuordileone, K. A. "'Politics in an Age of Anxiety': Cold War Political Culture and the Crisis in American Masculinity, 1949–1960." *Journal of American History* 87, no. 2 (2000): 515–45.
Dailey, Jane. "Sex, Segregation, and the Sacred after Brown." *Journal of American History* 91, no. 1 (2004): 119–44.
———. "The Theology of Massive Resistance: Sex, Segregation, and the Sacred after Brown." In *Massive Resistance: Southern Opposition to the Second Reconstruction*. Edited by Clive Webb, 151–80. Oxford: Oxford University Press, 2005.
Day, John Kyle. "The Fall of a Southern Moderate: Congressman Brooks Hays and the Election of 1958." *Arkansas Historical Quarterly* 59, no. 3 (2000): 241–64.
———. *The Southern Manifesto: Massive Resistance and the Fight to Preserve Segregation*. Jackson: University Press of Mississippi, 2014.
Defert, Daniel, ed. *Michel Foucault: Dits et écrits, 1970–1975*. Paris: Gallimard, 1994.
Delmont, Matthew, and Jeanne Theoharis. Introduction. *Journal of Urban History* 43, no. 2 (2017): 191–203.
Devore, Donald E., and Joseph Logsdon. *Crescent City Schools: Public Education in New*

Orleans, 1841–1991. Lafayette: Center for Louisiana Studies, University of Southwestern Louisiana, 1991.
Diamond, Sara. *Roads to Dominion: Right-Wing Movements and Political Power in the United States*. New York: Guildford Press, 1995.
Douglas, Davison M. "*Bush v. Orleans Parish School Board* and the Desegregation of New Orleans Schools." Teaching Judicial History Project, Federal Judicial Center. https://www.fjc.gov/sites/default/files/trials/sfj-bush_o.pdf.
Drews, Axel, Ute Gerhard, and Jürgen Link. "Moderne Kollektivsymbolik: Eine diskurstheoretisch orientierte Einführung mit Auswahlbibliographie." In *Internationales Archiv für Sozialgeschichte der deutschen Literatur*, vol. 1. *Sonderheft*. Edited by Wolfgang Frühwald, Georg Jäger and Alberto Martino, 256–365. Tübingen: Max Niemeyer, 1985.
Dudziak, Mary L. *Cold War Civil Rights: Race and the Image of American Democracy*. Princeton, NJ: Princeton University Press, 2000.
———. "Desegregation as a Cold War Imperative." *Stanford Law Review* 41, no. 1 (1988): 61–120.
Durham, Martin. "On American Conservatism and Kim Phillips-Fein's Survey of the Field." *Journal of American History* 98, no. 3 (2011): 756–59.
Elliott, Debbie. "Integrating Ole Miss: A Transformative, Deadly Riot." October 1, 2012. National Public Radio. http://www.npr.org/2012/10/01/161573289/integrating-ole-miss-a-transformative-deadly-riot.
Erickson, Ansley T. *Making the Unequal Metropolis: School Desegregation and Its Limits*. Chicago: University of Chicago Press, 2016.
Estes, Steve. *Charleston in Black and White: Race and Power in the South After the Civil Rights Movement*. Chapel Hill: University of North Carolina Press, 2015.
Evans, Sara M. *Born for Liberty: A History of Women in America*. 2nd ed. New York: Free Press, 1997.
Fairclough, Adam. *Race and Democracy: The Civil Rights Struggle in Louisiana, 1915–1972*. 2nd ed. Athens: University of Georgia Press, 2008.
Farmer, James O. "Memories and Forebodings: The Fight to Preserve the White Democratic Primary in South Carolina." In *Toward the Meeting of the Waters: Currents in the Civil Rights Movement of South Carolina during the Twentieth Century*. Edited by Winfred B. Moore Jr. and Orville V. Burton, 243–51. Columbia: University of South Carolina Press, 2008.
Fass, Paula S. "Cultural History/Social History: Some Reflections on a Continuing Dialogue." *Journal of Social History* 37, no. 1 (2003): 39–46.
Feldstein, Ruth. "'I Wanted The Whole World to See': Race, Gender, and Constructions of Motherhood in the Death of Emmett Till." In *Mothers and Motherhood: Readings in American History*. Edited by Rima D. Apple and Janet L. Golden, 131–70. Columbus: Ohio State University Press, 1997.
———. *Motherhood in Black and White: Race and Sex in American Liberalism, 1930–1965*. Ithaca: Cornell University Press, 2000.
Fields, Barbara J. "Ideology and Race in American History." In *Region, Race, and Reconstruction: Essays in Honor of C. Vann Woodward*. Edited by J. Morgan Kousser and James M. McPherson, 143–77. Oxford: Oxford University Press, 1982.
Findlay, James F., Jr. *Church People in the Struggle: The National Council of Churches and the Black Freedom Movement, 1950–1970*. Oxford: Oxford University Press, 1993.

Fischer-Lichte, Erika and Benjamin Wihstutz, eds. *Performance and the Politics of Space: Theatre and Topology*. New York: Routledge, 2013.
Formisano, Ronald P. *Boston against Busing: Race, Class, and Ethnicity in the 1960s and 1970s*. Chapel Hill: University of North Carolina Press, 2004.
Foucault, Michel. *The History of Sexuality*. Vol. 1: *An Introduction*. New York: Vintage, 1978.
———. *Die Ordnung des Diskurses*. 10th ed. Frankfurt am Main: Fischer Taschenbuch Verlag, 1997.
———. "Prisons et asiles dans le mécanisme du pouvoir." In *Michel Foucault: Dits et Ecrits, 1970–1975*. Edited by Daniel Defert, 523–24. Paris: Gallimard, 1994.
Foucault, Michel, and Colin Gordon. *Power/Knowledge: Selected Interviews and Other Writings, 1972–1977*. New York: Pantheon, 1980.
Fout, John C., and Maura S. Tantillo, eds. *American Sexual Politics: Sex, Gender, and Race since the Civil War*. Chicago: University of Chicago Press, 1993.
Fox-Genovese, Elizabeth. *Within the Plantation Household: Black and White Women of the Old South*. Chapel Hill: University of North Carolina Press, 1988.
Frankel, Philip. *An Ordinary Atrocity: Sharpeville and Its Massacre*. New Haven, CT: Yale University Press, 2001.
Frankenberg, Ruth, ed. *Displacing Whiteness: Essays in Social and Cultural Criticism*. Durham, NC: Duke University Press, 1997.
Fraser, Walter J., Jr. *Charleston! Charleston! The History of a Southern City*. Columbia: University of South Carolina Press, 1989.
Frederickson, Kari. "'As a Man, I Am Interested in States' Rights': Gender, Race, and the Family in the Dixiecrat Party, 1948–1950." In *Jumpin' Jim Crow: Southern Politics from Civil War to Civil Rights*. Edited by Jane E. Dailey, 260–74. Princeton, NJ: Princeton University Press, 2000.
———. *Cold War Dixie: Militarization and Modernization in the American South*. Athens: University of Georgia Press, 2013.
Fredrickson, George M. *The Black Image in the White Mind: The Debate on Afro-American Character and Destiny, 1817-1914*. 2nd ed. Middleton, CT: Wesleyan University Press, 1987.
———. *Racism: A Short History*. Princeton, NJ: Princeton University Press, 2002.
Freyer, Tony. *The Little Rock Crisis: A Constitutional Interpretation*. Westport, CT: Greenwood Press, 1984.
Friedan, Betty. *The Feminine Mystique*. 5th ed. New York: Norton, 2001.
Frühwald, Wolfgang, Georg Jäger, and Alberto Martino, eds. *Internationales Archiv für Sozialgeschichte der deutschen Literatur*. Vol. 1: *Sonderheft*. Tübingen: Max Niemeyer, 1985.
Frystak, Shannon. "'Ain't Gonna Let Nobody Turn Me Around': Oretha Castle Haley." In *Louisiana Women: Their Lives and Times*. Edited by Janet Allured and Judith F. Gentry, 303–23. Athens: University of Georgia Press, 2009.
———. *Our Minds on Freedom: Women and the Struggle for Black Equality in Louisiana, 1924–1967*. Baton Rouge: Louisiana State University Press, 2009.
Gates, Lorraine. "Power from The Pedestal: The Women's Emergency Committee and the Little Rock School Crisis." *Arkansas Historical Quarterly* 55, no. 2 (1996): 194–223.

Germany, Kent B. *New Orleans after the Promises: Poverty, Citizenship, and the Search for the Great Society*. Athens: University of Georgia Press, 2007.
Glass, Michael R., and Reuben Rose-Redwood. Introduction to *Performativity, Politics, and the Production of Social Space*. Edited by Michael R. Glass and Reuben Rose-Redwood, 1–34. London: Routledge, 2014.
Goddard, Terry D. "Race, Religion, and Politics: Rev. Wesley Pruden of Arkansas, Modern Day Jim Crow." *Pulaski County Historical Review* 54, no. 4 (2004): 107–18.
Godfrey, Phoebe. "Bayonets, Brainwashing, and Bathrooms: The Discourse of Gender, Race, and Sexuality in the Desegregation of Little Rock's Central High." Arkansas Historical Quarterly 62, no. 1 (2003): 42–67.
———. "'It's Time for the Mothers to Take Over': The Mothers' League of Central High and a Feminist Critique of the Historical Record." Unpublished manuscript, University of Connecticut, 2012.
———. "'Sweet Little Girls'? Miscegenation, Desegregation and the Defense of Whiteness at Little Rock's Central High, 1957–1959." PhD diss., Binghamton University, 2001.
Goffman, Erving. *The Presentation of Self in Everyday Life*. Garden City, NY: Anchor Books, 1959.
Goldstone, Lawrence. *Inherently Unequal: The Betrayal of Equal Rights by the Supreme Court, 1865–1903*. New York: Walker, 2011.
Gordon, Michelle Y. "'Midnight Scenes and Orgies': Public Narratives of Voodoo in New Orleans and Nineteenth-Century Discourses of White Supremacy." *American Quarterly* 64, no. 4 (2012): 767–86.
Grant, Nicholas. *Winning Our Freedoms Together: African Americans and Apartheid, 1945–1960*. Chapel Hill: University of North Carolina Press, 2017.
Grantham, Dewey W. *The South in Modern America*. Fayetteville: University of Arkansas Press, 2001.
Gregson, Nicky, and Gillian Rose. "Taking Butler Elsewhere: Performativities, Spatialities, and Subjectivities." In *Performativity, Politics, and the Production of Social Space*. Edited by Michael R. Glass and Reuben Rose-Redwood, 37–61. London: Routledge, 2014.
Gross, Neil, Thomas Medvetz, and Rupert Russell. "The Contemporary American Conservative Movement." *Annual Review of Sociology* 37 (2011): 325–54.
Guard, Julie. *Radical Housewives: Price Wars and Food Politics in Mid-Twentieth Century Canada*. Toronto: University of Toronto Press, 2019.
Hale, Jon. "'The Fight Was Instilled in Us': High School Activism and the Civil Rights Movement in Charleston." *South Carolina Historical Magazine* 114, no. 1 (2013): 4–28.
Hall, Jacquelyn D. "The Long Civil Rights Movement and the Political Uses of the Past." *Journal of American History* 91, no. 4 (2005): 1233–1263.
———. "Partial Truths." In *Southern Women: Histories and Identities*. Edited by Virginia Bernhard, Betty Brandon, Elizabeth Fox-Genovese, and Theda Purdue, 11–29. Columbia: University of Missouri Press, 1992.
———. *Revolt against Chivalry: Jessie Daniel Ames and the Women's Campaign against Lynching*. Rev. ed. New York: Columbia University Press, 1993.
Hall, Kermit L. "The Constitutional Lessons of the Little Rock Crisis." In *Understanding the Little Rock Crisis: An Exercise in Remembrance and Reconciliation*. Edited by Eliza-

beth Jacoway and C. Fred Williams, 123–40. Fayetteville: University of Arkansas Press, 1999.
Harold, Claudrena N. *New Negro Politics in the Jim Crow South*. Athens: University of Georgia Press, 2016.
Harris, Cheryl I. "Whiteness as Property." *Harvard Law Review* 106, no. 8 (1993): 1707–91.
Hart, Emma. *Building Charleston: Town and Society in the Eighteenth Century British Atlantic World*. Columbia: University of South Carolina Press, 2010.
Hawkesworth, Mary. "Confounding Gender." *Signs* 22, no. 3 (1997): 649–85.
Heale, M. J. *American Anticommunism: Combating the Enemy Within, 1830–1970*. Baltimore, MD: Johns Hopkins University Press, 1990.
———. *McCarthy's Americans: Red Scare Politics in State and Nation, 1935–1964*. Basingstoke, UK: Macmillan, 1998.
Heath, James O. *To Face Down Dixie: South Carolina's War on the Supreme Court in the Age of Civil Rights*. Baton Rouge: Louisiana State University Press, 2017.
Hendershot, Heather. *What's Fair on the Air: Cold War Right-Wing Broadcasting and the Public Interest*. Chicago: University of Chicago Press, 2011.
Hirsch, Arnold R. "Simply a Matter of Black and White: The Transformation of Race and Politics in Twentieth-Century New Orleans." In *Creole New Orleans: Race and Americanization*. Edited by Arnold R. Hirsch and Joseph Logsdon, 262–319. Baton Rouge: Louisiana State University Press, 1992.
Hodes, Martha. "The Sexualization of Reconstruction Politics: White Women and Black Men in the South after the Civil War." In *American Sexual Politics: Sex, Gender, and Race since the Civil War*. Edited by John C. Fout and Maura S. Tantillo, 59–74. Chicago: University of Chicago Press, 1993.
Hofstadter, Robert. *The Paranoid Style in American Politics, and Other Essays*. New York: Vintage, 1967.
Holden, Charles J. "'The Public Business Is Ours': Edward McCrady, Jr., and Conservative Thought in Post–Civil War South Carolina, 1865–1900." *South Carolina Historical Magazine* 100, no. 2 (1999): 124–42.
Houston, Benjamin. *The Nashville Way: Racial Etiquette and the Struggle for Social Justice in a Southern City*. Athens: University of Georgia Press, 2012.
Hunt, Lynn, ed. *The New Cultural History*. Berkeley: University of California Press, 1989.
Ignatiev, Noel. *How the Irish Became White*. New York: Routledge, 2009.
Inger, Morton. *Politics and Reality in an American City: The New Orleans School Crisis of 1960*. New York: Center for Urban Education, 1969.
Isenberg, Nancy. *White Trash: The 400-Year Untold History of Class in America*. New York: Penguin, 2017.
Jacoway, Elizabeth. "Down from the Pedestal: Gender and Regional Culture in a ladylike Assault on the Southern Way of Life." *Arkansas Historical Quarterly* 56, no. 3 (1997): 345–52.
———. Introduction to *Understanding the Little Rock Crisis: An Exercise in Remembrance and Reconciliation*. Edited by Elizabeth Jacoway and C. Fred Williams, 1–22. Fayetteville: University of Arkansas Press, 1999.
———, ed. *Southern Businessmen and Desegregation*. Baton Rouge: Louisiana State University Press, 1982.

———. *Turn Away Thy Son: Little Rock, the Crisis That Shocked the Nation*. New York: Free Press, 2007.
Jacoway, Elizabeth, and C. Fred Williams, eds. *Understanding the Little Rock Crisis: An Exercise in Remembrance and Reconciliation*. Fayetteville: University of Arkansas Press, 1999.
Jäger, Siegfried. *Kritische Diskursanalyse: Eine Einführung*. 4th ed. Münster: Unrast, 2004.
Jeansonne, Glen. *Leander Perez: Boss of the Delta*. Baton Rouge: Louisiana State University Press, 1977.
———. *Women of the Far Right: The Mothers' Movement and World War II*. Chicago: University of Chicago Press, 1997.
Jones-Rogers, Stephanie E. *They Were Her Property: White Women as Slave Owners in the American South*. New Haven, CT: Yale University Press, 2019.
Kaledin, Eugenia. *Mothers and More: American Women in the 1950s*. Boston: Twayne, 1984.
Katagiri, Yasuhiro. *The Mississippi State Sovereignty Commission: Civil Rights and States' Rights*. Jackson: University Press of Mississippi, 2001.
Kelley, Robin D. G. *Race Rebels: Culture, Politics, and the Black Working Class*. New York: The Free Press, 1996.
Kerber, Linda. *Women of the Republic: Intellect and Ideology in Revolutionary America*. Chapel Hill: University of North Carolina Press, 1980.
Kimmel, Michael S. *Manhood in America: A Cultural History*. 2nd. New York: Oxford University Press, 2006.
Kirk, John. "Arkansas, the Brown Decision, and the 1957 Little Rock School Crisis: A Local Perspective." In *Understanding the Little Rock Crisis: An Exercise in Remembrance and Reconciliation*. Edited by Elizabeth Jacoway and C. Fred Williams, 67–82. Fayetteville: University of Arkansas Press, 1999.
———. *Beyond Little Rock: The Origins and Legacies of the Central High Crisis*. Fayetteville: University of Arkansas Press, 2007.
———. "Daisy Bates, the National Association for the Advancement of Colored People, and the 1957 Little Rock School Crisis: A Gendered Perspective." In *Gender and the Civil Rights Movement*. Edited by Peter J. Ling and Sharon Monteith, 17–40. New Brunswick, NJ: Rutgers University Press, 2004.
———, ed. *An Epitaph for Little Rock: A Fiftieth Anniversary Retrospective on the Central High Crisis*. Fayetteville: University of Arkansas Press, 2008.
———. "Massive Resistance and Minimum Compliance: The Origins of the 1957 Little Rock School Crisis and the Failure of School Desegregation in the South." In *Massive Resistance. Southern Opposition to the Second Reconstruction*. Edited by Clive Webb, 76–98. Oxford: Oxford University Press, 2005.
———. *Redefining the Color Line: Black Activism in Little Rock, Arkansas, 1940–1970*. Gainesville: University of Florida Press, 2002.
———. "'A Study in Second Class Citizenship': Race, Urban Development, and Little Rock's Gillam Park, 1934–2004." *Arkansas Historical Quarterly* 64, no. 3 (2005): 262–86.
Klarman, Michael J. "How Brown Changed Race Relations: The Backlash Thesis." *Journal of American History* 80, no. 1 (1994): 81–118.

Kolchin, Peter. "Whiteness Studies: The New History of Race in America." *Journal of American History* 89, no. 1 (2002): 154–73.
Kousser, J. Morgan, and James M. McPherson, eds. *Region, Race, and Reconstruction: Essays in Honor of C. Vann Woodward.* Oxford: Oxford University Press, 1982.
Kruse, Kevin M. "The Fight for 'Freedom of Association': Segregationist Rights and Resistance in Atlanta." In *Massive Resistance. Southern Opposition to the Second Reconstruction.* Edited by Clive Webb, 99–116. Oxford: Oxford University Press, 2005.
———. *White Flight: Atlanta and the Making of Modern Conservatism.* Princeton, NJ: Princeton University Press, 2005.
Landphair, Juliette. "Sewerage, Sidewalks, and Schools: The New Orleans Ninth Ward and Public School Desegregation." *Louisiana History: The Journal of the Louisiana Historical Association* 40, no. 1 (1999): 35–62.
Landwehr, Achim. *Historische Diskursanalyse.* 2nd ed. Frankfurt am Main: Campus Verlag, 2009.
Lassiter, Matthew D. "De Jure/De Facto Segregation: The Long Shadow of a National Myth." In *The Myth of Southern Exceptionalism.* Edited by Matthew D. Lassiter and Joseph Crespino, 25–48. Oxford: Oxford University Press, 2009.
———. *The Silent Majority: Suburban Politics in the Sunbelt South.* Princeton: Princeton University Press, 2007.
Lassiter, Matthew D., and Andrew B. Lewis, eds. *The Moderates' Dilemma: Massive Resistance to School Desegregation in Virginia.* Charlottesville: University Press of Virginia, 1998.
Lau, Peter F. *Democracy Rising: South Carolina and the Fight for Black Equality since 1865.* Lexington: University Press of Kentucky, 2006.
———. "Mr. NAACP: Levi G. Byrd and the Remaking of the NAACP in State and Nation, 1917–1960." In *Toward the Meeting of the Waters: Currents in the Civil Rights Movement of South Carolina during the Twentieth Century.* Edited by Winfred B. Moore Jr. and Orville V. Burton, 146–55. Columbia: University of South Carolina Press, 2008.
Lee, Michael J. *Creating Conservatism: Postwar Words That Made an American Movement.* East Lansing: Michigan State University Press, 2014.
Lerner, Gerda. "Reconceptualizing Differences among Women." *Journal of Women's History* 1, no. 3 (1990): 106–22.
Lewis, Amanda. "'What Group?': Studying Whites and Whiteness in the Era of 'Color-Blindness.'" *Sociological Theory* 22, no. 4 (2004): 623–46.
Lewis, George. *Massive Resistance: The White Response to the Civil Rights Movement.* London: Hodder Arnold, 2006.
———. "Virginia's Northern Strategy: Southern Segregationists and the Route to National Conservatism." *Journal of Southern History* 72, no. 1 (2006): 111–46.
Little, Kimberly K. *You Must Be from the North: Southern White Women in the Memphis Civil Rights Movement.* Jackson: University Press of Mississippi, 2009.
Lodge, Tim. *Sharpeville: An Apartheid Massacre and Its Consequences.* Oxford: Oxford University Press, 2011.
López, Ian Haney. *Dog Whistle Politics: How Coded Racial Appeals Have Reinvented Racism and Wrecked the Middle Class.* Oxford: Oxford University Press, 2013.

Lowndes, Joseph E. *From the New Deal to the New Right: Race and the Southern Origins of Modern Conservatism*. New Haven, CT: Yale University Press, 2008.

MacKinnon, Catharine A. "Intersectionality as Method: A Note." *Signs* 38, no. 4 (2013): 1019–30.

Mallon, Florencia E. "Time on the Wheel: Cycles of Revisionism and the 'New Cultural History.'" *Hispanic American Historical Review* 79, no. 2 (1999): 331–51.

Margolick, David. *Elizabeth and Hazel: Two Women of Little Rock*. New Haven, CT: Yale University Press, 2012.

Martin, Bradford D. *The Theater Is in the Street: Politics and Performance in Sixties America*. Amherst: University of Massachusetts Press, 2004.

Maxwell, Angie, and Todd Shields. *The Long Southern Strategy: How Chasing White Voters in the South Changed American Politics*. Oxford: Oxford University Press, 2019.

May, Elaine T. *Homeward Bound: American Families in the Cold War Era*. 2nd ed. New York: Basic Books, 2008.

Mays, David J., and James R. Sweeney. *Race, Reason, and Massive Resistance: The Diary of David J. Mays, 1954–1959*. Athens: University of Georgia Press, 2008.

McCammon, Holly J., Karen E. Campbell, Ellen M. Granberg, and Christine Mowery. "How Movements Win: Gendered Opportunity Structures and U.S. Women's Suffrage Movements, 1866 to 1919." *American Sociological Review* 66, no. 1 (2001): 49–70.

McGirr, Lisa. *Suburban Warriors: The Origins of the New American Right*. Princeton, NJ: Princeton University Press, 2001.

McMillen, Neil R. *The Citizens' Council: Organized Resistance to the Second Reconstruction, 1954–64*. 2nd ed. Urbana: University of Illinois Press, 1994.

———. "White Citizens' Council and Resistance to School Desegregation in Arkansas." *Arkansas Historical Quarterly* 30, no. 2 (1971): 95–122.

McRae, Elizabeth Gillespie. *Mothers of Massive Resistance: White Women and the Politics of White Supremacy*. Oxford: Oxford University Press, 2018.

Merritt, Keri Leigh. *Masterless Men: Poor Whites and Slavery in the Antebellum South*. Cambridge: Cambridge University Press, 2017.

Metress, Christopher. *The Lynching of Emmett Till: A Documentary Narrative*. Charlottesville: University of Virginia Press, 2002.

Meyer, David S., and Debra C. Minkoff. "Conceptualizing Political Opportunity." *Social Forces* 82, no. 4 (2004): 1457–92.

Meyer, David S., and Suzanne Staggenborg. "Movements, Countermovements, and the Structure of Political Opportunity." *American Journal of Sociology* 101, no. 6 (1996): 1628–60.

Meyerowitz, Joanne. "Beyond the Feminine Mystique: A Reassessment of Postwar Mass Culture, 1946– 1958." *Journal of American History* 79, no. 4 (1993): 1455–82.

Miletsky, Zebulon Vance. "Before Busing: Boston's Long Movement for Civil Rights and the Legacy of Jim Crow in the 'Cradle of Liberty.'" *Journal of Urban History* 43, no. 2 (2017): 204–17.

Miller, Rachel H. "North Little Rock Six." *Encyclopedia Of Arkansas History and Culture*. Arkansas Historic Preservation Program, Butler Center for Arkansas Studies. http://www.encyclopediaofarkansas.net/encyclopedia/entry-detail.aspx?entryID=5566.

Moore, Leonard N. *Black Rage in New Orleans: Police Brutality and African American*

Activism from World War II to Hurricane Katrina. Baton Rouge: Louisiana State University Press, 2010.
Mouffe, Chantal. "Feminism, Citizenship, and Radical Democratic Politics." In *Social Postmodernism: Beyond Identity Politics*. Edited by Linda J. Nicholson and Steven Seidman, 315–31. Cambridge: Cambridge University Press, 1995.
Murray, Gail S., ed. *Throwing Off the Cloak of Privilege: White Southern Women Activists in the Civil Rights Era*. Gainesville: University Press of Florida, 2004.
Neidhardt, Friedhelm, and Dieter Rucht. "The Analysis of Social Movements: The State of the Art and Some Perspectives for Further Research." In *Research on Social Movements: The State of the Art in Western Europe and the USA*. Edited by Dieter Rucht, 421–64. Frankfurt am Main: Campus Verlag, 1991.
Newby, I. A. *Black Carolinians: A History of Blacks in South Carolina from 1985–1968*. Columbia: University of South Carolina Press, 1973.
Newman, Mark. "The Catholic Church and Desegregation in the Diocese of Baton Rouge, 1961–1976." *Louisiana History: The Journal of the Louisiana Historical Association* 51, no. 3 (2010): 306–32.
———. *The Civil Rights Movement*. Edinburgh: Edinburgh University Press, 2004.
Nicholson, Linda J., and Steven Seidman, eds. *Social Postmodernism: Beyond Identity Politics*. Cambridge: Cambridge University Press, 1995.
Nickerson, Michelle M. *Mothers of Conservatism: Women and the Postwar Right*. Princeton, NJ: Princeton University Press, 2012.
Nielsen, Kim E. *Un-American Womanhood: Antiradicalism, Antifeminism, and the First Red Scare*. Columbus: Ohio State University Press, 2001.
Noble, David W. "Conservatism in the USA." *Journal of Contemporary History* 13, no. 4 (1978): 635–52.
Nolan, Mary. *The Transatlantic Century: Europe and America, 1890-2010*. Cambridge: Cambridge University Press, 2012.
Oakley, Ann. *Sex, Gender, and Society*. London: G. Maurice Temple Smith, 1972.
O'Brien, Michael. "'The South Considers Her Most Peculiar': Charleston and Modern Southern Thought." *South Carolina Historical Magazine* 94, no. 2 (1993): 119–33.
Painter, Nell I. *Southern History across the Color Line*. Chapel Hill: University of North Carolina Press, 2002.
Parkinson, John. *Democracy and Public Space: The Physical Sites of Democratic Performance*. Oxford: Oxford University Press, 2012.
Patterson, James T. *"Brown v. Board of Education": A Civil Rights Milestone and Its Troubled Legacy*. Oxford: Oxford University Press, 2001.
Peirce, Neal R. *The Deep South States of America: People, Politics, and Power in the 7 Deep South States*. New York: Norton, 1974.
Peltason, J. W. *Fifty-Eight Lonely Men: Southern Federal Judges And School Desegregation*. New York: Link Harcourt, Brace and World, 1961.
Phillips-Fein, Kim. "Conservatism: A State of the Field." *Journal of American History* 98, no. 3 (2011): 723–43.
Poché, Justin D. "Religion, Race, and Rights in Catholic Louisiana, 1938–1970." PhD diss., University of Notre Dame, 2007.
Preskill, Stephen L. "The Developmental Leadership of Septima Clark, 1954–1967." In

Toward the Meeting of the Waters: Currents in the Civil Rights Movement of South Carolina during the Twentieth Century. Edited by Winfred B. Moore Jr. and Orville V. Burton, 222–38. Columbia: University of South Carolina Press, 2008.

Quint, Howard Q. *Profile in Black and White: A Frank Portrait of South Carolina*. Washington, DC: Public Affairs Press, 1958.

Reagon, Bernice J. "Gender & Race: The Ampersand Problem in Feminist Thought." In *Inessential Woman: Problems of Exclusion in Feminist Thought*. Edited by Elizabeth V. Spelman, 114–32. Boston: Beacon Press, 1988.

Reed, Roy. *Faubus: The Life and Times of an American Prodigal*. Fayetteville: University of Arkansas Press, 1997.

———. "Orval E. Faubus: Out of Socialism into Realism." *Arkansas Historical Quarterly* 54, no. 1 (1995): 13–29.

Richards, Jeremy M. "The Political Life of Stanley Fletcher Morse." PhD diss., University of South Carolina, 2005.

Roark, James L. "American Black Leaders: The Response to Colonialism and the Cold War, 1943–1953." *African Historical Studies* 4, no. 2 (1971): 253–70.

Roberts, Diane. *The Myth of Aunt Jemima: Representations of Race and Region*. London: Routledge, 1994.

Robnett, Belinda. "African-American Women in the Civil Rights Movement, 1954–1964: Gender, Leadership, and Micromobilization." *American Journal of Sociology* 101, no. 6 (1996): 1661–93.

———. *How Long? How Long? African-American Women in the Struggle for Civil Rights*. Oxford: Oxford University Press, 1997.

Roediger, David R. *Towards the Abolition of Whiteness: Essays on Race, Politics, and Working Class History*. London: Verso, 1994.

———. *The Wages of Whiteness: Race and the Making of the American Working Class*. Rev. and expanded ed. London: Verso, 2007.

Rolph, Stephanie R. "The Citizens' Council and Africa: White Supremacy in Global Perspective." *Journal of Southern History* 82, no. 3 (2016): 617–50.

———. *Resisting Equality: The Citizens' Council, 1954–1989*. Baton Rouge: Louisiana State University Press, 2018.

Roy, Beth. *Bitters in the Honey: Tales of Hope and Disappointment across Divides of Race and Time*. Fayetteville: University of Arkansas Press, 1999.

Rucht, Dieter, and Friedhelm Neidhardt. "Towards a 'Movement Society'? On the Possibilities of Institutionalizing Social Movements." *Social Movement Studies* 1, no. 1 (2002): 7–30.

Ruoff, John C. "Southern Womanhood, 1865–1920: An Intellectual and Cultural Study." PhD diss., University of Illinois, 1976.

Schechner, Richard. *Performance Theory*. Rev. and expanded ed. London: Routledge, 2003.

Scott, James C. *Domination and the Arts of Resistance: Hidden Transcripts*. New Haven, CT: Yale University Press, 1990.

Scott, Joan W. "Gender: A Useful Category of Historical Analysis." *American Historical Review* 91, no. 5 (1986): 1053–75.

Sharenow, Robert. *My Mother the Cheerleader: A Novel*. New York: Laura Geringer Books, 2007.

Sitkoff, Harvard. *A New Deal for Blacks: The Emergence of Civil Rights as a National Issue*. Vol. 1: *The Depression Decade*. New York: Oxford University Press, 1978.
Smith, Bonnie G. "Women's History: A Retrospective from the United States." *Signs* 35, no. 3 (2010): 723–47.
Smyth, William D. "Segregation in Charleston in the 1950s: A Decade of Transition." *South Carolina Historical Magazine* 92, no. 2 (1991): 99–123.
Soja, Edward w. *Postmodern Geographies: The Reassertion of Space in Critical Social Theory*. London: Verso, 1989.
Spelman, Elizabeth V., ed. *Inessential Woman: Problems of Exclusion in Feminist Thought*. Boston: Beacon Press, 1988.
———. "Woman as Body: Ancient and Contemporary Views." *Feminist Studies* 8, no. 1 (1982): 109–31.
Spitzberg, Irving J. *Racial Politics in Little Rock, 1954–1964*. New York: Garland, 1987.
Stockley, Grif. *Ruled by Race: Black/White Relations in Arkansas from Slavery to the Present*. Fayetteville: University of Arkansas Press, 2009.
Taylor, Joe G. *Louisiana: A Bicentennial History*. New York: Norton, 1976.
Taylor, Ula. "The Historical Evolution of Black Feminist Theory and Praxis." *Journal of Black Studies* 29, no. 2 (1998): 234–53.
Thompson, E. P. *The Making of the English Working Class*. New York: Pantheon, 1963.
Thorndike, Joseph J. "'The Sometimes Sordid Level of Race and Segregation': James J. Kilpatrick and the Virginia Campaign against *Brown*." In *The Moderates' Dilemma: Massive Resistance to School Desegregation in Virginia*. Edited by Matthew D. Lassiter and Andrew B. Lewis, 51–71. Charlottesville: University Press of Virginia, 1998.
Tyler, Pamela. *Silk Stockings and Ballot Boxes: Women and Politics in New Orleans, 1920–1963*. Athens: University of Georgia Press, 2009.
van West, Carroll. "Clinton Desegregation Crisis." *The Tennessee Encyclopedia of History and Culture*. Tennessee Historical Society, University of Tennessee Press. http://tennesseeencyclopedia.net/entry.php?rec=279.
Vervack, Jerry J. "The Hoxie Imbroglio." *Arkansas Historical Quarterly* 48, no. 1 (1989): 17–33.
Wallace, David. "Orval Faubus: The Central Figure at Little Rock Central High School." *Arkansas Historical Quarterly* 39, no. 4 (1980): 314–29.
Ward, Jason Morgan. *Defending White Democracy: The Making of a Segregationist Movement and the Remaking of Racial Politics, 1936–1965*. Chapel Hill: University of North Carolina Press, 2011.
Webb, Clive, ed. *Massive Resistance: Southern Opposition to the Second Reconstruction*. Oxford: Oxford University Press, 2005.
———. *Rabble Rousers: The American Far Right in the Civil Rights Era*. Athens: University of Georgia Press, 2010.
Weise, Julie M. *Corazón De Dixie: Mexicanos in the U.S. South since 1910*. Chapel Hill: University of North Carolina Press, 2015.
West, Candace, and Don H. Zimmerman. "Doing Gender." *Gender and Society* 1, no. 2 (1987): 125–51.
West, Carolyn M. "Mammy, Sapphire, and Jezebel: Historical Images of Black Women and Their Implications for Psychotherapy." *Psychotherapy: Theory, Research, Practice, Training* 32, no. 3 (1995): 458–66.

White, John. "Managed Compliance: White Resistance and Desegregation in South Carolina, 1950–1970." PhD diss., University of Florida, 2006.

———. "Providers of the Moral Compass: Conservative Women and White Resistance in South Carolina, 1947–1972." Unpublished Manuscript, College of Charleston, SC, 2012.

———. "The White Citizens' Council of Orangeburg County, South Carolina." In *Toward the Meeting of the Waters: Currents in the Civil Rights Movement of South Carolina during the Twentieth Century*. Edited by Winfred B. Moore Jr. and Orville V. Burton, 261–73. Columbia: University of South Carolina Press, 2008.

Wickberg, Daniel. "Heterosexual White Male: Some Recent Inversions in American Cultural History." *Journal of American History* 92, no. 1 (2005): 136–57.

Wieder, Alan. "One Who Stayed: Margaret Conner and the New Orleans School Crisis." *Louisiana History: The Journal of the Louisiana Historical Association* 26, no. 2 (1985): 194–201.

Wihstutz, Benjamin. Introduction to *Performance and the Politics of Space: Theatre and Topology*. Edited by Erika Fischer-Lichte and Benjamin Wihstutz, 1–14. New York: Routledge, 2013.

Wilhoit, Francis M. *The Politics of Massive Resistance*. New York: George Braziller, 1973.

Williams, C. Fred. "Class: The Central Issue in the 1957 Little Rock School Crisis." *Arkansas Historical Quarterly* 56, no. 3 (1997): 341–44.

Williams, Juan. Introduction to *An Epitaph for Little Rock: A Fiftieth Anniversary Retrospective on the Central High Crisis*. Edited by John Kirk, vii–ix. Fayetteville: University of Arkansas Press, 2008.

Woods, Jeff. *Black Struggle, Red Scare: Segregation and Anti-Communism in the South, 1948–1968*. Baton Rouge: Louisiana State University Press, 2004.

———."'Designed to Harass': The Act 10 Controversy in Arkansas." *Arkansas Historical Quarterly* 56, no. 4 (1997): 443–60.

Workman, William, Jr. Introduction to *The First Republican Belle*, by Mary Badham Kittel, i–xii. Columbia, SC: R. L. Bryan, 1969.

Wray, Matt. *Not Quite White: White Trash and the Boundaries of Whiteness*. Durham, NC: Duke University Press, 2006.

Wray, Matt, and Annalee Newitz, eds. *White Trash: Race and Class in America*. New York and London: Routledge, 1999.

Zelizer, Julian E. "Rethinking the History of American Conservatism." *Reviews in American History*, 38, no. 2 (2010): 367–92.

INDEX

Note: Page numbers in italics indicate illustrations.

POLITICS AND CULTURE IN THE TWENTIETH-CENTURY SOUTH

A Common Thread: Labor, Politics, and Capital Mobility in the Textile Industry
BY BETH ENGLISH

"Everybody Was Black Down There": Race and Industrial Change in the Alabama Coalfields
BY ROBERT H. WOODRUM

Race, Reason, and Massive Resistance: The Diary of David J. Mays, 1954–1959
EDITED BY JAMES R. SWEENEY

The Unemployed People's Movement: Leftists, Liberals, and Labor in Georgia, 1929–1941
BY JAMES J. LORENCE

Liberalism, Black Power, and the Making of American Politics, 1965–1980
BY DEVIN FERGUS

Guten Tag, Y'all: Globalization and the South Carolina Piedmont, 1950–2000
BY MARKO MAUNULA

The Culture of Property: Race, Class, and Housing Landscapes in Atlanta, 1880–1950
BY LEEANN LANDS

Marching in Step: Masculinity, Citizenship, and The Citadel in Post–World War II America
BY ALEXANDER MACAULAY

Rabble Rousers: The American Far Right in the Civil Rights Era
BY CLIVE WEBB

Who Gets a Childhood?: Race and Juvenile Justice in Twentieth-Century Texas
BY WILLIAM S. BUSH

Alabama Getaway: The Political Imaginary and the Heart of Dixie
BY ALLEN TULLOS

The Problem South: Region, Empire, and the New Liberal State, 1880–1930
BY NATALIE J. RING

The Nashville Way: Racial Etiquette and the Struggle for Social Justice in a Southern City
BY BENJAMIN HOUSTON

Cold War Dixie: Militarization and Modernization in the American South
BY KARI FREDERICKSON

Faith in Bikinis: Politics and Leisure in the Coastal South since the Civil War
BY ANTHONY J. STANONIS

Womanpower Unlimited and the Black Freedom Struggle in Mississippi
BY TIYI M. MORRIS

New Negro Politics in the Jim Crow South
BY CLAUDRENA N. HAROLD

Jim Crow Terminals: The Desegregation of American Airports
BY ANKE ORTLEPP

Remaking the Rural South: Interracialism, Christian Socialism, and Cooperative Farming in Jim Crow Mississippi
BY ROBERT HUNT FERGUSON

The South of the Mind: American Imaginings of White Southernness, 1960–1980
BY ZACHARY J. LECHNER

The Politics of White Rights: Race, Justice, and Integrating Alabama's Schools
BY JOSEPH BAGLEY

Massive Resistance and Southern Womanhood: White Women, Class, and Segregation
BY REBECCA BRÜCKMANN

CPSIA information can be obtained
at www.ICGtesting.com
Printed in the USA
LVHW091742151122
733217LV00004B/619

9 780820 358628